BETWEEN KING COTTON AND QUEEN VICTORIA

UNCIVIL WARS
Series Editors

Stephen Berry, University of Georgia
Amy Murrell Taylor, University of Kentucky
Fay Yarborough, Rice University

Advisory Board

Joseph Beilein, Pennsylvania State University, Behrand
Brandi Brimmer, University of North Carolina at Chapel Hill
Maria Angela Diaz, University of Illinois Urbana-Champaign
Gregory Downs, University of California, Davis
Megan Kate Nelson, megankatenelson.com
Kristen Oertel, University of Tulsa
Joshua D. Rothman, University of Alabama
KT Shively, Virginia Commonwealth University
David Silkenat, University of Florida

Between King Cotton and Queen Victoria

*How Pirates, Smugglers, and Scoundrels
Almost Saved the Confederacy*

Beau Cleland

THE UNIVERSITY OF GEORGIA PRESS

ATHENS

Material from the Lyons Papers and Arundel Castle Archives is used with the permission of the Duke of Norfolk, who owns the original manuscript material.

Published by the University of Georgia Press
Athens, Georgia 30602
www.ugapress.org
© 2025 by Beau Cleland

All rights reserved

Set in Garamond by Westchester Publishing Services

Most University of Georgia Press titles are
available from popular e-book vendors.

Printed digitally

EU Authorized Representative Easy Access System Europe—Mustamäe tee 50, 10621 Tallinn, Estonia, gpsr.requests@ easproject.com

Library of Congress Cataloging-in-Publication Data
Names: Cleland, Beau author
Title: Between king cotton and Queen Victoria : how pirates, smugglers, and scoundrels almost saved the Confederacy / Beau Cleland.
Other titles: Uncivil wars
Description: Athens : The University of Georgia Press, [2025] | Series: UnCivil wars | Includes bibliographical references and index.
Identifiers: LCCN 2025021179 | ISBN 9780820375250 hardback | ISBN 9780820375267 paperback | ISBN 9780820375274 epub | ISBN 9780820375281 pdf
Subjects: LCSH: Non-state actors (International relations)—Political activity | Privateering—Political aspects—Atlantic Ocean Region | United States—History—Civil War, 1861–1865—Blockades | United States—History—Civil War, 1861–1865—Participation, Foreign | Confederate States of America—Relations—Bahamas | Confederate States of America—Relations—Bermuda Islands | Confederate States of America—Relations—Canada | Great Britain—Colonies—America
Classification: LCC E600 .C54 2025 | DDC 973.7/5—dc23/eng/20250701
LC record available at https://lccn.loc.gov/2025021179

For Aylin.
I wouldn't have done it
without you.

CONTENTS

List of Illustrations ix
Acknowledgments xi

Introduction 1

CHAPTER ONE
"That Nation of Pirates":
Private Violence and the North American Origins
of Confederate Informal Diplomacy, 1837–1861 13

CHAPTER TWO
King Cotton and King Conch:
Informal Diplomacy, Anglo-Confederate Relations,
and Blockade Running in the Bahamas, 1861–1863 43

CHAPTER THREE
"I Risk with All Concerned":
Bermuda and the Fight to Control Blockade Running, 1863–1864 68

CHAPTER FOUR
"The Heartless Slave-Dealers in America":
Strikes, Spies, and the Failures of Confederate Influence
in Bermuda and the Bahamas, 1862–1864 97

CHAPTER FIVE
"The Like Was Not Practised in the Previous
Conflicts of Civilized Nations":
Divided Sovereignty and Paramilitary Violence in the
Colonies and at Sea, 1863–1865 120

CHAPTER SIX
"Informal Propositions Coming from Irresponsible
and Unofficial Persons":
British North America and the Perils of Informal Diplomacy,
1864–1865   149

CHAPTER SEVEN
"Schemes of Deviltry Concocted in Canada":
Public Causes and Privatized Violence from Canada, 1864–1865   167

Conclusion   193

Notes   203

Bibliography   243

Index   267

ILLUSTRATIONS

Images

Portrait of John Anderson   23
Portrait of Henry Adderley   46
Georgiana Gholson Walker and her children   80
Black workers on the Nassau waterfront, 1864   117
Portrait of Benjamin Wier   127
Portrait of George N. Sanders   161
The St. Albans Raiders at the Montreal jail, 1864   173
Jefferson and Varina Davis in Montreal, 1867   197

Maps

British America and the United States, 1861   xv
The Bahamas and the Southern Coast, 1862   55
The Maritime Provinces and the Route of the *Chesapeake*, 1863   132
Pro-Confederate Attacks and Plots Linked to British Colonies   178

Table

Table 1. Annual Trade Values in the Bahamas, 1860–1864   48

ACKNOWLEDGMENTS

In some respects, writing a book like this is akin to hunting in western North America. The most demanding part is done alone, under forbidding conditions, and though I did not have to crawl through snow or worry about bears in the archives, it sure felt that way sometimes. It's isolating and grueling, and it requires that you fight your own shortcomings as much as anything outside factors might throw in your way. But then you get home and remember that you didn't do any of this by yourself. A hunter has mentors, guides, and tradition to set them on the right path, and community, family, food, stories, and fellowship when they return, whether or not they were successful. This book came out of a similar process, and while I was frequently lonely, thousands of miles from my family on archival visits, or toiling silently over a keyboard, trying to find the words to bring this story to life, I was never alone. I have an army of people who helped me carry this project from an inchoate idea into a (hopefully) polished and enjoyable piece of scholarship and writing.

Some of those people, who likely won't ever see these words, were literally an Army. The roots of this project lay in Afghanistan, alongside a little bit of my youthful joie de vivre and the blood of some friends. To the men of 2–4 Infantry, 5–25 Field Artillery, ODAs 321, 325, our Afghan interpreters, and everyone who ever set foot at Firebase Cobra, this is for you. Turns out, not knowing who we're fighting or why is not remotely a unique experience in history. To the community of veterans in my generation who have turned to academic history, thanks for being models of how experience can inform good scholarship. Eric Burke, Rob Williams, Angela Riotto, Eddie Valentin, and Kate Dahlstrand stand out in my mind as examples to follow.

This book has benefited from the patience, feedback, and assistance of many people, across too many years, in my meandering course across graduate school and academia. I owe Eliot Cohen and Tom Keaney at the Johns Hopkins School of Advanced International Studies (SAIS), both now retired, for pointing me toward academic history as the appropriate outlet for my energy and the early version of this project. To Steve Seabrook, my partner in crime and staff rides, thanks for sticking with me across the miles and years. I also owe a debt of gratitude to Brandon Bowen and his family for hosting me in London during research trips, long after our SAIS years together.

I was lucky to have an amazing and supportive community of friends and fellow graduate students in Calgary. Shannon Murray showed me how to feel at home in a (slightly) foreign land. John Woitkowitz and Erna Kurbegovic shared the ordeals of comps and dissertation writing, and were courteously quiet in their suspicions that my research visits to Bermuda and the Bahamas in the winter may have been boondoggles. Will Pratt, Andrew McEwen, Mikkel Dack, Stuart Barnard, and Victoria Bucholtz made this whole thing fun somehow.

I of course have to thank the very many librarians, archivists, researchers, and support staff who made this work possible. I do not know the names of most of them, but the people who keep the records organized and the doors open deserve recognition all the same. Archivists and librarians were invaluable to this project on (and between!) two continents. At the University of Calgary, Nadine Hoffman and the rest of the library staff helped keep me up to my ears in books and microfilm. The staff at the Southern Historical Collection in Chapel Hill, North Carolina; the South Caroliniana Library in Columbia; and the South Carolina Historical Society in Charleston were very helpful to a fresh PhD candidate who didn't quite know what he was looking for. The people at the National Archives in College Park, Maryland, and in Washington, D.C., were great, as were the staff of the Manuscript Division of the Library of Congress. Rebecca Hughes, then of the Arundel Castle Archives, guided me around Lord Lyons's personal papers, while Karla Ingemann and Andrew Baylay at the Bermuda Archives were very accommodating. The staff of the Bahamas National Archives does amazing work on a shoestring budget. I was very impressed at the efficiency of the archivists and staff at the National Archives in Kew, United Kingdom, as well as at the British Library in London. The National Maritime Museum in Greenwich was a wonderful place to work and an interesting venue to explore whenever I needed a break from deciphering old handwriting. I also wish to acknowledge the institutional support I received from the University of Calgary, along with the support I received through the Post-9/11 GI Bill. I earned that particular bit money the hard way, but thanks all the same to the Department of Veterans Affairs.

I had so much, and such high-quality, academic support for this project that it's difficult to know where to begin, and I apologize in advance to those I inevitably forget or cannot list. I presented little pieces of this work at a wide variety of conferences and workshops, including at annual meetings of the Southern Historical Association, the Society of Civil War Historians, the Society for Military History, and BrANCH, as well as at workshops in Asheville, North Carolina, and in Calgary and Banff in Alberta, Canada. The feedback from other historians at those venues helped me turn a vague notion about transnational rebels into a viable book. Laura June Davis, Angela Diaz, Charles Wexler, Claire Wolnisty, and Pat Kelly all had an impact on this book at these venues, as did Matt Karp, Niels Eichorn, Duncan Campbell, Anna Holloway Gibson, and Andy Slap. I also want to thank Matt Stanley, John Quist, David Gleeson, Matt Hulbert, Trae Welborn, Patrick Lewis, and Joe Beilein for making me feel welcome at these venues, even when I was new to everything. Jay Sexton has been particularly generous with his time, providing feedback on this project at conferences and during its life as a dissertation. I also wish to thank Amie Kiddle, Jewel Spangler, George Colpitts, Nancy Janovicek, John Ferris, and Maureen Hiebert for their help in shepherding this book along its way. Nadine Zimmerli generously read an early version, and her comments were tremendously helpful. Thanks as well to everyone at the University of Georgia Press (though I am obliged by tradition to say "THWG"—Go Jackets!), especially Mick Gusinde-Duffy and my series editors, Stephen Berry and Amy Murrell Taylor, as well as the anonymous readers of my proposal and manuscript, whose reports were nice enough to make me doubt, just for a moment, the horrors of the proverbial Reviewer 2.

Most of all, this project was nurtured academically by Brian Schoen and Frank Towers. It is fair to say that I was practically clueless about the world of academic history when I started this. Brian and Frank have been incredible teachers, supervisors, mentors, and now friends. Brian stepped in and helped me think more broadly about transnational history in the Civil War era, and how questions of influence, sovereignty, and diplomacy can benefit from holistic analysis that goes beyond diplomatic records. His knowledge and eye for connection helped make this project a systematic study rather than a series of geographically isolated episodes. As for Frank, I credit him with making me into an actual historian. I've never met anyone with a better knack for getting at the heart of a historical argument, and he demanded (fairly) that my work do the same. Along the way he was unfailingly generous with his time, his knowledge of the business side of academic history, and his wisdom about the realities of finding work and getting published in this field. I'm a better writer and historian because of him.

I'm a transnational historian, so naturally my acknowledgments have to cross borders. My friends back in the States helped keep me connected with home, and they spared no effort in keeping my ego and self-regard in check. Joe, Sean, Chris I., Chris J., Amanda, Andy, Ty, Amy, Erica, Adam, and all the rest—thank you. Go Gators, even though I never attended. Thanks to my friends and family in Canada for helping to make me feel at home up here—especially my better half's Canadian family. Deniz, Kyra, Hüsnü, and Annik, you helped make this happen.

Last but certainly not least is my family. As I write this, a nine-year-old boy is peering over my shoulder and giggling. He wasn't around when this began, and neither were his big and little brothers. After three boys, five cats, four dogs, and a wedding (not necessarily in that order), this book is finally done. My boys made this project both meaningful and, at times, seemingly impossible, trying to write with an infant, a two-year-old, and a four-year-old at home, or doing research while missing them so much I thought I might die. Teddy, Raymond, and Bernie, I love you to pieces. Thanks for putting up with grumpy dad while he wrote a book with no pictures. To my parents, thanks for all your love, support, and occasional continent-spanning babysitting. To my brothers, Wade and Zach, thanks for only occasionally giving me grief about living in Canada and being the world's slowest writer.

To my wife, Aylin: Je t'aime, mon petit lapin. You are relentlessly hardworking, tenacious, talented, and beautiful. God only knows why you picked me, but I'm forever grateful you did. I quite literally couldn't have done this without you, and I wouldn't have wanted to anyway. Thanks for being the glue that holds it all together for our menagerie. Like I promised you that August day so long ago: through dogs and cats and, now, at least one book, even if you probably won't read it.

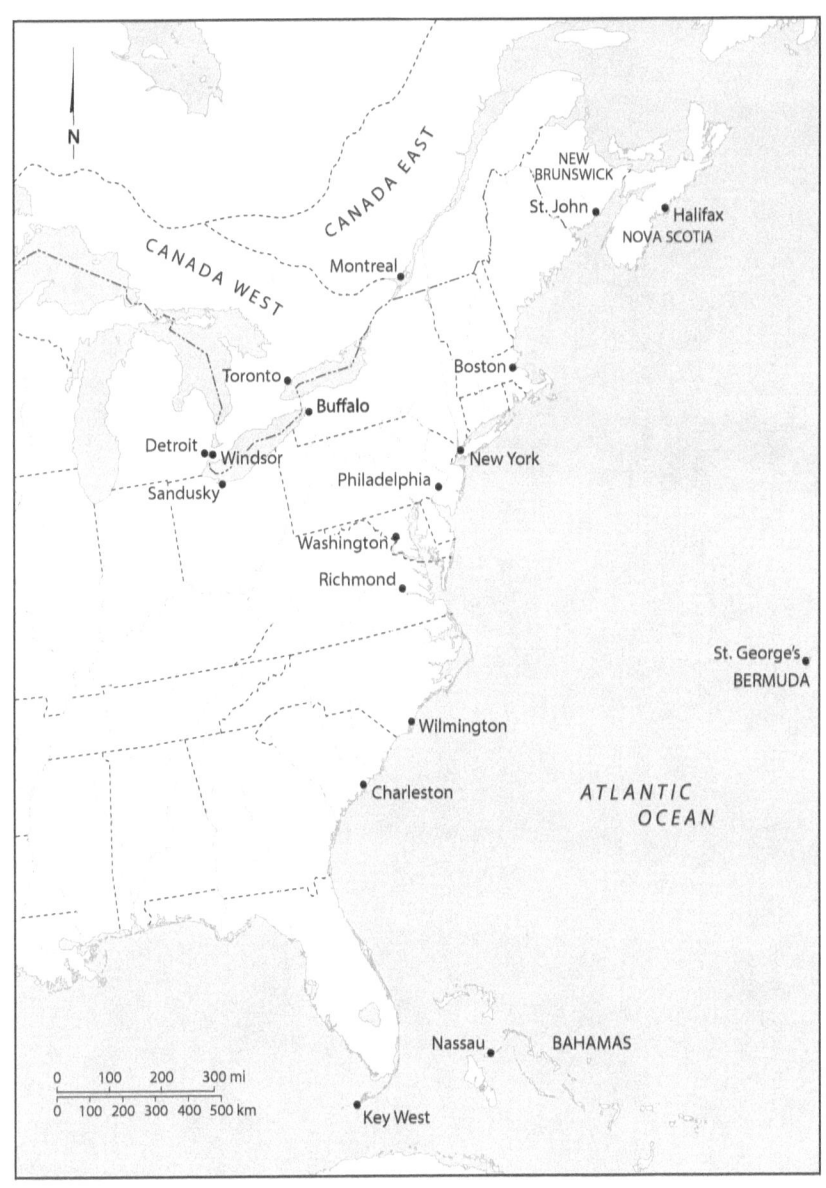

British America and the United States, 1861

BETWEEN KING COTTON AND QUEEN VICTORIA

Introduction

All concerned were laboring under the honest delusion that they were
engaged in a legitimate, belligerent act.
—Judah P. Benjamin, Confederate Secretary of State

AFTER JOHN WILKES Booth shot Abraham Lincoln on the evening of April 14, 1865, many accused him of being a puppet, acting on behalf of Jefferson Davis and the Confederate government.¹ No direct evidence of this has yet been discovered, but following Booth's "strings" is revealing nonetheless, often in unexpected ways. If we lift up the gossamer threads tying the assassin to the Confederacy, they lead not just south but north, into Canada, as contemporary observers immediately noted.² Lift a bit further and—like a fine net slowly drawn up from the water by its middle—they appear to spread in all directions, crisscrossing North America and gathering around rocks and places of shelter. This mesh was a vast, transnational network, anchored around the colonies of British America and composed of Britons and Confederates in nearly equal measure. This network, and the ties between the aspiring Confederacy and the British colonies it represented, proved to be vastly consequential to the course, duration, and aftermath of the American Civil War.

Booth likely would not have been in a position to assassinate the president without the logistical support and assistance of people in the pro-Confederate network in Canada. That network, to which he was personally introduced in Montreal in fall 1864, was hosted and facilitated by willing colonials across the hemisphere. Many of its Confederate members arrived in British North America via a long-established transportation and communications network built around British colonies, especially Bermuda and the Bahamas, whose primary purpose was running the blockade. The U.S. blockade, declared by President Lincoln on April 16, 1861, threatened to capture or destroy any vessel bound to or coming from rebel-held ports. While the blockade's effectiveness has been much debated, it was essentially impossible for large ships to enter Confederate harbors directly from Europe after 1861, and those seeking to move goods in and out of the Confederacy turned by necessity to nearby British colonies.[3] It is difficult to overstate how essential blockade running was for the rebellion's survival, and it would have been impossible without the aid of sympathetic colonials. Exploring the origins, operation, and importance of that network is the purpose of this book. Often dismissed piecemeal as quixotic side quests or amusing but ultimately inconsequential anecdotes, the operations of this informal, semiprivate network were of enormous consequence for the course of the war and its aftermath, and our understanding of the "international" Civil War is incomplete without a deeper reckoning with the power and potential for chaos of these private networks imbued with the power of a state.

Confederate observers recognized the importance of their friends in British America, and they often found colonial governments and courts to be quite sympathetic to their cause. James P. Holcombe, a Virginia law professor who was in Halifax on official Confederate business, wrote that among the elites of Nova Scotia, "the wish for our success is almost universal, and is freely expressed." Nearly everyone recognized "the almost self-evident truth that the future independence of these provinces is bound up" with the fate of the Confederacy. "The clergy, the bar, the press, are unanimous or nearly so in our favor. The sentiment is stronger still in the army. The acting governor, General Doyle, is our friend . . . and expressed to me warm wishes for our success." The colonies, in Holcombe's estimation, were home to people who knew "the true interest of England," in stark contrast to the perfidious government in London.[4] Individual colonials likewise garnered praise for their "generous sympathy and liberal contribution" to the Confederate cause. Holcombe told his superiors in Richmond that prominent men in Halifax "have given money, time, and influence without reserve, as if our cause had been that of their own country." In the midst of the war, Confederate president Jefferson Davis presented his personal thanks to several British Americans for their aid to the rebellion.[5]

Influential figures in both the Union and Confederate governments saw British colonies in North America as sites of active support for the Southern cause. Union observers judged the value of that aid to be immense. Secretary of State William H. Seward called these colonials "willing agents and abettors of the enemies of the United States, and their hostility has proved not merely offensive but deeply injurious."[6] Massachusetts senator Charles Sumner, in a speech rejecting the Johnson-Clarendon Convention of 1868, estimated that British support may have doubled the duration of the war and added $2 billion to the cost of defeating the insurgency.[7] Even if Sumner exaggerated these figures for negotiating purposes, British resources were, in fact, essential to the rebellion's survival. In the face of a blockade that after 1861 made direct imports nearly impossible, the overwhelming majority of the arms and supplies that the Confederacy received from abroad passed through British colonies en route from Europe, usually on British-flagged ships, consigned to British merchants, and paid for with cotton that followed the same path out of Southern ports.[8] Without the advantage provided by British (and, to a far lesser extent, Spanish) colonies, the Confederacy had no prayer of military victory. The colonies were unsinkable, unassailable refuges in an enemy-controlled sea.

The private parties that Seward denounced and Davis praised worked toward a Confederate victory in a transnational effort that deeply involved the colonial subjects of the British Empire in North America. Informal diplomacy—that is, the broad universe of international contacts not undertaken by formal agents of a state yet working broadly toward that state's interests—played an important role in developing a widespread network of merchants, politicians, sailors, minor officials, and conservative elites that worked closely in support of the Confederate rebellion across the ocean and land frontiers of North America. The cotton embargo of 1861–62—a citizen-led effort to prevent the export of cotton with the goal of forcing the British and French governments to intervene on behalf of the rebels—was orchestrated by a domestic network of merchants, planters, and citizens' groups. Most informal diplomatic networks, however, were transnational undertakings that involved British subjects alongside Confederate citizens, especially in the critical endeavor of blockade running. British colonies, not Europe, were the beating heart of Confederate international trade—practically everything, going in or coming out, had to flow through them. The Confederacy's informal diplomats and local partners built communications networks, modified local laws, provided introductions, and peddled influence on behalf of the Confederates. These unofficial representatives of the rebellion, it is no exaggeration to say, accomplished far more for their cause in practical terms than the official envoys ever did. This book seeks to center the importance of private, informal diplomacy and international violence, and show that they—and the colonial spaces that hosted and sheltered them—were inseparable from the Confederacy's formal war effort.

This Confederate reliance on private parties in the transnational aspects of the war came amid a transformative period for international law and colonial governance. Positivism, the view that law was "fundamentally a human creation" and bound by strictures of utilitarian rules and rational state interests rather than universal precepts of natural law, was the dominant trend in the developing regime of international law, especially regarding war.[9] In the nineteenth century, Britain was the leading advocate for a reformed international legal regime that firmly placed the state as the only legitimate purveyor of violence. Best exemplified by the 1856 Declaration of Paris, which among other things banned privateering (state-sanctioned private warfare at sea) and formalized requirements for blockades and the capture of neutral shipping, Britain sought a positivist, rules-based international order.[10] This "rage for order," as legal historians Lauren Benton and Lisa Ford termed it in their book of the same name, made the imperial government the implacable foe of filibusters, privateers, pirates, and other elements of international entropy—a position quite at odds with much of North America's contemporary experience. However, the reform of settler-colonial governance in the nineteenth century granted most of British America the ability, if not the uncontested right, to defy imperial preference and policy when local interests diverged from the metropole. This phenomenon was the most developed in British North America after 1841, and it manifested itself across British American colonies repeatedly during the Civil War as colonial officials and courts undermined the pursuit of raiders, pirates, and filibusters on the international margins of the war. Functioning and independent colonial court systems had tremendous leeway to interpret the law, and they often did so in ways that protected Confederate (and usually, by association, local) interests and promoted rather than discouraged the very behavior that the British government wanted to stamp out. Even if, as Jan Lemnitzer argues, it was the legal regime embodied in the Declaration of Paris rather than changing technology that stifled formal Confederate privateering, the parallel development of colonial governance gave it room to breathe in a less regulated, more chaotic form.[11]

The "traditional" history of Confederate foreign relations typically focuses on diplomacy with the great powers of Europe. This is entirely appropriate and has been ably covered over the years by notable historians from E. D. Adams to Howard Jones.[12] Other recent scholarship has greatly expanded the scope of historical investigation, reimagining the Civil War era as an international and transnational crisis, and it is in this vein that I write.[13] The failures of Confederate diplomacy were numerous and well-documented, from the ill-starred reign of King Cotton to the repeated failure of rebel diplomats to obtain recognition in Europe's halls of power. London and Paris, however, were not the only places where the Confederacy could forge international connections. Southerners could and did find influence and success far closer to home, particularly in the colonies of British America.

Civil War Southerners did not have to cross the Atlantic to interact with the British: they could do so in colonies a mere stone's throw away. Nassau, Bahamas, and St. George's, Bermuda, were only hours or a few days away from Charleston by steamer, while Southerners could (and did) ride the rails to Canada across the Suspension Bridge at Buffalo, incognito of course. What Confederates and their colonial partners quickly developed was a complex public-private commercial-diplomatic network, built on connections between British, colonial, and Southern merchants. The nodes of this network were anchored by wealthy and influential colonial merchants like Henry Adderley in Nassau and Benjamin Wier in Halifax, who worked (often quite literally) alongside Confederates like shipping agent John B. Lafitte, minor officials such as Lewis Heyliger, and mid-rank military officers like Maj. Norman S. Walker.

This informal network was crucial to Confederate military and diplomatic fortunes. Perhaps most importantly, it provided the foundation and the backbone for blockade running, the bulk of which was done by privately owned vessels and firms, but it also became the chief Confederate avenue for sending communications and people abroad. This network also facilitated extensive covert subversion and military action, particularly in British North America, whose shared border with the Northern states made it an attractive launching point for a wide variety of activities, ranging from recovering escaped prisoners of war, to politically interfering in Northern elections, to outright raiding. This commercial-diplomatic network proved vital for coordinating the movement of arms and supplies from Europe to the shores of the Confederacy, and for protecting the local interests of the Confederacy from both Union and British interference.

This story is just as much a colonial one as it is Confederate. The individual histories of the colonies most involved and their specific local social and political conditions deeply affected the depth and nature of their involvement in Confederate schemes. Poverty and greed played a significant role, but other factors were also important, especially the nature of local governance and the relative power of pro-Confederate elites in local power structures. Some colonials found the potential riches of blockade running too alluring to pass up. Others, particularly former slaveholders, sympathized with Southern racial and social hierarchy. Many who were otherwise opposed to slavery romanticized the Southern cause and embraced their struggle for "liberty" seemingly without irony. The preeminent failure of Confederate informal diplomacy in British America, perhaps not surprisingly, was among people of color, who found themselves torn between the ready availability of work along the wharves and the odious cause their employers supported. White Southerners in the colonies and their local friends brought about labor strife with Black workers through mistreatment and suppressed wages that in some cases resulted in catastrophic sabotage and low-level violence, along with occasionally heroic efforts by Black colonials to aid the United States against the rebel network. Despite this, the Confederate cause found influential friends among the white elites of British America, many of whom took substantial risks on its behalf.

In the following chapters, several broad patterns emerge that attest to the significance of the Confederate-colonial connection and the importance of including this transnational relationship into the narrative of the "international" Civil War. The first is Confederate reliance on merchants and business connections to develop the networks that supported blockade running, communication, and covert action. The Confederate government proved more than willing to tolerate wildcat foreign policy from merchants and local officials who coordinated the informal cotton embargo of 1861–62. In this tradition, Confederate citizens worked with friends and partners in British America on a variety of schemes and efforts connected to foreign policy and diplomacy, with little or no encouragement from Richmond. Relatedly, there emerged substantial subcontracting of diplomatic functions, sometimes out of necessity, to British colonial subjects. Influential colonists acted as "cutouts" (a term for those who lent Confederates their identities and addresses and sometimes acted as their proxies) for the Confederate government, appealing for help or asking for favors from both colonial and British imperial governments, which would offer a British subject aid that would have been denied to a Confederate citizen. The public-private nature of blockade running and Confederate overseas communications was not uncommon in nineteenth-century governance, and in this case, it was a product of Confederate preference for private action, as well as necessity. The strength of Confederate mercantile circles went a long way in making up for their government's institutional weaknesses in logistics and diplomacy. Once established by the summer of 1862, these commercial-diplomatic networks of trade proved to be remarkably resilient, if not efficient. They also proved very resistant to later Confederate efforts to exert greater direct control.

This book also addresses the substantial exploitation of the divided sovereignty inherent in the colonies, as practiced not only by Confederates but by colonial subjects. The British government under Lord Palmerston, who had only a precarious majority in Parliament, was fundamentally cautious in its foreign policy, and it sought to remain neutral in the conflict, in order to preserve international and regional order, and to tend to its own commercial and political interests in North America.[14] North and South each had their partisans in Parliament and the administration, but Palmerston and his foreign secretary, Lord John Russell, settled on a neutrality tailored toward maritime power, which, even if Americans like William H. Seward did not realize it, tended to favor the Union by making privateering and commerce raiding more difficult.[15] Local elites and government bodies often frustrated the policies of the imperial government, whose reach and power were limited by the structure of colonial governments, especially the relative independence of their courts and elected assemblies. The people of British North America in particular jealously guarded their hard-won prerogatives of "responsible government" and judicial independence, often to the frustration of authorities in London and Washington.[16]

The Confederate government likewise found it challenging to control those acting on its behalf in the colonies. Reliance on private individuals for governmental and paramilitary tasks made it very difficult for Confederate authorities to control freelance military or quasi-filibustering activities. Confederate inability to create much legitimate privateering, for example, drew British colonials like John C. Braine and Vernon Locke into nebulous or outright illegal actions against Union ships on the high seas, which resulted in tighter restrictions on actual Confederate warships. All of this combined to substantially complicate our understanding of the nature of British neutrality, which was far from uniform and constantly contested by both British subjects and Confederate citizens. Neutrality served as a ragged and patchwork edge, rather than a sharply defined line, between colonial Britons and participation in the American Civil War.

This Confederate-colonial relationship serves as an important reminder of the contingency of abolition in the Western Hemisphere—an achievement that was nearly as fragile as the wave of revolutions that accompanied it after 1861.[17] Although many historians remind us that slavery was not inevitably doomed to extinction, in popular memory there still persists an often unstated assumption that somehow it would eventually fade away. The friendly reception of Confederates in places across the British empire reveals a world where a successful rebellion might have secured a lasting future for its evil institution. Confederate proslavery internationalism might have harmoniously coexisted with the ostensibly abolitionist empire at its very doorstep, aided by self-interested merchants in Britain and intraimperial discord in British America.[18]

Finally, this book aims to draw greater attention to the importance of informal and privatized warfare on the margins of Civil War America. Privatized warfare here means organized violence carried out by private parties rather than uniformed persons regularly enlisted in the armed forces of a government, such as guerillas, privateers, and filibusters. Privateering—essentially state-authorized piracy by privately owned ships against enemy commerce—formed the centerpiece of early Confederate naval strategy, and it was subject to fairly rigorous domestic and international regulation.

By land, Confederates took the heart of filibustering—the exploitation of neutral territory to launch unauthorized military expeditions—and modified that tradition to suit the needs of the moment. In the taxonomy of private violence, filibustering—that is, illegal armed expeditions launched from neutral territory—loomed especially large in the public imagination in 1861. Karl Marx, in his explanation of the origins of the American Civil War to the readers of the Vienna newspaper *Die Presse* in the autumn of 1861, explicitly linked filibustering to the survival of a slaveholder's republic. He wrote that "only by acquisition and the prospect of acquisition of new territories, as well as by filibustering expeditions, is it possible to square the interests of these 'poor whites' with those of the slaveholders, to give their restless thirst for action a harmless direction and to tame them with the prospect of one day becoming slaveholders themselves."[19] Marx, who was unusually perceptive for a foreign observer of the war, understood the importance of privatized violence in the geopolitical affairs of mid-nineteenth-century North America and the ubiquitous nature of filibustering and other species of extralegal raiding in both spreading and attacking slavery. To Marx, who had ebulliently praised John Brown's own raid against the slave South, the "unceasing piratical expeditions of the filibusters" were inseparable from the proslavery occupants of the antebellum U.S. government and the quest to secure an empire for slavery in the Western Hemisphere. Marx's assessment was largely correct—filibustering flourished with the support, or at least the noninterference, of proslavery expansionists. While the form of pro-Confederate privatized raiding differed from antebellum filibusters, both were supported by many of the same evangelists for slavery who moved on to form the Confederate States.[20]

The clash of armies in the war may have drowned out the buzz of filibustering, privateering, piracy, and other forms of raiding, but privatized warfare flourished on the boundaries of the continent and at sea, encouraged by the Confederate government. As their sponsors lost control, they threatened incredible disruption and chaos. Many Southern politicians who rose to prominence in the Confederate government supported filibustering in the antebellum era, particularly the future Confederate secretary of the navy, Stephen R. Mallory, and Southern support for privateering in 1861 was widespread. Traditional privateering floundered after the first year of the war, but a fusion of it with filibustering-style attacks from neutral territory offered a brief glimmer of hope to Mallory, Judah P. Benjamin, and Jefferson Davis. Confederate leaders hoped to harness private enterprise and unconventional warfare to offset Union military and naval advantages and, perhaps, strike a blow that would change Confederate fortunes for good. These operations required international shelter, and Confederates found it—plus substantial assistance—among the territory and peoples of the British American colonies. British subjects in the colonies were, in many cases, participants in the Civil War rather than observers, and the colonial theater of war had far greater potential to disrupt regional peace and order than many historians have been willing to admit.

Ultimately, this book calls attention to the peripheries of power and makes the case for the enduring importance of private actors for our understanding of international violence and diplomacy in the Civil War era. British colonial merchants and businesses demonstrated the power to resist or alter the policies of even the world's most powerful state, and they would help shape the emerging dichotomy between settler dominions and conquered colonies within the British Empire for decades to come. The Civil War likewise marked an inflection in the dynamics of privatized violence in North America and beyond. In the antebellum era, such violence existed outside or in cooperation with the state, as with filibustering and privateering, but during the war, Confederates looked for new ways to bind private military action to private enterprise and state authority as a response to changes in international law and technology that disrupted the older traditions of transnational violence like privateering and filibustering. After the war, the emergence within the United States of parallel structures of private and public violence is understandable as part of this trend, and similar structures—think of entities like the United Fruit Company, the Pinkertons, and the U.S. Marine Corps in Latin America—were instrumental in building the formal and informal U.S. empire in the Caribbean basin and the Pacific in the late nineteenth and early twentieth centuries, with the slow-motion seizure of Hawai'i by a combination of planters, merchants, and a sprinkling of government force as perhaps the greatest example.[21] Filibustering did not disappear, as events like the Fenian raids of the immediate postwar years attested, but governments increasingly found alternative and more internationally acceptable methods of adventurism that maintained at least a veneer of international order and state monopoly on violence.

This book is divided into seven chapters, proceeding roughly chronologically from the antebellum era through 1865, with chapters 2 through 7 also organized geographically to focus on particular colonies and themes. Chapter 1 examines antebellum relations between the South and Britain, with a focus on the colonies as sites of conflict, particularly over slavery. Chapter 2 examines the critical importance of British colonial support for the establishment and sustainment of Confederate blockade running from 1861 to 1863, including the largely unexamined role of local elites like Henry Adderley in the Bahamas in creating favorable conditions for the most critical Confederate logistical campaign of the entire war. The difficulties surrounding Confederate government efforts to take control over blockade running are the focus of chapter 3, along with the social interactions of Confederates and

Bermuda society. Chapter 4 turns to the ambivalent relationship between the rebellion and Black colonials, especially in Bermuda and the Bahamas, and the social dynamics that influenced if, when, and how they opposed the pro-Confederate network in the colonies. Chapter 5 examines the case of the *Chesapeake* hijacking as an example of the increasing fusion of privateering and filibustering by pro-Confederate raiders. Chapters 6 and 7, set largely in Canada, explore how Confederates embraced the logic of informal warfare and diplomacy in 1864–65, with increasingly chaotic results.

It is also necessary to mention what this book is *not*: it is not an exhaustive history of British colonial involvement in the American Civil War. I have left to the side, for example, the extensive enrollment of British North Americans in the U.S. Army and most other colonial interactions that involved only the North or the U.S. government, as the focus is decidedly on the Confederacy and the British Empire. The Union response to Anglo-Confederate interactions is included where it is particularly relevant to the quasi-war in the colonies—the Union navy's pursuit and seizure of the *Chesapeake* in Nova Scotia territorial waters, or the implementation of a passport system along the Canadian frontier after the St. Albans raid, for two examples. For similar reasons of narrative focus, I have mostly excluded Confederate interactions with Mexico and with non-British colonies such as Cuba. While they mattered for the course of the war and played a role in blockade running, they do not have as much to tell us about specifically British imperial governance and private parties.

Caught between King Cotton and Queen Victoria, the colonies of British America occupied a place of ambiguous loyalty and ambivalent neutrality during the American Civil War. Many British Americans simultaneously took pride in their place in a mighty empire and resented that empire's interference in their affairs. Colonists almost everywhere claimed to oppose slavery, yet many actively supported a slaveholder's republic in the name of freedom. Confederates, for their part, shared in the inconsistency. Government officials insisted on respecting the neutrality of British territory provided there was gain in it, diplomatic or otherwise. An ad hoc commercial-diplomatic network bound the colonies and the rebellion together on the basis of trade, sentiment, and occasionally kinship, and hinted at the possibilities for future Anglo-Confederate cooperation had the rebellion succeeded. And in the midst of it all, freelance rebels—privateers, adventurers, and swindlers among them—carried the Confederate torch beyond Southern shores, starting fires along the way, often ignorant or heedless of international law, Confederate policy, or the strictures of neutrality.

A Note on Terminology

For the sake of clarity and consistency, I have attempted to adhere to contemporary names for cities and colonies. Of note, "Canada" refers to the United Province of Canada, which, prior to 1841, had been Upper Canada and Lower Canada—present-day Ontario and Quebec. The two portions were renamed Canada East and Canada West, although the old names remained in use.[22] "British North America" refers to the collective colonies of Canada, New Brunswick, Nova Scotia, and Prince Edward Island.[23] "British America" is the term I have chosen to cover all of these plus Bermuda and the Bahamas. The term thus excludes some British colonies in the Western Hemisphere, primarily those in the West Indies, plus British Honduras (Belize) and the Hudson's Bay Company territory.[24] To distinguish the non-Indigenous residents of these places from residents of Great Britain proper, I refer to them as "colonists" or "colonials."

In a work such as this, which features cooperation and a sometimes hazy distinction between private citizens and the Confederate government, it can be difficult to properly label those people involved and avoid confusion over their often-muddled roles. The general term "Confederate" applies to citizens of the Confederate States, regardless of whether they held a government position. "Pro-Confederates" were noncitizens (usually colonists) working in support of the rebellion. When referring to the government or individuals acting in their capacity as government officials, I specifically refer to them as such. For example, "Confederates expected British intervention, but the Confederate government did little to prepare for an extended war if Britain remained neutral." "Confederate government" refers to the general government and not state or local entities unless specified otherwise.

CHAPTER ONE

"That Nation of Pirates"

Private Violence and the North American Origins of Confederate Informal Diplomacy, 1837–1861

I do not look upon filibustering as the worst crime in the world. I do not think highly of the 1818 [neutrality] law. It was wise, no doubt, in our state of weakness, but it is useless to us now.
—Sen. Stephen Mallory

WHEN WILLIAM HOWARD Russell, the famed correspondent of the London *Times*, visited Montgomery, Alabama, in late spring of 1861, he encountered the seat of the Confederate government in the chaotic throes of organizing itself, an army, and a foreign policy. Russell interviewed several important Confederate leaders, including Jefferson Davis, but he also described the conditions in the city and the characters falling into the new government's orbit. The hotel Russell stayed in, filled beyond capacity along with the rest of city, required him to share one room and three beds with five men, and his shared room was "full of tobacco smoke, filibusters, and conversation."[1] These filibusters—veterans and supporters of unauthorized military expeditions—seemed at ease with the highest officers of the Confederate government, and many found places in the army or, in the case of John T. Pickett, the Confederate diplomatic corps.[2] While filibusters and self-appointed revolutionaries like George N. Sanders ("a learned pig" in Russell's jaundiced opinion) vied for Russell's attention, the Confederate government sought out his opinion on the issue of privateering.[3] William Montague Browne, the assistant secretary of state, intimated to Russell that the government had received hundreds of applications for letters of marque, and later asked if Russell would help them create such letters, as Browne and Judah Benjamin, then attorney general, could not find an example. Russell declined, begging that the duties of neutrality forbade him from giving such assistance.[4] Russell's brief sojourn to Montgomery hinted at recurring (and understudied) factors in the wider American Civil War: the Confederate government's comfort with privatized warfare, the unconventional and unprepared nature of its diplomacy and foreign policy, and its inescapable need for help from British subjects.

This chapter addresses two related themes in the immediate antebellum era and the early months of the American Civil War, glimpsed in Russell's experience at Montgomery: the relationship between the South and British Empire, including public opinion, and the widespread pattern of privatized diplomacy and transnational violence in antebellum North America and the early months of the war. Anglo-Southern relations were often fraught in the antebellum era. Tensions over slavery and abolition loomed over Southern, and later Confederate, attitudes toward Britain, and Anglophobia persisted throughout the United States, particularly around elections. Nevertheless, populist Anglophobia often gave way to realism in the course of foreign policy, particularly if it allowed the U.S. government to harness British power in its own interests, as with the Clayton-Bulwer Treaty of 1850, which prevented exclusive British control of a transisthmian canal in Central America and forbade further British territorial claims in the region.[5] The opinion of the British government toward the South, especially with regard to phenomena like filibustering and privateering, influenced how the empire's representatives on the margins of the conflict responded to Confederate provocations later in the war. The state of colonial popular opinion toward the Confederacy likewise affected the extent and enthusiasm of their support for the rebellion. Few, if any, colonials in British North America, Bermuda, or the Bahamas expected the Civil War to assume such gigantic proportions, and the colonies found themselves inexorably drawn into the conflict. Whether they liked it or not, colonial territories and subjects became active participants in the war.

Mid–nineteenth-century patterns of privatized transnational diplomacy and violence in North America likewise provided the basis for the Confederate laissez-faire approach to its informal agents in the colonies. A wide spectrum of privatized violence persisted on the frontiers of the United States and British America in the antebellum era, which influenced prewar public opinion and later the course of the informal warfare and diplomacy in these border regions. Filibustering garnered the most attention, but violence over the fate of fugitive slaves and widespread kidnappings by private detectives and other nonstate actors weakened the efficacy of borders and coastal waters as obstacles to transnational violence. Many prominent Southerners who went on to influential positions in the Confederate government had, in the 1850s, embraced the practice of filibustering when it suited their interests. Some went so far as to reject the premise that such adventures should be illegal under either U.S. or international law. Even the famously rigid "constitutionalist" Jefferson Davis regarded filibusters like William Walker with ambivalence rather than revulsion, and Davis never completely rejected the idea of private adventurism. The closer that privatized violence came under the wing of the state, the more enthusiastically future Confederates promoted it. Southerners (and many Northerners for that matter) embraced privateering as a weapon of war in 1860, even as the powers of Europe moved to banish it from the seas with the 1856 Declaration of Paris.[6] The changing environment of maritime law in the nineteenth century, along with the shift from sail to steam power, made privateering a disappointment to Confederate leaders and drove the Confederates to innovations of increasingly dubious legality in an effort to harness private enterprise to the war at sea. Alongside this private violence, the Confederate government tacitly encouraged private citizens to shape its foreign policy. In the first months of the war, this manifested itself in the informal cotton embargo. Later, the influence of private merchants, promoters, and self-appointed agents deeply affected the structure of key Confederate operations, including blockade running in the colonies.

These somewhat disparate threads provide the background necessary to understand the crucial role that informal diplomacy and private military action played in sustaining the rebellion. They also illustrate the indispensable role of British colonial territory and subjects in support of the Confederate project. The establishment of large-scale blockade running required the conjuncture of British colonial governance, with its inherently divided sovereignty, and the network of business and family connections between colonial ports of British America and the South. Bereft of their usual connection to transatlantic shipping and communications routes through Northern ports like New York, Confederate merchants turned to colonial ports to facilitate the crucial trafficking of weapons and cotton across the saltwater frontier and the Union blockade. Colonial ports and territory also provided essential shelter and launching points for a variety of pro-Confederate military actions, from facilitating the arming of commissioned warships like the CSS *Florida*, to raiding across the land frontier from British North America, to acts of outright piracy. The informal diplomacy and war in and around British America happened as it did because of the conditions and popular opinion of the immediate antebellum era. White Southerners remained suspicious of the British Empire, but their attitudes toward the colonies were more flexible; they could be imagined simultaneously as British and American, in the broadest sense of the word.

Many antebellum Southerners viewed Britain with a mix of paranoia and contempt. Slaveholders widely feared a British-sponsored abolitionist conspiracy, particularly in the years between British abolition in the West Indies and the Mexican-American War.[7] Although these fears softened in the 1850s, many Southerners replaced them with an assumption that greed and dependence on cotton would force the British to submit quickly in the event of war—or to recognize and aid an independent South in the event of secession. Attitudes toward the colonies proved far more flexible—Southern observers projected their needs and assumptions onto the colonies as circumstances required. The colonies could be both entirely British—a stand-in for the empire at large, or they could be regarded as a thing apart and a vulnerability to be soothed or exploited. The colonies did not occupy a place of importance in Southern discourse during the secession crisis. On the other side of things, strong growth and the "settler revolution" led the colonies, especially British North America, to the cusp of vastly increased independence from London.[8] While colonial public opinion was largely united against slavery, abolitionism's luster had faded a bit in the intervening years, and individual colonial governments were poised in 1860 to take advantage of the impending crisis, even if it conflicted with London's prerogative over foreign affairs.[9] At the same time, the Royal Navy and the Foreign Office gave significant attention to the threat of filibustering, up to and after the start of the Civil War. Their concern should serve as a reminder of the disruptiveness of privatized warfare and the prominent place it had in popular imagination in 1860–61. British authorities did not assume it would simply fade away, and they were right.

British attitudes toward the United States, slavery, and the Confederacy have been widely studied. The Palmerston government treated the United States with diffidence. Palmerston himself disliked the United States and republican governance in general, but his cabinet did not seek out conflict and, within the bounds of national honor, conciliated the Americans where it could.[10] Popular opinion varied widely by social class, religion, and political affiliation, as studies by R. J. M. Blackett and Peter O'Connor show, but most literate Britons identified American slavery as a national rather than a sectional institution. The Confederacy's supporters in Britain tended to be political conservatives, often aristocrats, as well as merchants or those who stood to gain from the cotton trade. They also tended to view slavery as a peripheral issue.[11] Nevertheless, once the war began, the Confederacy's unapologetic embrace of slavery proved to be a diplomatic millstone around their neck, preventing many Britons who might otherwise have been sympathetic from supporting their cause. In most ways, opinions in the colonies toward the South approximated those of metropolitan Britain, with some important exceptions.

British colonials did not mirror the South's angst toward them, but antislavery sentiment certainly affected attitudes, especially in British North America. Canada, if anything, became more staunchly abolitionist in the wake of the Fugitive Slave Law of 1850, and slaves seeking freedom were met with welcome, however lukewarm and segregated. Canadian Reformers, led by the newspaper editor and sometime politician George Brown, hoped to witness the "overthrow of two equally baleful dominions—the Slavocracy of the South, and the French Priestocracy of the North," although he could hardly have known that the "priestocracy" would become a staunch supporter of the Confederacy.[12] Public opinion in British North America soured quickly on the Union once the war began, on the twin influences of the *Trent* affair and the initial refusal of the Lincoln administration to proclaim emancipation as a war aim. Even before the war began, however, Canadian conservatives, some descended from United Empire Loyalists who proudly traced their lineage to Tory refugees of the American Revolution, had not forgotten Northern support for the Canadian rebellions of 1837–38 and leaped to the South's defense in spite of slavery, while even the Union's supporters in Canada found themselves caught against the tide of pro-British (or at least anti-American) sentiment.[13] The island colonies, many suffering from post-emancipation economic stagnation and political or racial unrest (a source of schadenfreude for some proslavery observers), offered a more welcoming climate of opinion, particularly as steamship traffic increasingly passed them by. Although their commercial ties had shifted somewhat toward the North—especially New York—by 1860, the white mercantile elites of both Bermuda and the Bahamas maintained some cultural affinity with the South, and trading and kinship networks linked them with Southern port cities, especially Key West.[14] Many of the leading figures of these colonies—especially the Bahamas—had vociferously opposed British emancipation and resisted the growth of political rights for the large Black populations of their colony.[15] These island territories, despite their place in Southern imagination as outposts of abolition, harbored great potential for friendship with a slaveholding Southern Republic, regardless of the empire's official stance on slavery or the Civil War.

Indeed, abolitionism (as a cause, if not as an ideology) had lost some of its influence in British society by the 1850s. In Britain, membership and activism in abolitionist groups waned as a consequence of their own success at home and their relative powerlessness to influence non-British slavery—a symptom of the emergence of an "anti-slavery pluralism" that permitted disagreement over race, equality, and governance even as it remained unified in opposition to holding humans as property.[16] Colonial governments in the West Indies struggled with racial animosity and economic stagnation, and many in the white minority sought to preserve their social and political power at the expense of former slaves and their descendants in ways that would have warmed the hearts of the architects of Jim Crow, even to the point of abolishing representative government in favor of direct rule by a Crown-appointed governor.[17] While they held out little hope of reestablishing slavery, the white mercantile and planter elites of the islands openly supported white supremacy, and few, if any, among them looked with anticipation toward the prospect of emancipation in their continental neighbor to the northwest.

Antebellum Southern sentiment toward the British colonies was ambivalent at best, not least because of lingering Anglophobia and the effects, real and imagined, of British emancipation. Southerners pointed to conditions in the colonies to reinforce their proslavery arguments and even, in some cases, to advocate for the reopening of the transatlantic slave trade.[18] South Carolinians, in the context of the earlier nullification crisis, expressed fears that West Indian emancipation portended the same fate for the South at the hands of a distant majority, which invited if not insurrection then economic loss, and the tales of Jamaican planters and comparisons to Saint-Domingue found receptive audiences.[19] South Carolina planter Edward B. Bryan's tract *The Rightful Remedy*, published in 1850, painted Northern and British abolitionism as one and the same—a dishonest, hypocritical ploy to impoverish the

South for their own benefit, with secession being the remedy for this situation.[20] Bryan's work for the Southern Rights Association highlights what historian Edward Rugemer called Southerners' "conspiratorial view of British abolition," and the widespread suspicion of British motives as anything but humanitarian.[21] High-profile incidents, like the self-liberation of the slaves aboard the *Creole*, who reached the Bahamas and freedom, or John Brown's raid on Harper's Ferry, which received substantial support in Chatham, Canada West, soured the attitude of many Southerners, especially planters and fire-eaters, toward their most proximate British neighbors.[22]

British colonies, especially in the West Indies, appeared frequently in proslavery arguments as examples of the evils and dangers of emancipation, and evinced fears of "black-a-moor regiments" (i.e., the British West India Regiments garrisoned there) threatening the South in the event of war with Britain.[23] Antebellum Southerners looked out from the shore and saw, as John C. Calhoun put it, the "[Royal] navy, sheltered in the commanding positions of Halifax, Bermuda, and the Bahamas, ready to strike a blow at any point she may select on this long line of coast."[24] Those inclined to Anglophobia saw the colonies as a beam holding, in the form of the Royal Navy, the Sword of Damocles over the South—and the United States as a whole. As late as 1859, U.S. senator Stephen R. Mallory of Florida spoke of the oppressive net of British colonies in the Atlantic and Caribbean that threatened American expansion and commerce and formed part of their effort to "undermine us in every part of the earth."[25]

Yet contradictorily, others saw the colonies as a weakness waiting to be exploited in the event of war. During tensions over the Maine boundary dispute in 1839, the New Orleans *True American* predicted that Britain's "West India possessions populated by hosts of free blacks will rise against the home government" and "join the Santo Domingo league." Canada, likewise, was "ripe for rebellion" in the still-roiling aftermath of the failed uprisings of 1837–38 and would also "raise the standard of revolt."[26] Neither of these outcomes seems likely, but they indicated a willingness on the part of Southern observers to project attributes on the colonies that suited the needs of the moment. In 1850, Edward Bryan sarcastically applauded the "defenceless" state of Britain's post-abolition colonies, their weakness being, naturally, the result of freeing the slaves.[27] As sectional tensions over slavery mounted in the late 1850s, some Southerners found meaning anew in the colonies as "weak and dependent" pawns of the British Crown, deliberately kept in a state of helplessness and serving as an example for Northerners in their supposed efforts to subjugate the South.[28] In their bad moments, the colonies were fully British and indistinguishable from the evils of the mother country. When the need arose, however, they could be considered in isolation, as entities separable from Britain itself.

Anxiety over abolitionism lay behind much of the Southern dislike of British colonies in the 1840s and 1850s. The *Creole* is the most famous example of a series of cases involving American ships carrying slaves that landed, for one reason or another, in British territory, resulting in the liberation of their human cargo. It became a matter of British policy that, after 1834 and emancipation, any slave reaching British territory immediately gained freedom. Several ships engaged in the intrastate slave trade—the *Comet*, the *Hermosa*, and the *Encomium*—arrived in the Bahamas as a result of storms while en route from the Upper South to New Orleans, as did the coastwise slaver *Enterprise* in Bermuda. Passage through the shoals and narrow straits of the islands could be treacherous even in good weather. Bahamian authorities freed slaves who arrived at the islands, whatever their provenance or cost—indeed, the Bahamas frequently became the new home for Africans liberated by the Royal Navy from slavers bound for Cuba.[29]

The *Creole*, a brig bound from Virginia to New Orleans with a cargo of slaves intended for sale, came to the Bahamas deliberately, after a party of slaves rose up against the crew, killing one and taking control of the ship in early November 1841.[30] They forced the remaining crew to sail to the Bahamas because some of the slaves on board knew they would be free if they could reach the islands. One of the leaders of the uprising, Madison Washington, had escaped slavery and lived for some time in Canada, near Toronto, and he was certainly aware of the safety offered by British soil. He had returned to the South that summer with the aid of abolitionists to attempt to free his wife, who was still held in bondage, but slavers recaptured him and put him on the *Creole* to be sold. A number of the other slaves on the *Creole* came from the same plantation as those freed from the *Hermosa*, so it is likely they also knew that the Bahamas could give them refuge. The brig reached Nassau on November 9, and the slaves informed local authorities of what had transpired. Governor Cockburn, who was an imperial appointee, and George Anderson, the resident attorney general of the Bahamas, allowed most of the slaves on board the *Creole* to go free, feeling that precedent coupled with pressure from a large group of Black Nassau residents gave them little choice. The threat of mob violence—small boats full of armed Black men had surrounded the *Creole*—underlined the actions of Bahamian officials, who later showed themselves quite sympathetic with slavery when it did not threaten their personal or professional safety. When the *Creole*'s first mate protested the impending release, Anderson told him, "You had better let them go quietly ashore; if you object I am afraid there will be blood shed."[31] The governor detained only the nineteen suspected of being involved in the "mutiny." A detachment of Black troops from the West India Regiment garrison foiled an attempt by a party of Americans to retake the *Creole* by force, and the authorities allowed the vessel to continue to New Orleans, less its human cargo.[32]

White Southerners reacted angrily to the release of the slaves and demanded that the so-called mutineers be extradited to the United States. The Colonial Office, after consulting with the Crown law officers in London, determined in January 1842 that piracy had not occurred, and thus the case was ineligible for trial in any British court. Despite this, the Nassau vice-admiralty court—staffed with local judges who were often of uneven quality—examined the matter in April, perhaps at the insistence of the U.S. consul, but it adhered to Crown policy and determined that it held no jurisdiction over crimes of mutiny and murder that occurred on the high seas, and the so-called mutineers walked free, further enraging the proponents of slavery.[33] Their rage might have burned even brighter had they known that in the late 1840s, John Brown invited Madison Washington to join him in his early plans for a strike against slavery. Washington declined, but throughout the 1840s and 1850s he persisted in abolitionist imagination as a romantic and heroic figure, and in slaveholders' imaginations as a symbol of British perfidy and of the persistent threat posed by British colonies as outposts of free soil on the American periphery.[34]

Suspicion of British motives drove Southern opinion and, frequently, U.S. foreign policy in the 1840s. Led by John C. Calhoun, the annexation of Texas arose out of a long-simmering fear of British abolitionism swooping onto the continent, based on the failings—real and imagined—of British emancipation, the struggles of West Indian economies under free labor, and interference with the intrastate slave trade.[35] The negotiations over what would become the Webster-Ashburton Treaty also suffered because of Southern concerns over slavery. President John Tyler, a Virginia slaveholder concerned with the safety of the coastwise slave trade, annoyed British negotiators with his demands for an apology and guarantees against future recurrences of cases like the *Creole*, but Britain would not budge on the issue of returning slaves to bondage.³⁶ All Tyler achieved regarding the *Creole* was a vague promise to avoid "officious interference" with American vessels that sought shelter in British ports, and a promise that British colonial officials would not encourage slave mutiny or revolts. An exchange of notes to this effect reassured enough Southern senators that the treaty passed, and they received further reassurance in 1855 when an arbitrator awarded the owners of the *Creole* slaves a substantial judgment against the British government in compensation.³⁷

Perhaps most importantly, the contentious atmosphere illustrated by the *Creole* and similar cases ensured that the extradition provisions of the Ashburton Treaty remained unsettled and vague. Article X allowed for extradition only in the case of seven ostensibly nonpolitical crimes, chiefly murder, robbery, piracy, and forgery, but because they were not explicitly defined, it remained an open question whether a British court would consider any of these a crime if committed by a slave seeking their freedom. The 1841 case of Nelson Hackett, who escaped slavery in Arkansas by reaching Canada West, only to be extradited back into slavery on allegations of theft, had united opinion in Canada and Britain against extraditing fugitive slaves. Hackett was extradited only because he engaged in theft that the governor of Canada believed to be in excess of what was required to make his escape, and British interpretation of the Ashburton treaty and Canadian statutes made it ambiguous whether other crimes tied to escaping slavery would be considered sufficient for extradition.³⁸ In 1843, a Bahamian court narrowly avoided deciding the issue in an extradition proceeding against seven slaves accused of killing a white man in Florida before reaching the Bahamas via the "saltwater railroad." The court released the men for lack of evidence but in its decision implied that it would have considered sending them back to the United States if the proof had been sufficient.³⁹ The matter remained troublingly unsettled until the question came up again in Canada on the eve of the secession crisis. The relatively muted Southern reaction to the case of John Anderson, another fugitive slave facing possible extradition to the United States in 1860, can be explained by the distraction over the political crisis in the United States, but it also reflects the softening attitude of many Southerners toward Britain and British America.

John Anderson, who killed a white slaveholder in Missouri during his escape in 1853, was one of the thousands who made their way north of the border after the Hackett case. Anderson reached Canada with the aid of

John Anderson, photographed in Montreal before he traveled to Britain in 1861. Credit: William Notman, "Mr. John Anderson, Montreal, QC, 1861," I-0.55.1, McCord Stewart Museum.

abolitionists, eventually settling in Brant County, where he lived relatively quietly until early 1860, when someone informed a local police magistrate of the killing committed by Anderson during his escape, a crime that fell under the terms of Article X and made extradition a possibility. The magistrate issued a warrant against Anderson, and a justice of the peace arrested him in March 1860. Word quickly reached Windsor, just across from Detroit, where Anderson's pursuers had lost his trail in 1854. Slave catchers frequented the Detroit-Windsor corridor, hoping to get word of potential victims, and one of them, James Gunning, learned of Anderson's arrest and decided to use the as-yet untested extradition treaty to recover his employer's "property." Secretary of State Lewis Cass formally requested Anderson's extradition in October from Lord Lyons, recently arrived as British minister in Washington, who forwarded the request to London and British North America. Anderson faced an extradition hearing in Brantford, where a justice of the peace heard arguments in the case. The magistrate, under guidance from Attorney General John A. Macdonald to require "evidence of criminality sufficient to sustain a charge according to the laws of this Province," signed a warrant of commitment for Anderson. Now only Macdonald and the governor-general stood between him and certain death in Missouri.[40]

Ironically, Southern observers paid little attention to the very case that might, at long last, give them a weapon to recover the "property" that Anglophobes said Britain schemed to deny them. When the three-judge panel in Toronto gave its ruling, the public in and around the courthouse erupted with anger. They ruled, two to one, that sufficient cause existed for Anderson to be held for extradition. Canadian and British abolitionists expressed fury at the possibility of Canada and Britain being turned into "tools of the slave-catchers" and organized a widespread campaign of petitions to the government, particularly the Colonial Office, urging them not to send Anderson to be "[burned] alive by a slow fire."[41] The editor of the Richmond *Daily Dispatch* praised the decision and the preparations by the Canadian government to prevent a rescue attempt, comparing it favorably against mob actions in Boston. Though "just as deeply tainted with abolitionism as the Yankees," the Toronto mob faced "a government that allowed no trifling with its laws."[42] Anderson and his attorneys again appealed, with Macdonald's blessing, to the Court of Common Pleas, also in Toronto.

Meanwhile, in London, two parallel actions concerning Anderson's case threatened to upend two decades of relative comity and increasing independence in Anglo-Canadian relations. A British abolitionist group, fearing that the court in Toronto was about to send Anderson to his death, appealed to the Court of the Queen's Bench in London for a writ of habeas corpus, which would require Anderson to appear in person, rendering him momentarily safe from extradition. In an extraordinary series of legal missteps, the court issued the writ in the erroneous belief that British courts still held authority in colonies with their own legal systems. A special courier raced for Toronto with the writ, hoping to arrive in time. At the same time and in complete ignorance of the court proceeding, the Colonial Office issued an order to Governor-General Head that he was, under no circumstances, to hand over Anderson.[43] Both of these measures were a clear usurpation of colonial judicial independence and responsible government. Both governments desired the same thing—to avoid handing over Anderson—but the Canadians did not welcome unwarranted and, as they saw it, illegal meddling in their affairs, even in a cause they agreed was right. The vague wording of the Ashburton Treaty threatened imperial harmony at a moment of crisis in North America.

Ironically, the wording of the treaty also became Anderson's savior. The Court of Common Pleas heard the case for and against Anderson's extradition and gave every appearance of agreeing with the earlier ruling. The judges then issued their decision: Anderson was free to go. The initial warrant for his extradition was invalid because of a technicality in its wording. The affidavits from witnesses in Missouri only accused Anderson of stabbing and killing his pursuer.[44] Since other crimes not included in the treaty, such as manslaughter, could have occurred, the court deemed the request invalid. The courier from London arrived before the announcement and served the writ for Anderson to the sheriff in Toronto, who sat on it, unsure of its legality and unwilling to interrupt while the court prepared its decision. Observers of every political stripe put aside their bickering briefly to condemn London's usurpation of local judicial authority. Had they learned of the Colonial Office orders to Head, their anger would have been even greater.[45] Interestingly, one of the Confederacy's strongest eventual friends in Canada, George Taylor Denison, authored a pamphlet praising the release of Anderson and the denial of his extradition on legal and humanitarian grounds.[46] Abolitionists, fearing rearrest under a correctly worded warrant, immediately sent Anderson to Britain, where he was feted at huge gatherings before being shuffled off, apparently less-than-enthusiastically, to Liberia, where he vanished from the record. Anderson's ordeal foreshadowed several cases that followed involving the possible extradition of pro-Confederate raiders, which provoked similar themes of colonial-metropolitan conflict over legal and treaty responsibilities. Over the next four years, colonial courts repeatedly turned to technicalities of questionable validity in order to avoid making unpopular rulings.

The secession crisis drowned out Southern (and now Confederate) reaction to the Anderson case. The Buchanan administration, paralyzed by resignations and incompetence, did nothing, and most influential Southerners, who might otherwise have cared deeply about the opportunity seemingly afforded by the Anderson case, had already left the federal government as their home states seceded. The *Mobile Evening News* reported on the Anderson verdict in one terse sentence, in an issue dedicated largely to Jefferson Davis's arrival in Montgomery and the proceedings of the provisional government there.[47] The new Confederate government, bereft of even a rudimentary diplomatic bureaucracy and lacking official recognition from Britain, could not hope to capitalize on the opening the case provided for retrieving fugitive slaves, and its attention was elsewhere in any event.

Ultimately, the Confederacy benefited from the willingness, demonstrated in the Anderson affair, of colonial subjects and officials to ignore or honor in the breach imperial directives that conflicted with colonial prerogatives or popular opinion. Struggles with London over governance pervaded British settler colonies around the world in the mid-nineteenth century, and the imperial government frequently accepted colonial endeavors as a fait accompli or otherwise compromised in some way with the issue at hand. Again and again, colonial interpretations of "British" governance and rights differed in ways large and small from their metropolitan counterparts, shaped by local history, climate, and political conditions, and this affected the relative power and level of imperial control over legislation, governorships, and the judiciary in the colonies.[48] The fractures between colony and metropole over issues of sovereignty, even on an issue of overwhelming agreement like opposition to slavery, hinted at the advantages the Confederacy might find in the colonies, particularly through low-level engagement and an informal diplomacy led by merchants and minor officials.

Legal and diplomatic disputes over slavery were far from the only sources of tension on the margins of the United States and the British Empire in the antebellum era. A persistent tradition of private transnational violence shaped

British policy and tempted Americans, particularly Southerners, with a ready (yet easily disavowed in the case of trouble) tool of empire. British imperial and colonial officials regarded the United States, and the South in particular, as a continuing source of violence and disorder in the hemisphere. Antebellum filibustering, usually but not always led by American citizens, caused endless headaches for British governors, diplomats, and the Royal Navy. On the eve of the Civil War, it was private, unauthorized extraterritorial violence that captured the imaginations of these officials and seemed to pose the greatest threat to the positivist international order pursued by Britain, perhaps best embodied by the 1856 Declaration of Paris. The British foreign secretary Lord Clarendon, in Paris to negotiate that agreement, raged at the conduct of the Americans, particularly in Nicaragua. He warned that this "nation of Pirates" would threaten everyone with "insolence" and disorder unless convinced that it would face "a universal league to compel them to observe the usages of civilized nations."[49] If state-sanctioned privateering posed such a threat to order that the powers of Europe could be induced to forbid it, then unsanctioned adventurers conquering territory required the attention of Britain, the power best poised to suppress it if the United States could, or would, not.

Filibustering caused the British government no end of trouble in the twenty-five years preceding the Civil War. American filibusters joined in the rebellions in Canada in 1837–38, which threatened to wrest away the largest settler colony remaining in the empire. Filibustering expeditions also threatened Spanish Cuba and British territorial claims in Central America in the 1840s and 1850s, especially William Walker's remarkably successful forays into Nicaragua. Walker's adventurism also threatened British strategic interests in the region, especially cross-isthmus access to the Pacific Ocean, negotiations over the fate of the Bay Islands, and the unsettled treaty arrangements with the United States regarding a future interoceanic canal.[50] A detailed history of filibustering need not be presented here. Rather, the intent is to demonstrate its ubiquity as part of a spectrum of private international violence in the immediate antebellum era. British officials considered it a real menace, while American officials and influential future Confederates were often happy to embrace it if it suited their ends.

Filibustering from "that nation of Pirates" consumed the attention of British officials and shaped the empire's approach to international law, as well as its military response to the secession crisis. Walker alone moved British legal opinion and naval policy regarding private violence further down the spectrum toward exclusive state control, continuing the trends seen at Paris in 1856. Previously, in 1854, the Crown's law officers issued an opinion stating that when dealing with filibusters, "the military or naval forces of friendly states not immediately concerned should not actually and directly attack, or engage any but pirates and banditti."[51] This excluded filibusters from categorization as *hostis humani generis* ("enemy of all mankind"—a legal appellation from admiralty law applied to pirates and, in this era, slave traders at sea) and thus from capture or attack by the Royal Navy. Yet in 1858, following the European accord against privateering in 1856 and Walker's serial invasions of Nicaragua, Britain changed course, and the Admiralty issued instructions for the navy to render assistance to local forces in repelling any filibuster attacks along the coast of Central America.[52] British ships never had to act on these orders, but they demonstrated the increasing concern of the British government over the metastasis of violence from the United States.

During the secession crisis and the early months of the Civil War, filibustering remained a primary concern of colonial governors and Royal Navy officers in North America. Vice Admiral Alexander Milne, the recently arrived commander of the North American and West Indies Station, expressed relief at the capture and execution of William Walker in September 1860 and the return of the remnants of his expedition to New Orleans. Milne's ships were indispensable in both, and he "confidently hoped that the organized system of Filibustering that has for so many years distracted those unhappy [Central American] countries has received its death blow."[53] Yet almost immediately the governor of Jamaica asked for further protection against a possible renewal of filibustering.[54] Other governors and officials echoed those concerns in the following months, in some cases in fear of direct attacks on their own colonies by Northern filibusters after Anglo-American tensions spiked amid the *Trent* affair in late 1861.[55]

While filibustering was perceived, then as now, as a chiefly American phenomenon, the participants in (and targets of) filibustering expeditions were far from homogeneous, and British subjects in North America often took a very different view of filibustering if imperial policy diverged from their interests. Europeans, including Britons, formed a large portion of Walker's first expedition into Nicaragua, and it was at the invitation of British colonists, upset at the impending return of their settlement in Ruatan to Honduras, that Walker undertook his fateful, final mission in 1860.[56] More markedly, the British participants in the Aroostook "War" in Maine, which wavered on the spectrum between vigilantism, filibustering, and state-sponsored warfare, came almost entirely from New Brunswick. The participants in filibuster expeditions launched from the United States came from all sections of the country and from a wide variety of backgrounds.[57] Filibustering and private military adventurism transcended borders in antebellum North America. The Civil War obscured but did not alter that formula.

The eventual leaders of the Confederacy held shifting and occasionally conflicting attitudes toward filibustering. Jefferson Davis generally disapproved of adventurers like William Walker, although some historians have argued that this disfavor stemmed in part because slaveholders held the most powerful positions in the federal government for much of the 1850s, and thus Davis, among others, felt that control over foreign policy offset the usefulness of supporting filibusters.[58] That argument hinges on the interpretation that the protection, rather than the extension, of slavery mattered most to Davis and other like-minded slaveholders. Walker, for his part, boldly proclaimed the necessity of expanding slavery within and without the United States, and he explicitly tied his Nicaraguan adventures, ex post facto, to the battle over slavery in Kansas.[59] Stephen Mallory and Judah P. Benjamin—the other two most important figures in the eventual use of private, extraterritorial violence in the Civil War—usually, though not always, spoke supportively of filibustering in the 1850s. In 1858, Mallory told the Senate, "I do not look upon filibustering as the worst crime in the world. I do not think highly of the 1818 [neutrality] law. It was wise, no doubt, in our state of weakness, but it is useless to us now."[60] The policy motivation for Davis, Mallory, and Benjamin matters less than the fact that they were perfectly willing, if the situation required it, to embrace private, perhaps even extralegal, violence. Davis spoke ambivalently about filibustering in the Senate, proclaiming his disfavor for the tactic and those involved yet questioning the wisdom of the Buchanan administration in interfering with Walker's latest foray into Nicaragua, as well as its legal power to do so. Davis's fellow senator from Mississippi, Albert Gallatin Brown, went further and praised Walker and his volunteers as "patriotic men—not lawless and piratical men as is now charged"—who sought to restore Walker to his rightful position. Future Confederate secretary of state Robert Toombs, in the same debate, compared Walker favorably with Hungarian revolutionary Lajos Kossuth.[61] Future Confederates framed their debate over Walker in terms of municipal neutrality laws of the United States. They tended to pay little attention to what international law might require in suppressing armed expeditions.

The debates over Walker presaged the later Confederate interpretation of neutrality laws and the obligation to prevent armed expeditions against another state. Republican and some Northern and border state Democratic senators pointed out repeatedly that Walker's expedition was prima facie a violation of U.S. neutrality laws, as well as "a flagrant and outrageous violation of the laws of nations."[62] Jefferson Davis proved to be more cautious than some of his future cabinet—he agreed with calls for a more stringent, if temporary, neutrality law to tamp down on filibustering in Central America, although he only tepidly spoke against the expedition itself. Still, Davis and Alexander Stephens supported Southern expansionism, and Davis praised Walker's Nicaraguan expeditions because they "gave hope to the South of the expansion of her institutions."[63] John Slidell, while condemning Walker, went the other direction and proposed repealing or modifying the neutrality law to permit private adventurers to join in conflicts when it suited the interest of the United States, using a theoretical Spanish intervention in Mexico as an example. Alexander Stephens likewise supported the repeal of neutrality laws and unabashedly praised filibustering expeditions of all stripes.[64] Walker's defenders argued his innocence by reading the neutrality law as narrowly as possible, in a manner that would effectively exempt from it hostilities not actively begun from the United States—an interpretation that Confederate operatives in Canada would mirror in 1864. Confederates, particularly Mallory, used this narrow legalism effectively on the British Foreign Enlistment Act during the war to launch raiders like the *Alabama* and *Florida* from British shipyards. Mallory and Benjamin later used the same reasoning to justify raids and hijackings using British colonial territory, having finally convinced Davis to actively support them (see chapters 5 and 7). The roots of their support for events like the St. Albans raid or the hijacking of the steamer *Roanoke* in 1864 were plain to see in future Confederate support for William Walker and filibustering.

While American filibustering to the south received the lion's share of public and official attention, other species of casual and unauthorized violence thrived in the borderlands between the colonies and the disintegrating United States. On the northern border, unauthorized violence flourished in the tumultuous few years surrounding the Canadian rebellion and originated on both sides of the line.[65] Such marauding faded as Canadian political violence eased in the 1840s, but other parties kept the fire burning. Police and private detectives frequently seized fugitives and spirited them across the border without authorization. On some occasions, these men resorted to violence when their quarry resisted. Some of these incursions were little more than informal, if technically illegal, extraditions by police officers from one side of the border, facilitating police from the other side as a favor or professional courtesy. Sometimes the victim was a petty criminal or prisoner who escaped over the border to elude pursuit, but fugitive slaves and political or military figures became targets as well. While not all cross-border violence was linked to international or American sectional strife, even the portion linked to ordinary criminality serves to remind us that the antebellum northern border was no impenetrable obstacle but rather the frequent scene of illicit violence.

Low-intensity fighting, raiding, and arson happened relatively frequently along the border between the United States and British North America in the antebellum era and vividly illustrates that illegal cross-frontier violence was not merely the province of Americans and occurred within living memory of the Civil War.[66] Deaths from this violence were rare, but beatings and arson were commonplace. English Canadians crossed the frontier on several occasions during and immediately after the 1837–38 rebellions, seeking to kidnap *patriote* refugees hiding in Vermont or seeking vengeance for similar attacks by *patriotes*, Hunters' Lodges, and American filibusters.[67] The most famous incident was the *Caroline* affair, where a party of Canadian loyalists crossed the Niagara river to burn the *Caroline*, an American steamer hired to transport supplies to Canadian insurgents on Navy Island. The *Caroline*'s attackers were civilians, but they acted under the orders of a British officer, leading to a long-running diplomatic feud and the retaliatory burning of the British steamer *Sir Robert Peel* by American filibusters.[68] Rumors abounded of plots to kidnap leaders of the rebellion who sought shelter in the United States, including William Lyon Mackenzie while he lived in Rochester, New York.[69] Low-level violence also accompanied the so-called Aroostook War, as settlers and lumberjacks from Maine and New Brunswick clashed over possession of disputed land along the poorly defined border. The private violence, mostly involving fisticuffs and, according to legend, a patriotic black bear attack, threatened to involve British and American troops before cooler heads prevailed.[70] The violence largely subsided by 1843, as political reforms in Canada and the settlement of the Maine boundary dispute removed some of the sources of grievance. A decade or so later and far to the west, border disputes and a series of confrontations by British and American settlers culminated in the 1859 murder of an "unruly hog" by private parties in the San Juan Islands and once again drew in armed forces from both sides. A British farmer on the island lamented that "an American shot one of my pigs for Trespassing!"[71] The farcical beginning devolved into a relatively tense joint occupation of the islands by British and American troops that persisted through the Civil War and beyond. In the interim, other forms of private violence persisted in the northern borderlands.

Kidnapping and what one historian has termed "irregular rendition" were also commonplace in the era.[72] Fugitive slaves were often the target of the most sensational cases, and they resisted ferociously, echoing similar violence within the United States. Escaped slave and abolitionist writer William Wells Brown recalled how in 1835 a slave catcher hired a party of men to kidnap a family of escaped slaves living in St. Catharines, Upper Canada. Brown made no mention of the nationality of the kidnappers, but they seized the family violently only to be caught and trounced by a large party of Black citizens across the border in Buffalo, who liberated the family.[73] Kidnapping attempts in Canada occurred throughout the antebellum era. In some cases, American citizens seized their victims personally; in others, they attempted, with mixed success, to induce Canadians to do their dirty work for them with promises of financial reward. John Anderson's case was exceptional in that it used formal extradition as its tool. In other instances, the expectation was to work outside the law.[74] The editor of the *Montreal Gazette* excoriated a Baltimore constable, John H. Pope, who openly attempted to bribe city police officers into helping him trick or otherwise coerce fugitive slaves to the border so he could seize them.[75] Pope's brazen offer to the Montreal chief of police and his mocking letter in response to the *Gazette*'s editor, in which he bragged of the ease of inducing Canadians to aid him, suggests that this kind of arrangement was fairly common, and that widespread antislavery sentiment in Canada was not necessarily an obstacle to colonial participation in illegal violence across the border.[76]

Private violence existed on the maritime boundary as well. As was so often the case in the United States, people of color were frequently victims. On the eve of the Civil War, a Southern ship captain took advantage of the geographic isolation of the Bahamas—and the relatively weak British naval presence—to kidnap a pair of Black Bahamian boys and sell them into slavery in Georgia. John Stirrup and Samuel Edwards were with a group fishing on the Bahama Banks in March 1861, when an American schooner, the *Hebe*, hailed them. The captain of the *Hebe* invited Stirrup and Edwards to come aboard and join two other boys, brought over by a white crew from the British ship *Leazer*, for some refreshment. While the crew plied the teenage boys with alcohol, the white British sailors shoved off, leaving their two boys behind. Someone on the *Hebe* set Stirrup's boat adrift, leaving them no way off the ship. When one of the boys noticed and raised the alarm, the crew seized Stirrup and Edwards. Their companions leaped overboard to avoid capture, but one of them died in the water, possibly from two gunshots fired from the *Hebe*. The captain and his partner, a Florida man named Frederick Clark, hid the captured boys in the forecastle until the ship reached Florida, where the pair were sold into slavery for $800 each.[77]

The kidnapping of Stirrup and Edwards was not unusual, but the consequences showed just how difficult it was for British and American authorities to police these areas, especially as federal control over the South unraveled, and how easy it was for attackers to escape even the slightest consequences for their actions. The governor of the Bahamas learned of the kidnapping rather quickly and alerted authorities in London and Lord Lyons, the British minister in Washington, but he could do little else—the Bahamas are a huge archipelago, and the governor had no authority beyond the three-mile limit of territorial waters. He could not have pursued the kidnappers even if he had the ability. The Royal Navy could have given chase under its authority to suppress the slave trade, but Nassau was a minor port with no permanent naval presence. The *Hebe* escaped cleanly. Lyons made substantial efforts, with American cooperation, to locate the boys, but the difficulties were enormous, and the Confederate government could be of no help. In other such cases, the Colonial Office felt restricted from contacting the Confederate government for the release of wrongly held slaves because it would be tantamount to recognition.[78] Stirrup escaped from a Georgia plantation and reached Union forces, eventually ending up on the Sea Islands working for the U.S. Navy, where Lyons found him and provided him transportation home in 1863. Edwards remained enslaved for the rest of the war, only returning home permanently in 1870. Frederick Clark faced trial for the kidnapping after the war, but he ultimately avoided conviction because the court lacked much of the evidence contained in State Department and Foreign Office files. Neither Clark nor the captain of the *Hebe* were punished in the end, and the British sailors involved in the initial kidnapping avoided charges altogether.

While these cases of unsanctioned, international cross-border violence were not as widespread as they were along the internal boundary between slave and free states, they still occurred with some regularity and illustrated a long-standing willingness to violate international frontiers.[79] Both American citizens and British subjects involved themselves with these affairs, not only because the relative inability of authorities to police the border made it unlikely they would be caught but also because that very weakness made it inconvenient or impossible to follow the required legal process in the case of fugitives. When raiders, fugitives, and others engaged in illicit violence and depredations on the margins of North America during the Civil War, they were the continuance of a long tradition of private parties engaging in extraterritorial violence. They were also, more broadly, a reminder that the Confederate government, for all its innovation in developing state power, retained significant features of eighteenth-century military practice with regard to privatized warfare, in defiance of the prevailing trends of the nineteenth century.[80]

Confederates sought desperately to join the "family of nations" in 1861, and in most respects, they accepted the existing regime of norms and responsibilities. It offered a road to recognition and thereby legitimacy, prestige, and the possibility of foreign assistance. Yet the emerging Confederacy was far less enthusiastic about following Britain and the powers of Europe in limiting the nonstate use of force—especially after 1863, when their hopes of prompt recognition faded. In 1861, the Confederate general and state governments organized huge conventional armies and a bureaucracy with extraordinary speed in a remarkable feat of state building, but they leaned on private parties in ways that differed sharply from their opponents and the major powers they aspired to join. The Confederacy did not, in other words, uniformly rush to embrace the prevailing movement of the time toward a positivist international order that concentrated authority and legitimacy under the state, especially regarding the use of force. The absence, rather than the presence, of state authority was the norm in North American borderland regions before Southern secession; it follows that the same species of private behavior would fill that vacuum during the war.

Private initiative and relationships played a crucial role in the early months of Confederate diplomacy, foreign policy, and naval operations, yet their importance is often obscured in traditional diplomatic histories. Early Confederate experiments with the cotton embargo, committees of safety, privateering, and "destructionists" illustrate the crucial role these people played in creating, executing, or disrupting official government foreign policy at a time of acute bureaucratic weakness and turmoil. Private initiative became the tool of choice and necessity in naval affairs and trade policy, not least because it reflected the ideological and economic preferences of the planter and merchant classes of the Confederacy. By the end of 1861, the precedents for encouraging private participation in practical foreign policy had been set, and the Confederate government would find it exceedingly difficult to assert control over its affairs in British America as the war dragged on. In the early moments of the Confederacy, however, private engagement with foreign policy and extraterritorial violence served the ends of the rebellion efficiently.

Observers, then and now, characterized Confederate foreign policy in the first year of the war as "King Cotton diplomacy." The widespread assumption that the British and French desire for cotton would, through venality, greed, and realpolitik, force them to quickly recognize an independent Southern Confederacy colored the decisions of Confederate leaders and diplomats. It also shaped the decisions of Southern citizens with no role in government who, in an atmosphere of enthusiasm and confidence, undertook a freelance foray into international trade policy through the so-called cotton embargo. Even though the embargo undermined another key goal of Confederate diplomacy—demonstrating the ineffectiveness, and therefore illegality, of the federal blockade—Jefferson Davis, his revolving door of cabinet officials, and the Confederate Congress acquiesced in the wildcat foreign policy of the embargo. Whether because of states' rights ideology, persistent Anglophobia, or simple benign neglect, the Confederate general government did little to guide the embargo or move it into conformity with any coherent foreign policy until financial and military shortfalls made cotton exports a necessity. By the winter of 1861–62, the fortunes of war and the Union blockade forced Confederates to look beyond the coast for aid and shelter to address persistent financial and material shortfalls. Confederates found comfort in the arms of nearby British America, despite their lingering suspicions, and discovered that many colonists were, in fact, eager to assist the rebellion.

Many prominent Southerners fully expected Britain to race to their aid in the event of war. They would do so, contended James Henry Hammond, among others, out of pecuniary interest in maintaining the flow of cotton from Southern ports to the factories of Lancashire. This reliance on King Cotton diplomacy has been ably explored by historians. Frank L. Owsley, in his eponymous work, judged Southern assumptions about the power of cotton to be logical, and based on a regional culture "clinging to the rationalism" of the Enlightenment. In his account, Southerners drew upon mounds of evidence, from speeches to trade statistics, to build their foreign policy assumptions.[81] More recent studies tie the Southern fascination with the power of cotton into broader global networks of trade and capital.[82] Brian Schoen, for example, argues convincingly that "Deep South disunionists assumed that potential European allies and northern adversaries shared their conviction that cotton ruled global trade," and that secession suggested not "a rejection of economic realism ... but an overabundance of faith in it."[83] Whatever the cause, this abiding faith in the strong international influence of an independent South, to paraphrase historian Scott Marler, colored perceptions both of the nature of its desired partner—the British Empire—and of the expected course of Southern trade and diplomacy in the event of civil war.[84]

The logic of King Cotton diplomacy held that by denying the powers of Europe access to the South's staple export, their hands could be forced into recognizing and supporting Confederate independence. The tool of choice for achieving this outcome—an embargo on cotton exports—showed the power of private parties in Confederate foreign policy in the early days of the war, as individuals and businesses drove the practical application of King Cotton diplomacy. Public opinion in 1861, at least as expressed in newspapers, supported a cotton embargo nearly unanimously.[85] Merchants in New Orleans, the South's most important commercial city, expressed an understandable desire for stability in the 1860 lead-up to the election, and the city's voters went overwhelmingly for John Bell and Stephen Douglas in November. The commercial class of New Orleans nevertheless identified strongly with the institution of slavery and, conscious of their intense dependence on the products of slave-labor agriculture, embraced secession.[86] After Louisiana cast its lot with the new Confederacy, the merchants of New Orleans needed a prompt return to stable trade, and quick recognition by Britain and France offered a seemingly easy means to that end. Stung by the failure of Britain to swiftly recognize the Confederacy and sweep away the blockade, yet sustained by their "abiding faith in cotton," in July 1861 a large body of the city's most influential merchants took foreign policy into their own hands and imposed a de facto embargo on cotton shipments from New Orleans. Within a few weeks, most of the major cotton ports in the Confederacy followed suit.[87]

Confederate farmers and planters shared this faith in the power of Southern agriculture to bring Europe to their aid, and many cooperated in suppressing cotton exports.[88] The editor of the *Mobile Advertiser and Register* scorned "the many discontented subjects of King Cotton" in England and declared, "Our planters and our Government will see that" cotton exports are prevented, "so that [while] England may have 'the will' to get the staple, 'the way' will only be such a way as suits us."[89] Confederate merchants did not limit their interference in trade policy to cotton. The Safety Committee of Wilmington, North Carolina—dominated by merchants like Armand DeRosset—discouraged the export of local staples, such as turpentine and naval stores, in order to keep them out of Northern hands. The editor of the *Wilmington Journal* lamented the local army commander's inability to interfere with trade and called for private action instead: "It therefore rests, for the present, with the citizens of Wilmington—with the merchants of Wilmington, to say whether any more shipments be allowed" for export. "The Safety Committee—the people—the merchants must act in this matter for the present."[90] Merchants in and around Charleston, Savannah, and other ports echoed these sentiments as well, even as they called for the Confederate Congress to take action to make the embargo a matter of law.[91]

This wildcat imposition of trade and foreign policy by merchants was not necessarily at odds with the ultimate goal of the Confederate general government, but it caused suspicion and confusion as to what actually constituted the government's official policy, both at home and abroad.[92] Many people wrote to Jefferson Davis and various cabinet officials, requesting permission to ship cotton out through an embargo that did not officially exist. Simultaneously, the massive drop in cotton exports—shipments from New Orleans, the South's most important port, fell by 99 percent between the 1860 and 1861 seasons—torpedoed Confederate claims in London that the British should ignore an ineffective, and therefore illegal, Union blockade. British observers, while erroneously attributing the embargo to the Confederate general government, were not fooled in the slightest as to the cause of the drop in cotton exports or its objective, and many expressed indignation at Southern presumptions about British venality.[93]

Foreign confusion over Confederate policy was understandable. Judah Benjamin worked behind the scenes with Louisiana congressman Duncan

Kenner to promote the embargo, even as he quietly helped Davis discourage Congress from actually passing legislation to that effect. State governments added to the turmoil by periodically interfering with cotton exports, often by unilateral actions by governors such as Thomas Moore of Louisiana and especially John Milton of Florida, or by the various Committees of Safety in the Confederacy's major port cities.[94] Confederates, whether private citizens or government officials, accepted the existence of the extralegal cotton embargo and carried on this informal foreign policy well into 1862, despite the intense frustration of British consuls and shipowners. The Confederate government, at all levels, was quite comfortable with private parties, rather than the state, taking the lead on matters of foreign policy. A similar situation prevailed regarding warfare at sea.

While Confederate officials tacitly encouraged private parties to shape and enforce its foreign policy, especially through the cotton embargo, their embrace of privatized warfare beyond the South's borders in 1861 displayed no such coyness. Confederate leaders fully expected to make up for their section's dramatic naval disadvantage by embracing the long tradition of privateering in North America. For decades privateers in the service of many nations had brought wealth and naval success to Southern ports, alongside an occasionally cavalier disregard for U.S. customs and neutrality laws.[95] Civil War privateering, however, never became the panacea that its proponents hoped for.[96] Just as in the antebellum era with cross-border pursuit of fugitives (one might think of them as a species of privateers seizing people), cumbersome rules at home and in the colonies, coupled with a vacuum of authority in many areas of the Atlantic littoral, drove many privateers to either abandon their trade or abandon the rules. As in previous centuries, "the line separating privateer from pirate was, more often than not, indistinguishable," and the common practice of "no prey, no pay" served to drive privateers toward piracy simply to keep their crews placid.[97] Confederate control over its private military forces abroad was tenuous from the very start, and when they failed to produce the success that Davis and so many others had predicted, Confederate leaders found themselves faced with a choice: they could abandon privateering as a lost cause, or they could embrace the efforts of their citizens and supporters who sought a fusion of privateering and filibustering. The events of 1861–62 hinted strongly that they would choose the latter.

The early capture of Confederate privateers created a crisis over the legitimacy of private violence on the margins of the Civil War. The initial Union reaction to the capture of privateers from the *Jeff Davis* and the *Petrel* was to treat them as pirates rather than prisoners of war, which carried the possibility of a death sentence. The question before the Union government was simple: if the rebels were a true belligerent power at war with the United States, the captured men should be treated as prisoners of war; if they were not, then they were criminals guilty of either treason or piracy. International law theorists such as Vattel and Wheaton, preeminent at the time, showed plainly that rebellions reaching sufficient strength had claim to the status of a belligerent power, but it took Northern courts several years to finally reach that conclusion.[98] To complicate matters, four Britons were among the crew captured from the privateer *Savannah*, causing Britain, not for the last time, to intercede on the behalf of pro-Confederate combatants and demand they not be executed. In the meantime, Jefferson Davis reacted sharply and threatened retribution on Union captives for any harm visited upon the imprisoned privateers. Lincoln conceded rather than risk a cycle of retribution on prisoners, and Davis established a precedent of lending his government's protection and legitimacy to private parties caught engaging in hostile behavior on its behalf.[99]

Although the Davis administration successfully forced the Union to accept Confederate privateering, the British persuaded the rest of the world to shut the door in their face by closing their ports to captured prizes. This policy more than any other factor crippled Confederate privateering. Britain recognized Confederate belligerency and, by extension, its right to issue letters of marque, but international law did not require neutral nations to allow their prize courts to be used by contending parties to condemn captured ships for sale, nor did it require them to admit captured vessels into their harbors except in cases of distress.[100] This policy, utterly predictable given Britain's efforts to outlaw privateering in 1856, somehow came as a shock to Confederate authorities, and it formed the nucleus for years of bitter complaint by Jefferson Davis of British partiality toward the Union.[101] Most privateers gave up, but some decided to ignore the increasingly inconvenient rules and engaged in illegal cargo sales, plunder, and, later in the war, hijackings by "stratagem"—that is, boarding civilian ships in the guise of passengers or distressed seamen. This last practice was adapted from Confederate guerilla raiding along the Chesapeake. It was prima facie an act of piracy for civilians to do it on the high seas, but Davis and the Confederate government chose to uphold and justify the practice rather than disavow it (see chapter 5).

Confederate comfort with privatized warfare and frustration with the failure of traditional privateering led directly to state-supported piracy more reminiscent of the Elizabethan era than the increasingly legalistic norms of nineteenth-century warfare.

In general, the Confederate government in 1861 appeared overconfident in its diplomatic situation and disinclined to centrally coordinate the two most important and potentially conflicting goals of its foreign policy: keeping Southern ports open in the face of superior naval strength, and using (or at least passively allowing) economic coercion in the form of dramatically restricted cotton exports to Britain, as previously discussed. Efforts at accomplishing the former took three forms: encouraging private armed vessels to attack Northern commerce, building or buying a naval force capable of breaking through a blockading squadron, and convincing the powers of Europe, mainly Britain, that a Northern blockade was ineffective and thereby illegal under the terms of the 1856 Declaration of Paris. Only the second of these required serious government effort; private ships and merchants would have to take care of the others. Meanwhile, if private commerce succeeded in easily penetrating the blockade, then the Confederate government would be hard-pressed to explain the lack of cotton exports as anything other than economic blackmail. The Confederate government painted itself into a corner, diplomatically, before the war even started, practically guaranteeing sour relations with London, although not necessarily with all corners of the empire.

British officials recognized some of the difficulties that private parties caught up in privateering, filibustering, and the blockade might present to them, and they raced to formulate policies to deal with them during the secession crisis and the early months of the war. Both the imperial garrison in Canada and the North American fleet received reinforcements to discourage adventurism, authorized or not, from either belligerent.[102] The queen's neutrality proclamation, issued on May 17, 1861, recognized Confederate belligerency, thereby clarifying the issue of the legality of the Union blockade and the legal status of blockade runners and privateers, who were to be treated as legitimate combatants.[103] The proclamation applied to all British territory, as did the Foreign Enlistment Act. Together they were intended to prevent blatant interference in the war by British subjects. Privateering was dealt with by an additional announcement, on June 3, that prizes of either side would be excluded from all British ports—a move calculated to both make privateering more difficult and avoid Union cutting-out expeditions into British ports.[104] The Admiralty sent directives to Vice Admiral Milne to avoid "any measure or demonstration likely to give umbrage ... or to have the appearance of partizanship" to either side of the conflict.[105] Similar orders went out to Canada and to Lord Lyons in Washington.[106] Despite the earlier fears from places like Jamaica of revenge attacks "for the fate of [William] Walker ... on the part of the lawless adventurers who abound in the S[ou]th[ern] United States," the Colonial Office worried more about the danger to Canada from regular or irregular attacks than other colonies.[107] British preparations for trouble in early 1861 conformed to their nineteenth-century experience with the Americans: the chief threats were filibustering, privateering, and a possible invasion of Canada.

In general, British policies were directed at discouraging external attacks on the colonies and lawlessness at sea rather than preventing neutrality violations from their own possessions, and the legal tools for prosecuting those were consequently limited. The normative changes in international law and British policy that problematized previously accepted species of private violence, especially filibustering and, after 1856, privateering, had not been accompanied by the necessary means to crush them out. The Foreign Enlistment Act, for example, did not anticipate the covert arming of ships in colonies or at sea, and no system existed for the reliable transmission between colonies of warrants for violations of the act. The neutrality declaration likewise did not forbid British subjects from breaking a blockade, and the authorities rightly assumed their robust participation in that trade, although not perhaps the vast pro-Confederate network that emerged from it. These policies did not anticipate the ambiguity of nationality for ships and people who moved along the maritime periphery of North America, or how colonials would use that to shield themselves from capture and prosecution by Britain or the United States.

As 1861 drew to a close, the groundwork had been laid for expansive economic and military interaction between the Confederacy and British America, which was conducted largely by private parties. While mercantile and military pragmatism swamped the old slaveholders' Anglophobia, white British colonists likewise found reasons to downplay or ignore the prevailing antislavery sentiment and assist the rebellion in the fractured United States. Black colonials, by contrast, found themselves torn between genuine antislavery activism, the very real legal and physical danger of aiding the United

States, and the economic relief that blockade-related work offered their impoverished communities. The proximity of British colonies made them, by necessity, the most important and accessible safe territory for a wide variety of Confederate activity, especially blockade running. For their part, newly empowered colonial elites were ready to cooperate with Confederates, with or without London's permission. Ironically, the Anderson case demonstrated just how much freedom the North American colonies had to contest or ignore imperial policy because it affirmed the powerlessness of British courts to overrule colonial judges, even in cases involving foreign affairs, where imperial prerogative otherwise remained supreme.

British America's importance for the rebellion probably came as a surprise to many Confederate observers, not least because of their unrealistic expectations about the international power, influence, and therefore legitimacy of the South once divorced from Washington. King Cotton and the Slave Power—his rhetorical cousin—did not fare well on their own abroad despite long-standing expectations of Southern influence, especially among the architects of secession and the leaders of the new Confederate state. Indeed, the stubborn colonial allies of the Confederacy only became important *because* of the failure of King Cotton to bend John Bull to his will in 1861. Nassau and Bermuda would hardly have mattered at all if the Royal Navy had swept away the blockade. In late 1861 and early 1862, Confederate merchants and purchasing agents finally recognized the necessity of shipping cotton out in order to finance both civilian and military imports, and the virtual impossibility of doing so by direct trade with Europe in the face of the rapidly improving Union blockade. Confederate transatlantic commerce turned by necessity to the nearest neighbors: foreign colonies just off the coast, especially the Bahamas and Bermuda.

CHAPTER TWO

King Cotton and King Conch

Informal Diplomacy, Anglo-Confederate Relations, and Blockade Running in the Bahamas, 1861–1863

The Bahamas Islands are a constant source of anxiety to me. Considering that the Bahamians push to the extreme limit the advantages their position gives them for running the blockade, they are hardly reasonable in expecting to find U.S. Captains always in good humour with them.
—Lord Lyons, British Minister to the United States

IN EARLY 1862, the acting governor of the Bahamas welcomed the arrival of "numerous strangers from the neighbouring continent," as Confederates and their supporters flowed into Nassau to open a critical and lucrative trade with the nearby Confederate coast. Their friendly reception in Nassau was not simply an accident of geography.[1] In an unlikely triumph of informal Confederate diplomacy, merchants, planters, and ship captains on both sides created ties of trade, self-interest, and genuine sympathy and sustained them against pressure from both the Union and the imperial government. This was a diplomacy of personal acquaintance, business relationships, and shipping routes, rather than one of formal envoys, and these informal networks gave the Confederacy a rare success in international affairs. By using British colonial partners, the Confederacy's ad hoc collection of minor officials, merchants, and shipowners pressed claims on the British government—and through them, the Union—in ways that their formal diplomats could not. In doing so, they formed and protected the blockade-running enterprise that sustained much of the Confederate war effort, and they created the means for expatriates and foreign allies to materially aid the rebellion. This Confederate commercial-diplomatic network extended across British America, from Toronto and Halifax to British Honduras and numerous places in between, but it had its greatest success in Nassau.

This reassessment of who mattered and what constituted "success" in Confederate diplomacy is important for bringing scholarship on Civil War diplomacy in line with the broader deinstitutionalization of diplomatic history.[2] It is also an opportunity to reconsider how and why individuals and subnational groups shaped the course of the war and international relations in the nineteenth century—and to push back against the paradigm of the state as the most important actor, a perspective that underlies even the "new" diplomatic history of the Civil War.[3] Whatever the relative claims over state capacity in this era, it was still a time of comparative bureaucratic weakness and agonizingly slow and unreliable communication. We must embrace the trend in histories of empire and sovereignty that increasingly deemphasize the role of the state by centering the diplomatic history of the war not on the State Department or the Foreign Office but on the people who personally shaped the transformation of state policy into action and, perhaps more frequently, vice versa.[4]

This approach allows us to ask different questions about things like blockade running. Rather than just assessing how much it helped the Confederacy in material terms or what it meant for formal diplomacy, we have the opportunity to reassess the actual importance of formal state power, both in blockade running and in the "international" Civil War. The merchants, supercargos, and minor officials who conducted the informal diplomacy that enabled blockade running are but one aspect of a broader universe of filibusters, ad hoc militias, settler colonists, and others who mobilized private resources and violence on behalf of (or in resistance to) empire building in mid-century North America.[5] While they have often escaped the notice of historians, these grassroots foreign policy actors deeply affected the course of the Civil War and the shaping of sovereignty and empire.

The U.S. government certainly took notice of the Confederacy's friends in the Bahamas. Secretary of State William Seward noted that "among those British subjects who were the first to institute a contraband trade with the insurgents, in violation of our laws, and in contempt of the Queen's proclamation [of neutrality], is a house established in Nassau and Liverpool, under the name of Adderly & Co." Seward, with undisguised anger, referred to the head of that firm, Henry Adderley, as "a person who is so vicious as to dishonor his own country and send desolation abroad to mine upon the motive of commercial gain. I desire that the British nation may understand that ... we do not confound the just and the good with the unjust and depraved."[6]

Henry Adderley, whom blockade runners dubbed "King Conch," excited such a strong reaction from Seward because he represented an enduring source of frustration for Union authorities, who could do little to curtail the Adderley firm's crucial support for blockade running and other Confederate endeavors in the Bahamas.[7] Yet Seward underestimated the sources of motivation for Adderley, and others like him, who risked their commercial and political fortunes in order to extend the cover of their British nationality to shield Confederate operations from the Union. The potential financial gains were enormous, but long-standing ties of culture, kinship, and a lingering sympathy for slaveholding also prompted Adderley and many like him to support the rebellion.

More broadly, as Seward alluded to, Adderley is illustrative of the importance of colonial partners to the Confederate war effort, and of the deep reliance by the Confederate government on private parties to create their trade and diplomatic policy in the Bahamas. This was critical to Confederate survival; the overwhelming majority of the arms and supplies that the Confederacy received from abroad passed through British colonies en route from Europe, usually on British-flagged ships, consigned to British merchants, and paid for with cotton that followed the same path out of Southern ports.[8] When Confederates needed arms shipments from Britain, Adderley received them. When Confederates needed harbor space in Nassau, Adderley provided it. When Confederates needed crewmen for a warship, Adderley & Co. rounded them up. And when Confederates needed local regulations changed or the aid of the British government, Adderley and his partners used their positions and influence to deliver it. The Colonial Office watched in frustration as figures from the governor down to local customs inspectors acted as enablers in word and deed for the Confederacy, often under the influence of the Nassau mercantile elite. The Adderley firm, and how it came to be the indispensable assistant to Confederate operations in the Bahamas, offer a window through which to examine the importance of informal diplomacy and the limitations of both the Confederate and British governments in their efforts to control events in the contested islands and waters of the Bahamas.

Mr. Henry Adderley, M.H.A., one of Nassau's leading merchants in 1844. Later a member of Executive Council.

Henry Adderley, in an undated photograph from the centennial issue of the *Nassau Guardian*. Source: *Nassau Guardian*, 23 Nov. 1944, 2. Image courtesy of Library of Congress.

Diplomatic histories of the Civil War mostly overlook the Bahamas—and British colonies generally—as sites of meaningful diplomatic action.[9] This is understandable for histories of formal interstate diplomacy: the Bahamas, like other colonies, had no independent foreign policy. London controlled the empire's external relations except in areas expressly delegated to colonial governments by act of Parliament. For many of the prominent histories of Civil

War diplomacy, British colonies in general are, unsurprisingly, an afterthought.[10] This relative lack of attention suggests the need for a study that emphasizes informal diplomacy as a way to measure the true importance of the Bahamas—and British America—to the Civil War. Informal diplomacy is necessarily a broad term, but it refers here to the sum of official and semiofficial relations between two states or territories that generally occur without the use of accredited diplomats.[11] Informal relations mattered greatly to the Confederacy: as an unrecognized state with a hastily cobbled together State Department, it had no credentialed diplomats and only a handful of men who served de facto as such, almost all of whom served in one European capital or another. Thus, the burden, to paraphrase historian Charles Hubbard, of Confederate diplomacy in the colonies fell primarily upon minor officials, private businessmen, trading and shipping firms, and sailors.[12] These people developed and maintained relations between the Confederacy and the Bahamas throughout the war, sustaining an indispensable part of the Confederacy's network of links to the outside world in the process. Histories of both the Civil War and the Bahamas often ignore how Confederates and their allies built their logistical and diplomatic network in cooperation with colonial merchants in Nassau.[13] Other works address conditions on the islands more directly, though few examine the details of the Confederate-Bahamian connection.[14] Much of the recent work on blockade running continues the debate around the effectiveness of the blockade and its economic impact on the Confederacy, incorporating new data and interpretations while giving correspondingly little emphasis to local diplomatic and political structures in colonial ports.[15]

Once the war began, Nassau, on the island of New Providence, became a critical node in the Confederate foreign logistical and diplomatic network. The descendants of slave-owning Loyalist planters constituted the political and economic elite of the colony, and their Nassau mercantile establishments provided the foundation of Confederate blockade-running infrastructure. Bahamian commerce increased exponentially from blockade-related traffic (see table 1), with a nearly thirtyfold expansion in exports between 1860 and 1864.[16] This explosion in trade, which likely undercounts the true totals in volume and value due to smuggling and bonded warehouses, reflects the importance of Nassau as a logistical hub for the Confederacy.

TABLE 1. Annual Trade Values in the Bahamas, 1861–1864

Year	Total Imports (millions)	Total Exports (millions)
1860	£0.23	£0.16
1861	£0.27	£0.19
1862	£1.25	£1.01
1863	£6.29	£3.37
1864	£5.35	£4.67

SOURCES: Compiled from data reported by the colonial government in its annual Blue Books of Statistics, 1860–1864, in CO 27/59 through CO 27/62, TNA. For background on Blue Books, see Sarah Preston, "Colonial Blue Books: A Major Resource in the Royal Commonwealth Society Library," *Bulletin of the Friends of the Cambridge University Library* 26–27 (2006–2007), accessed 29 Apr. 2021, https://www.lib.cam.ac.uk/collections/departments/royal-commonwealth-society/projects-exhibitions/colonial-blue-books-major.

NOTE: These sterling valuations are almost certainly an undercount due to the cotton price estimates used and rampant smuggling. In 1864, 62,617 bales of cotton were entered, duty-free, at Nassau, almost all of which were re-exported to Britain. Exports to the "Southern States of America" were listed at a mere £4,460, only because clearance papers almost never listed the true destination of ships bound for the Confederacy.

For its part, the Confederate government exercised little control over the development of blockade running through Nassau and instead allowed private parties almost unlimited leeway well into 1863. Merchant houses such as John Fraser and Co. of Charleston and Henry Adderley and Co. of Nassau, often controlled by some of the wealthiest men in their respective cities, cemented the relationship between Nassau and the new Confederacy.[17] This connection, reinforced by private citizens and Confederate government representatives deployed to Nassau, provided the most important conduit for goods, people, and communications between the Confederacy and the outside world. By relying heavily on private individuals and firms to maintain this network, the Confederate government displayed adaptability in the face of necessity and managed to mitigate some of its fundamental bureaucratic weakness. This benign neglect served them well early in the war because of the flexibility and low risk that outsourcing diplomatic and commercial authority offered. A hands-off approach also empowered a variety of Confederate citizens and supporters to conduct freelance diplomatic and military activities, interacting with the colonial authorities, Royal Navy officers, and occasionally the British government without the sanction of the Confederate government, albeit occasionally to the detriment of a coherent military and diplomatic policy. This pragmatic approach enabled the rapid establishment of blockade running and transshipment operations in places like Nassau. All of this makes clear that private parties and minor officials dictated the course and nature of the enterprise's development. The state played only a minor role.

Bahamians provided essential support to their "new" neighbors for several reasons. The colony struggled economically in the mid-nineteenth century, and colonists of all backgrounds welcomed the influx of money and employment opportunity that secession and war brought.[18] While financial gain was probably the chief motivator for Bahamian cooperation with the Confederacy, it was far from the only one. The colony's elite had a shared cultural heritage with Southern planter society, despite the relative failure of plantation agriculture in the Bahamas earlier in the nineteenth century. An honor culture remarkably similar to that of the antebellum South persisted among the Bahamian elite, and many white Bahamians "saw the South's secession movement as deriving from kindred sensibilities" about honor and local prerogatives.[19] Many of the older members of the Bahamian mercantile elite also shared with Southerners the experience of slaveholding, had not welcomed abolition, and worked hard to maintain their position of racial and economic hegemony within the colony.[20] Supporting a slaveholder's republic provided little moral dilemma for them.

The cultural connections between the Bahamas and the South were at least as old as the Republic itself. In the waning days of the Revolution, thousands of Loyalists fled the United States and ultimately settled in the Bahamas.[21] Southerners made up most of those who settled in the Bahamas, and people from Georgia and South Carolina alone made up about 70 percent of those who settled and received grants of land.[22] The influx of refugees and their slaves doubled the population of the Bahamas between 1783 and 1786 to almost nine thousand people, two-thirds of whom were Black and largely enslaved.[23] Thus established, the planter class and its descendants dominated the politics of the islands for decades. Although many Loyalists eventually left the Bahamas after their plantations failed, enough remained to maintain political control, even after the empire-wide abolition of slavery in 1834, and many shifted their households to Nassau and went into business as commission merchants or shippers.[24] Some of the most important local supporters of the Confederacy came from this group, who had intermarried with Bahamian families. Henry Adderley and his partners were perhaps the most prominent in terms of wealth, influence, and aid to the rebellion.

Henry Adderley, born in 1802, did not inherit much land from his wealthy father, and he took up his grandfather's trade as a shipping merchant in Nassau.[25] He augmented his connection with Southern slaveholders by marrying Mary Ann Perpall, the daughter of John Perpall, a Loyalist who came to the Bahamas in 1785 with twelve slaves.[26] Adderley was representative of the fusion of Loyalists and local planters into a merchant elite based in Nassau during the first half of the nineteenth century. Labeled "Bay Street" for the main thoroughfare along Nassau's waterfront, this "white Bahamian agrocommercial oligarchy" controlled the affairs of the colony.[27] This commercial elite provided the backbone of colonial support for the rebellion, lending their financial and political support to the cause.

That merchants in Nassau in 1861 might support the Confederacy is not surprising, purely for financial reasons, but for Henry Adderley it went beyond monetary considerations. Adderley, like many West Indian slaveholders, bitterly opposed emancipation, which was being considered just as he began a three-decade career as a member of the House of Assembly of the Bahamas, the elected lower house of the colonial government. He opposed emancipation so vociferously that the colonial governor fined him fifty pounds and sentenced him to a brief stint in jail in 1832, which Adderley avoided by paying the fine and apologizing.[28] By 1860, former slaveowners or their sons still dominated the House of Assembly, owing to strict property requirements for suffrage and plural voting rules that effectively disenfranchised poor whites and almost all Black Bahamians. Likewise, former slaveholders composed the majority—and were the most powerful members—of the appointed Executive Council of the Bahamas. Five of the eight members in 1861, including Attorney General George C. Anderson and Colonial Secretary Charles R. Nesbitt, owned slaves at the time of British emancipation.[29] In a modest preview of Reconstruction, white elites across the British Caribbean used the law to enforce their dominance over former slaves from the earliest days of West Indian emancipation, during which Black victims of white landowners often found themselves punished for "insolence."[30] Given their efforts to maintain, to the extent possible, the pre-abolition racial and social status quo, Adderley and many of his fellow ex-slaveholders no doubt thought the strict racial hierarchy of the South a social principle worth preserving.

Widespread support for secession and the Confederacy appeared in the Bahamas before any windfall of cash, although Union naval activity and interference with trade boosted pro-Confederate sentiment. While Henry Adderley's wealth and influence made him the most frequently noted Confederate supporter, he was far from the only one. Samuel Whiting, newly appointed as the Lincoln administration's U.S. consul for Nassau in the summer of 1861, noted that "the strongest prejudice exists here among the British officials in favor of the Secession movement and the same spirit exists among the mercantile portion of the community."[31] This "spirit" was plainly manifest well before blockade running began to enrich those merchants in earnest in 1862.[32] The actions of the U.S. government cemented the existing pro-Confederate attitudes of Nassau's "merchant princes," whose support predated the polarizing events of the *Trent* affair. When U.S. Navy Captain Charles Wilkes seized James Mason and John Slidell from the British mail packet *Trent* on November 8, 1861, colonists and metropolitan Britons alike united in outrage. British military officials in Nassau were similarly moved, according to recently arrived Confederate agent Lewis Heyliger: "The affair of the *Trent* I find creates a universal feeling of indignation among the Britishers [in Nassau]. I heard an officer say that if Government did not resent it becomingly he would forever renounce his title as an Englishman."[33] Blockade enforcement added to many colonists' displeasure. Some of the U.S. Navy's earliest and most contentious captures of suspected blockade runners were of Bahamas-bound vessels. The case of the *Bermuda*—captured by a U.S. warship as it sailed from Bermuda to Nassau, loaded with arms and ammunition for the rebels—attracted a great deal of attention, as did several others. The detention and, in some cases, loss of these ships did not endear the Union to many Bay Street merchants regardless of the legality of the seizures. They had money and their pride as British subjects at stake, not just their interpretation of their rights as supposed neutrals.

Despite these promising signs, Southern opinion toward the Bahamas before the war had not been uniformly positive, and vice versa. There was a great deal of resentment toward British colonial officials who freed slaves that ended up on Bahamian soil and toward the Black Bahamians who aided slaves in petitioning for freedom upon their arrival. Despite lingering proslavery sentiment, imperial officials in the Bahamas consistently upheld emancipation for any enslaved people who reached British soil, a prospect that frightened and annoyed Southern slaveowners.[34] Several recent histories have elaborated on the hemispheric awareness of Southerners, particularly with regard to the causes and consequences of British emancipation in the Caribbean, and the celebrated (for slaveholders, notorious) case of the *Creole* in 1841 drew Southern attention to the Bahamas in a decidedly negative fashion.[35] On the balance, however, elite opinion in Nassau was firmly in favor of the Confederacy throughout the war, while Southern sentiment was not so inflamed as to overlook the obvious advantages to be found in the Bahamas. A North Carolina journalist's 1864 travelogue, for example, presented a generally positive assessment of the utility of Nassau for the Confederate cause, while painting a derisive portrait of the condition of the large Black population of New Providence and the supposed shortcomings in their manner of treatment by Bahamian whites.[36] Confederates separated their antipathy for metropolitan British antislavery from the colonial subjects best positioned to aid their cause and their pocketbooks.

In addition to these ties of sentiment and kinship, Bahamians of all stripes supported the Confederate cause because they stood to gain from the economic opportunities offered by the Civil War and the blockade. The fierce resistance of Black Bahamians to the attempted recapture of the enslaved people on the *Creole* suggested that support from the nonwhite majority in the Bahamas was not guaranteed in 1861, but many found employment on Nassau's docks and wharves, whatever their opinion about the Confederates. The start of the war and the declaration of the blockade brought a swift (and temporary) turnabout in the economic fortunes of the Bahamas. On the crest of this boom, the colony quickly repaid its public debt and was able to raise the salaries of public officials substantially after years of stagnation, although often not by enough to offset the drastic price increases brought on by the flood of easy money.[37] The war years were, economically, perhaps the best the Bahamas had ever seen, or would see again for almost sixty years, when rum-running during Prohibition again made Nassau a popular destination for those seeking to bring illicit cargoes to the U.S. mainland.

Like the blockade itself, blockade running through Nassau started slowly and haphazardly but promptly involved local merchants and authorities in questions about British policy and neutrality. The first Confederate visitors to Nassau after the outbreak of war were not dedicated blockade runners or diplomats but private shipowners and captains who forced Bahamian authorities to make decisions about the crisis on the mainland without the luxury of consulting the Colonial Office or the Foreign Office in London. One of the first arrivals to excite comment was the schooner *William H. Northrop* of Wilmington, which arrived in Nassau on June 20, 1861, displaying "an unacknowledged flag which is known only as having recently been raised in rebellion to the United States."[38] The U.S. consul protested to the acting governor, Charles R. Nesbitt, who replied that flying an unrecognized flag was not against British law and would not prevent such vessels from using the ports and facilities of the Bahamas. The Law Officers of the Crown had anticipated such a problem during the secession crisis and ruled that an unrecognized flag was not a reason to exclude ships from British ports so long as their papers—such as shipping manifests, home port clearance, and ownership records—were in order, although they carefully specified that local port regulations could overrule this.[39] Nesbitt also declined to interfere with Southern captains who failed to present their vessel's papers to the consul as required by U.S. law, calling it a jurisdictional matter in which he had "neither right nor power to interfere."[40] This was not true, according to the Law Officers' opinion, though it is not clear if authorities in the Bahamas were aware of it. Nesbitt, in his caution, essentially opened the Bahamas to Confederate ships with an unrecognized country of register.

Despite being able to enter Nassau under the Confederate flag, most Confederate shipowners chose another course. Following Abraham Lincoln's declaration of a blockade of the states in rebellion on April 16, 1861, risk-averse Southern shipowners sought shelter from capture by the Union Navy by obtaining British registry. One of the first of these, the schooner *John Hancock* of New Orleans, visited the Bahamas in June 1861. This attempt at swapping flags was so blatantly fraudulent that even Nesbitt rejected it as illegitimate.[41] By the terms of the 1854 Merchant Shipping Act, in order to obtain a British flag, a vessel had to have a legitimate British subject as the owner, with the actual controlling interest in the ship also in British hands. A short time later, however, Nesbitt granted British registry to the very same vessel when the attorney for its Confederate owner found a willing local, Archibald Forsyth, to "purchase" the vessel. Nesbitt did so despite his own admission that the original owners almost certainly retained control of the vessel and Forsyth could not possibly have come up with the £5,000 purchase price. Forsyth, though born in the Bahamas, was a naturalized U.S. citizen who had lived for decades in Philadelphia working as a sailor and sea captain. Nesbitt knew this as well.[42] The Bahamas thereafter did a brisk business in changing ship registries.

Private Confederate citizens had once again forced British colonial authorities into making policy decisions that had cascading effects. The decision to be relatively permissive in granting British registry was upheld by the Board of Trade, and the case was distributed as a circular to colonial governors around the world, establishing it as the precedent they should follow; not every colony had been as forthcoming with granting Confederate ships a British flag, but this forced their hand.[43] The circular made it clear that colonial officials were not responsible for ensuring that the sale of these vessels to British owners was legitimate. This enabled a massive "flight from the flag" for both Union and Confederate merchant ships, as they sought protection from commerce raiders and blockaders, respectively, aiding the disintegration of the U.S. maritime carrying trade.[44] In this case, colonial officials in the Bahamas had effectively decided British policy worldwide.

The Confederate government's connection to Nassau developed from the commercial links maintained by these troublesome schooners, which made up the bulk of blockade running ships in 1861.[45] Direct cooperation came when the Confederate government needed to move large military cargoes from Europe. John P. Baldwin, a Confederate commissary officer who was born in Nassau and lived for many years in Key West, wrote to Henry Adderley in July 1861 seeking assistance in forwarding a cargo of arms on behalf of Secretary of the Navy Stephen R. Mallory.[46] Key West had largely been settled in the mid-nineteenth century by white Bahamian "conchs" like Baldwin, and they maintained familial and business connections to Nassau that opened the door to blockade running.[47] The personal nature of the connection is quite clear from the letter's tone, as is the expectation by Baldwin that he would soon meet with his "friend" Adderley in person. Ultimately, Baldwin did not go to Nassau, likely because the letter in question came into the hands of Union authorities and was published. In response to an inquiry by the British government on the matter, Adderley sarcastically replied, "I am rather surprised that the American Government should have countenanced the intercepting of letters passing through their Post Office. For your information, I beg leave to state that no warlike stores have been consigned to me from Great Britain for transport to the Confederate States, or to any

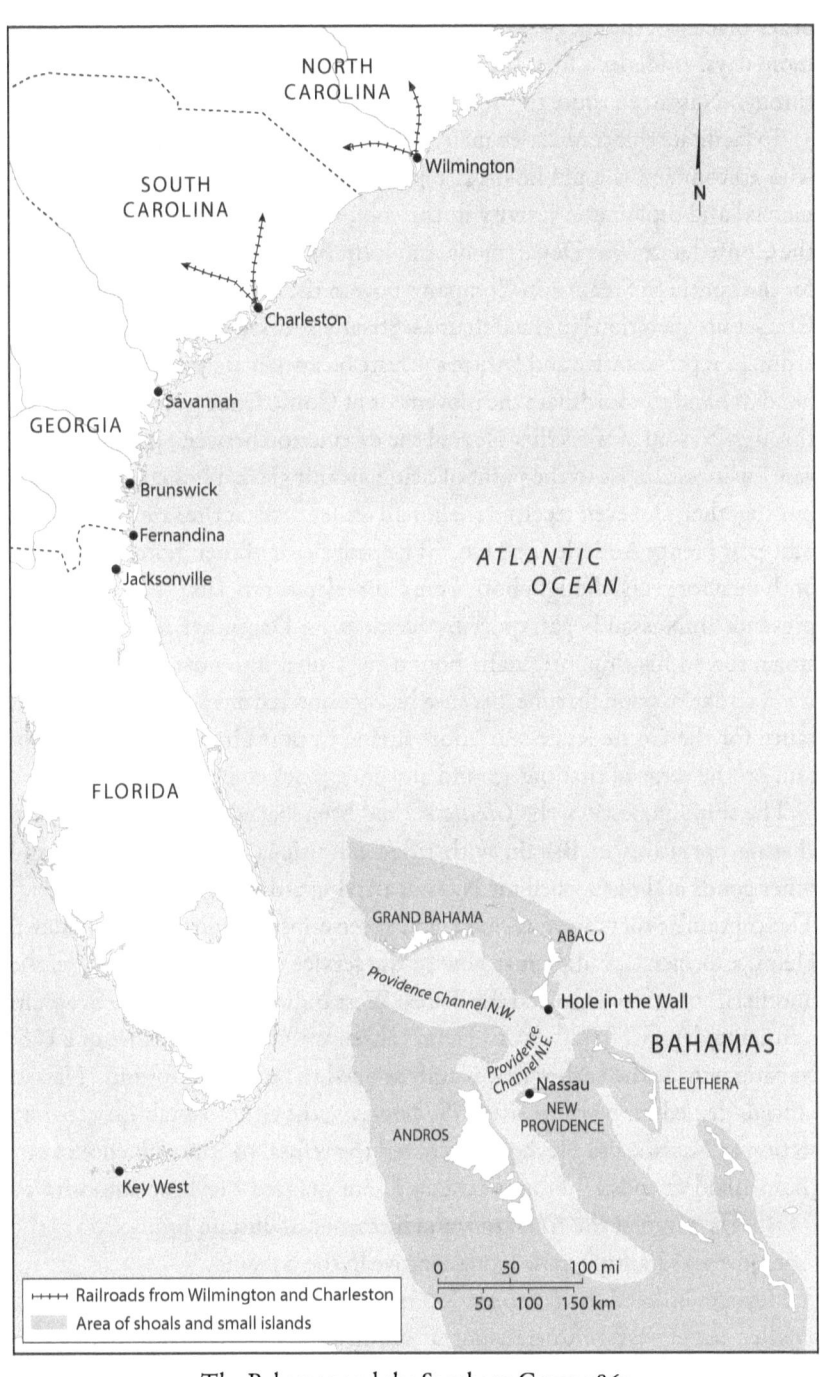

The Bahamas and the Southern Coast, 1862

other place."⁴⁸ Adderley's statement may have been true, but only for a few more days. Adderley's firm soon received the first major arms shipment sent through Nassau en route to the Confederate armies.

To facilitate this traffic, two men arrived in Nassau in the winter of 1861–62 who epitomized the public-private partnership behind Confederate commercial and diplomatic activity in the colonies. Lewis Heyliger, an agent of the Confederate War Department, and John Baptiste Lafitte, a former agent for the Southern Steamship Company, now in the employ of John Fraser and Co., set up operations in the Bahamas. Strictly speaking, Heyliger was a government representative and Lafitte a private businessman, yet the two worked hand in hand to coordinate the movement of Confederate government stores through Nassau in ways that blurred the distinction between public and private business almost to the point of being meaningless. They coauthored letters together, and even received their mail under cover at the same place—the offices of Henry Adderley and Co.⁴⁹ The proprietor of their hotel, who knew both men for years, thought both were Confederate officials.⁵⁰ Heyliger's long presence in Nassau began quite by accident on December 10, 1861, after a storm forced his ship, originally bound for Cuba, into port for repairs.⁵¹ It was a stroke of good fortune, because he encountered a vessel of great importance for the Confederate war effort sitting in port aimlessly, with its captain on the verge of turning around and going back to Britain.

The ship in question, the *Gladiator*, had been loaded by Confederate purchasing operatives in Britain with rifles, munitions, medical supplies, and other goods and dispatched for Nassau, arriving only a day before Heyliger.⁵² The captain's orders were to meet and receive instructions from Charles J. Helm, a former U.S. diplomat now in the service of the Confederacy as the unofficial consul to Cuba and the British West Indies. The *Gladiator*'s captain refused to depart Nassau due to Helm's absence and the appearance of a U.S. warship outside the harbor that plainly seemed to be waiting for him. Nassau officials denied the warship, the USS *Flambeau*, the right to establish a coaling station at Nassau, and Heyliger attributed the refusal to "the influence of our [Bahamian] friends."⁵³ From Havana, Helm granted Heyliger authority to oversee the cargo of the *Gladiator*, and he earned an instant promotion as the Confederacy's multipurpose representative in the Bahamas.⁵⁴

Heyliger ordered the *Gladiator*'s cargo to be divided and transferred onto smaller, faster vessels for transportation into the Confederacy—a practice known as breaking bulk. Nassau was the obvious place to do this because of its proximity to the Southern coast, its noninterfering government, and the friendly presence of Henry Adderley's firm, the partners in which all served in positions of influence in the Bahamas government.[55] The usual route from Nassau was approximately 650 miles to Charleston and 740 miles to Wilmington, and a steamship traveling an average of 12 knots could cover the distance in as little as two or three days.[56] In response to a request for help from Judah P. Benjamin, then acting secretary of war, John Fraser and Co. dispatched several fast steamers to Nassau to take on the *Gladiator*'s cargo and sent Lafitte there as their agent. Lafitte arrived on February 16, 1862, and immediately set to work with Heyliger.[57]

This public-private partnership between the Confederate government, Adderley, and John Fraser and Co. became the linchpin of the Confederate commercial-diplomatic network, which rapidly expanded to include many other firms and individuals around the coasts of North America and the Caribbean. The case of the *Gladiator* is instructive in this regard because it set the tone for most subsequent supply operations through the blockade. Despite the critical military nature of the supplies it carried and the importance of getting them through a screen of enemy naval vessels safely, everyone involved on behalf of the Confederate government still seemed to regard it as a *civil, mercantile* undertaking rather than a *military* one. It was standard practice in this era to rely on contractors and commission merchants to deliver supplies to the armed forces, but asking them to do so through the blockade was rather more unusual—and more expensive. The queen's neutrality proclamation precluded armed Confederate vessels from taking on the *Gladiator*'s cargo, but government-owned merchant vessels could come and go largely as they pleased. Still, Benjamin and Heyliger contracted John Fraser and Co.'s vessels to haul in the *Gladiator*'s freight instead of buying or even seizing the ships for government use. Rather than setting up their own transshipment and servicing operation in Nassau, they leaned on Henry Adderley and Co., and later a host of smaller contractors as well. Traders and speculators from Britain joined in, some leveraging their contacts with influential pro-Confederates to gain access to persons of influence.[58] Within the space of a year, Henry Adderley and his firm stood at the center of a vast commercial network, dominated by private merchants and working for profit on behalf of the Confederacy across the Atlantic Ocean and the Gulf of Mexico.

Merchants in Charleston, and later Wilmington, seized on the opportunity to restore some of the commerce lost when their regular connections to the North and Europe were severed. The link with New York broke down gradually, corresponding with the end of postal and telegraph service to the North and the haphazard early implementation of the blockade. Charleston merchant Charles O. Witte's letter book shows frequent correspondence with New York and points abroad through May 1861, but the volume of letters slowed in June and came almost to a complete halt by July.[59] The replacement connections to British colonies came slowly at first. Witte's business, for example, came almost to a standstill in the second half of 1861, and he slowly built up a trade through Nassau in late 1862, buying up cotton and shipping it out to the Nassau firm of Saunders and Son. Witte also availed himself of the neutral status of Nassau and its colony-subsidized steamship service to resume his correspondence with New York, using Saunders and Son as a cut-out (i.e., a neutral proxy figure to hide the true sender's communications).[60] This tactic was mimicked widely, and British mail packets became the backbone of Confederate overseas communication.

Such correspondence introduces an important contribution of the Anglo-Confederate commercial-diplomatic network in the colonies: access to the machinery and protection of the British government and mail. People in and outside the Confederacy found it difficult to communicate reliably across the blockade. As regular mail and telegraph service with the North was interrupted, people sought secure and reliable means of communication with the outside world. In those early days, Judah Benjamin himself begged the British minister in Washington, Richard Bickerton Pemell Lyons (addressed as Lord Lyons), to help him forward letters and money to his wife and daughters in Europe.[61] Lyons declined to make himself the tool of a Confederate cabinet official, but plenty of others in the colonies proved willing. The Confederate commercial-diplomatic network in the colonies became one of the most important conduits for mail and information from outside the United States.[62] This postal network was informal—no official Confederate courier or mail service existed beyond its shores. Once a letter reached the colonies—usually Nassau or Bermuda were the first stops—it went on to its destination far more reliably because it traveled under the cover of the British flag. Confederate communications were given invaluable protection by the simple expedient of being plausibly British once they reached the colonies. From colonial soil, Confederate letters could go on to their destinations easily, relayed via Halifax or even Northern cities like New York or Boston.

Local partners also gave Confederates access to the British government, often by proxy, and exploited the inevitable friction between colonial interests and metropolitan policy by demanding that British diplomats uphold their honor and rights as Englishmen even as they worked on behalf of the Confederacy. Confederate interests thus gained much from the contested sovereignty inherent in the British colonial system in America. The actions of the Bahamian local government, especially the House of Assembly and minor officials, show us just how complicated British neutrality was, as colonial subjects worked actively against imperial policy when it suited their interests and sympathies. The Confederate cause and the pocketbooks of merchants and blockade runners became the chief beneficiaries of this intransigence.

In 1861, the House of Assembly of the Bahamas had a long-established reputation for stubbornness and troublemaking.[63] Governor Bayley vividly illustrated the resistance of the Nassau agrocommercial elite in a long dispatch marked "separate and confidential" to the colonial secretary in 1863. He described the tendency of legislation in the Bahamas "to contravene, directly or indirectly, the intention of the Colonial Regulations and to defeat their practical enforcement." He pointed to restrictions on officeholders, including the registrar and police magistrates, to prevent them from doing their duties or filling in for absent or vacant officeholders, and other measures he perceived as intended "to place the Legislation of the Colony more and more in the hands of the Nassau storekeepers." Bayley sneered at the merchants as "destitute of anything like liberal education" and possessing "very sordid notions" about governance and civil service pay, but he despaired of weakening their control over civil service appointments and salaries.[64] The queen's representative struggled throughout the Civil War era to exercise any sort of control over Bahamian legal and regulatory affairs.

The Confederacy benefited from the divisions inherent in the Bahamian colonial-metropolitan relationship in several ways. Confederate merchant firms leaned on their influential local allies to appeal to the British government for redress of grievances, most frequently in relation to blockade running. In several cases, the governor forwarded these complaints to the Colonial Office, the Foreign Office, and the Board of Trade, bringing them to the attention of the British cabinet in a way that a traditional diplomatic approach would not have achieved. The actions, or inaction in some cases, of the Bahamian House of Assembly and courts also helped maintain the permissive legal and customs environment necessary for profitable large-scale blockade running. In 1862, the House of Assembly, goaded on by Adderley, repealed the tax on ship registrations retroactive to May 1861, easing the process of gaining British registration for foreign ships.[65] It also studiously ignored repeated pleas from the receiver general and Governor Bayley to increase the resources available to customs inspectors to combat rampant smuggling and to keep tabs on the increasing numbers of bonded warehouses in Nassau.[66] The Bahamas judicial system also did its part to tilt neutrality toward its Confederate friends. A Nassau court in 1863 tried several Black harbor pilots for violating the Foreign Enlistment Act for merely serving as pilots for U.S. Navy warships, even as similar and far more frequent violations by pro-Confederates passed unnoticed.[67] Colonial courts also shielded their countrymen from the imperial government in support of blockade running. In 1863, the Board of Trade and the Foreign Office attempted to force Henry Adderley's nephew Edwin and son Augustus to pay restitution for costs incurred by the British consulate in New York for the subsistence of the crews of the captured blockade runners *Ella Warley* and *Nassau*, but a Bahamian court ruled in the Adderleys' favor, leaving the British government to foot the bill.[68] The Bay Street elites who dominated the government attempted to protect their own financial interests while simultaneously guarding their political power from the increased attentions of London. Their sheer intransigence was sometimes enough to dissuade the governor from actions that would provoke controversy.[69]

Colonial partnerships also helped Confederates contest their blockade-running losses and U.S. trade restrictions using the machinery of British diplomacy. Confederate merchants could not show up at a Union prize court to contest the proceedings, and they had no diplomatic service of their own to assist them in getting redress in the "foreign" courts of Key West or Philadelphia. Nassau, instead, provided an opportune place to press their grievances via the colonial governor, particularly when the incidents occurred in Bahamian waters or involved ships going to or from Nassau. In doing so, they relied on the fig leaf of British nationality to press their colonial hosts' bureaucracy into service on Confederates' behalf. International law was still in a state of ferment, and Confederates rode British coattails as "intra-imperial law and inter-imperial compromise" molded the form of maritime policing.[70]

An early example involved the seizure of the previously mentioned *Bermuda*, which the U.S. Navy captured in April 1862.[71] The incident came to the attention of the British government shortly thereafter, when Henry Adderley and Co. sent a letter to Governor Bayley to "express our indignation at so gross an outrage upon the rights of British subjects and so flagrant an insult to the British flag," and asked him to "promptly take such steps as in your judgment may be necessary to protect the interests of her owners and secure proper indemnity for the serious loss sustained."[72] Adderley and Co. did not, of course, mention that the ship was owned by a Confederate-controlled merchant house or that it carried Confederate munitions. Bayley forwarded the letter both to the Colonial Office and directly to Lord Lyons in Washington. In a private letter to Lyons about the matter, Bayley also mentioned that the harbor at Nassau "is full of English and quasi-English steamers," indicating that he was under no illusions as to the real ownership of the *Bermuda* and similar ships, but he accepted this quasi-Englishness as sufficient to merit his intervention.[73] Lyons correctly thought that the *Bermuda* would be condemned by the prize court for having contraband aboard but forwarded the issue to Vice Admiral Sir Alexander Milne, commander of the Royal Navy's North American and West Indies Station, for his consideration.[74] The Colonial Office also forwarded Adderley's letter to Lord Russell, thus ensuring that the complaint of a Confederate merchant reached the eyes or ears of nearly every relevant major British official in London and North America. James Mason could hardly have hoped to do the same. The use of prize court cases by Bahamian, Confederate, and English merchants offered a way to challenge the British government's recognition of the legitimacy of the Union blockade, as well as the blockade's legality within U.S. courts.[75] In this instance, the interimperial compromise between the Union and Britain, unknowingly on Confederate behalf, favored the Union, as Britain acquiesced to the capture and, eventually, the "continuous voyage" doctrine that did not permit stops at intermediate ports to remove liability of seizure for intent to break a blockade.[76] Further examples followed, directed at ship seizures as well as U.S. trade restrictions with the colony that dragged in Lord Lyons and the Foreign Office.[77]

The cozy relationship between Confederates and the Bahamian elite sometimes gave direct naval benefits to the rebellion, as in the case of the *Oreto*, the future CSS *Florida*. In 1862, under pressure from Union authorities, Commander Henry Hickley of HMS *Greyhound* seized the ship for potentially violating the Foreign Enlistment Act, which forbade the provision of warships to a belligerent power. It is noteworthy that it was Hickley who seized the

Oreto, not Bahamian authorities, who had repeatedly declined the American consul's requests that they do so.[78] Bahamian attorney general George C. Anderson, a former slaveholder widely suspected of pro-Confederate sympathies, did not investigate the case particularly energetically, despite local merchants openly recruiting sailors for the warship on the streets of Nassau.[79] Anderson's other job as Henry Adderley's attorney may have encouraged his lethargy. The judge deciding the case at the vice-admiralty court, John Campbell Lees, had attended dinners thrown by Heyliger and Lafitte celebrating Confederate naval officers John Maffitt (who went on to command the *Oreto/Florida*) and Raphael Semmes.[80] Lees released the *Oreto*, which immediately left Nassau for a nearby anchorage to receive its armament, crew, and commission as a Confederate warship.[81] The escape of the *Oreto*, followed by the release and escape of a pro-Confederate pirate arrested for illegally selling prize cargo, increasingly put the Bahamas and Governor Bayley in the military and diplomatic crosshairs of the United States and his own Colonial Office.[82]

Bayley, perhaps more than any other colonial governor, found himself caught between the competing pressures of metropolitan policy, his own distaste for Yankee insolence, especially from U.S. consul Samuel Whiting, and local intransigence against the requirements of neutrality. The pressure on Bayley peaked in 1863, sparked by a speech wherein he castigated Northern hypocrisy on neutral rights and free trade, while reminding members of the House of Assembly that they enjoyed "the right of engaging in commercial operations with each or either of the belligerents."[83] Northern journals howled that this smacked of favoritism toward the Confederacy, and the Colonial Office agreed.[84] Internal comments by Colonial Office officials called the speech "a great indiscretion" and suggested that even the appearance of officially promoting or condoning blockade running as a "right" rather than a species of smuggling "is a clearly *unfriendly* act . . . to the blockading power."[85] The colonial secretary himself, Henry Pelham-Clinton, 5th Duke of Newcastle, wrote directly to Bayley and rebuked him for "laying yourself open to a charge of unfriendly conduct towards a neighbouring power" and "impairing the position of the Government you serve." The remarks deeply stung Bayley, and he wrote a lengthy rebuttal, attempting to explain his comments, which Newcastle did not accept.[86] He was certainly in a difficult position. As Newcastle said, Bayley's speech "was very acceptable to the inhabitants of the Colony, who are naturally anxious to make the most of what are apparently the advantages of their present position relative to the Seat of War."[87] Unfortunately for Bayley, his speech went unrewarded by Adderley and the House of Assembly, as they refused most of his subsequent proposals to increase the size and effectiveness of the departments tasked with enforcing customs and bonded warehouse inspections despite an epidemic of smuggling by blockade runners to avoid paying duties.[88]

Their deliberate inaction made Bayley appear to Union eyes as either weak and ineffectual or complicit in sustaining the cause of the rebellion by facilitating blockade running. The governor had little recourse, however, because of the effective informal diplomatic connections between the Confederates and the Bahamas commercial elite. The deep partnership between the Confederacy and his own colonial legislature and subjects, dominated by Bay Street merchants like Henry Adderley, managed to subvert both his neutrality and his power and influence over affairs in the Bahamas. Perhaps to ease opposition to his duties, Bayley remained attentive to the demands of the Nassau merchant community, particularly in passing along their grievances to London and to Lord Lyons in Washington, as previously noted. The commercial-diplomatic network effectively tied Bayley's hands when it came to municipal affairs—as late as 1864, he still complained to the Colonial Office that "the mercantile members of the House [of Assembly] are not ignorant" of problems with customs enforcement and cargo inspections of blockade running traffic, but "I fear they are not averse to its continuance."[89] Bayley pleaded for a Royal Navy officer, immune from the House of Assembly's power, to be appointed harbor master, to no avail. George Harris, a partner in Adderley and Co. and Henry Adderley's son-in-law, was conveniently also the chairman of the Board of Pilotage for the Bahamas and rejected Bayley's request out of hand.[90] Like other colonial governors of the era, Bayley had been forced away from actively managing or mediating local politics and into a "quasi-monarchial" role as a supposedly neutral arbiter of the Crown's authority.[91]

Bayley continued to play that role by conveying his subjects' complaints against foreign interference to the Colonial Office and Lord Lyons. He transmitted yet another complaint, signed by over fifty merchants and members of the House of Assembly, to Lord Lyons in May 1863, once again protesting the use of bonds against goods shipped from New York, though Seward and Treasury Secretary Salmon P. Chase refused to budge on the matter, despite strong protests from Lord Russell.[92] Bayley also forwarded a forbidding pile of correspondence, mostly gathered by Lewis Heyliger, on the affair of the *Margaret and Jessie*, a "British" blockade runner shelled by a U.S. warship, supposedly in Bahamian territorial waters. This package included a letter from the owner of the *Margaret and Jessie* himself, George A. Trenholm, asking for redress. The inclusion of the Trenholm letter is hard to explain as anything but overconfidence or incompetence, because it blew apart the mutually agreed-upon fiction that the ship, like so many blockade runners, was British and not Confederate. Further insistence on the matter by James Mason came to naught, although Lafitte and Trenholm lobbied for compensation even after the war ended, much to the annoyance of the Foreign Office.[93]

Curiously, on at least one occasion the commercial-diplomatic network in Nassau welcomed the assistance of Governor Bayley and the British government against the Confederacy, in an example of how loose, decentralized control could cause it to work at cross purposes with the government in Richmond. In early 1863, a Confederate court in Wilmington seized the schooner *Harkaway*, arriving from Nassau under a British flag, because the vessel had once been owned by a Confederate citizen. It had been captured by the blockade, condemned by a U.S. prize court, and sold at auction to new British and French owners. Writing to Benjamin, Lewis Heyliger said the case "has made a very unpleasant impression here, as parties will naturally hesitate to purchase vessels condemned before a prize court, and in this proposition are the means diminished of finding suitable craft to run the blockade."[94] Governor Bayley obligingly forwarded the protest of the *Harkaway*'s nominal owner to the Colonial Office, which sent it along to Lord Russell requesting the intervention of the British consul in the area.[95] Both Heyliger's and the British consul's attempts to intervene met with harsh rejection, victims of Confederate frustration with lack of diplomatic recognition. Benjamin told Heyliger that once the British and French governments recognized the Confederacy, they "will be listened to with respect when presenting claims of their citizens for indemnity on account of injuries suffered. Till that period, the subjects of those powers must submit to the consequences of the delay caused by the action of their own governments." The secretary of state ordered him to "decline to make yourself in future the channel of communication for foreigners with this Department."[96]

Thus, the arms of the Confederate public-private partnership were not immune from friction, disagreement, and divergence of opinion as to the relative importance of smooth blockade-running operations and diplomatic respect (or lack thereof). The French and British owners of the *Harkaway* attempted, in effect, to use the Confederate commercial-diplomatic network in reverse to influence Confederate government behavior, and the Richmond authorities rather ironically resented the attempt at manipulation. Frustrated by the failure of formal diplomacy in Europe, beset by financial ruin, and disillusioned with the power of King Cotton, the Confederate government finally, though haltingly, attempted to exert greater control over their diplomatic and trade connections with the colonies. Benjamin's rebuke of Heyliger was a small move in that direction, but it took nearly a year before the Confederate Congress took any meaningful action to control private trade.[97]

Confederate informal diplomacy, such as it existed in the Bahamas and elsewhere in the colonies, succeeded precisely because it did not rely primarily on Confederates to carry it out. In the Bahamas, the Confederates had on their side the biggest fish—Henry Adderley, his son, the attorney general, and more—in a very small pond, and they exercised their pro-Confederate influence without particular direction from Richmond. The Confederacy's friends in Britain, though powerful, had no similar level of influence on the Palmerston government or among the elite. In fact, the Confederacy's very insistence on official meetings, recognition, and formal correspondence hamstrung James Mason and his predecessors, as the prime minister and his cabinet would not consent to officially meet or correspond with diplomats from an unrecognized government.[98] Lewis Heyliger and his associates operated under no such constraints in the Bahamas, and indeed his one attempt at making his presence officially known to Governor Bayley was stiffly rebuked, and they went back to merely being constant fixtures on the Nassau social scene who enjoyed unfettered access to most of the Bahamian government.[99] Informality amplified and extended Confederate influence because it did not force their colonial counterparts to keep them at arm's length.

By the end of 1863, the Confederate experiment in Nassau had become both a beehive of intermingled private and government activity centered on running the blockade and the centerpiece of a network of supporters and suppliers that stretched around the coast of British America that included much of the white mercantile, political, and social elite in places like Montreal, Halifax, Bermuda, and British Honduras.[100] The active intervention of local merchants and government proved essential in creating and sustaining the trade in the face of U.S. naval and diplomatic pressure. The imperial government supported its Bahamian subjects ambivalently, torn between preserving

British rights and prestige and maintaining a posture toward the blockade that would protect their naval advantage in a future war. Supplies consistently flowed into, and cotton out of, the Confederacy, providing critical support to the finances of the government and the combat power of the rebel armies. Such a large proportion of Confederate arms and supplies came through blockade runners that Charles Sumner later estimated that they added two years to the duration of the war.[101] By war's end, 60 percent of the Confederacy's modern rifles, one-third of the lead for Confederate bullets, and two-thirds of the saltpeter needed for manufacturing gunpowder had come through the blockade.[102] Confederate armies would have collapsed far sooner without the supplies pouring through colonial ports, Nassau above all. Informal diplomacy had been the indispensable enabler of the rebellion's military power.

The decentralized, quasi-private network centered in Nassau shepherded blockade running through the hazards of local regulations, British policy, and zealous Union blockading captains. It was not a foregone conclusion that a colonial port like Nassau could be used for blockade running: colonial legislatures could (and some did) ban the export of arms and ammunition to both belligerents, and they had substantial freedom to regulate their own harbors.[103] There was likewise no guarantee that a slaveholder's rebellion could avoid the active resistance of Black Bahamians, whose long-standing and aggressive stance against slavery contended with the relief from poverty brought by high wages and plentiful work.[104] The smooth and friendly environment in Nassau was no accident; it was rather the result of hard work, carefully cultivated relationships, and strong support by the white mercantile elite of the Bahamas, which overrode most overt resistance to blockade running. Central state authority had little to do with the success of blockade running in the Bahamas.

The significance of blockade running to Confederate military power and the utility of the Bahamas as a nearby shelter for Confederate ships, agents, and communications suggest that the informal diplomacy of the Anglo-Confederate commercial-diplomatic network was far more important to Confederate military and international fortunes than was previously understood. Colonial help made the rebellion viable, and it promised a postwar world where slavery need not have been a barrier to Confederate commercial and diplomatic fortunes. More importantly, it serves as a reminder of the limitations of state authority and the enduring power of private parties to shape the course of diplomacy, war, and empire.

Yet all was not well: in 1863, Nassau was overcrowded and ruinously expensive; U.S. Navy warships prowled the narrow passages of Bahamian waters, increasing the risks of blockade running; and the Confederate government, lacking control over wharfage and warehouse space, could not expand its operations when it became clear that relying chiefly on private firms would not meet the needs of the armed forces. Leaving blockade running in private hands had freed the Confederate government from managing a gigantic logistical program and resulted in vast quantities of supplies entering its ports. However, as the war dragged on and prospects of international recognition faded, the Confederate government began to look for ways to control or bypass its friends and proxies in the colonies in order to increase the military effectiveness of blockade running.

CHAPTER THREE

"I Risk with All Concerned"

Bermuda and the Fight to Control Blockade Running, 1863–1864

The adventurous spirit of English merchants led the way at the outset in blockade running, and it is much to be regretted that the Confederates themselves did not take the initiative in the matter.
—Letter to the *Bahama Herald*, March 23, 1864

IN MARCH 1862, John Tory Bourne, a middling commission merchant of St. George's, Bermuda, wrote to John Fraser and Co. of Charleston to extol the virtues of Bermuda as a transshipment point and his own virtues as a potential commercial agent for Confederate business. Bourne, who had assisted the CSS *Nashville* during its visit to the island the previous year, pronounced his dedication to the Southern cause and offered to take no commission on government shipments until "the acknowledgement of the Confederacy by the European Powers," and in doing so, "I risk with all concerned."[1] He soon received frequent business from the Confederate government and its private blockade-running associates across British America, and added his contacts in the Northern states and Nova Scotia to that burgeoning network.

Bourne and the merchants of St. George's integrated themselves into the pro-Confederate colonial network, although the changing circumstances of the war in 1863 and 1864 made their experience unlike that of Henry Adderley & Co. and their associates in Nassau. The Confederate government, though still dependent on local assistance and facilities, involved itself far more directly in blockade running through Bermuda, while the British imperial government retained greater influence over affairs in the colony because of its importance as a naval stronghold. The official Confederate presence in

Bermuda grew in 1863, driven by a growing divergence between the rebellion's military and financial needs and the preferences of private shippers. This presaged a much larger effort to regulate blockade running in 1864 by legislation and shipping restrictions that illustrated the practical limitations of informal diplomacy and the resistance of the colonial network to control by any government.

Bermuda in 1863 was a place of contrasts. Its splendid year-round climate was offset by the occasional appearance of horrific yellow fever epidemics. Its excellent harbors were surrounded by extensive and treacherous reefs. Its geography made it a refuge for groups operating on the maritime periphery of the Civil War, from blockade runners and adventurers to the Royal Navy and the Confederate government. Its isolation from the North American coast made it an attractive place to exploit the gray areas of the war in ways that ranged from the benign to the monstrous, from cultivating social relations to planning for biological warfare against Northern civilians. Officials in Richmond, looking to establish a government blockade-running depot, sought to avoid the overwhelmed facilities and swarming Union warships around Nassau, and Bermuda provided a suitable alternative base of operations. The Confederate government, attracted by the relatively quiet conditions in Bermuda, soon expanded its presence until the operation, based in the town of St. George's, became the most active official Confederate government establishment in all of British America.[2]

The structure of imperial British power in Bermuda, particularly the large British military presence, affected the composition of the pro-Confederate network there, while social connections helped develop and maintain its support. British Army and Royal Navy officers composed an important component of the island elite, and the governor and his deputy were both army officers. Lower-level officers frequently expressed their support for the Confederate cause in word and deed, although the most powerful officer in North America, Vice Admiral Sir Alexander Milne, was scrupulously impartial and moved quickly to suppress un-neutral behavior among his charges when he found it. Milne kept his winter headquarters in Bermuda, but due to his command obligations, he spent only a small portion of his time in the colony. Confederate citizens, including women, integrated into the social life of the island and created a welcoming atmosphere among Bermuda's military and social elite, who in turn helped the rebellion where they could with access to facilities, information, and protection from Union interference. White

Bermudians aided the Confederates for a variety of reasons, including commercial self-interest, anti-Northern sentiment (especially after the *Trent* affair), and perhaps even sympathy with Southern racial hierarchies. Confederate informal diplomacy proved less successful at cultivating support among the island's Black working class, whom they regarded with scorn and racial animus (see chapter 4). Confederate unwillingness to treat Black pilots, stevedores, longshoremen, and other laborers with respect and fair pay resulted in a costly strike, featuring arson and violence, that threatened to upend shipping operations in Bermuda.

The Bermuda link in the Confederate commercial-diplomatic network, with its prominent formal government presence, illustrated the advantage that could be gained by relying on a combination of private parties and colonial officials for access to shipping infrastructure and to facilitate the movement of people and communications. Separate Confederate state blockade-running operations, especially from North Carolina, also operated with local partners in Bermuda, adding a layer of complexity to the trade and to later efforts to regulate it. Colonial merchants and shippers were insulated from Confederate government efforts to fully control blockade running, and in 1864 they exploited the friction between the state and the general government to protect their operations. The long-delayed attempt to control blockade running shows that Confederate state centralization was less "all-encompassing" than some scholars, who focus mainly on the domestic realm, have suggested because of its transnational nature—the colonial participants in the trade were frequently integrated into government efforts and at least partly immune from its control.[3] The Confederate general government relied extensively on private parties and the forbearance of British colonials to conduct its foreign trade, and Jefferson Davis's attempt to take control of blockade running ultimately remained incomplete—cut short by yellow fever and undermined by organizational weakness and the longstanding predisposition toward informal and private control over operations in the colonies. Even at the peak of Confederate government involvement and regulation, private shippers remained indispensable to blockade running through the colonies.

The move toward greater state involvement in blockade running reflected a trend in Confederate governance with which historians have long grappled. Frank Owsley memorably chiseled "Died of State Rights" on the Confederacy's tombstone, attributing its defeat to a weak central government and the inability to cooperate with fractious state governors, particularly Zebulon Vance of North Carolina and Joseph Brown of Georgia.[4] Owsley's thesis fell by the wayside over the following decades, as scholars found that he perhaps overestimated the negative influence of irascible governors and underplayed the depth of centralization that occurred within the general and state governments of the Confederacy. Emory M. Thomas argued that during the war, the Confederate government "unwittingly" transformed itself from a loose confederation into a "centralized, national state" and that it was Jefferson Davis and his administration that "dragged Southerners kicking and screaming into the nineteenth century."[5] Thomas suggested that in addition to centralizing steps like conscription, internal passport controls, and the suspension of habeas corpus, the general government "all but nationalized the Confederate economy." Thomas traced the transformation of the Confederate government to the spring of 1862 and the opening of the Peninsular Campaign in Virginia, which provided the backdrop for conscription and other methods of expanded coercion in the name of security.[6] Military necessity likewise provided Davis and his cabinet the pretext for expanded economic intervention like the tax in kind, creating state-sponsored or -owned industries, and various other measures.[7] More recent scholarship differs on the extent of centralization, but the trend generally acknowledges the tendency of the government to expand the reach and scale of its interaction with its own citizens.[8]

Still, there is dissent on the extent and power of Confederate government control over its wartime economy, and this chapter is in sympathy with it. Michael Brem Bonner argues that the Confederate government settled into a pattern of "expedient corporatism" in managing its relationship between government power and private business, melding the public interest and private gain where possible.[9] This is a useful extension to the scholarly trend that finds that the political economy of warfare in the Civil War era was in a transitional stage, as Paul A. C. Koistinen has argued, between the minimal market-based mobilization that characterized American warfare prior to 1815 and the massive state intervention characteristic of mobilization for industrialized warfare in the twentieth century.[10] Koistinen argues that Confederate mobilization faltered in part because of the political dominance of the planter elite, and that their centralizing efforts, although effective, were hindered by an enduring laissez-faire, profit-driven ethos bent toward preserving private property.[11] This is in contrast to the relative independence and power of the

U.S. Army's Quartermaster Department and the mixed-military economy it created in the North, where military bureaucrats had greater freedom from political interference than did their Confederate counterparts.[12] These analyses point toward pragmatism as a guiding principle for many of the primary Confederate officials involved, but the complications imposed by private colonial business partners and competition with state governments made it particularly difficult to fully rationalize overseas purchasing and shipping, much less stop the frivolous loss of specie, cotton, and cargo space to luxury goods for the rich.[13] The flexibility of the privatized system was increasingly in tension with the Confederacy's financial and military difficulties.

Whether the change in Confederate governance was a conservative "revolution," as Thomas put it, or a more proactive "moment of possibility" for portions of the slaveholding elite bent on reform, as Michael Bernath argues, remains up for debate.[14] It is clear, however, that a revolution was neither necessary nor unprecedented when it came to controlling foreign policy and trade. Matthew Karp makes a persuasive case that antebellum Southern slaveholders exercised substantial control over American foreign policy in the decades leading up to the Civil War, and that they pursued an energetic expansionist agenda that was quite comfortable with the vigorous exercise of government power.[15] Karp's analysis, in combination with the findings of historians like Robert Novak and Brian Balogh on state strength in the nineteenth century, suggests that the Confederate general government should have been comfortable with strong control over trade policy, particularly if it served to protect slavery and the war effort. Max Edling demonstrates the existence of an antebellum fiscal-military state that gave precedent to aggressive means of war financing and argues that politicians ideologically opposed to centralized government had perhaps the most inclination to use aggressive state power.[16] The fact that the Confederate government waited for years to impose serious constraints on trade suggests that it was long comfortable with minimal oversight of the transnational network that operated the bulk of the Anglo-Confederate merchant marine.

From the very first days of their government's existence, Confederate leaders argued about the legality and propriety of active intervention, and as early as March 1861 the cabinet declined to take control of overseas cotton shipments in order to avoid interfering with private business.[17] The private interests of planters and cotton prevailed over military necessity far longer than practically any other segment of the Confederate economy. Despite precedent and constitutional authority, the Davis administration and the Confederate Congress both waited until relatively late in the war to intervene substantially in blockade running. The centralizing tendency in the Confederate government foundered against bureaucratic inertia, incoherent or conflicting policies within the general government and the War Department, and faith in free-market solutions to a military dilemma. Rather than being "the nearest thing to state socialism to appear in the nineteenth century," Confederate efforts to control blockade running remained inextricably bound up with private enterprise even at their zenith, and private citizens, as well as British subjects and officials in the colonies, played an essential role in creating and sustaining support for the rebellion in Bermuda and beyond.[18] Merchants and the government had long wrangled over the limits of trade policy in the early republic, and though mercantile influence waned somewhat by the Civil War era, the Confederate experience suggests that their power to contest the terms of international commerce remained significant.[19] While never fully returning to the "imperial" system of benign neglect and accommodation that historian Gautham Rao ascribes to post–Revolutionary era customs collection, the Confederate government largely deferred to merchants (including colonial and British partners) in the first years of the war and faced difficulties not unlike their Jeffersonian predecessors when attempting to shift from revenue collection toward more comprehensive surveillance and control over shipping entering and leaving its ports.[20]

Pro-Confederate activity in Bermuda started more slowly than in the Bahamas and featured a stronger government presence. Like the Bahamas, Bermuda had a long history with the South. In the early seventeenth century, ships bound for Virginia shipwrecked on the islands and provided Bermuda's first permanent human settlers. The Virginia Company initially oversaw the settlement of Bermuda, and places like Bermuda Hundred in Virginia earned the name in part as a promotional effort by the company.[21] By 1861, however, Bermuda's main commercial links were with New York and centered on the export of temperate crops like onions, potatoes, and arrowroot.[22] Although situated "in the eye of all trade" during the age of sail, steamships no longer had to pass by Bermuda when riding the Gulf Stream and trade winds back to Europe. The island's commercial fortunes seemed uninspiring until the Civil War intervened. As in the Bahamas, economic conditions in Bermuda made cooperation with blockade running an attractive endeavor, especially for the white mercantile elite.

Despite the inhabitants' readiness to work with the Confederacy, geography influenced the shape and pace of development for the Confederate commercial-diplomatic network in Bermuda and favored a larger government presence. Bermuda sat substantially farther out from the Confederacy's main Atlantic ports of Wilmington and Charleston than did Nassau. Although well-situated between North America and Europe in comparison to the Bahamas, the financial incentive for blockade runners to minimize coal loads in favor of cargo made Bermuda less desirable for profit-motivated private blockade-running firms. The larger blockade-running firms made a later appearance in Bermuda, allowing local merchants in some cases to take the lead. One of them, John Tory Bourne, styled himself as the Confederate agent in Bermuda, although he had no such formal appointment. Bourne, along with the vast majority of blockade traffic in Bermuda, operated from the town of St. George's. St. George's, described by one Confederate observer as "a primitive little place" with quaint houses, narrow streets, and buildings painted all in white, was more easily accessible from the open sea than the capital of Hamilton and became the center of the blockade-running business in Bermuda.[23]

This removal of blockade running from the center of colonial government, a distance of roughly ten miles, reduced the frequency of pro-Confederate interaction with the governor and legislature, whose most influential members lived in and around Hamilton. So unlike Charles Bayley in the Bahamas, Lt. Col. Harry St. George Ord, the governor of Bermuda, did not have to look out his window and see blockade running happening before his eyes. The imperial government presence on the islands also affected the choice of who filled that office. Bermuda's governor in this era was often a British Army officer, given the large military presence on the island, including a sizable garrison, a convict establishment overseen by the military, and the large Royal Navy dockyard facility that was the North American fleet's winter home. With their commission and career not particularly tied to their relations with colonists or the Colonial Office, the military governors of Bermuda were less solicitous of their legislatures and constituents than were the civilian governors of the Bahamas. Nonetheless, the governor could not afford to dismiss the interests and demands of his colony's elite.

Ord joined a long line of Bermuda governors who ran afoul of their colonial charges over differences on the reach and prerogative of royal (and therefore gubernatorial) authority. Fortunately for him, this resulted only in some rancor with the legislature and Privy Council (the appointed cabinet in Bermuda), rather than being beaten in the streets of Hamilton, which was the fate of Richard Coney, the first royal governor of Bermuda.[24] In 1863, at the height of Bermuda's involvement in the Civil War, Ord was angered by the postmaster of St. George's, who petitioned the House of Assembly for an increased salary despite the governor's express orders not to do so. Ord attempted to dismiss the man, but his cabinet and the legislature disagreed. Ord complained of the erosion of executive authority in Bermuda, but the Colonial Office handed him a Pyrrhic victory. They permitted Ord to suspend, not fire, the offending postmaster, and Ord thereafter proved reluctant to enter into open conflict with the legislature.[25] In the midst of the turmoil created by blockade running, the governor could not freely exercise his power, even over public servants in Bermuda, if the colonial legislature, dominated by merchants, resisted it. Although Bermuda's legislature carried perhaps less influence than its equivalent in the Bahamas, it could resist the imperial government if necessary. Fortunately for the Confederacy, the legislature and governor shared sympathy for their cause and embraced, within limits, a rebel presence in the colony.

Before 1863, Confederate government attention to Bermuda had been rather limited. The most visible presence was occasional visits by Confederate warships and commerce raiders. The CSS *Nashville*, a converted transport, stopped by in October 1861, seeking coal and some repairs. Its captain, Lt. Robert Pegram, tried to purchase coal from the Royal Navy dockyard, located at Ireland Island, but the commander there refused, citing the need to keep enough on hand for the North American fleet's anticipated arrival. Pegram then asked Ord to supply him from the garrison's stocks, but Ord refused and directed Pegram to proceed to St. George's and attempt to buy some there from private stocks. The U.S. consul, Frederick B. Wells, asked Ord to prohibit the "piratical" *Nashville* from coaling at all, but Ord rejected this consideration, as British law allowed foreign warships to purchase coal in neutral British ports.[26] The *Nashville* had asserted its right as a belligerent warship to enter Bermuda's ports, but Ord prevented both Confederate and Union representatives from gaining any particular advantage from the episode. Local friends of the Confederacy, however, did their best to put a thumb on the scale.

Confederate informal diplomacy aided the cause in Bermuda, although it was not as immediately effective as it was in the Bahamas. Ord and his attorney general proved far more cautious, for example, in granting British registry to Confederate-owned ships. Bermudians eager to drum up business solicited shipowners, North and South, to use Bermuda to obtain a British flag. Bourne, for example, told a Boston firm that "should any of the ship owners of your City wish British Register, I will be happy to assist them here," then detailed what paperwork was necessary.[27] Rather than granting these registries out of hand, as Charles Nesbitt did for Confederate ships in the Bahamas in August 1861, Ord refused initial attempts to do so and referred the matter to Lord Lyons in Washington and to authorities in London for further guidance. Events overtook him, however. The Colonial Office directed Ord to abide by the standards established by Nesbitt, which allowed blockade runners to easily use the British flag for cover.[28] Ord eventually came to sympathize strongly with the Confederate cause, especially after prolonged social contact with Confederates in Bermuda, but he remained relatively evenhanded at the outset of the war.

Despite Ord's careful initial approach to neutrality, white Bermudians were less inclined to evenhandedness. The November 1861 *Trent* crisis exposed pro-Confederate sympathy in Bermuda's House of Assembly and across the islands. The chief newspaper of the islands celebrated British war preparations and taunted the publishers of the pro-Republican *New York Times*.[29] The imperial government asked that colonial legislatures pass measures that would, upon a declaration by the queen, prohibit the exportation of arms and munitions. Charles Maxwell Allen, who had replaced Wells as U.S. consul, misinterpreted the act as "a very decisive stand" by Ord "against these islands being made a depot for . . . the rebellion."[30] The measure was actually intended to prevent weapons from reaching the United States in the event of war with Britain, but the Bermuda legislature also misunderstood its purpose. Fearing that it might interfere with the potentially lucrative blockade-running trade with the Confederacy, the House of Assembly inserted a two-year expiration date into the act, against the wishes of the imperial government, which nonetheless approved the bill rather than fighting to get a more acceptable version passed.[31] White Bermudians on Front Street and in St. George's exhibited the ability to shape imperial policy to better serve their own interests, and if that benefited their Confederate friends, so much the better.

Popular anger against the United States was likewise widespread, even after James Mason and John Slidell had been released into British custody. HMS *Rinaldo* carried the pair into Bermuda on January 9, 1862, after weather prevented them from reaching Halifax. Consul Allen, a New Englander who had taken up his post in October 1861, reported their arrival and declared that "the sympathy of the people of these islands is almost entirely with [Mason & Slidell] and their cause; and they are very bitter against the government of the United States."[32] They stayed in Bermuda only briefly, but the two enjoyed the hospitality of the governor and dined with Admiral Milne before departing on a warship for St. Thomas to catch the regular mail packet for England. Allen, like his counterpart in Nassau, reported frequent harassment and threats from local rowdies. On one occasion, someone raised the rebel flag on the consulate flagpole during the night, and Allen reported to his wife that Southerners and their local friends "have threatened to whip me." As the summer drew on, his situation did not improve: he was attacked in the street and in his office, and someone cut down the consulate's flagpole on July 3, preventing him from hoisting the Stars and Stripes on Independence Day. Allen did not identify his attackers' nationalities but found that "the general sentiment is, 'It's good enough for him; he's a damn Yankee.'"[33] By mid-1862, popular opinion among white Bermudians and the growing population of transients was decidedly against the Union and favorable to the rebellion.

Pro-Confederate colonists also managed to influence local policy in the wake of the *Trent* crisis. The Union navy, annoyed by the visit of the *Nashville*, wanted to maintain a presence off of Bermuda, but the distance from the mainland limited the endurance of steamers, which required frequent coaling. In hopes of overcoming this problem, the navy sent several cargoes of coal to Bermuda, consigned to the consul, Allen. Southern sympathizers leaped into action to prevent this, just as they had in the Bahamas. John Tory Bourne immediately protested the coal's arrival to the colony's receiver general, the chief customs officer, as "highly prejudicial to the mercantile interests of this Colony." Governor Ord initially rejected the petition, saying the consul had the same right as any other person to receive cargo. However, he changed his mind after learning of the Bahamas' refusal to allow a U.S. coal depot, and in his letter to the Colonial Office explaining his decision, he copied Bourne's phrasing exactly.[34]

Confederate informal diplomacy had helped to essentially exclude the U.S. Navy from the waters around Bermuda. In the absence of a nearby coal depot, Union warships generally could not hold their stations around the islands for more than a few days without having to return to the mainland to refuel. Indeed, when Charles Wilkes, of *Trent* notoriety, attempted to loiter with a group of warships in and around St. George's harbor in the fall of 1862, he caused a diplomatic incident and guaranteed strict enforcement, at least against American ships, of the restrictions on belligerent warships' use of British harbors. Governor Ord described Wilkes as "very insulting" and said his conduct "openly and willfully transgressed" British neutrality laws. Bermuda merchants expressed their anxiety to Ord that the presence of Wilkes's small fleet presaged the regular harassment of shipping, akin to the "blockade" of the Bahamas that had begun pushing some trade to St. George's. That this shipping was almost certainly involved in blockade running did not enter the conversation, but Ord could hardly have been unaware of it. Nevertheless, he asked the Colonial Office for a strong naval force to "preserve ourself from insult" and protect British neutrality and the colony's commercial interests.[35] The relative absence of Union cruisers also made Bermuda an attractive stop for Confederate commerce raiders like the CSS *Florida*, and they visited the colony as frequently as their situation, and the governor's tolerance, allowed. The Bermudians thus won a substantial informal diplomatic victory for the Confederacy by shielding vital shipping from Union interference and creating a lasting refuge for Confederate raiders.

Bermuda provided an essential shelter for pro-Confederate movement and communications, both intercolonial and across the blockade. Travelers bound between Europe and the Confederacy took advantage of regular mail steamer service that connected Bermuda and Britain, usually via Halifax, although they could also take passage, as the opportunity arose, on cargo ships going directly to or from Britain carrying blockade goods, coal, or cotton. Personnel movements of a more sensitive nature also took advantage of Bermuda's location in the central Atlantic, far from Union cruisers. Matthew Fontaine Maury, en route to Europe to procure ironclads and torpedo (underwater mine) components, passed through Bermuda. The exiled Democratic politician Clement Vallandigham, after being banished to the Confederacy, also made his way to Bermuda, where Maj. Norman S. Walker's office booked him passage to Halifax on the *Harriet Pinckney*, a government-owned vessel.[36] He proceeded, with Confederate assistance, to Canada West to resume his subversion of the Union cause. Shadier characters likewise favored Bermuda. A party of Confederate naval personnel traveled under cover through Bermuda in late 1863, returning from Canada after the first aborted attempt to attack the Union prisoner of war camp at Johnson's Island, in Lake Erie.[37]

Social connections facilitated Confederate movement through Bermuda and formed an underappreciated element in the success of Confederate informal diplomacy in the colonies. Women, particularly the wives of Confederate officials and businessmen, played an important role in facilitating connections between Confederates and sympathetic British subjects in the colonies through social events. Georgiana Gholson Walker, wife of Major Walker, joined him in Bermuda in 1863 and quickly established their household as the centerpiece of Confederate society on the islands. Despite being six months pregnant and in charge of three small children, she leveraged her social connections, which included her congressman father and a close friendship with Varina Davis, to book passage on a blockade runner out of Wilmington in March 1863. The wives of civilian merchants likewise attempted to cross the blockade, although the harrowing experience of Marie DeRosset illustrates the risk involved. Her husband, Louis H. DeRosset, the son of Wilmington merchant Armand DeRosset of the firm DeRosset & Brown, had gone to St. George's to oversee the firm's operations there, which included business with a variety of private firms as well as the Confederate government. Marie, with their infant child, attempted to join him on the blockade runner *Lynx*, but the blockading squadron off Wilmington spotted them and opened fire. A cannonball nearly missed decapitating her and wounded the helmsman, and she was struck in the head by fragments of the ship's wheel. She fled to the cabin, where her fleeting sense of safety vanished in the rising water—the ship had been hulled repeatedly. In a later letter to her mother, she wrote, "I stayed in the cabin until I could no longer keep baby out of the water, when the Captain sent us on shore." The *Lynx* was destroyed, but the crew and passengers managed to reach the shore near Fort Fisher. Marie DeRosset and her child survived the ordeal, were "cheered by the crew for our bravery," and reached Bermuda on the *Owl* a few days later.[38] There, she joined her husband in the business and social life of St. George's.

Georgiana Walker, an astute observer, kept a detailed diary during the war years that provides a revealing glimpse into how Confederates fit into the relatively intimate social life of Bermuda and how readily they mingled with the most prominent members of society and government. Bermuda, disrupted by the rush of the war, was "a funny little community," full of provincial eccentricities "but good for all that." Walker commented repeatedly on the quality of the social life she discovered, remarking that the people were "very

Georgiana Walker with her children, photographed in England. Two of her children were born in British colonies during the war: a son, Randolph, born in Bermuda in 1863, and a daughter, Edith, born in Halifax in 1864. Credit: Henry Ashdown, "Georgiana F. Gholson Walker and Children, ca. 1870," carte-de-visite, FIC2009.04390, American Civil War Museum, under the management of Virginia Museum of Heritage and Culture.

English," with parties that were "more numerous than magnificent" but that nonetheless "afford[ed] a really good society."[39] That "society" provided Confederates frequent opportunities to befriend important locals and develop useful relationships with officials everywhere, from the governor's mansion to the naval dockyard.

British military and naval officers, the governor, Confederate expatriates, and Bermudians mingled freely at social events. The Confederate presence at these events was not merely a formality—Charles Allen, the U.S. consul, did not receive similar invitations, and he was generally excluded from the island's polite society until after the war. The Walkers rented a house near St. George's that became a center of Confederate social life in Bermuda. A constant parade of Confederate officers, blockade-running captains, British army and navy officers, and island officials passed through the house. Norman Walker's office facilitated travel for a wide variety of Confederate personnel, and occasionally for figures like Vallandigham, while Georgiana hosted most of them for dinner and socializing as they awaited their opportunity to take passage on British mail steamers or blockade runners.[40] Blockade runners and merchants also enlivened island society and elicited further sympathy for their cause by sponsoring frequent parties and events. Walker recounted a well-attended party in 1863 on board the blockade runner *Cornubia* that featured numerous "redcoats that enlivened the scene" and entertainment by the band of the Thirty-Ninth Regiment of Foot, one of the main units of the island's garrison.[41] Local newspapers likewise reported glowingly on other social excursions, such as one led by the officers of the government-owned runner *Lady Davis* on the Fourth of July in 1863 that featured prominent toasting of Queen Victoria, Jefferson Davis, and the Confederate cause by both Southerners and British officers.[42]

British military officials in Bermuda, at least by their social calendar, appeared strongly sympathetic with the rebellion. The island's garrison and naval establishment frequently entertained, and were entertained by, Confederates. Walker noted, for example, that John Newland Maffitt, captain of the CSS *Florida*, "was very handsomely entertained at the mess of the 39th" shortly after his vessel arrived at the islands and exchanged cannon salutes with the garrison.[43] Vice Consul William C. J. Hyland, one of the few pro-Union white Bermudians, reported the salute to Washington in a dispatch on the *Florida*'s activities.[44] This exchange of salutes resulted in diplomatic wrangling, as William H. Seward reported the event as both evidence of pro-Confederate bias in Bermuda and an act that implied diplomatic recognition of the Confederacy. Ord scrambled to explain himself to the Colonial Office, for he had not only authorized the salute but failed to mention it in his dispatch reporting the arrival of the *Florida*. Ord claimed that "the omission was quite accidental and the result of my forgetfulness," and that he "unhesitatingly authorized" the salute because he understood it to be a routine courtesy extended to foreign warships. Some Colonial Office officials felt that Ord had overstepped his bounds, but the Colonial Secretary accepted his explanation.[45]

Ord was probably being less than forthright in this instance. It does not appear that any other Confederate warship ever received a salute in a British port anywhere on the globe, and they certainly had not in Bermuda prior to this occasion. Ord's unthinking and "unhesitating" greeting of the *Florida* may well have been an outgrowth of his warm sentiments toward the Confederacy and his frequent and positive social interactions with the Confederate diaspora on his islands. Governor Ord and his wife, for example, paid a social call on the Walker home, and they agreeably impressed Georgiana. Governor Ord reciprocated the warm feelings. At a dinner party at Mount Langton, the official governor's residence, in April 1864, Ord declared that Georgiana "had fully converted him to the Southern cause," which she dismissed as a mere pleasantry because "his Excellency needed no conversion."[46] Ord's sympathy to the cause was unambiguously clear to Confederate society in Bermuda.

Conviviality and hospitality not only made for pleasant evenings but had material benefits for the rebellion as well. In his official correspondence with London, Ord took great pains to point out when he refused Confederate warships the use of the Royal Navy Dockyard for repairs. He did not extend the same caution to, as Charles Bayley called them, "quasi-English" blockade runners. On at least eight occasions, Ord permitted blockade runners the use of the Royal Navy's facilities on Ireland Island, across the sound from Hamilton, for repairs. The commander of the dockyard, Captain Frederick Glasse, held authority over the use of these facilities, and he acquiesced to requests from Bermuda merchants operating or aiding blockade runners, including John Tory Bourne, to repair and assist the runners. Admiral Milne learned of the assistance to ships that were "more or less the property of the Govt of the Confederate States of America" from a careless remark by Ord, and he ordered it stopped immediately.[47] Milne, whose duties and good sense caused him to maintain a greater distance from the Confederate diaspora in the colonies, immediately realized the diplomatic dangers posed by such permissiveness. Milne urged the Admiralty and Palmerston's government to forbid the practice because it not only gave the impression of official support for blockade running but also ran the risk of providing official repairs to Confederate-owned vessels operating under British colors.[48] Fortunately for the officers involved, Union authorities did not learn of this direct assistance.

By integrating themselves into the social life of Bermuda, Confederates also helped to nurture informal connections with other colonies, particularly in British North America. As Confederate interest in British North America grew, Bermuda increasingly served as the most important gateway for Confederate access to the region. Numerous Confederates on both private and public business passed through St. George's, from the previously mentioned naval raiders, to legal advisers and so-called commissioners, to ostensibly private businessmen like Nathaniel Beverley Tucker and George N. Sanders, who nonetheless involved themselves in public affairs. Some of these men received their introductions to British North American society through friends of the Confederacy that had connections with Bermuda or the South. For example, Thomas Connolly, the Catholic archbishop of Halifax, made periodic visits to Bermuda as part of his duties. An avowed friend of the South, Connolly paid a visit to the Walker residence in May 1864, causing Georgiana to exclaim, "What a glorious man he is!" and declare that she "would vote for him for *Pope* tomorrow."[49]

Although Walker could not vote for pope, she could provide the setting for Connolly to meet Confederate agents and become acquainted with them. Fortuitously, the archbishop's visit to Bermuda coincided with the arrival of Confederate commissioners Clement C. Clay and Jacob S. Thompson, who were making their way to British North America to oversee a variety of clandestine missions for the Confederate government. Clay's wife was a good friend of Georgiana Walker, and she promptly hosted a dinner party for the archbishop to honor "the many hospitalities which he has extended to our countrymen while in Halifax."[50] The guest list included Clay and Thompson, along with the lieutenant governor of Bermuda (Ord was absent from the colony) and several members of the island's high society. Clay and Thompson doubtless began their relationship with Connolly in Bermuda, and he proved more than willing to aid them during their missions in the months that followed. The archbishop returned to Halifax on board HMS *Vesuvius*, and the two Confederates followed shortly thereafter in the Royal Mail steamship *Alpha*.[51] Confederate informal diplomacy proved effective in creating and maintaining active support in Bermuda among the white elite.

The cordial relations between Confederates and white government officials in Bermuda had other implications for informal relations between Britain and the rebellion. Bermuda's curious position as both a British naval base and a pro-Confederate stronghold led the imperial government to choose it as the site of sub rosa contact with the Confederacy in order to rid itself of a problem in another colony with a far less welcome Southern presence. The circumstances and diplomatic intrigue around the arrest and quasi-extradition of Confederate sailor Joseph Hester from Gibraltar to Bermuda played out almost entirely at sea, and in and around British colonies, and showed how the colonies could serve as a kind of interstitial space for interactions between Britain and an unrecognized government away from diplomatic complications and prying eyes. The British government hoped, in effect, to engage in some informal colonial diplomacy of its own.

Joseph Hester had been a warrant officer on the merchantman-turned-commerce raider CSS *Sumter*, which sailed from New Orleans in June 1861 under the command of Raphael Semmes. The ship spent several months attacking Union commerce on the high seas, but after Spanish authorities forced it out of Cadiz under Union pressure in January 1862 (Semmes blamed the "red Republican German refugee Carl Schurz" for the expulsion), the *Sumter* entered the British-controlled port of Gibraltar in need of coal and repairs.[52] Semmes found British authorities there "kindly" but "very particular in the preservation of their neutrality" and unwilling to allow him to use government coal or recruit crewmen despite widespread anti-Union sentiment—a stark contrast to the welcoming environs of Nassau or St. George's. Semmes proved unable to obtain coal from private sources because of what he called "a combination of [local] merchants (under the influence of the Yankee consul) against me."[53] Eventually Semmes and most of his crew left the *Sumter* to take up positions on the ship that became the CSS *Alabama*, leaving the former vessel with just a caretaker crew on board that included Hester. The Confederates eventually sold the *Sumter* off as a merchant ship, but not before trouble raised its head.[54]

After months of idleness at Gibraltar, the *Sumter*'s acting commander, Lt. William Andrews, caught Hester pilfering supplies on October 15, 1862, and Hester shot him three times. Andrews died within minutes, and Hester turned himself in to British authorities. The local coroner investigated and determined that Hester should be charged with murder.[55] Because the killing happened on board a commissioned warship, British authorities determined that they had no jurisdiction to try Hester themselves, but in the interest of justice, they sought to turn him over to the Confederacy for trial. With only a handful of seagoing ships, it was unlikely that the Confederate navy could pick him up at Gibraltar, so Secretary of State Judah Benjamin proposed that the Royal Navy deliver him to any Confederate port or, if that failed, hold him at Bermuda and a Confederate officer would pick him up.[56] Faced with the uncertain legality of detaining Hester, the Admiralty and the Foreign Office agreed to this proposal, and on May 5, 1863, the prisoner was loaded onto HMS *Shannon* and shipped for Bermuda.

Bermuda served as the destination for this unusual cargo for much the same reason that it appealed to blockade runners: it was isolated yet relatively near the Confederate coast, had a strong military and naval presence, and hosted a sympathetic population that included a number of Confederates who could facilitate a transfer. Bermuda was Confederate enough to permit ready, informal interaction with British authorities, and British enough to prevent Union interference and accusations of de facto recognition. Due to bureaucratic and communications delays, Hester arrived in Bermuda on June 1, before Governor Ord received notice from the Colonial Office that he was coming. Ord coordinated with Admiral Milne, then present at Bermuda, and they initially determined to keep Hester on board the *Shannon* to avoid having to release him if someone filed a writ of habeas corpus.[57] Ord appears mainly to have been concerned about being held personally liable for an illegal detention, for it is hard to imagine that the island's Confederates would have clamored for a murderer's release en route to the Confederacy for trial. Meanwhile, the American consul, Charles Maxwell Allen, did not note Hester's arrival or make any mention of him to either British authorities or the State Department. Bermuda appeared well-suited to his continuing quiet detention.

The question of detaining Hester indefinitely in Bermuda, however, quickly came to a denouement. Union authorities refused to allow the *Shannon* to cross the blockade to deliver Hester, but rather than hold him until a Confederate officer arrived and risk the unlikely but embarrassing scenario of a habeas corpus petition, the British government told Ord to set him free in Bermuda. On July 30, 1863, Hester stepped off the *Shannon* a free man, having literally gotten away with murder.[58] Unaware that Hester had been freed, the Confederate government sent a ship to Bermuda to take him into custody, which arrived a few weeks later. Lt. John Wilkinson, a Confederate naval officer who frequently commanded blockade runners, expressed surprise that Hester had been freed and asked Governor Ord to rearrest him, but Ord declined because he had no legal authority to do so.[59] Hester would not be the last murderer to escape into the colonies in the confusion of the war. He reappeared briefly on a blockade runner but disappeared from view until Reconstruction, where he played a role in hunting down Klan fugitives from the Carolinas.[60]

Despite a favorable climate of local opinion and a relative lack of Union warships, Bermuda did not see heavy blockade-running traffic until 1863.[61] Bourne, regardless of his lobbying, had initially not been able to drum up much business. James T. Welsman, a partner in John Fraser and Co., wrote that Bourne was "the very first, and for a long time was the only friend the Confederacy had in these islands," but the overcrowded harbor and facilities at Nassau finally persuaded Confederate officials in the War Department of the advantages of Bermuda, and by mid-1863, Bourne had no shortage of business.[62] Col. Josiah Gorgas, head of the Ordnance Bureau, organized a steamship line dedicated to bringing in government cargoes, and he chose St. George's as its colonial depot. Gorgas ordered Maj. Norman S. Walker to proceed there from England and set up operations.[63] Walker's duties initially centered on receiving and transshipping Ordnance Department goods from Europe, but he quickly fell into a role akin to Lewis Heyliger's in Nassau, acting as an informal agent at large for Confederate interests, despite having no official connection with the State Department or navy. Unlike Heyliger, however, Walker worked from his own offices and did not share his address or duties with any particular merchant house. Bourne worked with Walker's office frequently, as a consignee and agent, but they often butted heads about the extent of Bourne's duties and his "right" to send and receive Confederate cargoes. Private shippers followed in increasing numbers later that year, especially after the Union campaign against Morris Island effectively closed Charleston to blockade runners for several months.[64]

Bourne complained that Walker and his small staff, including George Black and Maj. Smith Stansbury, "not being businessmen," refused to pay the going local rates for freight and cargo, and "if it was not that I am afraid I may injure the cause" in Bermuda, "I would give up having anything to do with them."[65] Bourne was torn between his loyalty to the rebellion (and his large potential payoff if it survived) and his personal pride and immediate financial concerns.[66] Despite this friction, Bourne and other Bermuda merchants, including Nathaniel Butterfield (whose family name still adorns a prominent bank on the islands), worked closely with the civilian side of the informal Confederate network across the colonies, particularly with John B. Lafitte and the partners of Henry Adderley & Co. in Nassau.[67] Bourne also maintained prewar commercial ties to Halifax and may have helped connect Alexander Keith to the pro-Confederate network in that port.[68]

Confederate state governments also engaged in blockade running, most notably North Carolina. Acting independently of the general government, the state dispatched purchasing agents to Europe and the colonies, where they cooperated with much the same network of colonial merchants and officials as the Confederate general government. Governor Zebulon Baird Vance, a competent manager and a constant thorn in the side of Richmond authorities, ordered his agent in Europe, John White, to purchase a steamer, dubbed the *Advance*, and commence running cargoes between Bermuda and Wilmington. James H. Flanner, a Wilmington merchant, served for much of the war as the ship's purser and agent in St. George's, where he also worked with John Tory Bourne, as well as the firm of Lemmon & Co., who frequently received and reshipped cargoes for the state of North Carolina.[69] South Carolina, Virginia, and Georgia also conducted blockade running on their own account, using a combination of state-owned ships and charter contracts with private shippers. North Carolina's use of a state-owned ship to save on freight costs occurred nearly contemporaneously with a similar operation by the Confederate Ordnance Department.

Ordnance chief Josiah Gorgas arranged for agents in England to purchase or build a small fleet of steamers for the direct use of his department. Bourne's complaint about Confederate shipping rates points to a major advantage of this approach: the potential savings of up to £30 a ton in gold or cotton just in freight charges, in addition to the ability to ship out cotton entirely to the government's account. This move toward government-operated blockade runners coincided with the organization of the Erlanger loan in Europe.[70] Confederate finances abroad were in crisis by 1863, drained by huge purchasing contracts in Europe and ruinously expensive shipping arrangements in the colonies that often did not prioritize government stores. The move toward publicly owned and operated cargo ships was part of a broader reorganization of Confederate purchasing and shipping between the spring of 1863 and 1864.[71]

Gorgas's little fleet proved to be cost-effective and convenient, and the Confederate Quartermaster Department, responsible for supplying uniforms, tents, and other non-weapon items, soon sent their own representative, Maj. Richard P. Waller, to Nassau to arrange transportation for quartermaster supplies into Wilmington.[72] The government-owned steamers operated almost exclusively from Bermuda and were successful enough in their operations that by late September 1863, Secretary of War James A. Seddon called for the purchase of "all the steamers of the first class for running the blockade" that could be managed with the resources available, and encouraged all War Department agencies involved in overseas procurement to assist with and use the Ordnance Department's steamers. Seddon, who was so enthusiastic about their capacity for exporting cotton on government account, claimed that if he had twenty steamers, he "could probably render the Department independent of all foreign loans, and even aid the Treasury in rectifying the expansion of its paper currency here."[73] Seddon, Gorgas, and other officials believed they had found, in the harbors of Bermuda, a solution to their unceasing overseas supply headaches.

Seddon proved too optimistic about the risks and rewards involved in his department's attempt at blockade running. Bad luck and the U.S. Navy cost the effort several ships and cargoes, and competing purchasing and shipping arrangements hamstrung efforts to maintain an efficient shipping network.[74] Purchasing agents for state governments and even some general government agencies made competing contracts in Europe, and many earned commissions based on the total cost of the contract—a built-in incentive to choose the highest bidder. Once in the colonies, their goods competed for limited space in warehouses, wharves, and on ships—in some cases, under the care of the same agent, who had a natural incentive to prioritize the best-paying customer. Colin McRae, the Confederate Treasury agent in Europe, grew so exasperated with the swarm of private, state, and national government agents that he asked, "Why does not the Government take the subject of blockade running entirely into its own hands? Not a bale of cotton should be allowed to come out of the country nor a pound of merchandise go in except on Government account."[75]

McRae raised a crucial question: Why did the Confederate government not clamp down completely on blockade traffic, given the exigency of its financial situation? To do so seemed the logical complement to directly operating government steamers, but McRae perhaps underestimated the importance and influence of colonial shipping operations. The Confederate constitution unquestionably gave the government legal authority to do so, but powerful elements in Congress and the general government stubbornly clung to the use of private shipping and resisted government control over cotton, in part because of old suspicions of government tyranny and in some cases to preserve existing arrangements by state governments or other influential parties.[76] The War Department, the body most dependent on overseas supplies, advocated strongly for greater control over blockade cargoes in the summer and fall of 1863. Seddon, after finding the small War Department fleet of steamers "inadequate," appointed officers to posts in Charleston and Wilmington to oversee shipping on government account and worked with the local commanders—W. H. C. Whiting in Wilmington and Pierre G. T. Beauregard in Charleston—to pressure privately owned ships to voluntarily give cargo space to the government or face potential impressment. He succeeded late in the year in gaining a concession that one-third of each ship's outbound cargo space would be reserved for government use.[77]

Curiously, the Confederate Navy Department did relatively little to take charge of blockade running. Despite its almost complete reliance on overseas production for essentials like boilers, engines, and machinery, the department showed no interest in operating government cargo ships. Indeed, bureaucratic stovepiping characterized all Confederate shipping operations. Each department was funded by separate congressional appropriations and had to purchase and ship supplies on its own account. This frustrated Ordnance Department officers and frequently led to wasted space or bureaucratic wrangling over funding. To further complicate matters, the other main supply organizations for the army, the Quartermaster and Subsistence Departments, made separate contracts with private shippers to move goods on their behalf, adding to the multiplicity of actors working on both ends of the colonial trade network on at least partial government account.[78]

In the colonies, all these various state and general government operations worked through the same handful of local merchant houses, wharves, and agents. Many, especially the War Department and the State of North Carolina, favored Bermuda because it was less busy than Nassau and because Vance believed, tragically and erroneously, that Bermuda was less susceptible to yellow fever outbreaks and thus would spare his ships from being quarantined at Wilmington.[79] John Tory Bourne, for example, served simultaneously as an agent or consignee for the Confederate Ordnance Department, the state of North Carolina, John Fraser & Co. (the Confederacy's main shipping and banking partner in Charleston), Fraser, Trenholm & Co. (the Liverpool branch of John Fraser & Co.), Henry Adderley & Co. in Nassau, and numerous private British and colonial individuals and firms, from Halifax to Belfast to London.[80] Bourne's vast interconnections with public and private operations across the Atlantic typified the complicated structure of blockade running as managed by the pro-Confederate commercial-diplomatic network in the colonies. This intercolonial network kept supplies moving into the Confederacy and leveraged its connections within the South to resist attempts to centralize control and reduce profits.

As attempts at using government-owned vessels floundered due to losses and a scarcity of ships, the Confederate Congress finally took action when it returned to session in December 1863, searching for a method of "controlling private enterprise, without, however, depriving it of the stimulus to exertion."[81]

Members introduced several different bills in the House and Senate aimed at controlling blockade running.[82] The Senate Committee on Commerce reported three bills in mid-January to that effect, which proposed to "impose regulations upon the foreign commerce of the Confederate States," prohibit certain imports, and establish a new Bureau of Foreign Supplies.[83]

The resulting bills, passed on February 6, 1864, put stringent controls on import and export freight. In a move that particularly annoyed private shippers, the Congress prohibited importation of a dizzying variety of so-called luxuries, including alcohol, Roman candles, clocks, lace, and toys—all items with high values in ratio to their weight.[84] More importantly, the second act prohibited the export of cotton, tobacco, and other Southern staples such as naval stores "except under such uniform regulations as shall be made by the President of the Confederate States."[85] With these measures, Confederate authorities hoped to both force private shippers to bring in government-purchased goods and prevent the hemorrhage of cotton at rock-bottom rates. Private parties who purchased cotton in Confederate ports at six pence a pound could usually resell it in the colonies or in Britain for four or five times that amount. The Confederate government finally intended to take that margin for itself.[86]

With these expansive powers now in hand, the Davis administration laid out new regulations for blockade running that reserved 50 percent of the cargo capacity of each ship for the use of the Confederate government, at rates set at the government's discretion. Any state contracts with privately owned ships could use only the remaining half of the ship. The regulations offered inducements for private shippers to move more outgoing cargo on the government's behalf by increasing the freight payment they would receive, but insisted that freight on incoming voyages would be paid on delivery at a Confederate port.[87] This last portion was at odds with the prevailing custom of prepaying all or a portion of freight charges, and it did not sit well with private shippers who faced the prospect of losing a ship to the Union blockade with nothing to show for their efforts.

The private shippers and merchants in the colonies, especially at Bermuda and Nassau, did not welcome this Confederate government foray into controlling trade and its consequent reduction in their freedom of action and profits. Bourne groused to a business correspondent in England that "the restrictions put on the Blockade trade by the Confederate Congress is likely to cramp all connected in this Trade. The present holders of Cotton Bonds are the only persons likely to do any business with the Confederacy."[88] Another merchant's clerk wrote, "The blockade runners swear that they will not bring in a single cargo under the present arrangement viz one-half of the cargo. It is unjust and extortionate."[89] Even the stalwarts of John Fraser and Co. chafed under the new arrangements, particularly at Walker's handling of business in Bermuda.[90] At least initially, the regulations coincided with a decline in trips across the blockade, although the public outcry in Bermuda was limited; in fact, the main newspaper of the islands did not even mention the restrictions.

By contrast, merchants and blockade runners in Nassau loudly complained about the new regulations and pointed out that the government had deliberately left the trade to them in the first place. The staunchly pro-Confederate editor of the *Bahama Herald* called the new laws "prohibitory" and claimed they had an immediate "depressing effect on the market, and a general feeling of inactivity is observable."[91] He later wrote that the rules were overtly favorable to holders of cotton bonds then circulating in Europe from the Erlanger loan and put too much risk onto the heads of private shippers. He ardently hoped for Confederate victory, "but we cannot shut our eyes to the fact that supplies are imperatively required from European markets, and those supplies can only be had for ready cash," which was a straightforward swipe at not prepaying for freight charges.[92] Other writers were less circumspect in pointing out that Confederates left this vital operation in colonial hands and should not expect too much cooperation in taking it back. A Bahamian correspondent of the *Herald* asserted that "the adventurous spirit of English merchants led the way at the outset in blockade running, and it is much to be regretted that the Confederates themselves did not take the initiative in the matter" of transporting war supplies for their armies.[93]

Confederates felt compelled to defend the new rules publicly. One Confederate in Nassau, under the nom de plume "Justice," wrote in defense of the regulations, only to face heaps of abuse in the pages of the newspaper, as well as threats of violence.[94] One respondent castigated Justice for insisting that blockade runners foot the bill "in order to remedy the evil results of an imbecile management of his Country's Treasury and Navy Departments." The *Herald*'s editor hinted that someone had tried to intimidate him into revealing the identity of Justice and other writers who defended the Confederate attempt to control blockade running so that they might be targeted for retribution, and that some sort of interpersonal violence had occurred as a result of arguments over the regulations.⁹⁵ Lewis Heyliger himself felt compelled to intervene in the debate. Writing under his usual pseudonym of "X," Heyliger tried to calm the waters by directing the Nassau merchants' ire against the United States and the bond restrictions on commerce with Northern ports, and by promising that the new regulations, if found to be disadvantageous, could be reconsidered or modified.⁹⁶ The discontent among the blockade-running set was palpable, and they turned to other means to contest the government's imposition on their profits.

Private shippers resisted in some cases by resorting to smuggling, but the firms and individuals most deeply tied to the government generally acquiesced to trade restrictions.⁹⁷ This was due in no small part to the blizzard of existing government contracts that remained in effect for shipments under more favorable terms, but also because Confederate authorities in the colonies and on the continent did not strictly enforce restrictions on luxury goods. Many ships cleared St. George's with openly declared contraband like bonnets, pianos, and wine long after the restrictions on their import came into effect, which suggests either that private runners evaded the rules or that Confederate authorities did not (or could not) vigorously enforce them.⁹⁸ Private shippers also took advantage of the inherent conflicts of Confederate federalism. Despite efforts to centralize overseas purchasing, state governments—especially North Carolina—persisted in maintaining their own purchasing and shipping operations in Europe and the colonies, and private shippers turned informal diplomacy on its head by appealing to their state-level patrons for protection from the new regulations. Central authority in the Confederacy faced a combined challenge from state and nonstate competitors.

The greatest resistance to Confederate general government attempts to control blockade traffic did not come directly from private parties but rather from state government operations, especially the relatively efficient blockade-running service of North Carolina. Governor Zebulon Vance clashed frequently with Confederate authorities in Wilmington over control of the cargo space on state-owned or chartered steamers, and the state's agents in the colonies often mirrored this conflict on their end.⁹⁹ Vance wrote to Jefferson Davis in March 1864, shortly after the publication of the new rules, and took issue with the administration's new claims on cargo space, claiming that "the Regulations, if persisted in, will destroy the [blockade-running] trade absolutely" unless state-chartered ships received exemptions.¹⁰⁰ Davis, referring to his repeated sparring with Vance and other governors over control of cargo space, groused to Governor Joseph Brown of Georgia that blockade runners "attempted to interpose the State authorities between themselves and the General Government, and thus evade the regulations."[101] After treating blockade running as a commercial affair for so long, Davis and the executive branch faced an array of opponents who jealously guarded their commercial prerogatives.

Davis was not mistaken; agents for blockade-running companies did appeal to governors to shield them from the new regulations, and Vance for one did his best to work on their behalf. When Confederate authorities informed Theodore Andreae, agent for the Alexander Collie line of blockade runners, that they intended to take half the space of the steamer *Hansa* as it lay in port at Wilmington, Andreae sought help from North Carolina authorities because the *Hansa*, among others, used a portion of its capacity to carry freight on state behalf. Vance wrote to Richmond threatening that he would "fire the ship before I will agree" to the new rules.[102] Davis contended, in reply, that to offer exemptions to any ships other than those wholly owned by a state government would permit wholesale avoidance of the new regulations and defeat their intent. If a mere partial stake in a ship allowed it to escape the rules, "all the ships engaged in running the blockade would ere long be owned in part by the states, and there would be nothing left for the Confederate Government to regulate."[103] Davis, obstinate as ever, demanded compliance with the rules, and stated that he would not consider exemptions.

Vance's irritation stemmed in no small part from the way the regulations imposed on his existing contracts. In order to spread his state's risk across several vessels, Vance had sold a portion of the *Advance* to a merchant partnership in Richmond and Wilmington and then entered into a contract with the London merchant house of Alexander Collie to purchase a share of several more ships. The contract gave the state one-fourth of each ship's outbound cargo space, usually filled with cotton, and devoted the entire ship to state goods on the inbound leg.[104] The War Department's imposition on a third of each ship's cargo space beginning in late 1863 had counted state-owned space toward the government's share and had only a minimal impact on North Carolina's operations, but Davis's 1864 regulations removed this exemption, leaving the private partner only one-quarter of the ship's outgoing cargo space, rather than the two-thirds they had expected.[105] After the new regulations came into force, other governors likewise scrambled to mitigate the effects on their operations. South Carolina had an important ally in the person of

William Porcher Miles, chair of the House Military Affairs Committee, who replied to urgent telegrams from Governor Milledge L. Bonham at the close of the legislative session that month. Miles assured Bonham that Secretary of War James Seddon had "expressed every disposition to extend assistance" and would allow the state to ship cotton on the same terms as the Confederate Government, but that Davis would soon issue new regulations and that Bonham had better attempt to make arrangements with him directly.[106] Seddon had, in general, been conciliatory about excluding state cargoes from restrictions, but the new regulations moved control over cargo space to the Treasury Department, and Jefferson Davis rigidly opposed any modifications or concession to the states.

Vance and the other Atlantic coast governors, especially Joseph Brown of Georgia, joined together to pressure their congressional delegations to repeal or modify the restrictions on commerce at the next session.[107] They obliged, and in early June Congress passed a bill to modify the previous act to specify that "the Confederate States shall not interfere with steamers sailing on State account, either in whole or in part."[108] Davis vetoed the bill, and his statement explaining his decision focused its ire on the "foreigners" profiting at Confederate expense. He accused private shipowners of "depreciating our currency and exhausting our country" while benefiting from the use of public harbors and the protection of Confederate fortifications. He also alleged a conspiracy by private shippers, first to hold their vessels out of service to force the government to revoke the new regulations and, when that failed, to conspire with state governors to avoid Confederate imposition on their cargo space by transferring their vessels to the states.[109]

There is little evidence of such a conspiracy, however. Shipping contracts between state governments and British merchants predated the February 6 law, and despite the new restrictions, state governments did not purchase ships beyond what they already owned. Private shippers based in the colonies retained powerful influence over Confederate trade, despite what one historian called "radical socialistic" controls and "the most radical interference in the open marketplace ever seen in America."[110] The Confederate government succeeded in wresting some control over blockade running from private hands, but only after three years of war and increasingly desperate financial circumstances. The results were not a resounding success: from January through August 12, 1864, only 1,672 bales of cotton made it to Europe directly for Confederate account. Nearly twice as much cotton, even under the new regulations, went to pay for competing contracts with the Collie and Crenshaw firms, alongside large deliveries in payment of cotton-backed Confederate bonds to private purchasers.[111] Imports through the blockade were sufficient to keep Confederate armies in the field, but exports were far short of the six thousand bales that Maj. Thomas Bayne estimated were necessary to pay for those supplies.

Confederate operations in Bermuda came to an almost complete halt in the late summer of 1864, although the enemy this time was not the U.S. Navy or angry merchants. A horrific yellow fever epidemic erupted, likely carried in by blockade-running traffic, and swept through the island's population. Visitors suffered particularly heavily—out of 131 deaths in St. George's in the first month of the outbreak, only one person was a native Bermudian.[112] Those that could flee did so, and much of the blockade-running traffic removed to Halifax or Nassau to escape the ravages of the disease.[113] The island's garrison suffered severely, and the government ordered most of the soldiers to go to Halifax to wait out the epidemic.[114] Georgiana Walker and her children had fortuitously departed for England in June before the outbreak began in earnest, although a sailor on the ship carrying them died of the disease midway through the voyage.[115] The Confederate government presence on Bermuda nearly vanished, although local stalwarts like Bourne carried on their work in spite of the danger. The death toll, especially in St. George's, was heavy—nearly 10 percent of the parish population died of the disease. Across Bermuda, out of a population of around 6,400 (plus the island's garrison and transient population, which likely added several hundred more), island officials estimated that 2,732 people caught yellow fever, and 529 of those patients died—a loss of around 8 percent of the island's population in just a few months.[116] The epidemic did not entirely end Confederate involvement in Bermuda, but it marked a transition away from primarily logistical operations and sharply curtailed blockade running until cooler weather eased the epidemic in the autumn.

Bermuda served as the site of Confederate experimentation with direct government control of blockade running, first through ownership of a small fleet of steamers, and later by import restrictions that mirrored the increased regulations on shipping in Confederate ports. The move to greater regulation and direct involvement came only after military and fiscal crises in 1863 convinced Davis and key War Department officials that private carriers would not provide enough return, in terms of the price of exported commodities and the type and volume of war-related imports, to sustain the rebellion. In an effort to shape a uniform and effective trade policy, the Confederate Congress and the various executive branch agencies worked to overcome the opposition of coastal state governors and a widespread fondness for private enterprise, bureaucratic parochialism, and states-rights dogmatism. The inertia of reliance on private shipping enervated attempts to create an effective export control system. Private merchants in the colonies and their agents and partners in the South played South Carolina, Georgia, and especially North Carolina against the general government in Richmond. The resistance of nonstate actors like merchant firms showed that they remained powerful players in the blockade-running trade even after the implementation of the trade regulations of 1864. The Confederate general government succeeded in exerting greater control over imports and, to a lesser extent, cotton exports, but private contracts, cotton bond redemptions and a lack of available government-owned cotton, and smuggling ensured that private shipping remained a lucrative venture, to the detriment of Confederate finances.[117]

In Bermuda, Confederate informal diplomacy successfully cultivated relationships and sympathy with the Bermudian elite and British imperial officials, both civilians and military. Local merchants like John Tory Bourne provided introductions and intercessions for blockade runners and warships alike, while Confederate officials and their wives, especially Georgiana Walker, created a semblance of Southern society in their temporary homes. These efforts built goodwill with the most influential British subjects of the colony, which paid dividends in the form of small forbearances from the government and ready access to port and warehouse facilities. The Confederate government maintained a more overt presence in Bermuda than any other colony, and attempted its greatest direct involvement with blockade running, which endured until yellow fever nearly ended commerce in the colony in the late summer and fall of 1864. Ultimately, the example of Confederate attempts to control blockade traffic demonstrates the durability of the privatized model of blockade running and the ability of the Anglo-Confederate networks in the colonies to resist impositions by either government.

Informal diplomacy proved to be remarkably successful in cultivating ties with white colonials in Bermuda and the Bahamas. It floundered, however, with the large Black populations of these colonies, whose labor made transshipping operations for blockade running possible. It is to this important but understudied group that chapter 4 turns.

CHAPTER FOUR

"The Heartless Slave-Dealers in America"

Strikes, Spies, and the Failures of Confederate Influence in Bermuda and the Bahamas, 1862–1864

Is there a nation or a tribe more intruded upon or degraded than the Sons of Africa? Is there a people so friendless and so unprotected, except where Britain holds her sway[?] Look at the heartless Slave-dealers in America, who set them up at auction, as though they were cattle of some sort.... We are not conscious of half the sufferings of our oppressed brethren.
—Robert S. Evans, Bahamas Friendly Society

CONFEDERATE GRASSROOTS DIPLOMACY proved effective in creating and maintaining active support in the Bahamas and Bermuda among the white colonial elite. By contrast, it largely ignored the large Black and "coloured" share of the islands' population, with negative consequences for blockade running and beyond.[1] The Confederate diaspora in the colonies could never reconcile their proslavery worldview with the necessity of free Black labor for bringing it into being. When they could not ignore the Black workers surrounding them, they treated them as a despised and contemptible people. Visiting Confederate journalist Frank Wilson called Black Bahamians "a lazy, dirty, thriftless people[,] as they have ever been since the mistaken philanthropy of England emancipated them, and as they ever will be until they are returned to their natural condition, and their labor made compulsory."[2] Black colonial Britons took up the economic opportunities offered by blockade running, but they were hardly enthusiastic supporters of the slaveholders' project. Despite their widespread poverty, many actively risked their safety and freedom to support the United States by serving as informants, guides, ship pilots, and sailors. This active support became especially apparent after the issuance of the Emancipation Proclamation in January 1863. Others were willing to take pro-Confederate money to work at the docks, but they would not passively accept exploitation. Black workers' response to pro-Confederate labor exploitation was shaped deeply by their level of social cohesion and self-organization, as well as their level of economic independence. This peaked with a burst of labor militancy among Black workers in St. George's, Bermuda, in 1863, which resulted in a strike that featured violence, an assassination attempt, possible arson, and a lengthy disruption to Confederate supply operations in the colony.

It seems clear that Confederates in the 1860s did not understand the social organization or self-protection tradition of free Black people in the British Atlantic and West Indies, nor did they attempt to do so. They had little experience in dealing with organized Black waterfront labor—none existed in the primary blockade-running ports of Charleston and Wilmington before the war—and none at all in engaging on equal terms with a large body of independent Black mariners.[3] The willingness of Black Britons in these colonies to use all the tools at their disposal to provide mutual aid, education, and defense against predation by Americans was hardly a secret, yet there is barely a hint of it in any of the Confederate correspondence or accounts from the major blockade-running ports of the Civil War. When Confederates deigned to notice Black fraternal organizations such as the Odd Fellows or local friendly societies, the response was bemused scorn, as though they were unruly children playing like adults. The Confederacy's white colonial allies displayed a similar lack of interest in the affairs of their fellow islanders, who were largely excluded from formal political power through restricted franchise and other means. This lack of interest and respect would ultimately cost the rebellion money, time, cotton, and ships, as Black colonials engaged in resistance via strikes, informing, slowdowns, and even direct service for the United States.

The 1863 St. George's strike did not appear out of thin air, but historians have paid relatively little attention to how labor disputes, Black social institutions, and white racial attitudes shaped the diplomatic and military course of blockade running in Bermuda and the Bahamas. Scholars of the African diaspora and Caribbean history have shown that Black islanders in Bermuda, the Bahamas, and the West Indies had been organizing to protect and care for themselves and others for decades, and the islands featured a robust culture of friendly societies and fraternal organizations dating back to emancipation. These groups provided monetary support for their members and a sense of social rapport in their communities. They also served as powerful sites for fostering racial consciousness and a sense of solidarity with the African diaspora, including those still held in slavery in the United States.[4] These communities were complicated and multiethnic, owing to the settlement in the Bahamas of Africans liberated from illegal slaving voyages. Friendly societies and fraternal groups like the Odd Fellows and the Freemasons served alongside the church as one of the most powerful tools for community organizing and protection in the British Atlantic world, although they still reflected the ethnic and social divisions in their colonies.[5]

That organizing spirit helped protect Black communities in the islands, but these communities also demonstrated a willingness to act assertively, even aggressively at times, to liberate and protect enslaved Americans when they could. Historians have ably demonstrated Black Britons' hemispheric awareness of slavery, as well as their hostility toward it, and the fact that white Southerners were aware of this hostility even to the point of paranoia.[6] Although numerous studies have examined Black communities and these acts of liberation and support in the antebellum era, the thread is often lost amid the turmoil of the Civil War years.[7] However, there is a growing recognition that a broader revolutionary antislavery current was at work in the Atlantic world before and during the 1860s, and the Black residents of the Bahamas and Bermuda were very much a part of that network.[8] This chapter will address how that spirit manifested itself amid the complicated economic life of blockade-running ports, where Southern dockside labor practices had their first serious encounter with an entirely free Black workforce. The result was a manifest failure of Confederate influence that had real costs to the rebellion in terms of money, ships, cotton, and war materiel.

By the 1860s, friendly societies and fraternal groups were firmly established in the Bahamas, and these institutions served as catalysts for local action against slavery even after it had been abolished in British colonies. Black Bahamians established friendly societies almost immediately upon emancipation. The first of these, the Bahamas Friendly Society, was established in Nassau in 1834, with a membership mainly of creole or Bahamian-born Black men. By contrast, the Grant's Town Friendly Society, founded in 1835 and named after the mostly Black Nassau suburb, had a membership mostly of liberated Africans who had been resettled on New Providence from captured slaving vessels after 1825.[9] These societies, which were originally almost exclusively male, existed alongside one another throughout the antebellum period, augmented by several others on New Providence—many organized along ethnic lines by liberated Africans—as well as some on the Out Islands, which were organized by clergy.[10] These societies provided some limited financial benefit for their members while also serving as important social outlets and, on occasion, sites for political organizing during the 1860s.

Black Bermudian society was not isolationist in its protective mission: its leaders proved very willing to come to the aid of enslaved Americans when the opportunity presented itself. The 1835 case of the American coastal slaver *Enterprise*, forced by a storm into the harbor at Hamilton with seventy-eight enslaved people on board, provided an early chance for Black Bermudian activism. Richard Tucker, the head and founder of the local Young Men's Friendly Institution, filed a writ of habeas corpus for the slaves held on board the *Enterprise*, and a local judge promptly beamed the captives to freedom.[11] The judge, after granting the release of the captives, declared that "too much could not be said in praise of the Friendly society of colored people, who had thus generously exerted themselves to rescue so many of their fellow beings from cruel thraldom."[12] Despite years of diplomatic and legal wrangling, the people liberated from the *Enterprise* were allowed to remain in Bermuda, although compensation was paid to their former owners.[13] In the 1850s, others in Bermuda attempted, though without success, to leverage the British government to free Patrick Williams, one of their fellows held in slavery in the United States.[14] Williams had been kidnapped in New York in the 1830s and sold into slavery in Louisiana, where he languished for over two decades before succeeding in getting word to friends in Bermuda. Though their efforts failed (the testimony of Black Bermudians not being admissible in a Louisiana court), the case of Patrick Williams showed that Black Bermudians would pursue opportunities for liberation even decades after the fact.[15] Black Bermudian wreckers also brought a suspected American slaving vessel to the attention of the Royal Navy after heaving it off a Bermudian reef on the eve of the Civil War.[16] Given their history, it seems clear that the Black residents of Bermuda were unlikely to actively support the efforts of a proslavery rebellion.

Black Bahamians, through public speeches, spontaneous action, and a variety of social organizations, also demonstrated hostility to American slavery before the Civil War. Emancipation Day activities frequently referenced the conditions prevailing on the nearby continent. Friendly societies on New Providence usually held a parade through Nassau, which often included the delivery of a "loyal address" to the governor and crown that interlaced declarations of loyalty with occasional comparisons to the wretched conditions of their American counterparts. In 1849's address, the Friendly Societies asked the government to help gain for them "all the rights and privileges of British subjects," as "we are denied the privilege of admission into Foreign Ports on the footing of Her Majesty's subjects generally," which was plainly directed at the continuing ill-treatment of Black Bahamian mariners in Southern ports under the so-called Negro Seaman Acts, which were first used against Nassau sailors in Charleston in 1822.[17] At the 1850 celebration, children at a Baptist-run school shouted out three cheers for the queen and freedom, and three groans to slavery and the American consul E. B. Graff, who had recently printed a proslavery pamphlet.[18] This rudeness was met in the newspapers with disapprobation and a critique that closely associated calls for greater democracy with the institution of slavery. In 1859, Robert S. Evans, head of the Bahamas Friendly Society, gave a rousing Emancipation Day address that indicated both a deep hostility to American slavery and a broader, more radical pan-African abolitionist sentiment.

Evans's speech is worth closer examination. While it contained many of the features of loyal addresses of previous years, such as professions of loyalty to the British Crown and offerings of thanks for emancipation and political rights, Evans then turned, with fierce language, on their nearest neighbor. "Look at the heartless Slave-dealers in America" who sell off Africans to "some monster in human shape, who have no regard for God themselves . . . [who] will tell them that . . . their very souls with their bodies are their masters' property." He excoriated the "freaks of caprice" that tore families asunder in the American South. Evans then demanded to know, after his interlude on the treatment of slaves in the United States, "Shall the sons of Africa bear this yoke forever? Shall there be no hand to deliver them from their oppressors? Then where are we to look for help?"[19] But Evans went further, reaching around the world for examples of the complicity of Europeans, including Britain, in the slave trade and their enduring failure to grant Africans the rights and freedoms owed to them as children of God. Evans plainly, and likely to the discomfort of white audiences, called for liberation everywhere, not just in British territories. Rhetorically, Evans shows that influential portions of Black Bahamian society were not just aware of the conditions of enslaved people in America but actively questioning who would help achieve slavery's demise, not only there but everywhere it held sway.

For their part, Black Bahamians had long been prepared to move from rhetoric to action to liberate enslaved Americans who reached their shores, most notably in the case of the coastal slaver *Creole* in 1841. Friendly societies and other social organizations were the centerpiece of this activism. Black Nassau watermen of every variety were instrumental in bringing ashore the liberated people of the *Creole*, from the harbor pilot who brought the vessel into Nassau and encouraged small boats to surround the slaver, to the armed boatmen who removed the formerly enslaved and alerted the ship's guards of the imminent attempt by the white crew to retake the vessel.[20] In the later case of seven Florida slaves who escaped to the Bahamas via a small boat, the U.S. marshal sent to demand their extradition claimed that a Nassau friendly society had organized a legal advocate for the men and suspected their influence in the Nassau court's ultimate refusal to send the group back to the United States.[21] These efforts often met with success, although the heterogeneous nature of Black society on New Providence sometimes reduced the community's ability to act in a coordinated fashion.

Rivalries between Black people born in the Bahamas and the groups of liberated Africans periodically introduced after being liberated by the Royal Navy were not uncommon. Differences in language and culture created distinct fissures in the Black communities that surrounded Nassau, with the accompanying creation of competing social organizations, churches, and friendly societies. This dissension at times extended to the Black soldiers of the West India Regiment garrisoned in Nassau's barracks, and Nassau's harmony was periodically marred by ugly brawls involving factions of locals, which sometimes drew in the regiment's soldiers as well.[22] To further complicate matters, communication between New Providence and the Out Islands of the Bahamas was uneven at best—the colonial government struggled to maintain regular mail or passenger service between them. As a result, social organization was necessarily more local in these places.

Once blockade running began in earnest in 1862, Black Britons in the colonies were in a morally difficult position, with the potential economic relief of employment in the blockade-running apparatus on one hand, and their staunch opposition to slavery on the other. To compound their difficulties, they faced a hostile legal environment that tended to punish neutrality violations that favored the United States more than those that aided the rebellion. Yet despite these obstacles, many Black colonials chose to actively aid the United States by serving in such roles as informants, harbor pilots, guides, and sailors, and some of their social activities likewise reflected their public hostility to slavery.

Black social organizations continued their antebellum rhetoric and organizing against slavery despite the economic relief of the blockade-running boom. Friendly societies organized Emancipation Day celebrations every August 1, whose speakers typically emphasized the loyalty of Black subjects while commenting on issues of concern to their specific friendly society or community. Intriguingly, the Nassau Friendly Society gathered at Zion Church on Emancipation Day in 1864 to form a branch of the British and Foreign Anti-Slavery Society.[23] This was surely a considered message to the white pro-Confederate community in their city that the benefits of employment did not obviate their concerns for the millions of people their employers wished to keep in chains. This rhetorical and social opposition to the rebellion complemented direct action by others to help the United States, especially ship pilots and informers.

Black colonials, especially in the Bahamas, frequently provided direct aid to U.S. forces, particularly by serving as ship pilots, messengers, and as part of what was, in effect, an informal relay service between the consulate in Nassau and U.S. cruisers. American vessels operating in Bahamian waters relied heavily on local Black pilots to help them avoid the treacherous reefs and shoals of the archipelago. These pilots were not merely passive observers—they helped U.S. naval officers decide when and where to pursue suspected blockade runners, directly assisting in the damage, destruction, or capture of some of those ships.[24] The American commanders certainly appreciated their work—Commander Arthur Clary of USS *Tioga* inquired whether his pilot might be included when the prize money for the *Tioga*'s Bahamian captures was calculated, "he deserving [a share of the proceeds]."[25] Black pilots also, on occasion, resisted working for Confederates. The pilots of Nassau refused as a body to take the schooner *Prince Alfred* out of the harbor in August 1862 because it was carrying guns and ammunition for arming the *Oreto*, which had just been released by the court and was being prepared to transform into the CSS *Florida*. A white shipping agent was forced to guide it out himself instead.[26]

The network of Black colonials that opposed the Confederate operation in the Bahamas was composed of people in a variety of maritime occupations, including wreckers, who acted as scouts and couriers for the American consul and navy. At least one of *Tioga*'s captures, that of the blockade runner *Granite City*, was enabled by the aid of wrecker captain Matthew Lowe passing along timely information.[27] Black Bahamian wreckers—that is, ships and crews dedicated to salvaging stranded or wrecked vessels and their cargo in return for a share of its value—proved to be a dangerous opponent of the rebellion at times. Before the war, wreckers were widely viewed with suspicion and distaste in the United States and among the commercial class in the Bahamas: vultures at best, waiting to feed on the carrion of shipwrecks, or ant lions at worst, luring unwary prey into dangerous waters in order to feast on them. Yet this profession created something remarkable: an independent body of Black mariners "of intelligence and enterprise" who often commanded and even owned their own vessels.[28] In an environment where American ships faced strict and unequally enforced limits on entering and departing Bahamian harbors, wreckers had a tremendous advantage: they could come and go as they pleased, with no requirement to get customs clearance.

The wreckers' personal and regulatory freedom of movement could be a powerful tool, and both the U.S. and the pro-Confederate network tried to leverage it to their advantage. Seth Hawley, U.S. consul in Nassau beginning in March 1863, immediately noted the utility of wreckers for both sides and urged the U.S. government to hire them at a rate high enough to keep them from being bought off by the pro-Confederate merchants of Nassau. Although Hawley felt that the wreckers were generally immoral, unreliable, and in it for the money, his dispatches hint at the presence of genuine antislavery, if not anti-Confederate, sentiment among many of them. While he noted that the "wreckers are extensively used by our enemies to notify the blockade runners" of U.S. naval movements, he found that many were willing to fight the Confederate cause. Referring to one unnamed wrecking captain who refused any compensation for relaying messages, Hawley noted, "He has strong sympathy with his race in the southern states, which induces him to do this without pay."[29] The antislavery activism of Black Bahamians was alive and well in at least a portion of the Bahamian wrecking fleet, despite the best efforts of the Confederate network to buy them off.

The consequences to Black colonials for aiding the United States could be severe. Confederate officials in the Bahamas long suspected that an organized network of Black residents was aiding the United States, and they predictably chose suppression and coercion as the means to deal with their free Black antagonists. Lewis Heyliger, the main Confederate agent in Nassau, assured the colonial government that "there existed a regularly organized channel of communication between the [U.S.] consul and the gunboats, by means of lighthouse keepers, pilots, etc." Heyliger overestimated how organized this system was, but it certainly existed, and he leveraged his influence with the government and the white elite to suppress it, including publishing stolen letters highlighting its use in a Nassau newspaper, which printed the last name of at least one Black pilot, who had already been arrested for serving on a U.S. warship.[30] The pro-Confederate network in Nassau used a variety of means to suppress and punish Black Bahamians who tried to help their opponents, including both economic and legal coercion. Regarding his service to the U.S. Navy, wrecker captain Mathew Lowe claimed, "[It] brought me into disrepute, both with the wreckers and the community of merchants here [in Nassau]. I could not get work for my vessels or my self from any of these merchants . . . and I was for a long time thrown completely out of employment."[31] American consuls likewise suggested that the white Nassau merchants who owned wrecking vessels used their power to stop their Black captains from working with them.[32] In the case of pilots, the friends of the rebellion turned to courts and prisons to do their dirty work.

Ship pilots were particularly vulnerable because their knowledge of local waters was simultaneously so useful to the U.S. Navy and so dangerous for blockade runners. The mercantile community lost no opportunity to offer them up for prosecution for violating the Foreign Enlistment Act when they could be identified. Consul Seth Hawley warned that Bahamian pilots "will do well not to land at any point" in the Bahamas because of the risk of arrest.[33] His warnings were not idle. A Nassau court convicted two Black pilots, Thomas Dames and Alexander Price, for violations of the Foreign Enlistment Act in February 1863. These unfortunate men were sentenced to two years in prison at hard labor, which was a desperate cruelty in comparison to the legal invulnerability of the few white men arrested for aiding the Confederacy.[34] In Dames's case, he "cheerfully went from this port and found the [USS] *Tioga*," which he served aboard as a pilot for several weeks while the regular pilot was sick. Bahamian authorities seized him when he returned home to Nassau to visit his wife and two young children. The American consul presented these convictions as evidence of the "severity [with which] they punish all those who dare to give aid or comfort to the North," and pointed out that the consul and anyone he met with or tried to communicate with were under almost constant surveillance.[35] Pilots James Sweeting, Thomas Curry, and Stephen Roberts all suffered this fate in 1864.[36] The authorities had been after Curry for the better part of a year—he had angered the Nassau elite by serving as the pilot of the *Tioga* for several valuable captures.

The cases against these pilots are worth examining in further detail, as they are a stark example of the unequal treatment of Northern and Confederate supporters by Bahamian authorities. When white British subjects engaged in obvious violations of the Foreign Enlistment Act (alongside more serious crimes like smuggling and piracy), Attorney General George C. Anderson declined to even charge them with the crime. This was the case with the notorious raiders Vernon Locke and John C. Braine, both of whom engaged in outright piracy on Confederates' behalf, along with serving aboard Confederate privateers and warships. By contrast, when Dames and Price appeared before the court, Anderson more or less railroaded them. The editor of the *Nassau Guardian* remarked that these may have been the first-ever charges filed under the Foreign Enlistment Act anywhere in the empire.[37] Anderson requested, and Judge Stephen Lees granted, a special jury to oversee the case.[38] In nineteenth-century jurisprudence, this meant that a jury would be chosen from a more restricted pool, generally with much higher property qualifications than in a typical trial. This technique had links to the broader dispute over the behavior of free Black sailors in the Bahamas, especially around so-called collusive wrecking. Two years earlier, Bayley reported the case of the alleged cooperation between a Black pilot and a wrecking captain to deliberately run a merchant vessel ashore in order to gain salvage rights on its cargo. The Black members of the jury refused to convict the two men on the given evidence, and Bayley urged that measures be taken to prevent a preponderance of "the lower classes of Creole negroes" from serving on juries.[39] The use of the special jury system grew out of this suspicion that Black juries would not meekly uphold the interest of the Bay Street elites.

By allowing a special jury in these cases, the judge practically guaranteed that Dames and Price would face a jury of wealthy white merchants or their social equivalents—exactly the people whom their assistance to the U.S. Navy might hurt. Notably, Dames was defended by T. W. Dillet, one of only two nonwhite attorneys admitted to the bar in Nassau. Dillet argued, probably correctly, that the Foreign Enlistment Act, as written, did not apply to pilots who were engaged only temporarily on a warship and had not enlisted in the armed forces or participated in hostilities on behalf of a belligerent power.

Both Dillet and Price's attorney also pointed out the almost complete lack of evidence provided against their clients beyond rumor.[40] The special jury did not care—they returned a guilty verdict against each immediately. The prosecution of other pilots continued into the next year. Pilots Sweeting, Roberts, and Curry faced the same charges, and once again Anderson requested, and the judge granted, the use of a special jury. During their trials, the chief evidence against them was testimony from white crewmen who allegedly served aboard blockade runners captured by the U.S. ships these pilots served aboard. The blockade runners claimed to have recognized the pilots by sight during their captures. The special juries convicted all three, largely on the basis of this extraordinarily sketchy testimony.[41] Attorney General George Anderson, Judge Lees, and the pro-Confederate white elite of Nassau had firmly demonstrated that while they did not bother with a carrot for Black Bahamians, they were ready and willing to use the stick to prevent them from assisting the enemies of the rebellion.

This surveillance had some effect in suppressing open support for the Union and reducing the resources that might otherwise have been available to American officials in the Bahamas. In addition to discouraging and imprisoning pilots who might have helped the U.S. Navy, the pro-Confederate network in the Bahamas pressured others to deny their assistance to the U.S. government. Consul Samuel Whiting reported in early 1863, "Every movement I make to convey information to our cruisers is closely watched, and the Captains of the wrecking vessels are deterred from giving me any aid or assistance, while the schemes of the rebels find active and hearty support from all classes."[42] Whiting's remarks are revealing: most of the crew on wreckers were Black, and so were many of the captains, although white merchants often owned the vessels.[43] The suppression had some effect on the wreckers and sowed distrust. Some Black wrecker captains refused to leave messages for U.S. cruisers with other collaborators at Out Island rendezvous points out of fear of betrayal and arrest, preferring instead to deliver the messages only in person.[44] This hampered the coordination between the consul and the navy. On the whole, Heyliger and his local allies did not engage with Black Bahamians as a body worthy of influence. Instead, they bought off who they could and turned the power of the state against the rest, as was evident from the rash of pilot prosecutions in 1863 and 1864. Left to their own devices, the Black wreckers would readily aid the Americans, and U.S. consuls appear to have regularly chartered such schooners to find and bring information to U.S.

warships cruising Bahamian waters if their opponents did not intervene to prevent it.[45] Clearly repression and surveillance filled in for the pro-Confederate community of the Bahamas, where persuasion and sympathy had failed.

Because of the danger of openly supporting the Union cause, some colonial residents used more surreptitious means to oppose the rebellion and its local friends, such as relaying signals or messages and acting as spies and informants. Away from Nassau, Black colonials relayed messages for American cruisers and hoisted prearranged signals at key points on Abaco Island and Stirrup Cay (two points on the east and west ends of the Providence channel leading to Nassau) to alert U.S. Navy ships of the presence of blockade runners.[46] While the identities of colonial spies and informers for the United States are generally unknown to us, at least some portion of them were Black.[47] One anonymous party provided the U.S. consul in Nassau a packet of letters from Fraser, Trenholm, and Company to their agent, John B. Lafitte, in early May 1862, which contained information on the movement of ships containing arms and munitions for the Confederacy.[48] Informants also kept the consul apprised of the arming and crewing of the *Oreto*, which allowed the consul to alert the U.S. Navy as well as Governor Bayley, despite the latter's desperate wish to remain ignorant.[49] The *Oreto*'s steward, Charles Ward, testified as to the ship's character and the plans of its officers at its trial before the Nassau Vice Admiralty Court, but the judge specifically denigrated his testimony in his written decision to release the ship back to Adderley and Co.[50]

A similar situation occurred late in the war surrounding the steamer *Alexandra*, which had previously been the subject of a seizure and inquiry in England. Now renamed *Mary*, the ship was seized by Bahamian authorities on the insistence of the American consul Thomas Kirkpatrick. An informer revealed to the consul the presence of at least one cannon and ammunition on the *Mary*, and after dogged inquiry, he drove the authorities to take action. They did their best to avoid seizing the ship, insisting at first that there were no arms on board and, when that proved false, that the gun was unsuitable for naval use—a contention that likewise was untrue.[51] Kirkpatrick's informer, whom he described as "a faithful black, on board of [the *Mary*], at risk almost the whole time ... reported to me through another faithful negro pilot what" was happening aboard the ship. Kirkpatrick praised his unnamed informant, who "ran a very great personal risk, but he seemed to have no personal fears," and he hoped to reward the man "when all is over, for his faithful service to the Cause of our country."[52] Despite the efforts of Adderley and Co. to hide the arms and other suspicious equipment, the consul's informants were accurate and persistent, and the ship was seized, though it was ultimately released after blockade running had largely ceased. American consuls and naval officers regularly received information from Black colonials and sailors regarding pro-Confederate shipping and activities, and this cooperation repeatedly allowed the United States to hamper these efforts through military or diplomatic means.

Black colonials also provided material support to the United States in a variety of ways, especially in areas away from the eyes of pro-Confederate white residents. Frustratingly for pro-Confederate Bahamian officials, the Black residents of the Out Islands frequently provided fresh food, supplies, shelter, and information to U.S. warships operating in Bahamian waters. James Nibbs Brown, the police magistrate on Abaco Island, sent an alarmed report to Nassau that the U.S. steamer *Tioga* appeared to be a regular visitor to various ports on that island, despite this practice being prohibited. Furthermore, Brown reported that the *Tioga*'s arrival "was joyfully hailed by the Inhabitants who appeared to be well-acquainted with her," and this visit was only interrupted by the unscheduled presence of the magistrate, who forced the Americans to depart.[53] After further investigation, Brown found that residents of Abaco, the Biminis, and the Berry Islands all received U.S. warships on a regular basis, and the ships' "arrival is hailed with joy and hopefulness of gain," and that the people did not report the American presence to the governor as required.[54] Brown understated the case if anything—the American navy officer Charles O'Neil recorded frequent visits to various remote anchorages in the Bahamas on board the *Tioga*, which often remained for several days at a time, as well as the frequent receipt of supplies from wreckers.[55]

American warships regularly violated the restrictions on entering Bahamian coastal waters without the governor's permission in these isolated cays, banks, and sandbars with the cooperation of their largely Black populations, who benefited from their presence. On at least one occasion, the crew of the USS *Tioga* tipped off a wrecker and occasional pilot as to the location of a derelict ship so that their ally might get there first and claim salvage on the vessel.[56] Black crewmen on captured ships also received easier treatment from the U.S. Navy. An armed boat from the *Tioga*, operating near shore with the knowledge of locals, captured the schooner *Nonesuch*, owned by the Adderley company, near the Joulter Cays, situated on the northwest passage between

Nassau and the Florida coast. The *Tioga*'s crew deposited the Black sailors from the schooner on shore at Stirrup Cay but held the white sailors on board with the prize crew, then sent them off to Key West.[57] Confederate influence on the merchant elite of Nassau held little sway beyond New Providence.

Black residents of Bermuda had fewer opportunities for unobserved support for American warships owing to the islands' compact geography, but they lent material support in other ways. One example was simply providing the American consul, Charles Maxwell Allen, a place to rent lodging. Allen found the town of St. George's to be busy, cramped, and overrun with Confederates and their sympathizers.[58] He secured lodging with a Black family, and hired a boy to help him with housekeeping and meals. This was no small thing: Allen was almost entirely ostracized from white society in St. George's, with the exception of an English painter and passing Northern ship captains and sailors. The cooperation and shelter of Black Bermudians enabled him to remain at his post and do his job. It is also likely that he had informants among the laborers of St. George's given his robust knowledge of Confederate shipping through the port, but he gave little indication in his official correspondence of the sources of his information. He may also have had links to Bermudian harbor pilots, for on one occasion pro-Southern locals accused Allen of paying pilots to deliberately wreck a blockade runner on a reef, but Allen denied having anything to do with it.[59] The extent of direct support of Black Bermudians for the Northern cause remains somewhat ambiguous because of this, but given the almost complete absence of sympathy among white Bermudians, his support almost by default probably came from Black residents.

Black support for the Northern cause was not guaranteed, and there are indications that some in Bermuda and the Bahamas did not support the Union—especially early in the war. The willingness of Black colonials to work for blockade-running outfits might be considered a form of tacit support, or at least non-opposition, but this must be balanced against their poverty, the centrality of those operations to colonial economies during the war, and patronage networks that predated the war. There were a few incidents of public expression of support, often in the form of teasing or harassing Americans on the streets of Nassau or St. George's in the early days of the conflict, and further cases where white colonials insisted on the existence of widespread Black support for the Confederacy, although these last assertions lack much in the way of evidence.

White colonial elites occasionally insisted that their Black fellow subjects supported the Confederate cause. It is true that some U.S. naval officers treated Bahamians of any race with suspicion or contempt—one complained that "neither wreckers, spongers or fishermen, white or black, can be depended upon," and he "doubt[ed] even the pilots until they have been benefited by captures."[60] Bahamas governor Charles J. Bayley maintained that this support not only existed but was so severe as to provoke retaliation from the U.S. Navy. In August 1863, the U.S. Navy steamer *Mercedita* ran down and collided with the Bahamian schooner *Ellen*, cutting it in two and sinking it. Bayley alleged that the collision was deliberate and based on the skin color of the *Ellen*'s captain or crew. He wrote to the Colonial Office to allege that the *Mercedita* sank the schooner because of "the strong and unexpected sympathy of all our coloured population with the cause of the Confederate States, a sympathy produced by the known kindly treatment of the Negro in the Southern States compared with his normal humiliation and abject degradation in the great Cities of the North."[61] Bayley, himself an inveterate racist, so closely parroted Confederate racial rhetoric and allegations that the Colonial Office was alarmed. Newcastle directed his staff to "omit transmitting this to the [Foreign Office]" so that it would not appear in diplomatic correspondence, which was frequently printed and published, and he directed Bayley to decline to include such language in official correspondence in the future.[62] Bayley's theories about the sinking of the *Ellen* may have been influenced by reports of Black Bahamians being killed during the New York City draft riots earlier that summer, which he related to Lord Lyons.[63] Another incident, wherein a U.S. warship prevented Bahamian wreckers from collecting cotton bales thrown overboard by a fleeing blockade runner, was more believable as a potential source of conflict.[64] Nevertheless, these occasions were unusual, and most interactions between the navy and Black Bahamians appeared to be cordial.

More believably, Black colonials occasionally joined other pro-Confederate white residents in the verbal jostling of Americans on the streets of Nassau and St. George's, or joined in the general merriment surrounding the arrival of Confederate ships. Samuel Whiting, the American consul at Nassau until March 1863, reported that a crowd of "colored blockade-running seamen" gathered outside the consulate singing Confederate songs, egged on by a group of white "Southern rebels." Whiting, who was prone to outbursts and drunkenness himself, replied that "those who were so enthusiastic in behalf of the rebel flag had better read the advertisements in the Charleston Courier of the 20th February," offering slaves to be sold at auction.⁶⁵ Although Whiting was often accused—mostly by his antagonists in Nassau, including Governor Bayley—of intemperance and ill manners, he had no reason to lie about this incident, but it is not clear how he identified the men's profession. Just two months earlier, a white sailor on board the Confederate cruiser *Florida* recorded in a journal entry that upon their arrival in Nassau, "an entire boatload [of Black Bahamians] rowed around us, singing the Bonnie Blue Flag. They are all southern sympathizers." The Confederate suggested that "the amount of money we throw into the hands of the Nassauites *probably* influences their sentiments in our favor."⁶⁶ While it is impossible to definitively prove in the absence of firsthand accounts from actual participants, both Union and Confederate observers felt that the Black Bahamians who participated in public displays of support for the Confederacy did so in part because of the money they could make, not because of any affinity with the cause of the rebellion.

Perhaps more surprisingly, given the risks they faced in the Confederacy, some Black sailors served aboard blockade runners and Confederate warships, with varying levels of enthusiasm. The accounts of Black sailors going into Confederate ports must be treated with caution—the main sources are memoirs written long after the fact. Thomas Taylor, a British supercargo on several prominent runners, claimed that his Black steward accompanied the vessel on its voyages.⁶⁷ Confederate naval officer John Taylor Wilkinson, who frequently commanded blockade runners, claimed to have hired a Black Bahamian pilot who "was unjustly treated" in Wilmington on at least one occasion and had to be rescued by a white crew member.⁶⁸ Several Black sailors agreed to serve on the *Oreto* in the summer of 1862 in part because they were promised a bounty, but many of them declined to remain with the ship after it was seized and its character as a warship became clear. One Black Bahamian sailor told the *Oreto*'s recruiter, in reply to his urging to rejoin the ship after its release by the court: "I did not feel like going; I did not join her afterwards"—and neither did many of his compatriots, despite offers of up to $100 a month, some paid in gold.⁶⁹ When white Confederates and their local collaborators became tight-fisted, even that limited support could turn into damaging resistance, which was exactly the case in St. George's in the summer of 1863.

The 1863 strike by Black dockworkers was remarkable because it was a direct attack on the actual operation of blockade running in colonial British harbors, in a place with a comparatively smaller Black population than its island neighbors to the south. In 1864, Bermuda's permanent population was roughly 11,500, of whom around 6,500, or 56 percent, were listed as "coloured."[70] The clandestine war over Black support, especially in the Bahamas, tended to result in indirect action—the U.S. Navy capturing a runner at sea, or the Bahamian government (reluctantly, ineffectively) seizing a suspected Confederate cruiser or (enthusiastically, efficiently) arresting Black pilots who worked on U.S. warships. In Bermuda, the striking workers aimed their resistance directly at the Confederate office there and the merchants and ships who did business with them.

The strike itself was the result of low wages and the refusal of the Confederate shipping office, led by Maj. Norman S. Walker, to consider raises for the largely Black workforce on the docks of St. George's. That refusal to negotiate was deeply informed by racial attitudes. Walker's wife, Georgiana, criticized the state of race relations in Bermudian society in her diary, in much the same vein as other Confederate observers in the Bahamas. Her warm accounts of family affairs were interrupted by outbursts of racism directed at Black Bermudians. She criticized them as a people "born to be slaves & yet forced to be free" and interpreted Bermuda governor Harry St. George Ord's declaration that he was in Bermuda "to govern them & not to be governed by them" to be in reference to the island's Black and mixed-race population, ignoring that the governor's difficulties stemmed chiefly from the white minority. Walker railed against the supposed failings of the "African aristocracy," especially their demands for higher wages for work on the docks of St. George's.[71]

Georgiana Walker's racial animosity highlights an element of Confederate informal diplomacy that proved far less successful: relations with the Black islanders that made up the majority of the labor force in Bermuda and the Bahamas. Black stevedores, seamen, pilots, draymen, cooks, maids, and other workers, skilled and unskilled, provided an important part of the labor force that sustained blockade running, yet they appear infrequently in both contemporary accounts and the historiography of the blockade. The fruits of blockade running did not accumulate evenly, and although laborers did enjoy higher wages than normal, their cost of living likewise increased, often in excess of their pay. By comparison, white merchants, seamen, and officials often complained of their wages not meeting the inflated costs of island life, but they did not, in most cases, refuse to work. They enjoyed sympathy with the Confederate cause and had some hope of their grievances being redressed. Enslaved workers handled the vast majority of waterfront work in the antebellum South, and in places like Charleston, local merchants and authorities repeatedly acted against the interests of enslaved and free Black people, and even free white laborers, with few consequences.[72] It came as a shock to Confederates, therefore, that in July and August 1863, the Black workforce on the wharves of St. George's felt empowered to attempt a strike against their Confederate and pro-Confederate employers. Black fraternal organizations played a role in the strike. Masonic and Odd Fellows chapters had spread across Bermuda in the 1850s, serving as both social clubs and the site of potent Black political organizing dating back to emancipation.[73] Inkel Bell, the head of the St. George's chapter of the Odd Fellows, worked in Norman Walker's offices. Walker's wife, Georgiana, reserved special scorn for the Odd Fellows and other Black fraternal groups that dared to inconvenience her by having a parade and opening a temple.[74] Several violent encounters between Black dockworkers and white blockade-runner crews occurred in the midst of the strike, raising racial tensions in St. George's nearly to the boiling point.

Norman Walker tried to break the strike by traveling across Bermuda to recruit scabs, both white and Black, from the more remote areas of the islands. Georgiana blamed a large cotton fire on the striking workers, which burned perhaps three thousand bales as they sat on the wharf, but she claimed after a short time that the Black laborers begged to resume their jobs at their prior wages and meekly returned to work.[75] She vastly overstated their meekness and her husband's success in breaking the strike: during the affair, striking workers threatened Black scabs with violence, and the St. George's police suspected a "coloured" assailant in the attempted assassination of William Tudor Tucker, one of the white negotiators involved in the wage dispute.[76] A group of merchants and citizens of St. George's offered a £200 reward for information on the assailant, but this small fortune enticed no one to come forward.[77] It is not clear how the cotton fire started—dry baled cotton is very combustible—but some observers suspected arson because of a simultaneous fire among hay bales elsewhere in the town, perhaps set to distract firefighting efforts. Black onlookers reportedly watched as white people, including the crews of Confederate-owned blockade runners, attempted to extinguish the blaze, and few made any attempt to help.

The implication of this resistance is clear: poor labor relations, combined with racial animosity, had the potential to dramatically slow, disrupt, and even sabotage the blockade-running portion of the Confederate commercial-diplomatic network, even more so than covert resistance by Black colonials. Three thousand bales of cotton represented three or four runs through the blockade by a sizable steamer and hundreds of thousands of dollars in gold, even at wholesale prices—a substantial loss to the Confederate government and the private merchants associated with them. Shortly after the fire, Norman Walker and John T. Bourne, his local agent, reached a quiet accommodation with the striking workers by discharging the scabs and rehiring the others with a 20 percent raise, from five to six shillings per day.[78] Sabotage, work slowdowns, and other forms of labor resistance by Black colonials in Bermuda represented a failure of Confederate informal diplomacy in its dealings with an important, and usually overlooked, component of colonial society. Confederates and their white collaborators in Bermuda appeared to have never considered maintaining a happy labor force as a military or informal diplomatic objective, to their cost. Nearly a year after the strike, the editor of the *Royal Gazette* was still worried about incendiarism among the Black workers in St. George's. In an article on the St. George's fire brigade, he declared the brigade necessary due to both the high volume of flammable material in the town and on the docks, especially cotton, as well as "the highly inflammable tempers of many of those for whose labour in connexion with it there is so great a demand."[79] In other words, he and others were clearly still worried about deliberate cotton fires being set by unhappy Black workers.

The St. George's strike was not the only labor disturbance to affect blockade running. While details are scarce, there were several disruptions by workers in Nassau the following year, and it is entirely possible that workers there were aware of the successful labor action in Bermuda. Certainly the pro-Confederate editor of the *Bahama Herald* recognized the danger to both blockade running and white economic supremacy posed by Black labor action. The *Herald* printed a letter from "F.M.B.," ostensibly a Bahamian, that decried the ability of the "labouring population of Nassau" to purchase luxuries with their current wages and suggested that employers in the Bahamas should be protected from unannounced strikes by their (presumably Black) workers, as part of a plan to deal with the eventual end of blockade running.[80]

Other letters and articles complained of the rudeness and "defiance" of "our labouring classes" toward "respectable gentlemen" on the streets of Nassau, and of the ability of Black boatmen in the harbor to charge whatever they wished for hauling people or freight.[81] These reports came amid anxieties over the new Confederate shipping regulations, stricter enforcement of customs bonds on trade with New York, and the prosecution of several Black Bahamians for serving as pilots for the U.S. Navy.

At least one strike in Nassau took place in June 1864. There is no mention of it in the U.S. consular records, but the newspapers reported on it sporadically. Workers involved in cotton transportation—principally stevedores it seems but perhaps including draymen and other waterfront workers—organized a strike beginning on June 13. They demanded a raise to at least ten shillings per day, despite the supposedly unsolicited "justice and generosity" of the Nassau merchants who employed them. Workers who crossed the picket line on Bay Street, whether from ignorance of the plan or a lack of solidarity, were assaulted by the strikers, and it seems very likely that other forms of social pressure were also applied on the recalcitrant.[82] By the end of the month, the issue appeared to have been settled, and the *Herald* reported, "This movement [is] now entirely over, a good understanding existing between the Workmen and the employers which, it is to be hoped, will be of long continuance."[83] The terms of the agreement were not published, but presumably some concession was made to the workers in order to come to this "good understanding" and get them back on job, and later newspaper reports indicated that workers in Nassau earned around ten shillings per day.[84] This suggests that the strike succeeded in its goal.

The Nassau labor disputes differed from the Bermuda strike in several respects. For one, it was larger in scale, comprising a large portion of the dockside labor force, across multiple employers, although the available information is scant as to the total number of laborers engaged. It also featured less unity among the workers involved. The St. George's strike appeared only to have to contend with scabs recruited from outside the area. In Nassau, by contrast, the strikers reportedly meted out violence to their fellows who did not immediately join the strike, which may be indicative of the ethnic and cultural divisions among the Black communities in and around Nassau. The solidarity of the more socially homogeneous Bermudian dockworkers in St. George's was fairly complete, and their violence was directed at white employers and their property rather than at their fellow laborers, as in Nassau.

Black stevedores, longshoremen, and draymen working on blockade runners at the Nassau wharves, sketched in the months just before the June 1864 strike. Credit: Frank Viztelly, "Unloading Cotton from Blockade-Runners at Nassau, New Providence," *Illustrated London News*, 30 April 1864, 432. Image courtesy of Library of Congress.

Just as in St. George's, it seems clear that Black workers in Nassau won a victory over the pro-Confederate merchants, although their employers responded by taking action against independent boatmen and pilots. The Nassau elite, led by the Adderleys and other merchants, passed restrictions in the House of Assembly on what Nassau boatmen could charge for their services, and Charles Nesbitt appointed Augustus Adderley as commissioner of pilotage, giving the white elite greater control over harbor operations in the archipelago.[85] The Crown denied assent to the Boatman's Act because of its overly harsh penalties and its ban on "insolent" or "discourteous language," but the House of Assembly amended it in the subsequent legislative session, and it finally went into force in May 1865.[86] Despite these acts, Nassau dockworkers enjoyed higher wages until the end of blockade running, and they forced more money out of the merchants just as the "depression in trade consequent of President Davis'[s]" new Confederate shipping regulations hit home.[87] Judging by the squeals of merchants and runners in the newspapers, these workers timed their blow well and helped themselves while hurting the pocketbooks of the rebellion and its allies in the Bahamas.[88]

It should come as no surprise that white Confederates failed to gain comprehensive support from Black colonials in Bermuda and the Bahamas. The cultural and business links that served them so well in cultivating support with the white elite of the colonies only served to thicken the blanket of prejudice and disdain that already characterized their interactions with Black people, free and unfree. By contrast, Black islanders seemed increasingly willing to support the United States, especially after 1863 and the clear emergence of emancipation as a war aim via the Emancipation Proclamation. The result was a clear shift of support toward the North among Black Bermudians and Bahamians, differentiated by the social supports and community organizations available in each place, as well as geography and the extent of pro-Confederate surveillance against Black cooperation with the United States.

Black colonials may have been willing to work for the blockade-running businesses of the pro-Confederate network in the islands, but this was largely due to economic necessity and preexisting patronage networks. Insufficient wages, political repression, and vindictive and unequal legal prosecution by the white supporters of the Confederacy helped alienate them further. This failure of Confederate informal diplomacy helped push portions of the Black populace from indifference or tolerance of the Confederate presence to outright opposition. This manifested itself in various ways and included acting as informants on the movements of blockade runners, serving as couriers and messengers between consuls and U.S. naval vessels, serving as coast pilots aboard U.S. warships, and more. Labor action also resulted from pro-Confederate indifference to Black islanders, including costly and sometimes violent strikes at St. George's in 1863 and Nassau in 1864.

By 1864, the rebellion was faltering at the margins of the continent. The resistance of Black colonials contributed directly to the slow corrosion of uncontrolled private blockade running as a tenable choice for the Confederate government, which responded with a variety of measures aimed at controlling what entered Confederate ports at what price, while still leaving most of the burden of the effort in private hands. Elements within the Confederate government, particularly Stephen R. Mallory and Judah P. Benjamin, envisioned a similar transnational effort that might revive Confederate naval fortunes and provide some measure of revenge for perceived Northern "atrocities" and British diplomatic perfidy. Private enterprise and foreign citizens might yet, they hoped, transform the war on the maritime boundaries of North America.

CHAPTER FIVE

"The Like Was Not Practised in the Previous Conflicts of Civilized Nations"

Divided Sovereignty and Paramilitary Violence in the Colonies and at Sea, 1863–1865

Many of the people of Halifax are willing agents and abettors of the enemies of the United States, and their hostility has proved not merely offensive but deeply injurious.
—U.S. Secretary of State William H. Seward

It appears to have been a capture made for the benefit of the Confederacy by a body of men without any public authority, and who, with the single exception of a subordinate officer were British subjects.
—Confederate envoy James P. Holcombe

IN THE EARLY hours of December 7, 1863, Orin Schaffer lay dying on the deck of the U.S.-flagged merchant steamship *Chesapeake*, en route from New York to Portland, Maine. His fatal wound had come from a pistol shot, but the finger on the trigger belonged to a British subject, not a Confederate. Schaffer died before dawn, and the same British hands threw his body overboard. His death, and the subsequent escape from justice by everyone involved in it, demonstrated that some British North Americans were not merely observers of the American Civil War but active participants on the Confederate side.[1] The attack on the *Chesapeake* and its aftermath reflected the increased willingness of private parties, composed mostly of British subjects, to engage in privatized warfare at sea after mid-1863, and the readiness of the Confederate government to embrace and encourage such attacks. The success of this raiding depended heavily on exploiting the relative independence of the settler colonies of British North America, and the colonists' ability to circumvent British neutrality and law in support of the rebellion. The attack on the *Chesapeake*, like several others in the same period, was privately organized and executed across international boundaries, on state behalf yet without state sanction. These raiders, encouraged by elements in the Confederate government, created a fusion of the filibustering tradition of the mid-nineteenth century and privateering. The Confederate government seized on the hijacking and resulting trials as an opportunity to leverage its informal diplomatic network into something more activist and sinister by turning British neutrality and the contested sovereignty of the settler colonies into a weapon against the Union.

This chapter is centered on the hijacking of the *Chesapeake* by British subjects, mostly colonials from New Brunswick and Nova Scotia, and the spate of copycat attacks that followed in 1864 and 1865. Historian Aaron Sheehan-Dean recently wrote that "the nature of nationalism in mid-nineteenth century America required believers to pledge adherence to standards of conduct" that tended to limit violence, and that international norms, morality, and diplomatic pressure "compelled the Confederacy to participate in the war as a state rather than a guerilla republic."[2] The cases of the *Chesapeake*, the *Roanoke*, and others provide a compelling twist to this framing. When the combatants, in whole or in part, on these expeditions were not citizens or even residents of the belligerent polities, those standards of conduct were not so rigid. When the Confederacy lent its assistance to these ventures, it discarded state norms and behaved as a "guerilla republic." The transnational nature of the irregular conflict on the maritime periphery of North America, unlike much of the domestic guerilla war, brought even minor incidents to the direct attention of the highest Confederate authorities, particularly Jefferson Davis, Judah Benjamin, and Stephen Mallory.[3] They also attracted the notice of senior British colonial and imperial authorities, as well as those of the Union. A mere handful of murders, because of their location and perpetrators, brought forth complicated questions over international law, intraimperial sovereignty, and the use and abuse of neutrality. Disputes arose over both the obligation of colonial courts to uphold imperial primacy over foreign affairs and how traditional understandings of the rights and duties of neutrals should shift in response to attacks that attempted to fuse privateering and filibustering techniques into a new species of international maritime violence.

Development of the Confederate Network in the Maritimes

As the Confederate government struggled to assert control over blockade running and yellow fever ravaged Bermuda, much pro-Confederate activity shifted northward to Nova Scotia and the Maritime colonies of British North America. The Southern cause had widespread support in the Maritimes, particularly in Halifax, which one observer described as "a hot Southern town."[4] Local enthusiasm for the rebellion made itself manifest in the winter of 1863 with the *Chesapeake* hijacking, which had been planned in and launched from colonial territory, without the knowledge of the Confederate government. In its aftermath, the British government struggled to control the violence emanating from its possessions, while colonial governments and courts often openly permitted Confederate operatives and sympathetic ruffians to exploit the growing chaos on the war's periphery.

The Confederacy's operatives and supporters abroad—both official and informal—took advantage of the divided sovereignty inherent in the British colonies, seeking opportunities to exploit British neutrality in the war against the Union. These Confederates showed a savvy ability to identify sympathetic locals, including within colonial governments, and solicit their aid. As in Bermuda and the Bahamas, local merchants in places like Halifax worked with Confederates openly, despite taking liberties with British neutrality law. What distinguished British North America from the more southerly colonies was the degree of independence and the fierceness with which local authorities guarded their judicial prerogatives from imperial interference, even when the cases involved matters that fell ostensibly under London's authority, such as neutrality violations. Local courts repeatedly freed the perpetrators of raids and acts of piracy launched from British North American soil, often against the wishes of Crown officials, and residents sheltered and protected other fugitives from capture. The Confederate government seized upon this opening to launch further informal military and covert operations from the soil and waters of British North America, and sought in many cases to extend the protection of belligerent status to attackers who did not qualify for it under Confederate laws, such as the Partisan Ranger Act, or as privateers under the law of nations.

Confederate ambivalence toward direct control over informal diplomatic relations and trade created an environment, particularly in Nova Scotia and New Brunswick, that promoted and legitimized freelance action by both Confederate citizens and British subjects, often with unpredictable consequences. What began as commercial and logistical support for the rebellion moved, by late 1863, toward paramilitary operations that bore a significant resemblance to earlier patterns of filibustering: private international military adventures not done at the behest of a state and launched from neutral territory with the tacit support of the local populace. The possibility of filibustering greatly concerned British officials from the earliest days of the war, particularly in the aftermath of William Walker's last attempt in Central America in 1860. Admiral Milne personally visited Greytown (now San Juan de Nicaragua), the port town on Nicaragua's Caribbean coast that was the scene of Walker's late 1857 invasion, to oversee the situation at that time and repeatedly reinforced his squadron in the Gulf of Mexico as a result. Fears of filibustering reappeared during and after the *Trent* crisis, although it was *northern* filibustering that worried British observers.[5] The governor of the Bahamas professed fears of just such a "lawless expedition" as late as 1864.[6] Despite Milne's hopes that Walker's execution in September 1860 meant a "death blow" to filibustering, quasi-private warfare sprang up and threatened open conflict along the northern U.S. border in 1863 and 1864.[7] Imperial officials in London and North America discovered, to their alarm and frustration, that local courts prevented effective action to stop further raids and failed to bring to justice those responsible for violations of British neutrality and international law. The relative political maturity of Nova Scotia in some respects enabled rather than dissuaded violations of British neutrality.

Confederate engagement with the British Empire occurred almost entirely within what historians have variously termed the "Anglo world," "Greater Britain," or the British World. That is to say, the most consequential interactions—mercantile, military, and interpersonal—between Confederates and British colonial subjects took place within Anglophone territories from Gibraltar to Australia, and from the Cape Colony to Vancouver Island, controlled largely by white English-speaking settlers. Even the island colonies of the Bahamas and Bermuda, which in 1860 held substantial populations of former slaves and their descendants, had been majority-white settlement colonies for much of their history. These locations made sense as sites of Anglo-Confederate interaction because of language and geography, but their relatively privileged place within the empire lent them other advantages as well.[8]

The "Settler Revolution" of the nineteenth-century Anglo world—the phenomenal growth and development of British settler colonies, and in the case of the United States, former colonies, in comparison to the rest of the world—shaped the power relations between colony and metropole in the course of creating "a politically divided but culturally and economically united intercontinental system."[9] The demographic and economic growth of places like British North America, brought on by the Settler Revolution, gave weight to colonists' demands for greater self-government. Scholars differ over the precise reasons behind the grant of responsible government—that is, the extent to which the governors and their appointed councils were answerable to the elected lower house of the colonial legislatures—to the northern provinces, but their relative size, prosperity, and racial composition clearly mattered to London. Canada, for example, received self-governing status relatively quickly after the rebellions of 1837–38, while imperial officials spent decades considering whether to reduce Jamaica to direct control in response to both intransigence by the white minority government and unrest by its majority Black population.[10] Whether settler colonies received responsible government as a benign nod to their right to British institutions or as a piece of realpolitik to keep them within the empire without violence is immaterial, although it seems clear that race informed British assumptions about colonial self-government.[11] The result in either case was that colonies like Nova Scotia, New Brunswick, and Canada exercised political independence within the British Empire to a degree unseen since the American Revolution, and imperial administrators often felt they had little power over their charges, even to prosecute crimes that fell under London's jurisdiction.[12] The Confederate rebellion found opportunity in that independence.

The northern colonies provided other attractions for the Confederacy. British North America was too far north to be a major entrepot for blockade running, although some ships managed to run into Confederate ports from the Maritime colonies, mainly Nova Scotia and New Brunswick, and the two colonies were frequently listed as the false destination of blockade runners as they attempted to enter the Confederacy.[13] Despite its geographical disadvantages, Nova Scotia, and Halifax in particular, assumed an important role for the Confederacy as a communications and transit hub that the Royal Navy sheltered, albeit unintentionally. Because the North American squadron's main base and summer headquarters were at Halifax, a substantial garrison and naval presence discouraged the U.S. Navy from aggressively interfering with trade in the way that it did outside Nassau. Furthermore, Confederate messages to and from Europe often went via Halifax, under cover, in the mailbags of Cunard Line mail packets and even Royal Navy warships. Local political conditions in Nova Scotia also proved favorable for the Confederacy, not least because "[Nova Scotian] politics remained essentially a struggle between members of the mercantile and professional elites."[14] The Confederacy found important friends among both groups, and economic hardship made some influential Halifax merchants particularly receptive to aiding the Confederacy.[15]

Merchants made some of the earliest connections between the Confederacy and Halifax, as they did elsewhere in the colonies. Prewar ties and shipping routes provided one avenue for such arrangements. Shortly after Lincoln declared the blockade in 1861, a Savannah firm led by Andrew Low, a merchant and banker of English birth, proposed running provisions purchased in Halifax through the blockade under cover of their British nationality, acting on the erroneous assumption that this would shield them from capture.[16] The Confederate government also attempted to arrange the purchase of arms and equipment within British North America, although the meager returns discouraged much further effort in that department after 1861.[17] Likewise, Tom Hernandez, a Savannah harbor pilot captured while running the blockade and a friend, John Dickson, made their way from New York to Halifax after a prize court released Hernandez in December 1861. Using Dickson's family connections in Nova Scotia, they sought and found opportunity on the *Standard*, another blockade runner there.[18] The quest for economic gain, along with a romantic view of the Confederacy's efforts, seemed to have attracted the owners of the *Standard* and others to the cause, such as Halifax merchant Benjamin Wier and Alexander Keith Jr., a nephew of the more prominent brewer and merchant who shares his name and a future terrorist.[19]

Support for the Confederacy among the Haligonian elite was not restricted to merchants. Prominent physician Dr. William J. Almon supported the Confederacy in word and deed, sending a son to fight in the rebel army and physically aiding the escape of a prisoner in the *Chesapeake* affair during the winter of 1863–64.[20] The provincial attorney general, William Alexander Henry, and the provincial secretary, Charles Tupper—both powerful members of the Nova Scotia Executive Council—openly professed Southern sympathies.[21] Likewise, Thomas Connolly, the Catholic archbishop of Halifax, materially aided Confederate efforts in the colony, hosting Southern agents and officers and providing them with introductions and pleas for support from Catholics across British North America. These men formed a key portion of an informal pro-Confederate network that lent its effort and influence toward promoting the fortunes of the rebellion and increasingly sheltered and supported private raiding on behalf of the Confederacy.

The importance of this soft power came in large part because of the ad hoc nature of the Confederate state, especially in the early months of the Civil War. The recruitment of friendly and influential colonial subjects, who acted independently of the Confederate government but generally in its interest, helped counterbalance some of the institutional weakness of the young State Department. The Confederate tendency toward dispersed, informal diplomacy was on full display in British North America as white Southerners crisscrossed the provinces, representing themselves as agents of Confederate governments at all levels, often regardless of their authority to do so. Some were relatively prominent men, like Raphael Semmes and Dr. Luke Blackburn, but others were hustlers, self-promoters, and blackguards like Vernon Locke and John C. Braine. The chaotic first months after secession reflected the South's sudden loss of the bureaucracy, procedures, and relative discipline of the U.S. State Department.[22]

This tenuous control, and the freelance agents whom it encouraged, influenced the development of the pro-Confederate network in Nova Scotia. George N. Sanders, formerly a Kentucky Democratic politician and U.S. consul in London, was the most prominent example of such unofficial agents. He quickly engaged in a continuing series of informal negotiations, contracts, and other endeavors on Confederate behalf, to the intense frustration of officials in Richmond, because he held no official position with the government. Sanders's early efforts bore some fruit, particularly by gaining the interest of Benjamin Wier, a Halifax merchant and politician with a checkered past, who eventually served as one of the first members of the new Senate of Canada.[23] Sanders arranged a contract with Wier's firm for a courier and transport service between the Confederacy and Halifax under the cover of schooner trade with Baltimore. Sanders seems to have done so of his own volition, and not as a paid agent of the Confederacy, as evidenced by the government's later refusal to compensate him or his son Lewis for their efforts. Sanders succeeded in getting the Confederate government to adopt his scheme, but the trans-

Benjamin Wier, pro-Confederate merchant and politician from Halifax, photographed in Montreal in 1865. Credit: William Notman, "Benjamin Wier, Montreal, QC, 1865," I-17871.1, McCord Stewart Museum.

port line fell apart after Union authorities discovered it.[24] Nevertheless, Wier remained a consistent supporter of the Confederate cause in ways that went beyond mere hope for profits.

Wier and Company provided a variety of services for the Confederacy, including forwarding and receiving cargo and letters, repairing ships, and later serving as the terminus of the Canadian portion of the Confederacy's network to send escaped prisoners of war back to the South. Wier's activities were well-known to Union and British authorities, but the latter did little to restrain them, as his activities stayed largely within the letter of imperial law, and local authorities had neither the reason nor the inclination to do so either. Wier and other Maritime supporters of the Confederacy severely tested that forbearance in the winter of 1863–64, as they placed themselves squarely in the middle of a military, diplomatic, and legal battle over the fate of the steamer *Chesapeake*.

Pro-Confederate Networks and Privatized Violence at Sea

Perhaps no event better illustrates the Confederate exploitation of private initiative, divided sovereignty, and local sympathies than the so-called second *Chesapeake* affair of late 1863 and early 1864—the first *Chesapeake* affair, in Nova Scotian memory, was the capture of the USS *Chesapeake* by the HMS *Shannon* during the War of 1812.[25] This was not a random attack. Rather, it can be traced to Confederate promotion of privateering and adventurism in the earliest days of the war and to Confederate secretary of the navy Stephen Russell Mallory's ongoing quest "to create a branch of naval warfare which shall enable us to unite and employ private enterprise and capital against the enemy."[26] Private military action had a long history in British colonies and in North America generally, and the Civil War provided opportunity to those inclined to resume that tradition of unauthorized violence, often characterized by a loose interpretation of maritime law and open defiance of the government in London.[27] The attack on the *Chesapeake* represented a foreseeable, although unauthorized, extension of the logic of informal diplomacy and privatized warfare in the colonies.

The man chiefly responsible for the attack on the *Chesapeake* was Vernon Guyon Locke, originally of Sandy Point, Nova Scotia. Locke, born in 1827, was a sailor and captain who worked on vessels based in ports up and down the North American coast from Nova Scotia to North Carolina. When the

Civil War began, his sympathies lay with the South, as did his nose for personal gain, and he obtained access to a letter of marque from the owner of the privateer schooner *Retribution*, which he crewed with a group his victims described as "beach-combers, principally British subjects or escaped convicts." From his first moments as a privateer, Locke, who often sailed using the alias John Parker, was either ignorant or contemptuous of British neutrality and international law.[28] Like most Confederate privateers, he captured few prizes and faced the nearly insurmountable difficulty of trying to sail a captured vessel through the blockade and into a Confederate port to be sold as a prize. The queen's neutrality proclamation of 1861 forbade ships of either side from bringing ships or cargo captured as prizes into British ports, and the other major powers followed suit, effectively leaving Confederate commerce raiders the option of burning their captures or trying to bring them through the blockade.[29]

Locke responded to this difficulty by running a prize, the American schooner *Hanover*, ashore in one of the outlying islands of the Bahamas and bringing its cargo separately to Nassau for sale. He then loaded the *Hanover* with a cargo of salt for an attempt to run the blockade.[30] These actions were patently illegal by both British and Confederate law, but questions of legality did not slow down Locke, then or later. He subsequently seized the brig *Emily Fisher* and repeated his effort to land the cargo, allegedly in the presence of a local official on Long Cay who refused to intervene.[31] By ignorance or complicity, local Bahamian officials aided Locke in violating British neutrality.

Local sympathy, enhanced by Confederate informal diplomacy, aided Locke repeatedly during his colorful career. He escaped justice for his role in the *Hanover* affair by working with local friends in the Bahamas to conceal his identity and the character of his prize. Pressure from British and Union authorities eventually forced Bahamian officials to arrest Locke as he loitered in Nassau in May 1863. The local criminal court was not scheduled to resume until October, so the locals granted Locke the "surprisingly small and insignificant" bail of £200. William Seward protested, correctly, that Locke would gladly lose such a sum and skip town.[32] Even the Colonial Office remarked that the bail opened Bahamian authorities to suspicion of collusion, and like clockwork, when the court resumed its session, Locke failed to appear. The Colonial Office was furious with Bahamas governor Charles Bayley, and the Duke of Newcastle personally demanded an explanation.[33] Given the openly pro-Confederate proclivities of the Bahamian authorities in earlier cases, such as the trial and escape of the *Oreto/Florida*, it is unsurprising that officials made no meaningful effort to keep Locke from fleeing the colony, and ultimately neither Bayley nor the attorney general suffered for their laxity.[34] The indifferent attempts of Bahamas authorities to prosecute pro-Confederate figures like Locke and, later, John C. Braine contrasts sharply with their aggressive treatment of the Black pilots who worked with the U.S. Navy in the same period.

Locke's escape from the Bahamas made it clear to him and his associates that they could carry out legally dubious raiding and rely on a widespread network of friends and local officials to shelter them from the consequences. He even managed to sell the *Retribution* to a blockade-running firm before taking his leave of Nassau, which likely helped fund his next adventure.[35] If local authorities in the Bahamas had shielded him from British law and Union capture, Locke could certainly expect the same or greater assistance in his native province. He was not disappointed.

In early November 1863, Locke found his way to St. John, New Brunswick, from Nassau, and fell in with John Clibbon Braine, another British subject with ties to privateering and raiding.[36] Locke and Braine, along with Henry A. Parr, gathered a group of young men from Nova Scotia and New Brunswick and hatched a plan to seize an American steamship on the high seas and convert it into a privateer by using the commission and letter of marque from the *Retribution*, which Locke retained when he sold the ship. Locke offered his recruits shares of any spoils or prizes as an inducement to join the expedition.[37] They planned to maintain the legality of their attack by renaming their target the *Retribution II* once they gained possession of it. Locke and Braine seemed either ignorant or heedless of the rule that letters of marque applied to specific ships regardless of the name and were not transferable.[38] The group determined that the *Chesapeake*, a fast steamer that plied regularly up the New England coast, fit their needs. In an era that often openly celebrated filibustering, yet another party prepared itself to cross a foreign frontier for military action.[39]

The attack was a dramatic tale in its own right. Locke remained in New Brunswick while Braine led a group to New York and took passage, with weapons concealed in their baggage, on the *Chesapeake*, which was bound for Portland, Maine, with an assorted cargo. The ship left port on December 5, with Braine and a party of about twelve companions on board. Just after midnight on December 7, while the ship was off Cape Cod, the group attacked. The hijackers shot Orin Schaffer, the ship's second engineer, three times as he tried to escape from the engine room. The attackers wounded two other crewmen and narrowly missed the captain, and within the span of a few minutes they had control of the *Chesapeake* "in the name of the Southern Confederacy."[40] The hijackers steamed into the Bay of Fundy, between New Brunswick and Nova Scotia, where they put ashore the remaining civilians and picked up Locke, who took command.[41]

The seizure, which began smoothly, soon unraveled in the face of logistical difficulties and poor decisions. The crew immediately went to the U.S. consul in St. John, who alerted U.S. authorities of the hijacking via telegraph. Several warships—including the USS *Ella and Annie*, a speedy former blockade runner—began hunting for the missing *Chesapeake*, which lacked sufficient coal to reach a friendly port like St. George's or Wilmington. Locke sailed up the coast, making several stops in desperate search of coal and selling portions of the cargo as they went.[42] During one of these stops, at Shelburne, Nova Scotia, Braine left the ship and attempted to escape. The American vice consul in Liverpool, Nova Scotia, attempted to capture him, but local citizens interfered, and Braine got away.[43] Maritime colonists helped an obviously guilty man escape outside authority, and they would do so again before the *Chesapeake* affair ended.

The *Chesapeake* reached Mud Cove, near Sambro, Nova Scotia, on December 16, where it anchored, nearly out of fuel. Locke left the ship and traveled overland to Halifax, about fourteen miles distant, to secure a schooner loaded with coal, with the assistance of Benjamin Wier, who paid the expense out of Confederate accounts. The coal arrived late that night, but it was too late to save Locke's expedition. On the morning of December 17, the *Ella and Annie* discovered the *Chesapeake* lying inshore near the Sambro harbor entrance, the coaling schooner still alongside. The pirates, including Locke, knew they stood no chance and fled on shore, leaving one of their number, George Wade—the man who had shot and killed Schaffer—to be captured in his sleep on board the schooner. Union sailors also seized two Halifax men on board the *Chesapeake* who had sailed on the coaling schooner. After a ten-day search in foul winter weather, the Union again possessed the *Chesapeake*.

The *Ella and Annie*'s captain, however, had in his enthusiasm to capture the pirates actually violated British neutrality by seizing the ship within British territorial waters, which at the time extended one marine league, roughly

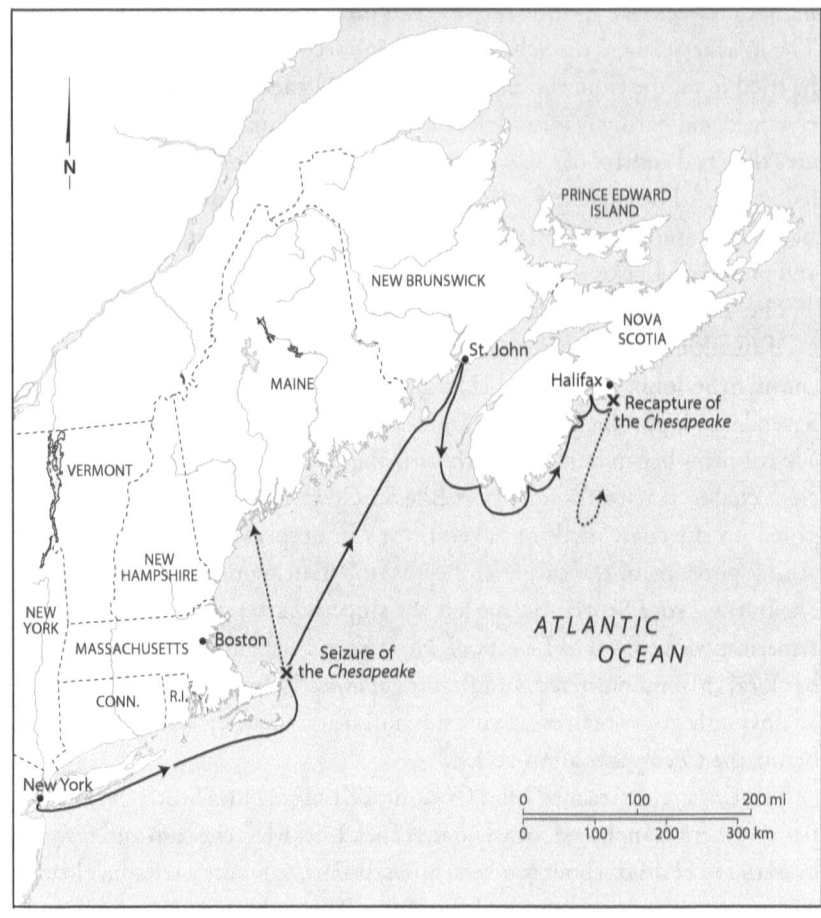

The Maritime Provinces and the Route of the *Chesapeake*, 1863

three miles, from shore. The Union naval commander on the scene, Commander A. G. Clary of the USS *Dacotah*, had a great deal of experience in skirting the rules about visiting neutral waters in the Bahamas and judged that this could not be safely concealed from British and U.S. authorities. He ordered the *Ella and Annie* to proceed to Halifax with the *Chesapeake* so that the seizure could be adjudicated. The small flotilla arrived in Halifax a few hours later and encountered a tense scene. Word spread quickly among local authorities, the British garrison, and the populace that the *Chesapeake* had been seized in British waters and that, furthermore, the U.S. Navy held several local men as prisoners on board their ship. The very real possibility of a diplomatic rupture or even armed conflict hung over Halifax harbor.

The official response to the arrival of the *Chesapeake* fell mainly to the garrison commander and the acting governor, Maj. Gen. Charles Hastings Doyle. Local politicians also involved themselves, particularly Dr. Charles Tupper, in his role as the provincial secretary. Doyle, like the other colonial administrators of British North America, had severely circumscribed powers. He could issue arrest warrants, for example, but their execution relied on local police forces and magistrates, and any warrant remained subject to habeas corpus proceedings and the decisions of the independent colonial judicial system. After a great deal of agitation in the 1840s and 1850s, the imperial government granted British North America the principle of responsible government.[44] The imperial government, through appointed representatives like Doyle, retained authority over external matters, the form of government, and public lands and resources, while generally acceding to colonial legislatures on most other matters. By necessity, the "problem of sovereignty was solved without precision, but with faith in the good sense and goodwill of all concerned" and the assumption that "there would be no great clashes over the demarcation of imperial and colonial questions."[45] Historian Phillip Buckner argues that responsible government in fact increased the power of the colonial executive (though not necessarily the governor) by imposing some form of party discipline on the elected assembly, and that it doubled as "a means of securing collaboration of the colonial elites in the perpetuation of Imperial rule."[46] Nova Scotia, the first colony granted responsible government, tested this faith in good sense and goodwill during the Civil War. Imperial sovereignty over foreign policy in the colonies proved far less supreme and unchallenged than the architects of responsible government expected.

The *Chesapeake* affair immediately confronted Doyle with navigating this division in sovereignty. The breach of British territorial waters by a U.S. warship clearly fell under Crown responsibility as a matter of foreign policy, as did, at least on its face, the extradition, under the 1842 Webster-Ashburton Treaty, of the men accused of piracy and murder. Colonial courts, however, bore the responsibility for adjudicating both the fate of the *Chesapeake* and its captors, and to date no one had been successfully extradited from British North America to the United States under the terms of the treaty—its practical application remained untested in 1863.[47] To further complicate matters, colonial courts had jurisdiction over local violations of imperial laws, such as the Foreign Enlistment Act, which inevitably had international repercussions. If colonial judges and juries differed with the Crown on how to handle the fallout of the hijacking, then a conflict would loom over the hazy boundaries of authority in British North America. The Confederate government and its local supporters acted quickly to bring such a conflict to life. As the U.S. warships entered Halifax harbor with the recaptured *Chesapeake*, the potential for conflict between Britain and the United States, and between London and the colonies, approached its peak.

The American prize crew duly handed the *Chesapeake* over to British custody without problems, although Doyle had the ship docked at the Queen's Wharf under armed guard in order to prevent any further mischief. Commander Clary agreed to Doyle's demand to hand over the prisoners and ordered a boat to transfer them ashore at 1 P.M. the next day. A crowd, angry that the Yankees had seized local men from British waters, waited as the American boat approached, and as Wade stepped onto the wharf, Confederate supporter William J. Almon told him to jump into a waiting rowboat. Wade needed no further encouragement. He leaped into the boat, and two oarsmen quickly pulled away from the wharf. Almon, Alexander Keith Jr., and Dr. Peleg Smith blocked the constable's attempt to aim his pistol at the escaping pirate, and the constable could only watch in frustration as the boat rowed away across the harbor and disappeared.[48]

The interference of three wealthy, prominent Haligonians in a prisoner transfer was hardly accidental, and it infuriated both Doyle and the Americans. All three publicly supported the Confederacy, and now they had openly defied British authority to aid the escape of a colonial subject who had engaged in violence on behalf of the rebellion. Their actions, however, stemmed not just from pro-Confederate sentiment but also from their sense of local patriotism. A wide swath of the Maritime population did not support the prosecution (and potential extradition) of a local man whom the Americans had seized while in violation of Nova Scotian—and by extension, British—territory and neutrality. They did not care that international law and British treaty obligations required otherwise. The stage was set for a conflict between colonial public opinion and imperial sovereignty.

The first point of contention between imperial and local authority was the fate of three of the pirates captured in New Brunswick. Although the ringleaders of the attack, Locke, Braine, and Parr, remained at large, the New

Brunswick authorities seized three local men who had not had the diligence or the foresight to stay hidden. New Brunswick lieutenant governor Arthur Gordon, in issuing the warrants for their arrest, plainly believed his power was circumscribed, and that once he issued the warrant, the matter lay entirely in the hands of local magistrates.[49] The pirates' initial appearance before a St. John police magistrate in January 1864 raised a series of difficulties for imperial authorities over jurisdictional and legal technicalities that repeated themselves in subsequent cases across British North America. Confederate sympathizers in Halifax and New Brunswick arranged for two prominent attorneys, including John Hamilton Gray, a former premier of New Brunswick, to defend the accused. They contested the standing of a lowly police magistrate to hear an extradition case, as well as the propriety and wording of the arrest warrant. A variety of witnesses appeared on the defendants' behalf, including Dr. Luke Blackburn, posing as a disinterested party, present merely to testify to the veracity of Jefferson Davis's and Judah P. Benjamin's signatures on "John Parker's" commission.[50]

The magistrate rejected all these claims and ordered the men held in jail, pending an appeal. Their attorneys promptly appealed to the New Brunswick Supreme Court, where justice William Johnston Ritchie agreed to hear the case. Ritchie, a future chief justice of the Supreme Court of Canada, was closely connected to the pro-Confederate elite in the Maritimes.[51] His brother, John W. Ritchie, had already consulted with Benjamin Wier about the case and represented the Confederate government before the Halifax vice-admiralty court when the *Chesapeake* came up for trial. Justice Ritchie was also the brother-in-law of W. J. Almon. After two weeks of hearings, Ritchie ruled not only that the arrest warrants were improperly filed but that the application for extradition itself was invalid because the American consul had submitted it rather than the U.S. government. He admonished the pirates for violating the Foreign Enlistment Act but did nothing else about their obvious crime, and ordered the men released on a writ of habeas corpus.[52] Ritchie thus managed to undermine both British municipal law restricting unsanctioned military activity as well as the treaty designed to ease cross-border tensions in North America, all in the service of protecting local men who more or less admitted to being guilty of a crime.

The Colonial Office anticipated that local courts might not cooperate and directed Lieutenant Governor Gordon to prepare new warrants in the event of the pirates' release.[53] Gordon instructed provincial attorney general John

Mercer to do so three days before the trial ended, but Mercer ignored the directive. The new warrants did not arrive, and despite a mountain of evidence that the three had been complicit in violations of both municipal and international law, the hijackers walked out of the St. John jail on March 10, 1864, as free men and promptly disappeared. It seems clear that the provincial courts and authorities, particularly Mercer and Ritchie, could have held the *Chesapeake* raiders on the evidence available by simply issuing a new warrant and ordering their immediate rearrest. Through deliberate inaction, they turned a botched and inept act of piracy into a marginal success for the Confederacy because they demonstrated that attacks planned, recruited, and launched from British soil could expect some level of protection from local authorities against imperial law or extradition to the United States. The interpersonal connections of the Confederate informal commercial-diplomatic network, extending through Ritchie, ensured the escape of the attackers.

The Confederate network in Halifax, meanwhile, worked in the vice-admiralty court to gain legal cover for the seizure of the *Chesapeake* by having it declared an act of war or legitimate privateering rather than simple piracy. John W. Ritchie and Benjamin Wier alerted Confederate authorities of the raid and pending trials as quickly as they could, via their connection with Norman S. Walker in Bermuda. Walker forwarded the news to Judah P. Benjamin and Jefferson Davis through the blockade. Wier told them he had secured the legal advice of "Mr [J. W.] Ritchie . . . one of our very best lawyers, and also a friend to Southern independence," for the captured men and hoped to secure some sort of evidence from Richmond that they acted as legitimate combatants in order to prevent their extradition to the United States.[54] Ritchie suggested that the capture might be found legitimate by the local vice-admiralty court, and the ship awarded to the Confederacy as a result.[55]

The trial of the *Chesapeake* opened to intense interest. The provincial attorney general, James William Johnston, represented the Crown, while Ritchie appeared on behalf of the Confederacy, despite not having any formal appointment as their agent. Johnston, himself a Confederate sympathizer and an uncle by marriage to William J. Almon, felt that the case should not have come to the court at all, and he remained relatively passive during the proceedings. Ritchie argued that the *Chesapeake* should be considered a lawful prize because it had been captured by Confederate citizens—a dubious claim at best since only one of the attackers, Canadian-born Henry A. Parr, had lived for any length of time in the South.[56] The presiding judge,

Alexander Stewart, rejected this claim out of hand as irrelevant, and exclaimed that "this Court has no prize jurisdiction" over Union or Confederate captures, and he could not entertain mere "vague assertions and rumours" that the seizure was a legitimate act of war, since the attackers did not see fit to appear and make their claim before the court.[57] Stewart therefore had no choice but to dismiss any latent claim to the vessel.

Stewart made this decision not least because Confederate encounters in other colonial possessions had set a precedent for neutrality violations involving captured ships and cargoes that the imperial government was eager to avoid repeating. The CSS *Alabama* had carried a prize into Cape Town in violation of the queen's neutrality proclamation and attempted the sale through subterfuge of the cargo of others in Mauritius. Officials in the Cape Colony and Mauritius initially abetted these attempts to avoid British neutrality regulations, but the Colonial Office sent clear guidance to colonial ports around the world, including Halifax, that further such incidents would not be tolerated. Doyle made sure that Stewart saw the relevant documents from the Colonial Office before the *Chesapeake* came to trial.[58] Any prizes brought into a colonial port that had not been condemned already by a Confederate admiralty court were to be seized and returned to their owner without trial.[59] In fact, just before the *Chesapeake* hearing began, the Royal Navy seized the CSS *Tuscaloosa*, formerly the American bark *Conrad*, in Cape Town on the same order.[60] Stewart made no decision as to the legal status of the captors themselves but emphasized that "the *Chesapeake*, if a prize at all, is an *uncondemned prize*," and the act of bringing such a vessel into a neutral port was an offense so grave that it "*ipso facto* subjects that prize to forfeiture."[61] Stewart released the ship and its cargo to their owners, prompting Doyle to write privately (and prematurely) to Lord Lyons in Washington that "the closing scene of the Chesapeake has at last taken place."[62] The *Chesapeake* appeared before the court primarily because of the American violation of British territorial waters during its recapture, however, and Judge Stewart left the legality of the seizure itself in question. His ruling did not proscribe future ship hijackings but instead clung narrowly to the confines of imperial policy regarding prize ships. The window for further attacks remained open.

Nova Scotian authorities, having disposed of the case of the *Chesapeake* before the vice-admiralty court, still had to deal with the fallout of George Wade's escape from custody. Although the trial of William J. Almon, Alexander Keith Jr., and P. W. Smith before a Halifax municipal court was purely domestic, the outcome had potential consequences for British neutrality and foreign policy. If another local court failed to punish the abettors (at least in American eyes) of a murderous attack on a civilian ship, it might encourage further hijackings and sour still-fragile Anglo-American relations. The hearings attracted intense public interest on both sides of the border, illustrating the inherent conflict between popular opinion in the colonies and official British policy.

The nature of Halifax's lower criminal court practically guaranteed that the case's outcome would be controversial. Elected city officials heard cases in Halifax and decided what, if any, charges the defendants would face. In this instance, the mayor, Philip Carteret Hill, also served as chief magistrate. Hill came from the same "Tory-Anglican-merchant establishment" of Halifax that had produced Almon, Ritchie, and many other Confederate sympathizers, and his impartiality in the case was questionable at best.[63] After some delay, the trial opened on January 11, 1864. As an indication of the imperial government's acute interest in the case, Doyle took the unusual step of ordering the provincial attorney general to be present at the proceedings and answer questions about the events on the Queen's Wharf on the day of Wade's escape.

The defendants, the constables, and numerous other witnesses testified before the court and presented a somewhat confused account of the day's events. The combined testimony suggests that Almon knew the details of the impending prisoner transfer and arranged for Wade's escape. It defies credulity that a manned, otherwise idle rowboat just happened to be waiting at the right slip at the right moment by sheer coincidence, and that it carried the prisoner beyond the Halifax city limits immediately, ignoring shouted orders to return. When testimony closed, Hill reluctantly ruled that the three should appear before the Halifax County Supreme Court in the spring session, but only on the lesser charge of interfering with a police officer rather than the far more serious count of aiding the escape of a prisoner. The defendants walked free after giving a small bond.[64]

During the Supreme Court's next session, a grand jury reviewed the case referred from Halifax and dismissed the charges due to a supposed lack of evidence. This confirmed the suspicions of many observers that no jury in staunchly pro-Confederate Halifax would convict local men for aiding the rebellion. Doyle remarked privately to Lord Lyons, "I strongly believe that Dr. Almon is so popular a person, and that there are so many sympathetic with the Southern Cause here, it will be very difficult to find a Jury who will agree in their finding. Nous verrons!"⁶⁵ By late spring 1864, everyone involved with the capture of the *Chesapeake* and the escape of the hijackers had either eluded pursuit or been acquitted altogether. The almost complete lack of personal consequences assured future attacks from neutral soil, and the near absence of diplomatic trouble for the Confederacy encouraged further sponsorship of unconventional warfare from British territory.

The Confederacy Embraces the Logic of Private Violence

When Davis and the cabinet in Richmond learned of the *Chesapeake* affair, they were unaware that most of the legal proceedings in the Maritimes that would determine the ship's fate were already underway. Nevertheless, Davis and Stephen Mallory immediately recognized the potential windfall that a favorable decision in the Halifax vice-admiralty court could provide. If the capture received legal sanction on British soil, it opened the way for an expanded campaign of hijacking against Union shipping that would be protected by law as legitimate privateering. This could reignite Confederate privateering and perhaps meet Davis's heretofore unfulfilled expectations for it. The "piratical" attacks on ships like the *Chesapeake*, the *Roanoke*, and the *Salvador*, to give three examples of varying legality, were not spontaneous crimes, invented out of thin air by their perpetrators. The Confederate government accepted the importance and legitimacy of privatized warfare such as privateering from the very beginning, and this preference for engaging private capital for the war at sea lasted throughout the war, although its form changed dramatically with the military and financial situation. Privateering proved unappealing to crews and owners who could not easily be paid, and the few ships and crews who attempted it generally had brief and unspectacular careers after the summer of 1861.⁶⁶

In response to the lackluster results of its privateers, the Confederate government tried several approaches to make up for its naval weakness. An overseas purchasing program to buy from European shipyards met with mixed success. Commerce raiders like the *Alabama* and the *Florida* hurt Union merchant shipping, but their success and the corresponding diplomatic uproar drove the Palmerston government to enforce the Foreign Enlistment Act stringently against further Confederate ships being built covertly in British yards.⁶⁷ Very few of the European-built warships intended for the Confederate navy ever reached their hands. As a corollary to this program, some Confederate officials and private citizens advocated an unconventional approach to naval warfare as a way to avoid the restrictions of formal privateering while still attracting private capital to fund and operate ships.

Southerners began proposing unconventional attacks at sea almost as soon as the war started. Many would-be privateers could not meet the conditions of Confederate law, which required a vessel to be on hand in a Confederate port and a substantial bond as a guarantee against misconduct before the government could issue a letter of marque. To avoid this, a Charleston resident named David Riker wrote to the Confederate government in July 1861 and proposed to go to Havana and hijack a steamship bound from there to New York. Robert Toombs, then secretary of state, did not definitively shoot down the idea but urged Riker and his men to obtain commissions in the state militia in order to protect themselves from piracy charges.[68] Their plan never materialized, but the attack on the U.S. mail steamer *Roanoke* three years later was almost identical, except that the hijackers were led by a British subject. By 1864, the Confederate government turned haltingly to encouraging hijackings and providing them with enough official cover to prevent the participants, if captured, from being hanged as pirates or spies (not always successfully).[69] The problem with this method, of course, was that it was usually illegal. Either the attacking parties, as bona fide servicemen, were guilty of launching attacks from neutral territory, or they were guilty, as civilians without a letter of marque, of piracy. Unsurprisingly, the parties of men who engaged in seizing merchant ships at gunpoint did not place a high priority on observing diplomatic and legal niceties, and even the attacks conducted by bona fide Confederate servicemen usually broke the neutrality laws of their points of origin.[70] The participants relied on the inability or unwillingness of their neutral hosts to prevent the attacks and prosecute them afterward. It was the structure of colonial governance and the aid of informal pro-Confederate networks that made this practice viable.

The news of the *Chesapeake* attack came to Richmond at a time when the Davis administration was experimenting with unconventional naval warfare and actively seeking new opportunities to seize ships by subterfuge. Confederate raiding parties had already used similar techniques with success against Union shipping in places like the Chesapeake estuary, and extending the practice beyond internal waterways seemed only logical. In early 1862, in the very midst of passing responsibility for government blockade running to merchant firms in Charleston and Nassau, Secretary of the Navy Stephen Mallory strongly and repeatedly advocated the use of a privatized "provisional navy" specifically organized to raid in this fashion.[71] Over the next year, Mallory lobbied the Confederate Congress to authorize such a force, and it finally passed a law creating the new organization, dubbed the "volunteer navy," on April 18, 1863. Jefferson Davis signed it a few days later.[72]

The new organization suffered, however, under some of the same restrictions that had choked off privateering, particularly the requirement to commission ships in a Confederate port, which made it exceedingly difficult to obtain suitable vessels. In the winter of 1863–64, Mallory, now less tied to long-standing antebellum norms for privateering, convinced Congress to modify the bill to permit ships to be commissioned abroad, during the same session in which they dramatically tightened controls over blockade running.[73] While the actual participation in the volunteer navy program was slim, Mallory's advocacy for it, and Congress's acquiescence, demonstrated an increased willingness to cede oversight of violence to private parties at a time when government control over all aspects of the war was generally increasing. Mallory in particular provided encouragement for this quasi-private raiding even when it fell outside the purview of the navy. He encouraged groups interested in operating as "independent river guerilla parties" in the West who sought to use government sanction to "secure to them the rights of prisoners of war, if captured," and offered to facilitate their applications to President Davis.[74] The *Chesapeake* affair and the events that followed demonstrated that Mallory and Davis had overcome any earlier hesitation about extending this style of warfare beyond Confederate shores. The legal and political environment in Richmond increasingly favored covert raiding, private initiative, and the use (and potential abuse) of neutral territory.

Davis, in earlier instances, refused permission for such operations. Mallory and others presented him with plans to attack the prisoner of war camp at Johnson's Island, located in Sandusky Bay, just off Lake Erie, on several occasions in 1862 and early 1863. The proposals required the use of Canadian territory, and Davis, who still clung to hopes of recognition and intervention, did not wish to antagonize the British government. By the late summer of 1863, he had abandoned his opposition in response to events abroad. British authorities acted, in Davis's mind, as pro-Union partisans in a number of cases, particularly the seizure of the so-called Laird rams—ironclad warships meant for the Confederacy that were under construction at the Laird shipyard near Liverpool.⁷⁵ The seizure of the Laird rams and the increasingly obvious unwillingness of the British government to recognize the Confederacy removed much of Davis's reluctance to violate British territory and sensibilities.⁷⁶ This was augmented by increasing Confederate hopes that France would emerge as their best chance for recognition, intervention, and the construction of warships.⁷⁷ Respect for neutrality, which had animated Confederate discourse on diplomacy and relations with Britain, suddenly became far less of a stumbling block for those who wished to take more direct action against Union targets on the periphery of North America.

Attacks like the one on the *Chesapeake* dovetailed with this increased appetite for unconventional warfare. Private military expeditions against countries nominally at peace with the organizing nation—that is, filibustering—commonly aided efforts at empire building, and the Civil War was no exception.⁷⁸ Historians have struggled on occasion to differentiate filibustering from other forms of interstate violence, not least because filibustering expeditions often received tacit encouragement and support from governments. One prominent historian defined the term "filibuster" rather tightly by emphasizing the private nature of the expedition as the most important characteristic. He excluded from the category any attack that received "implicit or explicit permission" from the perpetrator's government because these attacks "failed the test of privacy."⁷⁹ Yet numerous antebellum filibustering attacks received just such support from governments, from American attacks against Spanish Florida to Narciso Lopez's failed expedition to Cuba. In the case of the expedition against Florida, it is likely that President James Madison himself approved of the operation.⁸⁰ Because so many of these private expeditions received some sort of quiet government approval, it seems more practical to classify filibustering inclusively according to the relative *extent* and openness of government knowledge and approval, rather than the government's complete absence.

Several pro-Confederate raids fit into this modified category. The government in Richmond often did not know of these attacks in advance but nevertheless accepted the casual invocation of legitimacy by their organizers, and cabinet officials in Richmond, especially Mallory, as will be discussed, promoted them on numerous occasions. Vernon Locke waved around a Confederate letter of marque to persuade British colonists to join him in attacking a country with whom their own government was formally at peace. This was in the same tradition of filibustering as the parties of Americans who joined with the *patriotes* and Hunters' Lodges in 1838, crossing the border in the opposite direction to aid a rebellion in an ostensibly friendly territory.[81] John C. Braine and Thomas Hogg later took similar actions by using volunteer commissions in the Confederate navy, signed by Mallory, to attract crews for hijacking missions in neutral territory. The Civil War–era expeditions in British North America joined an often-overlooked history of private international violence along the northern frontier.

The *Chesapeake* was not the only example of maritime quasi-filibustering for the rebellion. Just weeks earlier, Confederate citizen Thomas Hogg and a party that included several British subjects hijacked the American merchant ship *Joseph R. Gerrity* out of Matamoras, Mexico, and sailed it into British Honduras (modern-day Belize). Hogg illegally sold the ship and cargo, then made his escape when British officials learned the truth and attempted to arrest him.[82] A similar attack from Canada in the fall of 1863 using Confederate naval officers was aborted at the last moment after being betrayed by an informant. The group planned to seize a steamer on Lake Erie and liberate the prisoner-of-war camp at Johnson's Island, Ohio.[83] When British authorities arrested several seamen involved in the capture of the *Gerrity* in Liverpool, James Mason, inspired by Confederate support for the *Chesapeake*'s captors, funded their legal defense, thereby demonstrating a willingness to legitimize filibustering and piracy ex post facto.[84] These incidents received remarkably broad support from Confederates who commented on them. Norman Walker, passing word from Bermuda, expressed disapproval of the *Chesapeake* attack's methods but recommended that the government support the captors nonetheless. Georgiana Walker, commenting privately, disapproved of the hijacking but stopped short of condemning it.[85] Clearly, Benjamin, Mason, and Davis agreed, and virtually no one in a position of power recommended that the Confederate government openly disavow the attacks. By early 1864, the Confederate cabinet demonstrated an increasing appetite for unconventional naval warfare and a tolerance for filibustering on its behalf, and the events in the Maritime provinces seemed ripe for exploitation in the service of building a slaveholding empire.

To that end, Davis dispatched University of Virginia law professor James P. Holcombe to Halifax, seeking some advantage in the pending trials over the *Chesapeake* and its captors, and to arrange a network to transport escaped Confederate prisoners of war home. Before Holcombe arrived, however, the Halifax vice-admiralty court released the *Chesapeake* back to its owners, thwarting Davis's hopes. Nonetheless, Holcombe claimed that the hijackers, now fugitives, should receive Confederate support, because they "imperiled life and liberty in an enterprise of great hazard, which they honestly believed was invested with the sanction of law." In part because of the hijackers "generous sympathy with our cause," Holcombe urged that the government give, ex post facto, official sanction for the raid.[86] The filibustering tail wagged the dog of Confederate foreign policy, as Davis and Benjamin agreed to provide such evidence.[87] The Confederate government supported these raiders not only out of a sense of moral obligation to those who took up arms on their behalf but also because they offered a cheap and disruptive weapon against Union commerce and naval power that could use non-Confederate manpower and ships. The utter failure of British courts to successfully prosecute the attackers in the *Gerrity* and *Chesapeake* attacks for either piracy or violating the Foreign Enlistment Act provided no disincentive for acknowledging or sponsoring further raids. More would follow in short order.

While the leadership of the Confederate government was generally unified about not openly disavowing these attacks, some officials did attempt to prevent those that were plainly illegal, as in the case of the *Roanoke*. In October 1864, the residents of St. George's, Bermuda, watched as the U.S.-flagged mail steamship *Roanoke* burned to the waterline and sank a short distance outside the harbor. This catastrophe was no accident. A group of hijackers—pirates, according to American authorities—led by John C. Braine of the *Chesapeake* attack, deliberately set the ship ablaze after Bermudian officials denied them entry to the port at St. George's. Awakened by the *Chesapeake* case and a further hijacking on the Great Lakes that September, the Colonial Office scrambled for a way to characterize these attacks. They were "a new feature which has sprung up in the present American war," and "the like was not practised in the previous conflicts of Civilized Nations."[88] The bulk of the party that seized the *Roanoke* in the name of the Confederacy had no official sanction or commission in the Confederate armed forces, despite their claims to the contrary, and acted as private citizens.[89] Many of them were British subjects as well. The *Roanoke* was one of at least seven attacks scattered around the North American maritime periphery, from the Pacific coast of Panama up to the Great Lakes, with a similar modus operandi but vastly different levels of official sanction. The attackers in this hybrid of filibustering and privateering, with the example of the *Chesapeake* before them, counted on neutral sites in the colonies to shelter them before and after their attacks.

In the case of the *Roanoke*, the locals rewarded this faith. Braine, fresh from his *Chesapeake* adventure and a visit to Richmond, presented himself to Charles Helm, the Confederate consul in Havana. He asked Helm for assistance in carrying out his plan to seize the *Roanoke*, which he claimed had the approval of the government. Braine misled Helm; he had an acting master's commission in the Confederate navy, provided by Mallory as a shield against hanging, but Mallory had approved seizing a ship from a northern port, not from Cuba.[90] Helm thought Braine's plan to launch an attack from Havana was both illegal and ill-advised, but he could not prevent the expedition's departure. Braine and his men seized the *Roanoke* on September 28, shortly after it departed Havana en route to New York. Greatly concerned that Davis or Mallory might actually have approved this plan, Helm wrote to Benjamin and pointed directly to the portions of the law of nations that this kind of action violated.[91] He cited Vattel, Kent's *Commentaries*, and Wheaton as all forbidding any attempt to set on foot an armed expedition, on land or sea, from neutral territory, even if the violence actually occurred beyond the limits of neutral land or waters, and he urged any future hijacking attacks to originate from a Union port. Helm also reported, erroneously, that he had dissuaded Thomas Hogg (captor of the *Gerrity*, who was also present at the time in Havana) from undertaking a similar venture. Hogg's mission had the full support of Mallory, as it turned out. In a stark demonstration of the impossibility of restraining these attacks, Hogg actually gave Braine and his men weapons, money, and exit passes from the Spanish authorities, which enabled them to carry out the attack.[92]

Braine took the *Roanoke* to Bermuda, where he received reinforcements and assistance from locals and the Confederate office in St. George's. Bermuda authorities refused to allow the ship into the harbor, their pro-Southern proclivities dampened by pressure from London to crack down on violations of neutrality rules after the *Chesapeake* fiasco, although they did not seize the ship as an illegal prize, as policy required. Out of fuel, Braine chose to burn the ship and merrily went ashore with the passengers and crew. Braine claimed that he and his men held commissions in the Confederate service, which was true only for Braine himself, the men having been recruited in Havana. Furthermore, Braine's commission was applicable only for a legitimate mission to New York, and he did not disclose that his attack on the *Roanoke* was not only unauthorized but actively resisted by the Confederate consul in Havana.[93] On the other hand, the Confederate office in St. George's, which certainly knew of Braine's misdeeds in the *Chesapeake* case, hired a ship in a futile attempt to refuel the *Roanoke* at sea and recruited crewmembers to go aboard and join Braine.[94] Bermudan authorities decided they would not arrest or prosecute the hijackers, who lingered for some time in St. George's, boasting of their exploits. Crown lawyers initially decided the seizure, while reprehensible, was not piracy, assuming Braine's commission was real, although the new colonial secretary, Edward Cardwell, scolded Lieutenant Governor William Hamley for failing to properly enforce the Foreign Enlistment Act and the rules against prize vessels entering British ports.[95] Before he could be arrested for these related crimes, Braine disappeared, off in search of another victim, while authorities in London and Washington raged at his easy escape from justice.

Braine struck again in Chesapeake Bay late in the war. In April 1865, he led a party that captured the schooner *St. Mary* by feigning distress in a small yawl and then seized the ship after being helped aboard by its crew. Braine evaded capture and made it to the Bahamas, where he sold part of the ship's cargo illegally. The improbably named Rawson W. Rawson, recently arrived to replace Charles Bayley as governor of the Bahamas, proved just as willing as his predecessor and his counterpart in Bermuda to accept Braine at his word and to ignore the *Chesapeake* attack (inexcusable, especially since Vernon Locke was on trial in Nassau at the time for that very event). Rawson refused requests from the U.S. consul to arrest Braine because he considered the *St. Mary* a legitimate prize and believed that its entry into British waters, normally prohibited, was allowable because the ship was supposedly in distress. Not surprisingly, the Nassau court acquitted Locke, and he and Braine went their separate ways, to the disgust of Union and British imperial officials.[96]

In contrast to Braine's self-directed raiding, the attack on the Pacific Mail Steamship *Salvador* quite certainly had the approval and support of the Confederate government. The *Salvador* ran regularly between Panama and California, often carrying gold, and Hogg persuaded Stephen Mallory to support an attack. The party was to board the ship in Panama and, like the others, seize the ship once it reached international waters and either convert it into a cruiser to attack further vessels or destroy it and make their escape. An informant tipped off the Union navy, and a substantial group of warships awaited the *Salvador* off the Pacific coast of Panama. On November 10, 1864, Union sailors boarded the ship and arrested Hogg and his men before they could even make their attempt. Ironically, the hijacking attempt with the greatest official legitimacy failed most ignominiously. The *Salvador* was not the last such attack, but the war ended before the Confederate navy could organize any more on such official terms. The *Salvador*'s hijackers, unlike Braine and Locke, had to face trial in an American court in San Francisco instead of in a welcoming colony.[97] Lacking a friendly colonial judge, they were convicted and given death sentences, which were later commuted to substantial stays in prison.

This fusion of filibustering and privateering was evidence of a North American cultural tradition of private transnational violence. From the Hunters' Lodges of the 1837–38 Canadian rebellion, to William Walker, to postbellum Fenian raiders, this was a continuity of what one might call grassroots foreign policy activists, engaging in violence in support of (if not at the behest of) an aspiring secession movement. This species of raiding also points to an enduring link between adventurism and private capital. Though driven by different circumstances, Southern support for Walker's Central American filibusters before the war was mirrored in 1863 and 1864 by Stephen Mallory, who, more than any other Confederate leader, promoted the fusion of private capital and violent means. After the war, the phenomenon reappeared in places like Baja California, where filibusters once again made themselves a nuisance with the support of English land speculators.[98] The cataclysmic war and concurrent state expansion of 1861–65 obscured this habit of private violence, but it certainly did not kill it.

The actions of private adventurers and filibusters shaped the Confederate government's behavior in the colonies and at sea, in large part because of the government's continued reliance on private parties to manage affairs in the region. James Mason took his cues from the trials in the Maritime colonies and funded the defense of the men on trial in England for seizing the *Gerrity*. Stephen Mallory promoted further hijacking operations because they offered the opportunity for minimal risk offensive actions with a good chance of success, and these attacks suited his desire to further engage private enterprise in the war at sea. In the months that followed the *Chesapeake* affair, hijackers claimed several more ships as victims, from the Pacific coast of Panama, across the British West Indies, and even on the Great Lakes. The attackers claimed Confederate authorization as cover for their deeds, truthfully in some cases, falsely in others. The Confederate government proved more willing, as their military situation worsened and the Union's "hard hand of war" struck home, to authorize or legitimize increasingly wild attempts at freelance diplomacy and violence on the British periphery of North America. These attacks relied implicitly on the shelter provided by neutral territory and on the relative immunity from consequences provided by colonial governance. The resulting chaos and public outcry demonstrated the depth and inordinate effect of the pro-Confederate networks across British America, as a relative handful of people caused problems for both Britain and the Union, all out of proportion to their numbers.

CHAPTER SIX

"Informal Propositions Coming from Irresponsible and Unofficial Persons"

British North America and the Perils of Informal Diplomacy, 1864–1865

It would be a fatal mistake, in my opinion, to abandon all effort to separate this section from the United States because no results have yet been achieved commensurate with our expectations.
—James P. Holcombe

AS THE CONFEDERATE military situation became more precarious in early 1864, the frequency and importance of informal military and diplomatic actions in the colonies increased. The province of Canada was the scene of the most dangerous events, but the maritime periphery of North America also saw continued action. Two Confederate "commissioners" to Canada, Jacob S. Thompson and Clement C. Clay Jr., arrived shortly after the resolution of the *Chesapeake* affair and joined James P. Holcombe. Their presence galvanized the pro-Confederate faction in Canada into action and led, directly or indirectly, to everything from peace negotiations with the Union government to attempts to influence the 1864 elections, as well as a wide variety of attacks, including direct raids, sabotage, arson, and assassination. Further hijacking-style attacks against Union shipping around North America augmented the chaos emanating from British North America. Their initial efforts in Canada, however, centered on informal diplomacy and efforts to subvert the U.S. government and influence the 1864 elections from the shelter of Canada, using both nonviolent and violent means. This chapter focuses on the former, which peaked in the summer of 1864 with the so-called Niagara Falls Conference and an attempt to lift the Copperheads, or Peace Democrats, to victory at the Democratic National Convention in Chicago.

The Confederate government, despairing of international recognition and intervention, began to abandon the norms of state behavior, particularly regarding neutrality, and indulged further in sponsoring and encouraging private parties to undertake international violence on its behalf. This was a gradual transition, slowed by persistent efforts by Confederate diplomats to gain recognition and linked to specific frustrations over supposedly pro-Union behavior by the British government. British detention of the Laird rams—powerful ironclad warships under construction for the Confederacy near Liverpool—in September 1863 led to the expulsion of the few remaining British consuls in the Confederacy and to Davis's approval of that fall's aborted raid on Johnson's Island through Canadian territory.[1] In June 1864, Secretary of State Judah P. Benjamin, angered by the "naked outrage" of the December 1863 seizure of the CSS *Tuscaloosa* by British colonial and naval authorities, called the Palmerston administration "a pretended neutral but really hostile Government" that engaged in such "insolent aggression" only because it did not fear a Confederate declaration of war.[2] Around that same time, the Confederate Congress approved a manifesto intended to be distributed to European governments declaring the South's indomitable spirit, blamelessness for the war, and desire for peace on the basis of independence. The manifesto did not mention recognition directly, nor did it give any particular call for action.[3] Three months later, Benjamin had "long ceased to expect from England any other action than such as may be dictated by our enemies to suit their own policy," and he conclusively abandoned hope of European intervention. Still, Benjamin held to the conviction that European recognition was forthcoming—perhaps from France—and would be enough to give the South victory.[4] By the fall of 1864, the Confederacy's formal diplomacy showed real desperation in Duncan Kenner's secret mission to Europe with an offer to abolish slavery in return for British recognition and support.[5]

Events in the colonies reflected the other side of that coin. The grim calculus of war led Davis, Benjamin, and Stephen Mallory to gamble that if their final efforts at gaining international recognition or a negotiated peace failed, the Confederacy had more to gain by provocation and subversion from British territory than it did from observing the niceties of interstate diplomacy.

This calculation had long been nascent in Confederate strategy. Privateering and the naval purchasing program overseas practically relied on avoiding or exploiting British and international law, and in the immediate antebellum period, future Confederate leaders had shown a tendency to interpret domestic and international law as narrowly as possible when it came to neutrality violations by filibusters. By 1864, this long-standing reliance on informal agents and preference for privatizing the war abroad set the conditions for a campaign against the Union that sheltered in British territory and brazenly violated international law as understood by the British and Union governments. Confederate officials in Richmond sponsored many of these attacks and gave ex post facto approval to others, which encouraged other outrages, including some that even the Confederacy's staunchest supporters considered beyond the pale.

The Confederate government embraced informal diplomacy and unconventional extraterritorial violence not simply because its hopes of formal statehood had faltered but because these were the traditional tools of grassroots empire building in North America—that is, the use of armed force by pioneers, settlers, filibusters, and the like who were not agents of the state in order to extend or secure control over territory. This approach was flexible and cheap, and the ambiguity over who bore responsibility for these actions shielded Richmond officials from blame when they went wrong. It seems unlikely, however, that this nebulous chain of command was entirely deliberate. Even with overland couriers and blockade runners, the Confederate leaders in Canada found communication with Richmond extremely difficult, and they were left almost entirely to their own devices when choosing their course of action. That the effort ended in atrocity rather than victory is only fitting, given its filibustering and privateering ancestors.

Historians generally have not been kind in their assessments of the Confederacy's activities in Canada. James McPherson dismissed them as "bizarre plots" beset by contradictory goals, while Robin Winks found that Confederate raiding had little immediate benefit for the rebellion, yet it turned public opinion in Canada against the South and handed Seward and the Union a diplomatic victory.[6] Brian Jenkins, the preeminent Canadian historian of Civil War diplomacy, argued that Confederate meddling in Canada further harmed the Confederacy's standing with the Palmerston government and served mainly to imperil the Reciprocity Treaty and to raise anxieties in both Canada and London about the security of the provinces from a revanchist

Union government.[7] Nevertheless, from a purely military standpoint the operations were an efficient use of Confederate resources. A relative handful of men and a small budget managed to create hysteria among the Union populace near the border and tie down several thousand troops and a great deal of diplomatic and surveillance attention. The Confederate leadership in Canada themselves thought these efforts at subversion were worth continuing, even after Lincoln's reelection.[8] Viewed in this way, the Confederate effort to combine the efforts of private enterprise and government leadership with North American traditions of privatized violence paid off. The international ramifications were largely negative, but the Confederacy did not live long enough to regret the spread of violence, disorder, and repression that followed.

Prior to 1864, Confederate operations in Canada were disorganized and largely the work of freelance troublemakers. Individual states in some cases sent agents there during the secession crisis and the early months of the war in search of supplies and arms, but few weapons were available for purchase, and Southerners had to compete with one another and with agents from many Northern states as well. Most of the small arms in Canada belonged to the militia or the British government, and the governor-general quickly forbade their sale or export.[9] These semiofficial agents soon drifted elsewhere with a few exceptions, leaving Canada to those wishing to help the Confederacy on their own terms. Some, such as the Reverend A. Crawford Walshe—an Anglican clergyman living in Hamilton, Canada West—pestered the governor-general, the Foreign Office, and the Colonial Office with allegations of pro-Union breaches of neutrality.[10] Walshe, despite being a relative nobody, tied down the attention of the imperial government and forced them to spend time investigating Union purchasing and "crimping," a term for illegal and occasionally coercive recruiting, in Canada. The Foreign Office took Walshe's allegations seriously, referring them to the Crown's legal advisers and causing Canadian authorities to investigate the claims, much to the annoyance of the Colonial Office. While the investigation dismissed many of Walshe's claims, it did result in increased pressure on Union crimps and recruiting within Canada, including a number of arrests.[11] Another group of conspirators caused more serious trouble by entrapping Joshua Giddings, then serving as U.S. consul general in Canada, in a scheme that resulted in his arrest by Canadian authorities.[12] Only one incident, the aborted late-1863 plan to attack the prisoner-of-war camp at Johnson's Island in Lake Erie, had the involvement and foreknowledge of the Confederate government. Nevertheless, the annoyance they caused for Union (and British) authorities hinted at the possibilities along the largely unsecured northern border.

Over the course of the spring of 1864, the Confederate cabinet moved to embrace the potential of British North America as a military and diplomatic pressure point against the Union. Encouraged by early reports on the *Chesapeake* raid and urged on by proponents such as Georgia senator Herschel V. Johnson, Jefferson Davis determined to send a pair of so-called commissioners to Canada to organize and coordinate the disparate pro-Confederate elements there. These included Confederate citizens such as escaped prisoners of war, exiles, transient businessmen, and a small group of aspiring but largely incompetent or inconsequential agents, including George N. Sanders and Nathaniel Beverley Tucker. British subjects formed a small but important component of the Confederate supporters in Canada, including some lower-level provincial officials, clergy, businessmen, and various others attracted by anti-Northern animus, a romantic view of the Southern cause, or a desire for adventure or personal profit. James P. Holcombe, whom Davis had already sent to British North America to examine the *Chesapeake* case and to set up a network to aid escaped Confederate prisoners in returning home, remained in place and awaited the arrival of reinforcements. Holcombe went out of his way to inform British authorities of his prisoner-transport mission in order to avoid "some misrepresentation by our enemies," and he assured Lord Monck that his instructions ordered him to "avoid most scrupulously any infringement of municipal or public law" or British neutrality.[13] His own government would quickly make a liar out of him.

Davis, despite his instructions to Holcombe, viewed the role of the mission to Canada as largely one of subversion. Herschel Johnson, writing to Davis in early January 1864, cited the returns of the 1863 elections in the North as evidence of the existence in the United States of "a powerful conservative element," particularly in the Old Northwest, that might be inclined to secede from the Union with the support of a "discreet and prudent agent" that could encourage such sentiment quietly.[14] Johnson, who had been Stephen Douglas's vice-presidential nominee in the 1860 election and one of the few southern Democrats who did not walk out of the Charleston convention, still retained hope that his old party in the North might come to the South's rescue, and he hoped to persuade Davis, whom he felt was "susceptible of flattery," that concrete action should be taken to this effect.[15] Johnson suggested that Congress could appropriate a substantial sum of money to underwrite a campaign to influence Northern politics and the upcoming elections. Davis, although skeptical of the prospects for success, agreed to try, and the Confederate Congress voted to appropriate nearly $5 million for "secret service" in February.[16] Roughly $1 million of this sum was dedicated to Canadian operations and its use left to the discretion of the as yet unchosen commissioners who would lead the venture.

At the outset, the mission to Canada was not intended to engage in traditional diplomacy. Davis, Johnson, and most prominent government officials opposed negotiations with the Union government, and Crown officials in British North America remained prohibited from recognizing Confederate envoys in any official capacity. The commissioners' objectives would necessarily have to be obtained by indirect and informal means. The position required discretion, organizational ability, and political acumen—particularly with Northern Democratic politics. To have any chance of success, Davis needed to choose his operatives carefully for the endeavor. Instead, he seems to have initially attempted to select political rivals for the job, in an echo of his disastrous choice of William Lowndes Yancey as a member of the first Confederate diplomatic mission to Europe in 1861. Yancey, a fire-eater and notorious proslavery advocate, was not only widely disliked in Britain but also a fierce critic of Davis and the government. Davis, who was often prickly and irritable, sent Yancey abroad at least in part to get him out of the way. In this vein, Davis considered his vice president, Alexander Stephens, and South Carolina senator James L. Orr for the Canadian mission. Both men were vociferous critics of Davis's administration and had connections to the Northern Democrats, but Stephens's health was too poor, and Orr declined. Davis eventually turned to Jacob S. Thompson and Clement C. Clay Jr. to join James P. Holcombe in British North America.[17]

Thompson, though not a devoted supporter of the Davis administration, was at the very least not among its vociferous critics. Born in North Carolina in 1810, he studied law at the University of North Carolina before moving to Mississippi, where he quickly became involved in Democratic politics. He served six terms as a U.S. congressman from Mississippi, and he was an occasional antebellum political rival of Jefferson Davis, to whom he lost the nomination for a Senate seat in 1855.[18] Thompson's close political connections with James Buchanan gained him the position of secretary of the interior in that administration, where he served as an influential cabinet member until his resignation during the secession crisis in 1860.[19] During the war, Thompson served in a minor role on the staff of General John C. Pemberton before taking up a position in the Mississippi state legislature in 1863. Davis summoned him from Mississippi to Richmond and offered him the Canadian mission, which he reluctantly accepted. Perhaps as an indication of his lack of optimism about the mission's prospects, Thompson transferred his vast property holdings to his son before departing.[20] Thompson was a capable choice for the position, with a demonstrated talent for organization and long experience in Democratic politics, although he had practically no experience in diplomacy or travel beyond the United States, and his military career had been short and undistinguished.

Clement C. Clay Jr., the second commissioner, was a former U.S. and Confederate senator from Alabama, but unlike Thompson, he and his wife were close friends of the Davis family. Clay had long experience with Democratic politics, although his connections to Northern Democrats had not been particularly strong even before secession. Beyond friendships with doughfaces like George Wallace Jones of Iowa, Clay's antebellum Senate career did not make him many Northern friends, even among Democrats. His accomplishments consisted mainly of insulting Charles Sumner and railing against supposed abolitionist schemes.[21] His unflinching sectionalism in the 1850s; his early support for the right, if not the act, of secession; and his steadfast support for the administration as a Confederate senator made him a politically reliable choice for Davis, although these same factors also limited his influence as a political agent aimed at the Old Northwest.[22] Clay had neither military nor diplomatic experience and had never traveled beyond the United States.[23] To make matters worse, he was a frail man, frequently beset by respiratory illness that left him unable to work for weeks or months at a time.[24] Clay himself doubted the wisdom of the appointment, deeming it one "for which I am not suited by my talents tastes or habits," and hoped for a partner in the mission who would "do the bargaining and bartering."[25] Clay and Thompson received verbal orders from Jefferson Davis at the end of April and began their roundabout journey north.

Thompson and Clay, along with their secretary William W. Cleary, ran the blockade out of Wilmington in early May 1864, traveling along the now well-established Confederate network in the colonies. They arrived in Bermuda, where they met with many of the rebellion's colonial supporters and received several useful introductions. Although neither man was Catholic, they found a particularly sympathetic friend in the archbishop of Halifax, Thomas Connolly, an Irishman by birth who happened to be visiting his Bermuda parishes at the time of the commissioners' arrival. Georgiana Walker entertained them at a gathering, along with a group of island notables, again highlighting the advantages of the social cachet that Confederates enjoyed in much of colonial high society.[26]

Thompson and Clay took passage on the British mail steamer from St. George's to Halifax on May 16 and arrived in Nova Scotia after a short passage.[27] They received a warm welcome from the city's pro-Confederate luminaries, including Connolly, who had preceded them to Halifax, and Benjamin Wier. The time spent socializing bore promising fruit, as Connolly wrote them a letter of introduction and an appeal to the Catholics of British North America to aid their mission. Connolly praised the Confederate cause as "command[ing] the respect and sympathy of the world" and called for "the attention and kindly services of every Catholic Bishop and Priest and layman with whom [Clay and Thompson] may come in contact."[28] Clay, hampered by illness, lingered in Halifax for two weeks while Thompson moved on to Canada, opening bank accounts in Montreal and Toronto to hold the mission's funds and taking up residence initially at the Queen's Hotel in Toronto, a popular destination for Confederates in the province.[29] Thompson networked with supportive Canadians upon his arrival, including George Taylor Denison, who hosted and sheltered a variety of Confederate figures during and after the war.[30] Clay and Holcombe met privately with Archbishop Connolly during their delay in Halifax, then moved on and settled initially in Montreal.[31]

George N. Sanders joined Thompson and Clay seemingly without invitation and promptly dragged the Canadian mission into the most famous case of informal diplomacy of the Civil War, the so-called Niagara Falls Conference. Sanders was a fascinating character, whose activities in the mid-nineteenth century prompted contemporaries to call him a "learned pig" and recent historians to describe him as everything from a "confidence man" to a "romantic realist."[32] Contemporaries were sometimes less kind, one such referring to Sanders as "a constant menace" to Confederate plans.[33] Sanders was born in Kentucky in 1812 and spent much of his life moving between Democratic politics and various business schemes.[34] As a leader of the Young America movement, he actively supported European revolutionaries in 1848, where he was rumored to have fought on the streets of Paris, and he oversaw a plan to export surplus arms from the Mexican-American War to support the uprisings on the continent. During a brief stint as U.S. consul in London in 1854, he urged the assassination of European monarchs, particularly Napoleon III, and the creation of a steam-powered guillotine. His excesses prompted the Senate not to confirm his nomination, thus removing him from office.[35]

During the Civil War, Sanders spent most of his time abroad hatching various schemes to procure weaponry for the Confederacy and money for himself. He also maintained his political activism, penning missives in which he defended a proslavery vision of states' rights at home as zealously as he had republicanism in Europe, with similarly poor results.[36] When he encountered Clay in Canada, Sanders drew him into a scheme to propose peace negotiations with the Union. Clay had learned of the scheme from afar, and at first dismissed it as "silly" and fervently wished that Sanders were in "Europe, Asia, or Africa" instead.[37] Thompson, deeply engaged with his plans for influencing Democratic politics in the West, declined to join, but Clay, homesick, credulous, and happy to finally have someone to "do the bargaining and bartering" for him, agreed, sweeping aside concerns that Sanders officially represented nobody but himself. Sanders ignored the fact that Clay, even though he was styled a "commissioner," had no authority of any kind to enter into negotiations, dragging him, along with Holcombe, into proposing peace discussions to the Lincoln administration via Horace Greeley, the influential publisher of the *New York Tribune*.

Sanders drew Greeley into the affair by blatantly misleading him as to the position and authority that he, Clay, and Holcombe possessed. In early July 1864, William "Colorado" Jewett, a Sanders associate as well as a swindler and political promoter, sent Greeley a letter claiming that the Confederate "ambassadors" in Canada held "full and complete powers for a peace."[38] Whether Jewett invented these powers himself or took his information from Sanders is not clear, but falsehood in service of the self was familiar territory for Jewett, whom a Colorado editor once described as having "diarrhoea of words and constipation of ideas."[39] Jewett, though born in Maine, sympathized with the South and spent a great deal of time in the early years of the war proposing peace and mediation plans to anyone in the North who would listen and many more who would not. He traveled to Europe in 1862 on a freelance diplomatic quest to gain intervention or mediation in the Civil War by the continent's monarchs. Jewett failed of course, and he returned to the

United States late in the year to continue promoting his peace plans through a blizzard of self-published pamphlets. He gained the attention of Horace Greeley in this way, who appeared to have a much more positive impression of Jewett than most others who encountered the man. Jewett spent the next two years floundering back and forth across the Atlantic and in British North America while appealing to uninterested and increasingly annoyed officials to adopt his latest schemes for mediation, one of which, a proposal from Louis Napoleon for French mediation in early 1863, had seized Greeley's imagination but went nowhere.[40] The opportunity from Sanders to, at long last, set up a peace mission must have seemed heaven-sent to Jewett, who by 1864 had become a firm Copperhead and correspondent of Clement Vallandigham.[41]

Thus did one self-appointed diplomat, Sanders, use another, Jewett, to foist a negotiation onto the president of the United States. Jewett's career of peace promotion, however incompetent, led him to Greeley, and it was the editor and Republican power broker who persuaded Lincoln to at least send an emissary to learn what the Confederates proposed.[42] Greeley traveled with John Hay, Lincoln's private secretary, to Niagara to hear what Sanders, Clay, and Holcombe had to say, arriving on July 17. Hay carried a missive from Lincoln addressed "To Whom It May Concern" that gave the conditions under which he would consider peace.[43] The negotiations, if they even deserve the title, went nowhere, just as they would months later near Hampton Roads, Virginia. They foundered on the implacable insistence by Lincoln that any peace must occur on the basis of reunification and recognize the abolition of slavery. After four days and only one brief face-to-face meeting between Hay and Holcombe, the "negotiations" ended amid accusations of bad faith.[44] Sanders and Clay supplied, through Jewett, selected correspondence to the Associated Press that made it appear as though Lincoln, in his "To Whom It May Concern" letter, had changed the terms of negotiation misleadingly, and painted him as a warmonger wholly opposed to peace, no matter the cost. They included a letter, obviously intended for public consumption, which hoped the Northern public would be inspired "to recall the abused authority and vindicate the outraged civilization of their country."[45] Greeley, in an attempt to allay accusations that he had interfered in Union diplomacy without authority, published additional materials related to the events at Niagara, including Lincoln's letter. In an indication of his rift with Lincoln over the affair, he printed the letters from Sanders in the *Tribune* without addressing their misleading context.

Historians have been largely united in labeling the Niagara Falls Conference a fiasco for the Union, and most argue that the fallout was a diplomatic and political success, to varying extents, for the Confederacy.[46] In terms of public opinion, Robin Winks argues that the failure of the Lincoln administration to respond to Confederate charges of insincerity tended to hurt its standing with Canadians, and the extended press coverage of the affair brought the Confederate presence in Canada to widespread attention in the North.[47] The Confederate aim, however, was to influence the Northern public and the Democratic Party away from Lincoln and toward peace. For Northern war skeptics, especially Peace Democrats, the Niagara negotiations provided potent ammunition for their campaign against Lincoln and the Republicans. A Copperhead newspaper feared that "tens of thousands of white men must yet bite the dust to allay the negro mania of the President," while Hay and John Nicolay, Lincoln's other private secretary, years later admitted that the Confederate letter proved "a not ineffective document in a heated political campaign."[48] Lincoln, drawn by Sanders and Clay into an explicit embrace of abolition as a peace condition, risked alienating people, including some Republicans, who were as yet unwilling to fight explicitly for the enslaved.

The Niagara Falls Conference highlighted at once the potential and the peril of the Confederacy's expansion of informal diplomacy. Sanders, Clay, and the others could propose peace negotiations with the Union precisely because they were away from Richmond and the control of Davis and Congress, regardless of whether the talks happened in good faith or as part of a plan to embarrass Lincoln and the Republicans. Davis, to the frustration of prominent critics like Vice President Alexander Stephens and Georgia governor Joseph Brown, had steadfastly refused to make peace overtures on any terms.[49] The commission's very distance from Richmond made the Niagara Falls Conference possible. By exaggerating the commissioners' authority, Jewett and Sanders torpedoed any chance at real negotiations before they even began, yet Sanders, Clay, and Holcombe managed to turn the affair into a public embarrassment for the Lincoln administration, giving the Confederacy a propaganda victory and handing Peace Democrats an easy way to accuse Lincoln of bloodthirsty duplicity. In this respect, it must be considered a success. For a negligible cost, the Confederate formal and informal representatives in Canada brought widespread attention to the notion that Lincoln, not the South, was the opponent of peace, and that he would carry on his war for abolition to the last extremity. The only recourse for Northern men who sought peace was the ballot or the bullet. With the main Union armies locked in bloody stalemates before Atlanta and Petersburg, this proved to be a persuasive argument, and Lincoln himself despaired of reelection until battlefield success buoyed his chances later in August.

Despite the short-term success, the Canadian mission's lack of coordination with any kind of coherent national policy objectives undermined Confederate efforts at formal diplomacy. The Niagara negotiations took the government in Richmond by surprise, and reactions across the Confederacy were mixed. Davis himself reduced the potency of the Niagara conference's portrayal of Lincoln as an unyielding tyrant by issuing similarly stringent terms to unofficial peace feelers offered by two Union representatives in mid-July. Davis took the bait, telling the men, in a statement aimed at both Union and Confederate audiences, that peace without Confederate independence and withdrawal of Union forces was impossible, and that the Confederacy would fight on, even "if we have to see every Southern plantation sacked, and every Southern city in flames."[50] Stephen Mallory hoped that Lincoln's peace preconditions might yield internal benefits against peace agitators like "our weak brothers in N.C. and Geo.," who, he hoped, "cannot fail to see that at present[,] peace with Lincoln means degradation."[51] Looking abroad, Judah P. Benjamin still believed that international recognition, even without intervention, could hand the Confederacy victory. Perhaps the Niagara Falls Conference fit with the mission of influencing Democratic politics in the Old Northwest and convincing European observers that the Confederacy would accept a reasonable peace, but enabling loose cannons like Sanders ensured that even Confederate officials on the scene had only limited control over the informal operations on the Union's periphery. This became increasingly clear in the coming months amid a parade of uncoordinated and largely illegal attacks from British territory.

While Sanders dragged Clay, Greeley, and Lincoln into the morass at Niagara Falls, Jacob Thompson and a network of Confederates and Copperheads worked to undermine Northern politics in anticipation of the upcoming Democratic National Convention in Chicago. Thompson's plan consisted of three potentially conflicting lines of operation. He planned to fund or even purchase sympathetic newspapers in order to influence public opinion. Simultaneously, Confederate operatives working for Thompson

George N. Sanders, self-appointed Confederate emissary and operative in Canada, photographed in Montreal in 1864. Credit: William Notman, "George N. Sanders, Montreal, QC, 1864," I-13580.1, McCord Stewart Museum.

were to provide funds, arms, and advice to subversive groups associated with the Democratic Party, particularly secret societies like the Order of American Knights and its successor, the Sons of Liberty. Finally, Thompson hoped to coordinate direct action against prisoner-of-war camps in the Old Northwest—like Camp Douglas in Chicago—to free a large body of Confederate soldiers that could either fight its way to freedom or support a Copperhead uprising.[52]

This "Northwest Conspiracy," as it was later dubbed, was in a sense a large-scale, more ambitious attempt at the sort of informal, substate diplomacy that served the Confederacy so well in the Bahamas, Bermuda, and Nova Scotia. Thompson and his lieutenants—particularly Capt. Thomas Henry Hines, a Kentucky cavalry officer from John Hunt Morgan's former command, dispatched to assist the Canadian mission—sought to leverage local self-interest and discontent into diplomatic and military advantage for the Confederacy. In this case, however, both the objective and the opposition were vastly more formidable. Henry Adderley was not at risk of being hanged for aiding the Confederacy in Nassau, and direct Crown authority was rather sparse there in any event. The Northwest, by contrast, fairly swarmed with Union authority, particularly through the provost marshal system that had been established to support and enforce conscription across the North. Provost marshal officials—and their hired detectives—also engaged in widespread surveillance in order to suppress sabotage, dissent, and similar behavior.[53] The Confederacy's supporters risked arrest, exile, or possibly execution if caught. The Confederate mission faced enormous challenges, and for it to succeed, it would have to cultivate dedicated support among at least a portion of the Northwest's populace.

Thompson's main avenue of influence with peace and separatist groups in the Northwest was through Democratic politicians like Clement Vallandigham. Vallandigham had been living in Windsor, Canada West, just across from Detroit, for nearly a year following his exile from Union territory and his brief unhappy sojourn in the Confederacy. He retained substantial sway in Democratic politics and remained the leader and most prominent member of the Peace Democrats—the faction of the party opposed to continuing the war for any reason. In June 1864, Thompson traveled to Windsor and met with Vallandigham to discuss his objectives and coordinate their efforts for the coming elections.[54] Although pilloried in the Republican press as little better than a traitor, Vallandigham refused to go along with Thompson's preferred objective—an independent Northwestern Confederacy. However, he accepted Thompson's offer of funds and even arms for groups affiliated with the Democratic Party as an augmentation for his own plans to return to Ohio. Vallandigham expected to be arrested upon his return, perhaps becoming a martyr and catalyst for a movement toward peace—or, if the federal response were too heavy-handed, an uprising.[55] This was less of a commitment than Thompson and Hines had hoped for, but they moved ahead with their plans.

There is only limited evidence as to the extent of the Confederate effort to influence Northwestern public opinion via newspapers, so it is difficult to assess the effectiveness of this approach. Clay, Thompson, Holcombe, and to a lesser extent Sanders and Tucker met in Canada with prominent Peace Democrats, including politicians and at least one newspaper editor, Washington McLean of the *Cincinnati Enquirer*. Holcombe also reported that they met with Ohio Congressman George Pendleton, former governor Washington Hunt of New York, New York Democrats Benjamin Wood and Leigh Richmond, former Buchanan administration attorney general and secretary of state Judge Jeremiah S. Black, Pennsylvania U.S. senator Charles Buckalew, former California governor and U.S. senator John Weller, Judge Joshua Bullitt of Kentucky, and Indiana Copperhead Col. John C. Walker, along with a "crowd of less distinguished persons."[56] Some of these politicians also presumably had influence over sympathetic newspapers. The extent of the purchasing or bribery campaign toward newspapers is unknown, owing to the destruction or loss of the relevant records and the clandestine nature of such a project.[57] Holcombe indicated in November 1864 that such efforts had been underway, and he thought that they could be effective if continued. He felt the Confederates in Canada should "employ money without stint to give this brooding resentment the proportions of anarchy and civil strife.... As far as practicable, [they should] subsidize leading presses, and through the ordinary channel of newspapers, as well as of campaign documents, enlighten and inflame the public mind."[58] In the postwar judgment of Hines, the scheme failed, though he blamed greedy war profiteers and Republicans rather than any particular failings on the part of Copperhead editors.[59]

Alongside the campaign to influence or purchase newspapers, the Confederate mission in Canada also coordinated a widespread campaign to fund, arm, and radicalize dissident organizations in the Old Northwest. Secret societies operating alongside or within the Democratic Party had long been active in the region. The most famous group in the immediate antebellum era was the Knights of the Golden Circle (KGC), a largely Democratic society with strong proslavery and expansionist aims. However, the KGC fractured badly during the early years of the Civil War, and by 1863 it was largely defunct. Another group rose in its stead: the Order of American Knights

(OAK), founded in Missouri in 1863. The group was not a direct descendant of the KGC, although there was some overlap of membership between them. Union authorities, for their part, worked to tie the groups together in the public mind in order to make them appear more dangerous and treasonable.[60] The OAK claimed an enormous membership approaching half a million, and their leaders led Thompson and Hines to believe that they were ready to consider armed insurrection if their political efforts failed.

The Confederates in Canada should have been a little less credulous about these claims. OAK members happily accepted Confederate funds in return for little more than vague assurances that they would cooperate against the Lincoln government. Copperhead groups drew the OAK into close association with the Democratic Party in early 1864, renaming it the Sons of Liberty (SOL) and installing Clement Vallandigham as its head. Political leaders associated with the SOL met regularly with Thompson in Windsor and Toronto, and with Holcombe, Clay, Sanders, and Tucker in St. Catharines, Niagara, and Montreal.[61] Politically, the goal of both the Confederates and their Democratic interlocutors was to prevent the nomination of George B. McClellan for president and put forth Vallandigham or another Peace Democrat in his stead.

Thompson tried to link his efforts in the Northwest with European diplomacy, penning a letter to Mason and Slidell advising them of the political situation there and requesting that they once again urge the British and French to intervene. Thompson, going beyond his mandate, made a naked appeal to geopolitical interest by assuring the two powers of the safety of Canada and imperial Mexico if they aided the Confederacy, while hinting that a weakened Confederacy might be forced into common cause with the Union and join with them in vigorously enforcing the Monroe Doctrine.[62] Clay drafted his own missive along the same lines, though he considered the Confederacy "without friends among the nations of the Earth" and the governments of England and France "practically our enemies." His letter also included the disturbing suggestion that wholesale mass murder of slaves might become necessary if European powers allowed the war to continue. The Confederacy might have to, "ere long, commence *ridding ourselves* of the male slaves above fifteen, to save our innocent women and children from destruction. It is a horrible thought, at which my heart revolts, but less horrible than the fate of the victims of their brutal passions, incited by our white foes of more cunning heads and more devilish hearts. Besides, their extermination is inevitable if the war continue[s] a few years more."⁶³ While clumsily drafted, the letters indicate that Thompson and Clay were aware that their mission was by necessity both diplomatic and political, and Clay's genocidal rhetoric hints at the unraveling of norms. They still held out hope for intervention and seem to have had little inkling that their presence and action on British territory had the potential to undermine the already slim prospects for it. Nevertheless, as long as they refrained from violence, the Confederate commission attracted little attention from Crown authorities.

The Confederates enjoyed some success in soliciting political cooperation with Copperheads. Vallandigham returned from exile in June 1864 to rally Peace Democrats before the start of the convention. To his surprise, federal authorities left him alone, spoiling his opportunity for further martyrdom. The Confederates, however, overestimated the strength of both the peace movement within the party and the stomach of the affiliated secret societies for actual violence.⁶⁴ The Peace Democrats, though somewhat successful in influencing the party platform at the convention, failed to prevent the nomination of George B. McClellan for president. Clay helped draft planks for the party platform that likewise went down to defeat, thus failing to bind McClellan to seek a negotiated end to the war. The long-planned paramilitary operation, coordinated by Hines and his colleagues, likewise failed to materialize. The relative handful of Confederate soldiers involved, sent by Thompson, could not hope to overwhelm the garrison at Camp Douglas from the outside and free the prisoners of war held there without the legions of Copperhead supporters that had been promised to them. When the Copperheads never arrived, Hines called off the attack, and the group dispersed into other endeavors, including a successful campaign of steamboat arson.⁶⁵

It was not a coincidence that the Confederate commissioners chose to use the KGC—with its deep links to antebellum filibustering, expansionism, and illicit violence—and its heirs in their plots to subvert the Union in 1864. It was another piece in the mosaic of unconventional, private, and illegal elements to the Confederate way of warfare and diplomacy in the colonies. Thompson, Clay, and the Confederates leaned on the OAK and the SOL out of expedience and their own relative weakness, but there remained the lingering preference for privatized action that characterized the fringes of the war. This was, in intention if not execution, a filibustering expedition, meant to create a new nation—in the form of either a diminished United States or a new Northwestern confederation.

Following the failure of the combined political and paramilitary plot in Chicago and the news of Union military success in Atlanta and beyond in August and September 1864, Clay and Thompson turned away sharply from their original mission. Having failed to achieve substantial results by political influence, the Confederate government representatives in Canada embraced direct action and violence. The two commissioners, still operating from separate locations, entertained proposals for a wide variety of plans to attack the Union, but they leaned, at least initially in the fall of 1864, toward operations that they could somewhat defensibly claim to be legitimate acts of warfare. Thompson's attention turned to reviving the long-standing plan to liberate Confederate prisoners of war at Johnson's Island, Ohio, while Clay contemplated raids across the land frontier, ultimately settling on the town of St. Albans, Vermont. Thompson also sponsored efforts of "incendiaries" to burn steamboats along the Mississippi River, which met with some success. In the following weeks, a wider arson campaign sprang up and struck across the north, from Brooklyn to St. Louis and as far south as New Orleans, and various arsonists presented themselves to Thompson seeking reward, though he declined to pay most for lack of proof.[66] The resulting attacks showed how effective such hybrid raiding could be, but they also demonstrated how badly the Confederates misjudged their political and diplomatic position within British North America. Informal diplomacy and privatized warfare were about to unravel into crime and atrocity. It remained an open question whether Canadians would be willing or able to suppress them.

CHAPTER SEVEN

"Schemes of Deviltry Concocted in Canada"
*Public Causes and Privatized Violence
from Canada, 1864–1865*

> Men say that our hearts are with them—
> That their loss or gain we share;
> That 'twixt friend or foe if we strike no blow,
> It is that we do not dare.
> Men know that their foes are ours—
> That their cause is all our own;
> And the breath of shame will blight our name
> If the South should fall alone.
> —"Sua Res Agitur," printed in the *Evening
> Telegraph* (Montreal), February 23, 1865

AFTER FAILING TO gain Peace Democrats the party's nomination, the Confederate network in Canada turned its energy and resources increasingly toward paramilitary action rather than influence and diplomacy.[1] These operations employed a combination of men who ran the spectrum from those who could plausibly claim to be bona fide soldiers, to British subjects, to people who in modern times might be referred to as stochastic terrorists—lone wolves, taking action on their own responsibility but inspired by the public and private goals of their cause. As the Confederate military and political situation grew more desperate, its adherents in the colonies did as well, with some embracing Clement C. Clay's genocidal rhetoric, and others changing their goals from military utility to revenge. The September 1864 raid on Johnson's Island, Ohio, represents one end of the continuum of legitimacy for Confederate operations out of Canada. It was bookended, seven months later, with a bullet to the head of the president of the United States.

The Johnson's Island raid is notable because it represented the Confederate government's embrace of the fusion privateering tactics pioneered by the attacks on the *Chesapeake* and the *Joseph L. Gerrity*, as discussed in chapter 5. In this case the attackers were mostly Confederate citizens, rather than British civilians, although Bennet G. Burley, a Briton and future pioneering war correspondent, joined in the attack.[2] Jacob Thompson chose John Yates Beall to lead the attempt.[3] Beall had experience in this kind of raiding, having led a partisan band in attacking Union shipping along the Potomac River in 1863, and he had connections among the Confederate exile community in Canada. Beall fled to Canada in 1862 while recuperating from wounds received as a Confederate infantryman in Virginia. He lived in Dundas, Canada West, for several months and made the acquaintance of Confederate exiles and escapees in the area.[4] The choice of Beall shows that the Confederate leadership preferred someone comfortable with irregular raiding—the first, aborted raid on the island featured a party made up entirely of regularly commissioned officers and sailors, but the next attempt used irregulars despite the availability of numerous young naval officers sitting idly in the South and abroad. Although styling himself as a captain, Beall held only an acting master's commission in the Confederate navy, which he obtained by appealing to Mallory after being invalided out of the Confederate army, and Beall had no experience of any kind in regular naval operations.[5] He was an officer in the mold of Mallory's volunteer navy—self-motivated, unpaid, and steeped in irregular warfare.

The plan for the raid was very similar to those previously proposed: a group of Confederates would seize a steamer on Lake Erie and, in conjunction with co-conspirators on the ground in Sandusky led by Charles H. Cole, attack the USS *Michigan*, moored at Johnson's Island; capture the warship; and liberate the prisoners on the island. The freed prisoners would then have a choice: fight their way south to freedom, escape to Canada, or join with the raiders in a campaign to wreak havoc along the American coast of the Great Lakes. Like most of the irregular attacks launched from the colonies, this plan displayed a variety of amateurish shortcomings. Most glaringly, the entire plot hinged on the ability of Cole, who falsely claimed to be an officer in the Confederate navy, to single-handedly distract or disable the officers of the

Michigan. Cole had lied to Thompson about his past—he may have been a Confederate soldier at some point, but he was not a naval officer—and he spent Thompson's money liberally on himself and a female companion posing as his wife while scouting Sandusky and Johnson's Island. His plan to distract the officers with a party, and perhaps to drug their food or drink, had virtually no chance of success, and in any event Cole appeared unlikely to endanger himself if he could help it.[6] Additionally, Beall had made no plans for fueling or provisioning the captured steamer, and there seemed to have been little consideration of what to do in the event Cole failed to incapacitate the *Michigan*'s officers. Nevertheless, the operation had the potential for success if the attackers acted boldly and achieved the element of surprise.

Despite these hopes, surprise was beyond their reach. As in the previous attempt to attack Johnson's Island, an informant betrayed the mission. On September 18, the provost marshal in Detroit learned of the attack just hours before it launched and alerted the garrison at the prison in Sandusky by telegraph. On September 19, Beall and his men boarded the steamer *Philo Parsons* at Windsor and two other towns along the Canadian shore, with their arms hidden in a trunk. They seized the vessel while underway on Lake Erie and raised the Confederate flag over the Great Lakes for the first and last time. After a comedy of errors, including a return to Middle Bass Island for fuel and the seizure and scuttling of a second steamer that came alongside them unsuspectingly, Beall and his party of roughly twenty men arrived off Sandusky after dark, awaiting the signal from Cole that the *Michigan*'s crew had been taken care of. After several hours of waiting, Beall's men mutinied and forced him to abandon the project. This may have saved their lives: the *Michigan*'s officers had arrested Cole earlier that evening, and the vessel was cleared for action, waiting to ambush Beall. The Confederates steamed back to Windsor, plundered some cargo and money from the ship and crew, and scuttled the ship under the watchful eye of a Canadian customs officer. All the Confederates escaped except for the bumbling Cole.[7]

The Confederate government, not for the last time, found itself vouching for the actions of its self-styled agents after the fact. The Union commander at Johnson's Island ordered Cole held as a spy rather than a normal prisoner of war—an understandable course of action given Cole's behavior. This prompted Thompson and Clay to address a joint letter to the camp commandant vouching for Cole's status as a regular soldier—they did not seem aware that Cole had lied to them about being an officer. The commissioners also sent a dispatch to Richmond, begging Davis to intercede on Cole's behalf. Davis directed Seddon to "let all practicable efforts be made in behalf of Mr. Cole" through the prisoner exchange cartel.[8] Beall also defended the raid as legitimate in a letter intended for a Canadian journal, claiming that it did not violate Canadian neutrality or the laws of war, although his statements about the raid not being planned or carried out from Canadian soil were patently false.[9] Ultimately Cole escaped trial and execution, the latest grifter and thief spared by government intervention, but he languished in custody until well after the war ended. Beall, Burley, and the others escaped capture, at least for the moment.

The raid had been doomed before it began by Cole and the informant, but it caused an uproar along the lake frontier and ratcheted up diplomatic tension between Britain and the United States. Cities from Buffalo to Chicago prepared frantically to repulse a Confederate attack, arming makeshift vessels with field artillery in violation of the Rush-Bagot limits. The governor-general of British North America, Lord Monck, reported the attacks to London with barely concealed frustration. In March 1864, amid other rumors of raiding on the Lakes, Monck had repeatedly asked for a patrol vessel of some sort for policing the lake frontier in anticipation of just such an event and had been rebuffed by Edward Cardwell, the colonial secretary. Other staff in the Colonial Office proposed a variety of prescient measures to combat the threat, including proposing a law allowing the expulsion of foreigners who threatened neutrality, but Cardwell declined to permit any further action.[10] Now Monck faced the prospect of an active force of Confederates, abetted in some instances by his own colonists, abusing Canadian neutrality to attack the United States, and he had few tools available to suppress their actions. Monck openly worried about maintaining peace between Britain and the United States in the presence of "a large number of refugees from the Southern States of America—hostile in spirit to the Government of the United States and prepared to give expression to that hostility in overt acts—coupled with the entire absence of any power on the part of the British Authorities to maintain an effective police on the British portion of the Lakes."[11] British concern with preventing conflict over the Rush-Bagot Agreement tied Monck's hands, and that restraint now threatened a breach of the peace because Canadian authorities lacked the tools to deal with an unruly Confederate "refugee" community bent on taking action. By the letter of the law, the Canadians could only prosecute violations of neutrality after the fact—

they had little power to interfere with or expel troublemakers before they acted.

A month later, Monck's fears were realized. On October 21, a party of about twenty men dressed in civilian clothes gathered in St. Albans, Vermont. Their leader, the young Kentuckian Bennett H. Young, announced that the town was under the power of the Confederate States, and his men robbed several banks and set fire to structures across the town. The townspeople raised the alarm, and the Confederates exchanged gunfire with some citizens, killing one before fleeing north with around $200,000 in stolen currency. A posse of soldiers, police, and civilians pursued the raiders up to and across the border with Canada East. The Americans captured one raider within Canada, but a British officer persuaded them to turn the captive over to him before the posse could beat their captive to death. British soldiers and Canadian police responded quickly and rounded up fourteen of the raiders, who appear to have thought themselves safe from capture within Canada and made little effort to hide themselves. The Canadian government sent the captured men, along with $90,000 in recovered money, to Montreal to face trial.[12] The remaining raiders escaped with the balance of the stolen money.

The raid was the work of Clay and Sanders, who embraced the suggestion of Young that Union border cities were vulnerable to attack. Young, who first met Clay and Holcombe upon their arrival in Halifax in the spring, had been persuasive enough that Clay sent him to Richmond to procure a commission from Secretary of War James Seddon. Young returned with a commission and joined in scouting for potential targets along the border region. In arranging the St. Albans attack, Seddon, Clay, and Sanders displayed the same interpretation of neutrality that underlay the Johnson's Island raid and mirrored antebellum defenses of filibustering. Because the raiders were all Confederate citizens, Clay, Sanders, and Young claimed that the attack was a legitimate act of war, ordered by belligerent authorities, and that there was nothing illegal about launching it from British territory and retreating thereto with their plunder. Once again, they alleged that the operation had the express approval of Davis and Seddon, and Clay and Sanders both wrote to Richmond, begging for documents, presumably postdated, that would bear out their story and prevent extradition for robbery and murder. The Confederate authorities in Richmond once again complied, lending their increasingly tenuous legitimacy to the attack.[13] A clerk in the Confederate War Department, clearly inured to his department forging such documents, remarked, "I doubt if such written orders are in existence—but no matter!"[14] The embrace of cross-border raiding showed the depth of Confederate misunderstanding of neutrality, as well as their miscalculation as to British and Canadian tolerance for violating the peace on the frontier.

This assertion of legitimacy by the Confederates in Canada was without merit, although the repeated lenience shown to pro-Confederate attackers across the hemisphere may have encouraged them in their legal approach. Certainly, both Clay and Thompson knew that their activities at the very least bordered on illegal, as their sometimes mutilated and destroyed correspondence indicates.[15] Lord Russell asked the Law Officers of the Crown to assess the St. Albans raid and the Canadian response, and their judgment was unequivocal. Operating with scant details, they ruled that the raid was legal only if the mission had not been planned or supported on British territory and if the attackers had not set foot on British (or Canadian) soil before the attack.[16] None of the raids and attacks sponsored or inspired by Clay and Thompson from Canadian soil met these requirements. Only the unwillingness or inability (through lack of evidence) of colonial courts to enforce the queen's neutrality proclamation had saved the likes of Braine, Locke, and Thomas Hogg from prison. Confederate abuse of this gap in enforcement threatened the peace along the Union's northern and maritime frontiers and eventually drove the British and Canadian governments to a far more robust suppression of pro-Confederate activities than in any other colony.

The Confederates and their friends still enjoyed some success with the colonial courts. While the Court of Queen's Bench in Toronto delivered Bennet Burley, of the Johnson's Island raid, for extradition to face trial in Ohio for robbery, the St. Albans raiders lived a life of near celebrity in Montreal. In the days following the attack, Canadian police and magistrates rounded up most of the raiders, including Young, and transferred them to Montreal to face an extradition hearing. Their lawyers requested time to obtain evidence of their positions as Confederate soldiers, and Judge Charles J. Coursol set a hearing for mid-December to allow a courier the opportunity to travel back and forth to Richmond. When the court resumed on December 13, Coursol—in a decision one observer called an "unaccountable and unprecedented failure of justice"—declared that colonial courts had no jurisdiction in extradition cases, and he set the prisoners free that very afternoon.[17] Coursol was wrong, but the Confederate raiders skipped town long before his decision could be overturned.

The captured St. Albans raiders, posing before the Montreal jail door. George Sanders, who coordinated their legal defense and escape, can be seen standing at rear center. Credit: William Notman, "St. Albans Raiders at the Jail Door, Montreal, QC, 1864," I-14018.1, McCord Stewart Museum.

Montreal chief of police Guillaume Lamothe stood ready to aid the newly freed men. No sooner had the judgment been announced than he handed the $90,000 in stolen money over to their representative, John Porterfield.[18] Porterfield, a Southern banker living in Montreal, was widely known to be involved with the Confederate diaspora there, and he had directly taken part in a scheme funded by Thompson to use gold purchases to collapse Northern finances.[19] Porterfield, for his part, had been introduced to Lamothe just the day prior by the ubiquitous George N. Sanders, who was in Montreal coordinating the prisoners' defense. Incredibly, Lamothe gave up not only the money captured with the raiders but also several thousand dollars of stolen St. Albans money that other parties had handed over to the court for safekeeping. The raiders thus left Montreal with more money than they had at the time of their capture. Another judge immediately issued a warrant for the prisoners' rearrest, but Lamothe purposely dawdled, giving Young and his compatriots a chance to flee or hide. Under pressure from Lord Monck, Canadian authorities worked to recapture the men and money, with mixed success.

Both Coursol and Lamothe were French Canadians and members of the Saint-Jean-Baptiste Society, a Francophone nationalist organization that emerged from the rebellions of 1837–38. The society was sympathetic to the rebellion, and its members helped a wounded St. Albans raider escape capture.[20] Some Quebecois nationalists clearly sympathized with a secession movement, for obvious reasons, even if they did not support slavery. The Catholic Church, as we have seen, also supported the Confederacy in British North America, and sympathetic French-Canadian priests repeatedly helped shelter Confederate fugitives in 1864–65, including John Surratt while he was a suspect in the Lincoln assassination.[21]

The Confederate collaborators paid a price for their help this time. Lamothe faced an immediate and hostile investigation by the city council. He made a variety of excuses for his inaction, but in the face of revelations about his obvious cooperation with the Confederates and his apparent personal liability for the missing money, Lamothe resigned his office on December 17. The city council, after somewhat acrimonious debate, accepted his resignation on January 3, 1865, in a vote divided sharply on ethnic lines—the Anglophone councilors voting unanimously to accept, and the Francophones voting to reject.[22] This split may have reflected Anglo-French tensions in Montreal more than either group's latent support for the Confederacy or

Union, as the *Evening Telegraph*, one of the chief English-language newspapers of the city, was a frequent advocate for the Confederate cause. Lamothe immediately went back to the aid of the escapees, helping to shepherd several out of Montreal and into a hiding place in the forests outside Quebec City, where they remained until Lamothe arranged a ship to carry them to Newfoundland.[23] Judge Coursol also faced consequences for his indefensible ruling. George-Etienne Cartier, attorney general for Canada East, ordered an inquiry into Coursol's conduct and removed him from the bench until it concluded. The investigation lasted through most of 1865, but it ultimately found insufficient evidence to further punish Coursol.

The diplomatic consequences in the following months were severe. In dire straits as Sherman tore his way across Georgia and Grant extended his grip around Petersburg and Richmond, the Confederacy launched a last, desperate bid for recognition. Davis sent Duncan Kenner to Europe with authority to offer the abolition of slavery in return for recognition. Kenner received his orders on December 27, 1864, and the Confederate courier network between Maryland and Canada helped move him covertly to New York to take passage for Europe.[24] In the meantime, Lord Russell took the unusual step of summoning Confederate envoy James Mason and demanding a halt to violations of Her Majesty's neutrality. The St. Albans raid and the bungled trial in Montreal poisoned any remaining hopes of success for the Kenner mission.

Confederate standing with Britain did not improve when James Mason met with Palmerston in March 1865 to present the Kenner proposal.[25] By then, word had reached Europe of the passage of the Thirteenth Amendment abolishing slavery, which weakened any appeal that the Confederate offer of gradual emancipation might have had, and Palmerston firmly denied that slavery was what prevented British recognition.[26] Lord Russell meanwhile ordered a legal review of the Confederate presence in North America, and the finding was uniformly harsh, particularly toward Thompson and Clay, whose presence as an "agent resident in Canada, for such [warlike] purposes, is a willful offence by that govt against the neutrality of this country, for which no excuse or palliation can be suggested."[27] Imperial authorities on both sides of the Atlantic had run out of patience with the specious Confederate interpretation of the limits of neutrality.

In Canada, the government at last took substantial measures to prevent a repetition of the raid. Lord Monck called out the militia to patrol the border regions, and he recalled the legislature ahead of schedule in January 1865 to respond to the crisis. The provincial legislature finally passed a bill along the lines of that proposed in March 1864 by the Colonial Office, and Monck raced to Quebec to promulgate it into effect on February 6. Known as the Alien Act, or in some publications as the "frontier outrages act," the law gave the Canadian government temporary and wide authority to round up and expel foreigners who threatened to disrupt the peace.[28] At last, Monck, Cartier, and John A. Macdonald—attorney general for Canada West—had the power to get rid of troublemakers before they struck rather than after the fact. Monck refused to meet with Clay and Thompson, who showed up at his door in an attempt to explain their actions, and he doggedly pursued rumors of further Confederate operations.[29]

This diligent pursuit disrupted an attempt by Thompson and Beall to seize or sink the USS *Michigan* using a locally purchased steamer, the *Georgian*, and in November 1864, Canadian detectives arrested Beall's associate Bennet Burley in Guelph, Canada West, as he prepared munitions for the raid. Thompson attempted to submit affidavits from Jefferson Davis and Stephen Mallory as evidence of Burley's status as a Confederate serviceman in order to save him, but this time the Canadians were unconvinced.[30] A Toronto court declared that the September hijacking of the *Philo Parsons* for the attempted raid on Johnson's Island was not a legitimate act of war, in spite of Jacob Thompson's pleas, and thus Burley was eligible for extradition. Monck and Macdonald handed Burley over to the United States under the Webster-Ashburton Treaty in February 1865.[31] Canadian authorities later prosecuted Col. George T. Denison, a Toronto dandy and Confederate sympathizer, under the Foreign Enlistment Act for his role in purchasing the vessel and hiding its true purpose.[32] The relative immunity that pro-Confederates had heretofore enjoyed in British North America had been swept away by early 1865.

Surveillance by Canadian and Union authorities made life miserable for the Confederate commissioners. Clay gave up on plans for further cross-border attacks after the St. Albans raid and prepared to return the Confederacy, essentially handing over the operation in and around Montreal to the increasingly reckless George Sanders. Macdonald, in his capacity as attorney general for Canada West, created a secret detective force to keep tabs on the security of the frontier, although his choice to lead the force, Gilbert McMicken, was a Confederate agent, and Macdonald was just as interested in the activities of the Fenian Brotherhood as he was the Confederates.[33] Nevertheless, in the aftermath of the St. Albans raid, Canadian and American surveillance of Confederate agents became almost suffocating. Thompson complained that the "bane and curse of carrying out anything in this country is surveillance under which we act. Detectives, or those ready to give information, stand at every street corner. Two or three cannot interchange ideas without a reporter." By December, Thompson had given up hope of achieving much by cooperation with Copperhead groups or direct attacks, but he saw promise in a campaign of destruction, arson, and incitement of Northern draft resisters.[34]

While other colonial governments, especially in Bermuda and the Bahamas, remained reluctant to interdict Confederate operations and filibustering, the Canadian government moved, belatedly but firmly, to curb operations from its soil. This clampdown came from two complementary movements: the push for the confederation of British North America, led by the coalition Macdonald government that entered office in 1864, and the military pressure from both the imperial government and (implicitly) a victorious Union Army. The Canadians were under enormous pressure from the War and Colonial Offices in London to pull their weight in their own defense, especially after the debacle of failed militia reforms earlier in the decade.[35] The crackdown on the Confederates was both a boon to and a consequence of the movement toward confederation. Unlike the Bahamas, the political leadership of Canada had more at stake than fleeting blockade-running profits. The imperial government insisted that the Canadians take on a greater share of the financial and military responsibility for their own defense, and the leadership had the ability and willingness to employ thousands of militia and dozens of detectives to suppress the expatriate rebels. There was much greater popular support for the Union in Canada than in the island colonies far to the south, and trade with the United States, bolstered by the Reciprocity Treaty, massively outweighed Canadian interests in blockade running. The Colonial Office, under pressure from Parliament to reduce expenditures related to the colonies, warmly supported the efforts to create a confederation of the British North American provinces as a way to reduce imperial obligations. The Charlottetown and Quebec conferences of September and October 1864, with delegates from each of the provinces in attendance, led to an agreement in principle on a federal union of the provinces. The specter of Union retaliation for Confederate raiding happening concurrently with those meetings

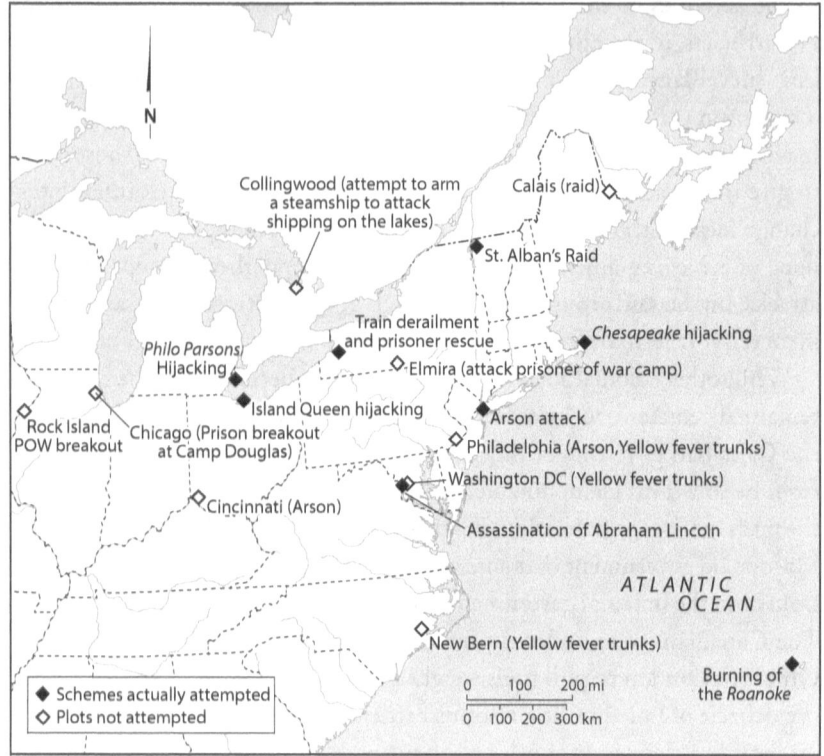

Pro-Confederate Attacks and Plots Linked to British Colonies

gave special impetus to confederation as a means of self-defense, while the militia reforms of 1863 and aggressive, if belated, legislation like the Alien Act gave the Canadians greater practical capabilities to repress bad-faith actions from individuals within or armies beyond their borders. While Bennett Young, George Denison, Guillaume Lamothe, and most Confederate collaborators ultimately escaped prison sentences, their repeated prosecutions contrasted starkly with the impunity enjoyed by pro-Confederate raiders elsewhere in the colonial periphery. As a Union victory became increasingly obvious, the prospect of a colossal, underemployed, and battle-tested army heading northward seemed more and more plausible to Canadian and British observers. The political leadership of Canada was not willing to let distaste for the Americans torpedo their burgeoning national ambitions.

The failure at Johnson's Island and the uproar following the St. Albans raid did not end Confederate efforts to attack the Union from British territory, but they were a watershed in the conduct of the war on the frontier. From that point on, pro-Confederate operations more or less abandoned any pretense at legitimate military action and moved toward retaliation, sabotage, and destruction.[36] Confederate authorities in Richmond and Canada made little effort to coordinate or control the remaining segments of the rapidly disintegrating apparatus that had been built in the colonies, and these men, acting alone or in small groups, carried on their freelance war, which continued in parallel with the more conventional operations sponsored by Clay and Thompson. Having received tacit encouragement to ignore and exploit neutrality and to violate the norms of nineteenth-century warfare, these parties attempted to carry out some of the greatest crimes and atrocities of the war, including the arson of New York City, biological warfare attacks using yellow fever, and the decapitation of the U.S. government. That these attempts largely failed should not obscure the horror that the perpetrators envisioned. The Confederate logic of decentralized, privatized foreign policy enabled and inspired attempts at terrorism that would not be out of place in the twenty-first century, and the events of the winter of 1864–65 strongly suggest that the Confederate government had lost control of its allies and agents in the colonies.[37]

These attacks also reflect the continuing erosion of the norms of nineteenth-century interstate warfare on the North American periphery. By late 1864, the Confederacy and its supporters in the colonies behaved more like a transnational insurgency than a conventional nation-state. The rebellion, which had largely though not exclusively remained within the borders of the United States and observed the forms of nation-state conflict, now featured a diaspora that conducted attacks across international frontiers from neutral territory and used borders as a shield against reprisal.[38] The attack on New York, like a subsequent attempt to kidnap Abraham Lincoln, was planned, funded, and coordinated largely from Canada and executed by men in civilian clothing who carried out their actions clandestinely and afterward sought shelter across international frontiers. Pro-Confederate operatives continued to exploit the border as a safeguard from arrest and interference by Union forces, but they abandoned the pretense of respecting neutrality. The weakness of the Confederate government allowed its citizens to navigate international boundaries and attempt to redefine the acceptable bounds of warfare in a way that was consistent with the American experience of privatized warfare in the Western Hemisphere throughout the century.[39]

The so-called yellow fever plot exemplifies the autonomy and disregard for the norms of warfare that Confederates embraced late in the war. The mastermind of the plot was Luke Pryor Blackburn, an ardent Confederate and prominent physician. Blackburn spent the first years of the war as the chief medical agent for Mississippi, charged with overseeing the health of the state's men in Confederate ranks. After Blackburn was denied a position in the Confederate army in 1863, the governor sent him to British North America to purchase supplies.[40] While in the colonies, Blackburn maintained close associations with other rebels he found there and involved himself in supporting the cause where he could, including testifying in support of the *Chesapeake* pirates during their extradition hearings in New Brunswick. Before the war, Blackburn had earned renown for his work combating yellow fever outbreaks. When the disease struck Bermuda in the summer of 1864, he traveled there to aid the local authorities. He worked with alacrity and disregard for his own safety during the outbreak, which proved particularly severe and lasted most of the summer. On top of praise from local officials for his "valuable assistance" and "humane conduct," the British Admiralty ordered that a gift—an engraved gold watch for Blackburn and a gold bracelet for his wife—be sent to Blackburn in thanks for his aid.[41]

It took some months to arrange the gift, and at last the lords commissioners of the Admiralty sent it on to the Colonial Office, to be forwarded to Blackburn, then known to reside at St. Lawrence Hall in Montreal. Almost immediately another dispatch followed, requesting in anxious terms that the watch be found and detained before it could be sent to Canada or word of its existence could reach the press or American authorities.[42] In the midst of the frantic investigation surrounding the assassination of Abraham Lincoln, American officials discovered a second conspiracy involving Blackburn. Confederates planned to spread yellow fever to Northern cities and coastal concentrations of troops—including New Bern, North Carolina, and Norfolk, Virginia—by sending trunks packed with the infected clothing and bedding of victims from the Bermuda outbreak. An informant in Canada alerted the Union consul in Toronto of the existence of the scheme on April 12, 1865, two days before the assassination. Separately and nearly simultaneously, a Confederate working in Norman S. Walker's office in St. George's approached the U.S. consul and offered information on the still-active plot. The informant, uncomfortable with the horrors planned, gave a very detailed description of several trunks of contaminated clothing, their location in a local boarding house, and their intended destination.[43] A quick investigation revealed that the trunks in question had been packed, stored, and ordered shipped at the behest of Blackburn.[44] The hero of Bermuda was revealed as a monster and a possible co-conspirator in the death of Lincoln.

The attempt to spread yellow fever to Boston, New York, Washington, and elsewhere failed, of course. Yellow fever requires *Aedes aegypti* mosquitoes for transmission from person to person, and soiled clothing and bedding cannot by itself be a vector for the disease. Nevertheless, Blackburn planned his attack using the best understanding of the disease available at the time. Physicians widely believed that yellow fever spread by "fomites," or through "miasma," fungi, or the presence of other diseases, such as malaria.[45] Blackburn would have been better served by directing blockade runners to those ports, as they were the culprits in spreading the devastating outbreak to Bermuda, the Caribbean, and portions of the Atlantic and Gulf coasts of the Confederacy that fall. Blackburn expected that his plan could work, and he engaged several witting and unwitting co-conspirators to accomplish the task, including Southerners hiding in Canada and several residents of Bermuda.

Blackburn enlisted Godfrey Hyams, a Southerner of English birth hiding in Canada, to help execute the scheme. Hyams was willing to help, but he proved unreliable as a co-conspirator in part because he was relatively poor, and Blackburn failed to pay him as he promised. The precise details of the plot remain somewhat uncertain, in part because Hyams may have lied in portions of his testimony and in part because those involved in the plot wished to hide their complicity as much as possible. It is certain, however, that Blackburn prepared at least three, and possibly as many as eleven, trunks of "infected" clothing to be distributed in Northern cities and areas of troop concentration in at least two separate visits to Bermuda. In the early summer of 1864, Hyams delivered a few of the trunks from Halifax as far as Baltimore or Washington and arranged for more to be sent to New Bern, claiming later that Blackburn gave him a "valise" of infected clothing intended for Abraham Lincoln, though Hyams may have fabricated that portion of the tale.[46] New Bern suffered a horrific yellow fever outbreak that summer, which may have led Blackburn to believe his efforts had worked. Hyams also testified that Jacob Thompson paid him $100 for expenses related to transporting the supposedly infectious trunks on behalf of Blackburn, linking Confederate government funds to the plot.[47] From the testimony of various witnesses, Hyams was regarded by the Southern community in Toronto as a contemptible figure, and Blackburn seemed to view him as an expendable agent, a "cock-eyed Jew from Toronto" who would be mourned by few if the fever claimed him during his mission.[48]

Curiously, Blackburn may have engaged the help of Joseph Hayne Rainey, a free man of color, to transport that first load of clothing from Bermuda to Halifax. Rainey was born a slave in Georgetown, South Carolina, but his father, a barber, saved enough money to buy his family's freedom while Joseph was young. Rainey lived and worked mainly in South Carolina, but after a stint as a forced laborer on Confederate fortifications in 1861, he took up a position as a steward on a blockade runner before settling in Bermuda with his wife. Rainey is best known for his career after the war, when he served as the first Black member of the House of Representatives, but he spent the war years operating a prosperous barber shop that catered to the blockade-running set in St. George's. Rainey, apparently well-known and liked around St. George's and Hamilton, made the acquaintance of Blackburn during the yellow fever outbreak in 1864. It appears that Rainey traveled with Blackburn to Halifax when the doctor made his departure from the islands, and he returned home to Bermuda several weeks later. When the yellow fever plot was exposed, two white Bermudians alleged that Rainey distributed trunks of fever clothing in New York and received a sizable payment from Blackburn for his services, which paid for his barber shop in Hamilton. The authorities in Bermuda did not find sufficient evidence to charge Rainey with any crime, as his accusers were themselves attempting to deflect blame in the matter, but his travels with Blackburn and his whereabouts after arriving in Halifax remained unexplained.

Rainey's involvement is a reminder that although, on balance, they strongly supported the Union, the free Black populace in the colonies was not always a monolithic obstacle to the Confederate cause, especially in places where the powerful sympathized with the rebellion. In Canada, where many Black residents had direct ties to family in the United States, a huge proportion of the eligible population crossed into the United States and joined the Union army.[49] Their opposition to the Confederacy was unambiguously demonstrated by their willingness to risk their lives to defeat it. In Bermuda and the Bahamas, by contrast, it was relatively difficult to reach Union territory to enlist, while large numbers of Black colonists benefited from the easy money, high wages, and patronage relations brought on by blockade running. Their opposition to the slaveholder's rebellion necessarily used more indirect means, and they faced far greater risks of economic and legal retaliation from the white elite on the islands, as in the example of the Black pilots repeatedly prosecuted for guiding U.S. ships.[50] Patronage networks and economic necessity made it almost impossible for Black residents on the islands to separate themselves from some connection to the pro-Confederate elite.

In this milieu, it is not impossible that Rainey assisted Blackburn, probably unwittingly given Rainey's treatment at Confederate hands in South Carolina in 1861, in carrying out his task. Like Godfrey Hyams, who was Jewish, Rainey was a member of a disfavored minority and probably struck Blackburn as particularly expendable. Blackburn returned to Bermuda in the fall of 1864 and gathered more clothing, but he decided to wait until the following year's warm season made an outbreak similar to the one in New Bern more likely. He left several trunks in the care of Edward Swan, a St. George's innkeeper, with instructions to hold them until he sent word with a destination. He told George Black, a clerk in Walker's office, to pay Swan $250, provided by Blackburn, upon delivery of the trunks.[51]

Blackburn's behavior, once it became known, met with some opposition from the Confederate community in British North America. At least one prominent Southerner in Canada, upon learning of Blackburn's plans, urged against it on moral grounds. The Reverend Kensey Johns Stewart, a former chaplain in the Confederate army whom Davis had sent to Canada to help organize a mission to rescue prisoners from the camp at Elmira, New York, apparently learned of Blackburn's plot.[52] Davis had had second thoughts about Stewart's suitability for secret service and declined to have him pursue the prison matter further, although Stewart remained in Canada as yet another freelance operative. In December 1864, after Blackburn again returned to British North America from Bermuda, Stewart wrote to Davis expressing his horror and concern at the nature of what he had learned of the plan. Stewart decried the "impious" nature of many of the Confederate agents in Canada and hoped that Davis was not "capable of desiring the blessing of God upon, or being associated with, the instruments and plans" of Blackburn. Stewart knew that Hyams intended to deliver trunks of what Stewart called "smallpox clothing" to Washington, and the minister felt sure that such an operation would bring the wrath of God upon the Confederacy. Stewart called Blackburn, whom he did not directly name, "well-meaning," but urged Davis to discourage further operations. Stewart also alluded to other campaigns of destruction against civilian targets then in progress and attributed their failure to divine disfavor.⁵³ Based on Stewart's letter, it seems likely that Davis was aware of Blackburn's plot, though there is no indication he knew or approved of it in advance.

Stewart was not the only one opposed to Blackburn's endeavor. Stuart Robinson, a Kentucky Presbyterian minister who fled for Canada in 1862, claimed that the senior Confederates in Canada likewise did not support the yellow fever plot. Robinson had gained some local notoriety by operating an informal church in Toronto frequented by Southerners (and a surprising number of Canadians) who came to hear his proslavery and pro-Confederate sermons.⁵⁴ According to Robinson, James P. Holcombe said that "if there was any sense in what [Hyams] was about, Davis would be the first man to hang him," and that Hyams had swindled his passage money to Halifax from Holcombe by pretending to be an escaped prisoner of war who wished to return to the Confederacy.⁵⁵ Jacob Thompson also supposedly rebuffed Blackburn as he prepared his second attempt in the spring of 1865 using the trunks of clothing stored in Bermuda. Thompson "was a man of family and had a reputation to sustain," and could not be associated with such a scheme. He warned Blackburn that "if he persisted in this undertaking it would make him infamous and that he would not furnish a dollar for any such purpose."⁵⁶ Blackburn, denied funds, remained in Montreal until his arrest in May.

Canadian authorities arrested Blackburn and charged him with neutrality violations under the Alien Act. Notably, the Confederate establishment in Canada gave evidence against Blackburn in an attempt to disavow his actions. William Cleary submitted an affidavit to the court that testified to Blackburn's role in the plot while claiming the Confederate government's innocence in the matter. With the end of the war, however, the prosecution lost urgency, and Blackburn, like the remaining St. Albans raiders, was acquitted for lack of evidence. In Blackburn's case, the obstacle to his conviction was that the yellow fever trunks had not actually been on Canadian soil, only Nova Scotian.⁵⁷ The Colonial Office hurriedly located Blackburn's gift from the Admiralty before it could become a source of embarrassment, and he never received it. The Admiralty considered his acquittal a matter of procedure rather than an affirmation of innocence and did not wish to be further associated with him.⁵⁸ And once the plot came to widespread attention, neither did the other Confederates in Canada.

While Blackburn acted with only ambivalent Confederate government sanction, Jacob Thompson redirected his organization to more nefarious ends. Never comfortable in his role and increasingly homesick, Clay arranged to return home after the St. Albans raid, leaving Thompson in charge of the Confederate mission in Canada. Stymied by federal suppression of attempts to orchestrate prison breakouts at Rock Island and Camp Douglas, Illinois, Thompson turned his thoughts to retaliation rather than military or political victory. He approved a scheme to commit widespread arson in Northern cities, including Boston, Cincinnati, and New York, to coincide with yet another planned Copperhead uprising on election day, November 8, 1864.[59]

The attack on New York coincided with increased calls by Confederates for retaliatory actions in response to supposed Union atrocities, especially Union general Philip H. Sheridan's campaign in the Shenandoah Valley of Virginia. In October, the editor of the *Richmond Whig* called for some enterprising Confederate, perhaps in Canada, to burn Northern cities in revenge, declaring that "it would not be immoral and barbarous" to do so.[60] Tipped off that uprisings were planned for election day, Union authorities reinforced New York with thousands of troops under Maj. Gen. Benjamin Butler. The Copperheads backed out once again, leaving the group of eight pro-Confederates led by Col. Robert Martin, who had made their way from Canada to New York, in want of a task. After learning from the newspapers that their compatriots in a parallel scheme in Chicago had been rounded up, the group decided to act on their own accord. John W. Headley, one of the participants, later wrote that their purpose was to "let the Government at Washington understand that burning homes in the South might find a counterpart in the North."[61] Robert Cobb Kennedy, who had escaped from the Johnson's Island prison in 1863 and joined the Confederate enclave in Toronto, likewise professed that "thus far the South had borne all the trials, endured all the privations, and that it was the purpose of turning the tables that these raids were undertaken. The ladies of the South ... have given up their luxuries and walk bare-footed over their own land, and it is about time for the women of the North to share their sufferings." Kennedy also claimed that Confederate authorities in Canada, though he does not say who, told him that "the object of the expedition was to retaliate upon the North for the atrocities of Sheridan in the Shenandoah Valley."[62] The little group of Confederates determined that fire was the appropriate purifier for Northern sins.

After obtaining "Greek fire,"—a liquid chemical that combusted when exposed to air—from a sympathetic Copperhead, the group launched their arson spree on the evening of November 25. Despite later efforts at self-justification that their raid was within the laws of warfare, their targets were almost entirely civilian and the attacks calculated to cause panic and death among the populace of Manhattan. They set fires in nineteen hotels across the city, along with Barnum's American Museum and a river barge filled with hay. Panicked shouts and ringing bells followed the men across the city, but by the next day Martin and his associates discovered that their fires had failed to spread much beyond the rooms they started in, and that the police were searching for the arsonists with the aid of descriptions from the hotels. The group traveled by rail to Niagara Falls and crossed back into Canada, where they rejoined Thompson in Toronto.[63]

Union authorities quickly laid the blame for the fires on Confederate operatives, although their failure to cause significant damage dampened the urgency of the Northern response and muted diplomatic conflict. Nevertheless, Northern officials, particularly Maj. Gen. John A. Dix, commanding the department that included New York, viewed the arson and Thompson's sponsored raids to free prisoners of war as criminal acts outside the legitimate bounds of warfare. When Union forces captured Robert Cobb Kennedy as he attempted to cross from Canada back to the South, they did not accord him the status of a prisoner of war.[64] Neither did they extend that status to John Yates Beall, who was captured by detectives in December after a particularly bumbling effort, led by Colonel Martin, to free some Confederate officers being transferred by rail in western New York. Both Beall and Kennedy were held and tried as spies and saboteurs before a military commission. Despite attempts at intercession by Thompson and others arguing that they were legitimate soldiers, not "guerilleros" or spies, the judges did not agree. Lincoln declined to interfere and both men were hanged at Governor's Island—Beall on February 24, 1865, and Kennedy the following month.[65]

The alarm surrounding the New York arson encouraged Jacob Thompson, who wrote to Benjamin, "The attempt on New York has produced a great panic, which will not subside at [Union authorities'] bidding." He planned continued efforts to destroy property and infrastructure across the North, and "to burn whenever it is practicable, and thus make the men of property feel their insecurity and tire them out with the war."[66] Holcombe and Thompson, independently of each other, both urged continued support of dissidents within the North to force a fracture among the Northern populace and perhaps strengthen Confederate armies. Neither placed any faith in Copperhead secret societies, whose repeated failure to carry out their promises to aid Confederate operations the preceding summer and fall had convinced Thompson and Holcombe of their uselessness, but both men remained optimistic that enough dissatisfaction remained among the people of the North that some kind of help could be forthcoming.[67] The Confederate government remained committed to funding irregular operations out of Canadian territory in spite of their increasing inability to direct their course.

Perhaps the ultimate symbol of that disruption between encouragement and control of irregular operations took place on the very night of the New York arson, standing on stage at the Winter Garden Theatre. John Wilkes Booth and his brothers headlined a performance of *Julius Caesar* in celebration of the tercentenary of Shakespeare's birth, although ironically John played the role of Marc Antony, while his brothers took the parts of the famous assassins Brutus and Cassius. Amid the second act, there literally arose the cry of "Fire!" in the crowded theater. Confederate agent John Ashbrook had just set fire to the neighboring Lafarge House hotel, and the smoke and activity of the fire department threatened to spread panic inside the Winter Garden. Theater staff and police urged the fearful crowd to return to their seats. The performance resumed, and the audience had no idea that one of the triumvirate standing before them was intimately connected with the organization behind the evening's terror. The next morning, Booth, already enmeshed in a reprisal plan of his own, sparked an argument with his brothers after defending the evening's arson as justified retaliation for Northern depredations in the Shenandoah Valley.[68] Booth had already accepted Confederate justifications for the attack, and he was surely aware through his own association with the network in Canada that government officials had supported it. He was justified in expecting similar aid.

The yellow fever plot and the attempted arson of New York may have failed, but the dislocation of private warfare from Confederate control had one last, catastrophic bullet in the chamber: Booth. Lincoln's assassination represents the logic of informal warfare and diplomacy taken to its extreme. This is not to argue that the Confederate government ordered or directly contributed to the assassination—other historians have examined the topic exhaustively and found no conclusive evidence.[69] What is clear, however, is that Booth and his associates carried out their attack in a milieu of Confederate desperation and a long-standing willingness by the government to countenance freelance action on behalf of the rebellion. After receiving both official funding and support for a plot to kidnap Lincoln inspired in part by revenge for the February 1864 Dahlgren raid on Richmond that supposedly meant to kill Jefferson Davis, it was not a great leap for Booth to adapt the plot into assassination.[70] The line connecting privateers, freelance pirates, "destructionists," and Booth is quite distinct.[71] When attempts to harness private enterprise for warfare in traditional forms failed to meet expectations, the Confederacy proved its willingness, over and over again, to accept and give legitimacy to private, illegal operations if they offered the prospect of success.

The last ripple of Confederate-inspired operations in Canada also proved to be the most shocking and consequential. On the evening of April 14, 1865, John Wilkes Booth assassinated Abraham Lincoln at Ford's Theatre in Washington. The Northern populace instantly suspected Confederate involvement, and Booth's movements and associations received intense and immediate scrutiny, even as the manhunt for the assassins, who had also badly wounded William H. Seward and targeted Vice President Andrew Johnson, swept across the District of Columbia, Maryland, and Virginia. Booth's movements in Canada created suspicion that the Confederate mission there had been involved in the assassination, and the United States issued warrants for the arrest of Clay, Thompson, George Sanders, Nathaniel Beverley Tucker, and William Cleary. Tucker had little to do with the covert operations in Canada, but his relative notoriety and association with Sanders and Clay were enough to tar him with the same brush.[72]

Speculation about the extent of Confederate involvement in the assassination was rampant at the time, and it has hardly died down since.[73] Confederate officials, particularly Clay, Thompson, and Judah Benjamin, destroyed much of the official correspondence regarding secret-service activities in Canada, so it is impossible to rule out some nefarious connection between the government in Richmond and Booth. However, it seems far more likely that Booth and his fellow conspirators acted in the same spirit as the other quasi-filibusters, arsonists, and raiders of the late years of the war. They certainly had contact with the Confederate network in British North America and received some funding and logistical support from it.[74] The assassination plot emerged from an aborted plan to kidnap and ransom Lincoln, which had substantial Confederate government involvement both in Canada and in the contested borderlands around Washington, northern Virginia, and southeastern Maryland.[75] Many of those involved in the assassination had been involved in the kidnapping plot, and Booth clearly leaned on the contacts and resources of that loose network in orchestrating the killing.

Booth famously visited Montreal for ten days beginning on October 18, 1864, ostensibly to arrange to have his theatrical wardrobe shipped to the South via blockade runner. In Montreal he stayed at St. Lawrence Hall, a hotel and hub for Confederate exiles and sympathizers in the city. He met widely with the Confederate community in the city, including Patrick C. Martin, a Maryland liquor dealer and occasional blockade runner who had spent much of the war in Montreal. Martin had cooperated with the aborted 1863 attempt to attack Johnson's Island and was a business partner of Alexander Keith Jr., of the Halifax branch of the Confederate network.[76] Neither Clay nor Thompson were in Montreal at the time of Booth's visit, but he met with George Sanders, who was still deeply involved in the Confederate operation there.[77] The St. Albans raid occurred just after Booth's arrival, creating a frenetic atmosphere, and Sanders left the city for St. Johns (Saint-Jean-sur-Richelieu) in order to attempt to help some of the captured raiders, but he returned before Booth left and took a room at the same hotel. This interaction with Sanders received particular scrutiny because of Sanders's earlier very public advocacy of assassination and his distress over the recent death of his son Lewis in a Northern prison. Booth conducted his business, including opening an account at the Bank of Ontario, favored by Confederate exiles, and taking out a sterling bill of exchange. Booth left Montreal and returned to the United States on October 28. Martin sailed for Halifax on one of his own blockade running schooners with Booth's wardrobe among the cargo, but his ship was lost at sea with all hands. Some have speculated that Alexander Keith sank the ship with a time bomb as part of a marine insurance fraud scheme. While this is conjecture, it is at least somewhat plausible given Keith's later infamy for a string of mysterious ship disappearances and the bombing of the passenger liner *Moselle* in Hamburg in 1875.[78]

One of Booth's co-conspirators maintained even stronger links to the pro-Confederate network in Canada. John Harrison Surratt did not participate in the actual assassination, but as a courier and frequent associate of Confederates in Canada and Maryland, he provided introductions and other support for Booth. At the time of the attack, he was in Elmira, New York, scouting the prisoner-of-war camp there at the behest of Edwin Gray Lee, a Confederate army officer (and distant cousin of Robert E. Lee) who had gone to Canada to replace the departed Clement Clay and James P. Holcombe. Upon learning of the assassination, Surratt fled to Montreal, where John Porterfield guided him to the same network of French-Canadian priests that had sheltered the St. Albans raiders. The priests hid Surratt for weeks until he could quietly book passage on a steamer for Britain. Surratt's case illustrates that the Confederate network maintained at least a loose connection with Booth and that its members were more than willing to aid the escape of a suspected assassin.[79]

Spooked by Booth's obvious ties to their network, prominent Confederates in Canada rushed to distance themselves from the assassination.[80] Tucker wrote a flurry of public letters declaring his own innocence and charging that anyone who claimed he was involved in the assassination "hath blackened his soul with diabolical perjury."[81] Tucker claimed never to have even heard of Booth before learning of the assassination and protested the innocence of his colleagues in Canada. Tucker and Sanders simultaneously published a joint response to the declaration from Andrew Johnson that they, along with Davis, Clay, Thompson, and William Cleary, were wanted in connection with the assassination conspiracy. They called the accusation "a living, burning lie," and accused Johnson of conspiring to murder "*our* Christian President," a reference to Davis and the supposed objective of the Dahlgren raid on Richmond the previous year. Their letter likewise claimed that neither of the men had ever met Booth, which was plainly a lie in the case of Sanders. Tucker went so far as to accuse Andrew Johnson of orchestrating the assassination himself in order to seize the presidency.[82] Cleary, Thompson's secretary and assistant, published a pamphlet protesting his innocence as well.[83] Clay, who had returned to the Confederacy just before the fall of Fort Fisher put an end to blockade running, turned himself in to Union forces in Georgia, and they imprisoned him alongside Jefferson Davis at Fortress Monroe. The other prominent Confederates in Canada, despite public boasts of their willingness to face Union authorities, decided to remain in exile for the time being.

The loud, angry denials of complicity by the Confederates in Canada illustrated the enduring problem of their mission: even a cursory investigation could plausibly tie them to violent acts by their associates, regardless of the actual extent of their involvement. By embracing private violence and ceding sovereignty over its use in a war for Southern independence, they implicitly encouraged illegal attacks, neutrality violations, and even assassination. By the same measure, they also opened the Confederate government to accusations of involvement in any of those schemes, however tenuous. Thompson (who had departed for Europe before the assassination), Sanders, and Cleary had every reason to fear that they might be arrested in Canada and either tried for neutrality violations under the recently passed Alien Act or extradited to the United States.[84] Their panicked denunciations showed that they recognized that their project had descended into illegitimacy and that they feared being held to account not only for an operation they had no control over but for one with which they could not deny association.

The long fuse—lit by privateering, Committees of Safety, and "destructionists" in 1861—had at last reached the magazine. Lincoln's assassination and the yellow fever plot were the logical endpoints of the persistent willingness of Confederate authorities to cede their authority over life and death, trade and commerce, and war and peace to private parties. The Canadian adventure, with far more direct Confederate control, participation, and funding than earlier colonial enterprises, nevertheless spun out of control in the hands of freelance evangelists for chaos like George Sanders. In the space of a few months, Jacob Thompson, Clement Clay, and their associates transformed their mission from one of informal diplomacy and subversion into one of direct action, revenge, and atrocity. When even quasi-legitimate operatives like Bennett H. Young, of the St. Albans raid, openly proclaimed revenge and reciprocity as their mission, how could the cloud of hangers-on, sympathizers, and grifters in the Confederate orbit in British North America and beyond fail to notice?[85] Luke Blackburn and John Wilkes Booth had every reason to expect that their crimes would be tolerated, though perhaps not approved of, by British colonials, and perhaps even embraced after the fact by the Confederacy. That was the lesson derived from the *Florida*, the *Chesapeake*, the *Roanoke*, St. Albans, and the many other cases where violations of the norms of warfare and international law received shelter in the colonies and sanction from the Confederate government.

That the Confederate mission to Canada failed to achieve a war-winning success should not obscure its troubling possibilities and the persistent bloody problem of transnational rebellions that it presaged. The Northern border certainly suffered years of turmoil as an indirect result of Confederate meddling in Canada. Northern detectives, rightly skeptical that Canadian courts would cooperate in extradition proceedings, attempted to kidnap former Confederates hiding in Canada on several occasions—Sanders himself narrowly avoided abduction in August 1865.[86] The Fenian Brotherhood, flush with recruits from the disbanding Union armies, made plans to hold Canada hostage in pursuit of freedom for Ireland, and American authorities did not hinder them until blood was shed on the Canadian side of the frontier.[87] Further west, the United States repaid British refusals to allow the U.S. army to pursue and "exterminate" Native Americans sheltering across the border from Minnesota during the Dakota War by encouraging kidnappings of two Dakota leaders in Rupert's Land, then a Hudson's Bay Company territory, and later allowing Métis leader Louis Riel to take refuge across the border.[88] The willingness of private citizens to disregard state authority along the border was, in 1864–65, a long-standing tradition, but the money, arms, and support of the Confederate government catalyzed it into action. Absent the organizational support of the Confederate apparatus in Canada for private, self-organized violence, it is an open question whether Booth would have attempted to assassinate Lincoln. The Confederates and their collaborators ensured that transnational violence far outlived their own ambitions.

Conclusion

Whatever Dr. Bratton's connection with Jefferson Davis, the Southern Confederacy or the Ku-Klux may have been . . . matters little to us here in Canada. We only know that he has been forcibly taken from beneath the protection of our flag, without permission or authority, which is a grave offense against the dignity, peace and welfare of our nation.
—*Hamilton Daily Spectator*, June 11, 1872

IT WAS A fitting irony that so many Confederates sought refuge in British colonies in the years after the Civil War. The places that Southerners railed against for harboring the "mutineers" of the *Creole* and countless fugitive slaves like John Anderson became the sanctuary for fugitive slavers, some of whom were very prominent men. Jefferson Davis, John C. Breckinridge, James Mason, John Bell Hood, Jubal Early, Luke Blackburn, Jacob Thompson, George Sanders, and many others spent months or years after the war in the colonies, mainly in Canada, while awaiting pardons or other opportunities to return home.[1] Davis came to Canada almost immediately after his release from Fortress Monroe in May 1867 to join Varina and their children, and he remained in the colony-turned-Dominion off and on for nearly two years. Despite a sizable pro-Union faction that included thousands of Union Army veterans both Black and white, there was little serious Canadian resistance to their presence, although an anonymous man shoved a paper with the word "Andersonville" scrawled on it into Davis's hand in Montreal that summer.[2] The victorious U.S. government did not, in general, pursue them or seek extradition, and most Confederates returned home eventually, pardon or no. A few stayed and started new lives, notably Confederate naval officer (and nephew of Jefferson Davis) John Taylor Wood, who settled in Halifax, the scene of his celebrated 1864 escape in the CSS *Tallahassee*—with the aid of a local pilot—from U.S. Navy pursuit. British North America, soon transformed into the Dominion of Canada, continued to offer a warm welcome to ex-Confederates.[3]

British territory occasionally sheltered Southern fugitives well into Reconstruction. In the closing days of the war, both Vernon Locke and John C. Braine—still wanted fugitives after their piracy in the *Chesapeake* and *Roanoke* hijackings—reappeared in the island colonies, and once again they escaped. Braine showed up in Jamaica in early July 1865 with the American schooner *St. Mary*, which he and his band had hijacked in Chesapeake Bay in March. Bereft of supplies and shorn of "all pretense of an insurgent authority" as cover for further misdeeds, he abandoned the ship and fled to Liverpool on a mail steamer, while the U.S. consul fumed at the governor's failure to arrest him. Braine returned to New York some time later and was arrested, but the government lost interest in his case and decided not to prosecute him further.[4]

A few years later, Canada again served as a refuge, this time for Ku Klux Klan members fleeing prosecution, but their pursuers were not above resuming the prewar practice of irregular renditions of fugitives. Joseph Hester—the very same murderer whose return from British custody into Confederate hands in Bermuda had been so troublesome in 1863—walked free and served in later years as a deputy U.S. marshal, operating against the Ku Klux Klan in North Carolina. Hester made newspaper headlines for bold captures of Klan members in Raleigh in 1871.[5] In 1872, he tracked Dr. Rufus Bratton—a murderer and fugitive Klan leader—to London, Ontario, where he allegedly chloroformed him, then stuffed him in a train compartment bound for Detroit.[6] The Canadian government protested at this violation of extradition rules, and the U.S. government reluctantly returned Bratton to Canada.[7] Hester, like so many previous cross-border vigilantes, escaped any consequences for his act. Indeed, the Supreme Court later ruled that kidnapping a person outside the United States was not a crime, freeing the Pinkertons and others to go on a spree of irregular renditions of fugitives.[8] Bratton's forcible return to the United States mirrored the process by which so many others—fugitive slaves and petty criminals alike—had been snatched back into bondage or custody in the nineteenth century, and his return to Canada on a legal technicality fittingly matched the safe haven received by Confederates in the preceding decade.

The British portion of the Confederate commercial-diplomatic network generally had better fortune than their Southern counterparts in the aftermath of the war. The U.S. government vigorously pursued firms and assets that could be definitively tied to Confederates, such as the Liverpool-based Fraser, Trenholm & Company, but colonial firms and subjects with their fingers in the blockade-running pie were mostly safe. In the Bahamas, Henry Adderley took his wealth and family and retired permanently to London, while his son Augustus and son-in-law George D. Harris remained prominent in the much-diminished affairs of Nassau, but also received knighthoods for their work in the London political and business community.[9] Henry Adderley died in London a very wealthy man in July 1875, leaving a substantial estate to his heirs.[10] John Tory Bourne fared less well. His gamble to delay taking a commission on his work until after a Confederate victory necessarily failed, and he returned to a slow and obscure mercantile life, trying to unload heaps of now-useless military supplies to the Royal Navy while managing a small import-export business.[11] Local historian William Zuill encountered Bourne's grandson in St. George's, Bermuda, in the 1920s and found he had little to show for his ancestor's efforts beyond a few letter books—valuable only to a historian.[12] The easy money of the heyday of blockade running did not last, but most of the Confederacy's mercantile friends on the island colonies survived the collapse of the trade in good order. The island colonies themselves likewise faded in importance, although Bermuda's military facilities ensured a greater share of imperial largesse than the Bahamas.

Some of the Confederacy's friends in British North America, for their part, played prominent roles in creating their own Confederation. Benjamin Wier supported the effort to unify the Northern colonies and served as one of Nova Scotia's first senators. J. W. Ritchie, who leaped to the defense of Confederate interests (and local pirates) in the *Chesapeake* case, gained an appointment to the Legislative Council of Nova Scotia as soon as that matter was resolved, and went on to become an influential voice in support of a British North American union.[13] His brother William Johnston Ritchie, who liberated the *Chesapeake* raiders in New Brunswick, was soon raised to the position of chief justice of the New Brunswick Supreme Court and later became a founding justice of the Supreme Court of Canada.[14] Thomas Connolly, the archbishop of Halifax, threw in his support as well, and called on the Catholic faithful to do the same.[15] George Taylor Denison—a wartime friend to and frequent visitor of Confederate exiles—went on to prominence as an advocate for British imperialism and a role for Canada as an active participant in building and maintaining the empire.[16]

British America had sheltered and sustained the rebellion's life and death. After Appomattox, it sheltered its rebirth and immortality as the myth of the Lost Cause arose to win in memory what the South had failed to achieve on the battlefield. Jubal Early wrote the first of his histories of the war while in Canada, laying the groundwork for a prolific postwar career as a premier Lost Cause writer.[17] Davis was not yet prepared to begin his own monumental (in size, not literary achievement) history of the Confederacy while living in Canada, but his wife, Varina—presaging the preeminent role of women in preserving and shaping the war's memory and legacy—smuggled the bulk of his personal papers out of the South and preserved them in a bank vault in Montreal while Davis languished in Fortress Monroe.[18] She ran the blockade, so to speak, with ammunition for the coming battle over the war's causes and legacy and found safe harbor, like so many arms-laden steamships, in the colonies.

While ex-Confederates began the struggle over the war's memory and legacy in the United States, the frontier between the provinces and the republic hardly returned to tranquility. The Fenian Brotherhood engaged in a series of filibustering attacks into Canada from the United States, hoping to spark an uprising and conquest, with the ultimate goal of trading the territory for the liberation of Ireland. The United States, still angered by Confederate exploitation of the colonies, indicated to the British government that if the Fenians succeeded, they would "acknowledge accomplished facts" and recognize an independent Ireland.[19] To the west, Native Americans used the border as a shield from the pursuit of U.S. troops, while Métis leader Louis Riel crossed in the other direction and sheltered from Canadian and British pursuit after his failed resistance in the Red River colony, and Fenians threatened yet another expedition amid the turmoil in Manitoba.[20] Across North America and the Caribbean, private military action—filibustering, transnational rebellions, banditry, and other species of violence—resumed its place in public attention, from Canada to Cuba, Jamaica, Mexico, and beyond. When U.S. authorities finally caught John C. Braine in 1866, he was trying to organize a filibustering expedition into the Caribbean, possibly against Haiti.[21] These incidents serve

Jefferson and Varina Davis, photographed in Montreal in 1867, after his release from Fortress Monroe. Credit: Unsigned, Notman Studio, "Jefferson Davis and Wife, Montreal, QC, 1867," I-28149, McCord Stewart Museum.

as a reminder that the quest for order and the remaking of sovereignty across the land and waters of the hemisphere were never quite complete and often failed to tame the traditions of grassroots international violence.

Private initiative and nongovernment actors deserve greater attention in our assessment of the Civil War's transnational conduct and legacy. The truly important diplomatic battles, once one looks beyond the objective of European recognition and intervention, were won and lost closer to home for the Confederacy. The ideological straitjacket of King Cotton diplomacy affected high-level Confederate assumptions and foreign policy goals in 1861–62, but within the Confederacy's borders, merchants, associations, Committees of Safety, and other private and semiofficial bodies created and sustained an unofficial export embargo. This was the most concrete early expression of Confederate foreign and trade policy, and the general government had little to do with it beyond some behind-the-scenes encouragement by Judah Benjamin and a few others. When the embargo loosened, it fell once more to private parties to work out where and how to move cargo out of ports and through the tightening blockade. British colonial help proved indispensable in this endeavor.

The queen may have declared neutrality, but colonial subjects and Confederate merchants, ship captains, and minor officials did much to determine its form and stringency, and they worked to turn it to their advantage. The decisions colonial officials, lawmakers, and judges made concerning the war frequently presented London with a fait accompli, and usually the Colonial and Foreign Offices upheld their choices—not least because of their long experience in the nineteenth century with difficult, fractious, and uncooperative populations in the American colonies. Conciliation and persuasion, rather than coercion, were the Colonial Office's tools of choice in dealing with them, and this gave colonists (and their Confederate partners) considerable freedom to push for favorable policies and resist or ignore those they disliked. Through their close association with colonial elites and social life, Confederates also made sympathetic friends among imperial officials and military officers. By these means, Confederates gained access to favorable import and export policies and low fees in the Bahamas, as well as occasional quiet access to Royal Navy repair facilities in Bermuda. Confederate informal diplomacy failed to find the same influence over the Black people of Bermuda and the Bahamas. Many of them proved willing to risk serious personal consequences to work against the slaveholder's rebellion and the financial interests of the colonial elite.

This nearly seamless connection between Confederates and the colonial mercantile elite also gave the rebellion access to the machinery and protection of British power. Some of this was apparent from what the Union chose *not* to do. No U.S. Navy cutting-out expeditions entered Nassau or Halifax to capture or destroy Confederate warships and blockade runners when they sheltered under colonial guard, yet a Union captain felt no compunction about ordering the same done in the Brazilian port of Bahia to seize the CSS *Florida*, whose career had begun two years earlier with the obliging help of locals in the Bahamas. Confederate passengers and communications likewise traveled with impunity aboard British ships—Union cruisers dared not seize people or mail from British mail packets after the *Trent* affair.[22] British diplomats and colonial officials likewise protected the "quasi-English" steamers of the blockade-running business and protested American depredations against them.[23] Colonial connivance and transnational partnerships made it difficult or impossible for British officials to differentiate between genuine British ships snapped up in the blockade and those owned in whole or in part by Confederate citizens. This occasionally descended into farce, as when future Confederate treasury secretary George A. Trenholm appealed to the Foreign Office to obtain redress for a U.S. Navy attack on a "British" steamer he owned, but more often the result was constant pressure from Lord Lyons on the United States to adhere to accepted rules on the capture of prizes and to refrain from egregious abuse of supposedly neutral shipping.[24] This co-option of British power was possible only with the aid of colonial friends and represents an underappreciated success of Confederate informal diplomacy and the privatized transnational blockade-running campaign.

Privatized warfare on the margins of the Civil War held enduring appeal for Confederate officials seeking an answer to the Union's naval and diplomatic stranglehold, especially Stephen Mallory and Judah Benjamin. Mallory, an old friend of antebellum filibustering, looked for ways to turn private enterprise into military effectiveness at sea. Mallory's volunteer navy program, which he developed in part at the urging of "private warfare" advocate Bernard Janin Sage, sought to mutate older privateering practices into quasi-state operations in order to evade municipal and international law.[25] The logic behind that program also motivated the government to offer sanction for pro-Confederate raiders on the margins of the continent and at sea, even when their attacks violated British neutrality or international law. Rather than explicitly disavowing men like Locke, Braine, or Thomas Hogg, the Confederate senior leadership offered them approval, protection in the form of volunteer commissions, and encouragement to continue their depredations. Colonial ports in turn offered them shelter, recruits, and credulous or sympathetic officials who, time after time, let them walk free despite their crimes.

Their impunity is a reminder that despite the massive growth and rationalization of international law in the nineteenth century, it still lacked reliable tools for enforcement and had no mechanisms of its own for enforcing justice and adjudicating legal questions.

Informal diplomacy and warfare received a close embrace from the Confederate government in the 1864–65 missions to Canada, but those operations unraveled in parallel with Confederate political and military fortunes. Jacob Thompson and Clement Clay Jr. at first seemed optimistic at their prospects of success in influencing the 1864 elections and bringing about the nomination of a Copperhead (Peace Democrat) and the defeat of Abraham Lincoln. Their initial charge having failed, Thompson and Clay—the latter having absorbed the free radical of George N. Sanders—moved toward raiding, sabotage, and revenge. In addition to sanctioned, if illegal, raids like St. Albans, Confederate officials supported projects of increasingly doubtful legitimacy, including arson attacks on Northern cities, and they looked the other way or provided logistical or financial help to schemes like the yellow fever plot and Booth's plan to kidnap Abraham Lincoln.

Canadian officials, absorbed in the project of a colonial union, had more to lose than their maritime counterparts and thus proved far less accommodating to Confederate malfeasance, especially when it came to violence. Bermuda may have been mostly immune from Union military pressure, but Toronto had been burned to the ground by American forces within living memory. Canadian and British officials regarded with deadly seriousness the prospect of a gigantic Union army on their doorstep. Despite strong support for the Confederacy among some Canadian colonials—especially elements of the French Canadian Catholic establishment—the Canadian government acted in concert with imperial authorities to crack down on Confederate raiding through legislation and enforcement, especially after the humiliating release of the St. Albans raiders in December 1864. This display of force came amid substantial progress toward Confederation, culminating in the British North America Act of 1867, which created the Dominion of Canada. Confederate informal diplomacy and Canadian anti-Northern sentiment could not overcome the combined pressure of Union diplomatic coercion, imperial desire for both reduced costs and the consolidation of international violence in state hands, and the broader desire for political and organizational reform in British North America.

Ultimately, the Confederacy's failures of traditional diplomacy in Europe and its military defeat should not obscure the absolute necessity and surprising success of its informal military and diplomatic efforts in North America. Relatively obscure figures like Lewis Heyliger, Henry and Augustus Adderley, Benjamin Wier, John B. Lafitte, Norman S. Walker, and many others did the thankless yet occasionally lucrative work of creating an informal Confederate network across British America. They created the logistical and regulatory framework for blockade running in the colonies that transported a huge proportion of the South's arms, equipment, and medicine, without which the Confederacy would have died with a whimper and in far shorter time. This network gave Confederates access to the tools of British power and the protection of the British flag over their merchant vessels and communications and protected pro-Confederate raiders and pirates from the worst consequences of their actions.

Although private military action in the colonies and at sea never realized the full ambitions of Davis, Mallory, and Benjamin to create a decisive break in Union naval strength or force an Anglo-American war, it nevertheless created an environment of chaos and fear along the northern frontier and at sea, and had lasting diplomatic and political effects.[26] The Confederate war from Canada, for example, was not the sole contributor to the abrogation of the Reciprocity Treaty, but it certainly helped seal its fate. The same could be said for both Canadian Confederation and the assassination of Abraham Lincoln, with enduring consequences for North America.

NOTES

Abbreviations and Nomenclature

ACA	Arundel Castle Archives, Arundel, United Kingdom
Alabama Claims	*Correspondence concerning Claims against Great Britain Transmitted to the Senate of the United States in Answer to the Resolutions of December 4 and 10, 1867, and of May 27, 1868*
BNA	Bahamas National Archives, Nassau, Bahamas
CSAR	Confederate States of America Records, 1854–1889, Manuscript Division, Library of Congress, Washington, D.C.
FRUS	*Foreign Relations of the United States* series. See *Papers Relating to Foreign Affairs* and related entries, 1861–1865, in the bibliography.
HDL	High Density Library, University of Calgary, Calgary, AB
LAC	Library and Archives Canada
LC	Manuscript Division, Library of Congress
MM	The National Maritime Museum, Greenwich, United Kingdom
NARA	The National Archives and Records Administration, Washington, DC
NARA II	The National Archives and Records Administration, College Park, MD
OR	*War of the Rebellion: The Official Records of the Union and Confederate Armies*
ORN	*Official Records of the Union and Confederate Navies in the War of the Rebellion*
PJD	*The Papers of Jefferson Davis*
SHC	Southern Historical Collection, Wilson Library, University of North Carolina
TNA	The National Archives, Kew, United Kingdom

Introduction

The epigraph is from Judah P. Benjamin to Henry Hotze, 5 May 1864, *ORN*, ser. 2, 3:1113.

1. Steers, *Blood on the Moon*, 223–25; "The Assassination Plot—Important Discoveries by the Government," *New York Herald*, 25 Apr. 1865, 4.
2. "Something to Be Looked After," *New York Times*, 19 Apr. 1865, 4.
3. Wise, *Lifeline of the Confederacy*, 58–66.
4. James P. Holcombe, private letter to Judah P. Benjamin, 26 Apr. 1864, in *ORN*, ser. 2, 3:1101–2.
5. Holcombe to Benjamin, 1 Apr. 1864, *ORN*, ser. 2, 3:1073–75; Benjamin to Holcombe, 20 Apr. 1864, in *ORN*, ser. 2, 3:1095–97.
6. William H. Seward to J. Hume Burnley, 14 Mar. 1865, *Papers Relating to Foreign Affairs, Accompanying the Annual Message of the President to the First Session, Thirty-Ninth Congress*, pt. 2 (Washington, D.C.: Government Printing Office, 1866), 96. Hereafter, documents in this series will be cited as *FRUS*, followed by the year of the documents concerned, as is the practice with subsequent collections published by the State Department's *Foreign Relations of the United States* series. (See history.state.gov/historicaldocuments/about-frus for details.)
7. Sumner, *Works of Charles Sumner*, 13:85–86. The Johnson-Clarendon Convention was an early attempt to settle damage claims between Britain and the United States arising out of the Civil War. These were later settled under international arbitration following the 1871 Treaty of Washington.
8. Wise, *Lifeline of the Confederacy*, 226, appendices 5–19.
9. Neff, *War and the Law of Nations*, 160–63.
10. Historians differ strongly as to why and how this ordering of international violence occurred but generally agree as to the chronology. Neff, *War and the Law of Nations*, 167–77; Benton and Ford, *Rage for Order*, 188–97; Thomson, *Mercenaries, Pirates, and Sovereigns*, 69–77, 140–42; Moss, *Marque and Reprisal*, 208–65; Lemnitzer, *Power, Law, and the End of Privateering*, 115–53.
11. Lemnitzer, *Power, Law, and the End of Privateering*, 115.
12. H. Jones, *Blue and Gray Diplomacy*.
13. Schoen, *Fragile Fabric of Union*; Doyle, *Cause of All Nations*; Karp, *This Vast Southern Empire*; Downs, *Second American Revolution*; Eichhorn, *Liberty and Slavery*; A. L. Tucker, *Newest Born of Nations*; Kiser, *Illusions of Empire*.
14. Krein, *Last Palmerston Government*, 4–5.
15. Krein, 44–54; Myers, *Caution and Cooperation*, 35–47; Jenkins, *Britain and the War for the Union*, 1:90–94.
16. Buckner, *Transition to Responsible Government*; McLaren, *Dewigged, Bothered, and Bewildered*.

17. Downs, *Second American Revolution*, 7–8.
18. Brettle, *Colossal Ambitions*, 4.
19. Karl Marx, "The North American Civil War," *Die Presse*, 25 Oct. 1861, in Marx and Engels, *Civil War in the United States*, 46.
20. Marx, 44.
21. Obert, *Six-Shooter State*, 44–62; Hutton, "Sleuthing for Mr. Crow."
22. Some, particularly Americans, used "Canada" as shorthand for all of British North America in the mid-nineteenth century. I have avoided or clarified such usage in this text.
23. Some writers include Newfoundland as well, but it was governed separately (i.e., not under the aegis of the governor-general of British North America) and in fact did not join with the rest as a part of modern Canada until after the Second World War. During the Civil War, British Columbia remained a part of the Hudson's Bay Company territory, while Vancouver Island was governed as a separate Crown colony.
24. I have chosen to separate Bermuda and the Bahamas from the British West Indies mostly as a matter of geography and contemporary governance. Slavery had been a more marginal presence on these islands than on the sugar-producing islands of the West Indies, and the white minority was substantially larger as a proportion of the population. They retained political power and legislative bodies even as their counterparts in the West Indies faced retrenchment and even a return to direct imperial governance. Other scholars consider them linked well enough to the West Indies by cultural and social factors to be grouped together (see, for example, Manning, "Nicknames and Number Plates in the British West Indies").

Chapter One. "That Nation of Pirates"

The epigraph is from Cong. Globe, 35th Cong., 1st Sess. 222 (1858).
1. Russell, *My Diary North and South*, 178.
2. Keehn, *Knights of the Golden Circle*, 152–54.
3. Russell, *My Diary North and South*, 167.
4. Russell, 170, 175–76.
5. Karp, *This Vast Southern Empire*, 43–44, 51–53; Sexton, "Anglophobia in Nineteenth-Century Elections, Politics, and Diplomacy," 110–16.
6. Lemnitzer, *Power, Law, and the End of Privateering*, 115–53.
7. Horne, *Negro Comrades of the Crown*, 133–63; Rugemer, *Problem of Emancipation*, 180–221.
8. On the "settler revolution" and colonial autonomy, see Belich, *Replenishing the Earth*.

9. C. Hall, *Civilising Subjects*, 338–79.

10. Krein, *Last Palmerston Government*, 32; Myers, *Caution and Cooperation*.

11. Blackett, *Divided Hearts*, 17–26; O'Connor, *American Sectionalism in the British Mind*, 13–16; Turner, *Stonewall Jackson, Beresford Hope, and the Meaning of the American Civil War in Britain*. This interpretation is not uncontested. See Campbell, *English Public Opinion and the American Civil War*.

12. Winks, *Civil War Years*, 9–10.

13. MacDonald, *Canadian Public Opinion on the American Civil War*, 82–89; Winks, *Civil War Years*, 16–17. Winks characterizes Canadians who opposed the Union as generally anti-Northern rather than pro-Southern.

14. Bahamas Blue Book, 1860, f109–15, CO 27/58, Blue Books of Statistics, etc., CO 27: Colonial Office and predecessors: Bahamas, Miscellaneous, TNA; Bermuda Blue Book, 1860, f171, CO 41/55, Blue Books of Statistics, etc., CO 41: Colonial Office and predecessors: Bermuda, Miscellaneous, TNA. The Blue Book compilations of trade statistics show that most of the colonies' trade by value and volume went to the United States, and customs entrance and clearance reports printed in the *Nassau Guardian* and the *Bermuda Royal Gazette* show New York as the most common port of exchange.

15. Craton and Saunders, *Islanders in the Stream*, 17–20; Themistocleous, "Merchant Princes of Nassau." On cultural similarities between the South and the Nassau elite, see Startup, "'Guardians of Our Own Honor.'"

16. Huzzey, *Freedom Burning*, 8–9. Huzzey disagrees with the idea that antislavery sentiment truly waned after 1834, although Catherine Hall, among others, contends that even if "anti-slavery sentiment was alive and well, it no longer dominated the public mind." C. Hall, *Civilising Subjects*, 390.

17. Ward, *Colonial Self-Government*; C. Hall, *Civilising Subjects*, 338–79; Huzzey, *Freedom Burning*, 185–86.

18. See, for example, Bryan, *Letters to the Southern People*; Schoen, *Fragile Fabric of Union*, 218–22.

19. Wilkins, "Window on Freedom."

20. Bryan, *Rightful Remedy*, 27–32.

21. Rugemer, *Problem of Emancipation*, 181.

22. Christy, "Cotton Is King," 23–24.

23. *North Carolina Standard* (Raleigh), 3 Nov. 1841, 1.

24. Calhoun, *Works of John C. Calhoun*, 4:32.

25. Cong. Globe, 35th Cong., 2d Sess. 1190 (1859).

26. *True American* (New Orleans), 22 April 1839, 2.

27. Bryan, *Rightful Remedy*, 28.

28. "British and Northern Slave Policy," *Charleston Mercury*, 13 July 1857, 2.
29. H. Jones, "Case of the Creole Slave Revolt," 31.
30. Perhaps the best recent account of the uprising itself can be found in Kerr-Ritchie, *Rebellious Passage*, 99–123.
31. Kerr-Ritchie, 137–41, 141. Several Bahamian figures involved in the *Creole* case remained in office two decades later during the Civil War, including Colonial Secretary Charles Nesbitt and Attorney General George Anderson, and issued repeated decisions that favored Confederate interests. See chapter 2.
32. Jones and Rakestraw, *Prologue to Manifest Destiny*, 81–89; Harrold, "Romanticizing Slave Revolt," 90–92.
33. Kerr-Ritchie, *Rebellious Passage*, 158–60; Craton, "Role of the Caribbean Vice Admiralty Courts in British Imperialism," 8–9. The fact that the court heard the case at all, given the Crown's legal opinion, shows that Bahamian courts and judges were willing to ignore or contest imperial decisions.
34. Harrold, "Romanticizing Slave Revolt," 101–2; H. Jones, "Case of the Creole Slave Revolt," 33–34.
35. Rugemer, *Problem of Emancipation*, 220–21.
36. Quoted in W. D. Jones, "Influence of Slavery on the Webster-Ashburton Negotiations," 48–52.
37. H. Jones, "Case of the Creole Slave Revolt," 43–47. The arbitration ruling did not admit that Britain had to return slaves or compensate owners in every case. The decision rested on the governor's order to have British troops board the *Creole*.
38. Murray, "Extradition of Fugitive Slaves from Canada."
39. Brode, *Odyssey of John Anderson*, 21.
40. Brode, 29–31; Finkelman, "International Extradition and Fugitive Slaves," 774–76. Finkelman overestimates the ability of the governor-general to overrule the wishes of the colonial ministers.
41. Abraham Fisher to the Duke of Newcastle, 9 Jan. 1861, f158, CO 42/631, CO 42: Colonial Office and predecessors: Canada, Original Correspondence—Secretary of State, reel B-451, HDL. CO 42/631 contains dozens of similar petitions.
42. "The Law in Great Britain and the United States," *Daily Dispatch* (Richmond), 19 Dec. 1860.
43. Sir William Fenwick Williams to Newcastle, 26 Jan. 1861, f60, CO 42/626, reel B-447, HDL.
44. Finkelman, "International Extradition and Fugitive Slaves," 777.
45. Brode, *Odyssey of John Anderson*, 87–99.
46. Denison, *Review of the Judgments of the Bench in the Anderson Extradition Case*.
47. *Mobile Evening News*, 18 Feb. 1861.

48. Cain and Hopkins, *British Imperialism*, 258–75; Dobson, *A History of Belize*, 124–25; Francis, *Governors and Settlers*, 239–41; McLaren, *Dewigged, Bothered, and Bewildered*, 43–46, 280–87.

49. Lord Clarendon to Cowley, 4 and 6 June 1856, quoted in Bourne, *Britain and the Balance of Power in North America*, 195.

50. Bourne, *Britain and the Balance of Power in North America*, 176–78.

51. Van Alstyne, "American Filibustering and the British Navy," 140.

52. Courtemanche, "Royal Navy and the End of William Walker," 352.

53. Vice Admiral Alexander Milne to the Secretary of the Admiralty, 4 Oct. 1860, in Milne, *The Milne Papers*, 2:110.

54. Courtemanche, *No Need of Glory*, 125–26.

55. Lord Lyons to Russell, 31 Dec. 1861, box 107, Private Correspondence, Lyons Papers, ACA; Charles J. Bayley to the Duke of Newcastle, 19 Aug. 1862, Governor's Despatches, 1861–1866 (microfilm), Bahamas National Archives; Lt. Gen. William Fenwick Williams to Lord Monck, 28 and 30 Nov. 1861, f157 and f174, CO 42/628, reel B-442, HDL.

56. Ruatan was the contemporary spelling of present-day Roatán.

57. May, *Manifest Destiny's Underworld*, 63–64.

58. Karp, *This Vast Southern Empire*, 195–96. The response of Davis, James Mason, and others to Cuban filibustering suggests that their aversion was practical rather than moral in this instance.

59. W. Walker, *The War in Nicaragua*, 275–79.

60. Cong. Globe, 35th Cong., 1st Sess. 222 (1858).

61. Cong. Globe, 35th Cong., 1st Sess. 217–21 (1858). Toombs served as the first secretary of state for the Confederacy and was the great-great-grandfather of entertainer and actor Roderick George Toombs, better known as "Rowdy" Roddy Piper.

62. Cong. Globe, 35th Cong., 1st Sess. 224–25 (1858).

63. May, "Irony of Southern Diplomacy," 77–78.

64. May, 78; Cong. Globe, 35th Cong., 1st Sess. 1541 (1858).

65. For the genesis of the violence among its French-Canadian participants, see Greer, *Patriots and the People*.

66. Stuart, *United States Expansionism in British North America*, 129–37.

67. Swanton, *North American* (Vt.), 1 July 1840, 2, and 25 July 1840, 3. *Morning Herald* (N.Y.), 28 May 1839, 2. Swanton was the site of fervent and vocal support for the Lower Canadian rebellion.

68. May, *Manifest Destiny's Underworld*, 10–13.

69. "Conspiracy to Kidnap and Abduct Wm. L. McKenzie, the Canadian Patriot," *Democratic Standard* (Georgetown, Ohio), 15 Dec. 1840, 1.

70. H. Jones, "Anglophobia and the Aroostook War." The story of the bear attacking British woodsmen is probably apocryphal.

71. Lyall, "From Imbroglio to Pig War," 73–77.

72. Unterman, *Uncle Sam's Policemen*, 48.

73. W. W. Brown, *Narrative of William W. Brown*, 71–77. Brown mistakenly identifies the year as 1836 in his memoir. Upper Canada (present-day Ontario) was renamed Canada West by the Act of Union in 1841.

74. "Kidnappers on Trial at Cleveland," *New York Times*, 8 July 1859, 5.

75. *Montreal Gazette*, 13 Jan. 1855. Reprinted in the *New York Times*, 17 Jan. 1855, 1.

76. *New York Times*, 7 Feb. 1855, 2.

77. Berwanger, "Case of Stirrup and Edwards."

78. Minute of the Duke of Newcastle, in Charles Nesbitt to Newcastle, 19 Aug. 1861, f47–48, CO 23/166, Secretary of State: Despatches, CO 23: Colonial Office and predecessors: Bahamas, Original Correspondence, TNA.

79. Harrold, *Border War*, 53–71.

80. Thomson, *Mercenaries, Pirates, and Sovereigns*, 69–77, 107–39.

81. Owsley, *King Cotton Diplomacy*, 1–14, 2.

82. See, most prominently, Beckert, *Empire of Cotton*.

83. Schoen, *Fragile Fabric of Union*, 10.

84. Marler, "'Abiding Faith in Cotton.'"

85. Owsley, *King Cotton Diplomacy*, 24–27.

86. Marler, *Merchants' Capital*, 81–84, 122–27.

87. Marler, "'Abiding Faith in Cotton,'" 263–67.

88. Hurt, *Agriculture and the Confederacy*, 9, 18–20.

89. *Mobile Advertiser and Register*, 3 Oct. 1861, 2.

90. *Wilmington Journal*, 17 Apr. 1861, 4; *Wilmington Journal*, 29 Aug. 1861, 2.

91. "A Back-Countryman," letter to the editor of the *Charleston Mercury*, 5 Oct. 1861, reprinted in *Southern Cultivator* 19, no. 11 (1861): 290; *Mobile Advertiser and Register*, 2 Oct. 1861, 2.

92. Hubbard, "James Mason, the 'Confederate Lobby' and the Blockade Debate of March 1862," 232–33.

93. *Economist*, 22 June and 21 Sept. 1861, quoted in Owsley, *King Cotton Diplomacy*, 40; Russell, *My Diary North and South*, 98.

94. Owsley, *King Cotton Diplomacy*, 32–38. John Milton to George Randolph, 25 June 1862; Milton to James M. Baker, 18 Aug. 1862, box 1, folder 11, Milton Letterbooks (1861–1863), State Library and Archives of Florida. Original held at Florida Historical Society, Cocoa.

95. Head, *Privateers of the Americas*, 5–8, 60–64.

96. For a broad survey of Confederate privateering, see W. M. Robinson, *The Confederate Privateers*.

97. Chet, *Ocean Is a Wilderness*, 37.

98. Weitz, *Confederacy on Trial*.

99. Sheehan-Dean, *Calculus of Violence*, 57–62.

100. Lemnitzer, *Power, Law, and the End of Privateering*, 132–33.

101. Speech of Jefferson Davis at Jackson, 26 Dec. 1862, in *PJD*, 8:576.

102. Dundas to Alexander Milne, 4 May 1861, in Milne, *The Milne Papers*, 2:275–76; Jenkins, *Britain and the War for the Union*, 1:96–97.

103. Jenkins, *Britain and the War for the Union*, 1:14.

104. Jenkins, 1:100–101.

105. Secretary of the Admiralty to Alexander Milne, with enclosures, 22 Dec. 1860, in Milne, *The Milne Papers*, 2:177–79.

106. Jenkins, *Britain and the War for the Union*, 1:88.

107. Charles Darling to Commodore Hugh Dunlop, 22 Oct. 1860, in Milne, *The Milne Papers*, 2:189–90; Jenkins, *Britain and the War for the Union*, 1:64–67.

Chapter Two. King Cotton and King Conch

The epigraph is from Lord Lyons to Lord John Russell, 30 Dec. 1862, box 107, Private Correspondence, Lyons Papers, ACA. A version of this chapter originally appears in the *Journal of Southern History* 89, no. 1 (2023): 61–88.

1. Charles R. Nesbitt, speech before the Bahamas Assembly, 18 Feb. 1862, f247, CO 23/168, CO 23: Colonial Office and predecessors: Bahamas, Original Correspondence, TNA. Nesbitt was the longtime colonial secretary of the Bahamas and on this occasion was filling in for the absent governor, Charles J. Bayley.

2. Bloemendal, "Conclusion"; Hunt, "Internationalizing US. Diplomatic History"; Paterson, "New Diplomatic History."

3. For example, many of the recent syntheses on Civil War diplomacy take a fairly state-centered approach even as they consider cultural and social factors. Herring, *From Colony to Superpower*, 224–64; Myers, *Caution and Cooperation*; H. Jones, *Blue and Gray Diplomacy*; Doyle, *Cause of All Nations*; May, "Irony of Southern Diplomacy."

4. Cain and Hopkins, *British Imperialism*; Belich, *Replenishing the Earth*; Darwin, *Empire Project*; Hopkins, *American Empire*.

5. Sexton, "Steam Transport, Sovereignty, and Empire in North America"; Tuffnell, "Expatriate Foreign Relations."

6. William Seward to J. Hume Burnley, 13 Mar. 1865, in United States, *Executive Documents Printed by Order of the House of Representatives, during the First Session of the Thirty-Ninth Congress, 1865–'66*, pt. 2, 95. In this correspondence, Seward had misidentified another man, a B. Adderly, as Henry Adderley, but his reaction was genuine.

7. J. Wilkinson, *Narrative of a Blockade Runner*, 140–41; Craton and Saunders, *Islanders in the Stream*, 19. "Conch" or "Conchy Joe" is a colloquial term for white Bahamians.

8. Wise, *Lifeline of the Confederacy*, 226, appendices 5–19.

9. Crook, *North, the South, and the Powers*; Foreman, *World on Fire*; Mahin, *One War at a Time*; Myers, *Caution and Cooperation*.

10. Jenkins, *Britain and the War for the Union*, 1:76–77, 117–19, 284; H. Jones, *Blue and Gray Diplomacy*, 83, 193; Owsley, *King Cotton Diplomacy*, 249–51, 300–301. Owsley mentions the Bahamas chiefly as a conduit for information for Confederate diplomats and to argue the ineffectiveness of the blockade. Jones mentions the islands only in passing, and the word "Bahamas" appears only twice in the entire text. By contrast, Jenkins gives Nassau attention as a site of blockade running and potential tension between Britain and the Union, credits the port's rise to prominence as a result of its usefulness as a coal depot, and attributes its friendliness to the Confederate cause as a product of greed.

11. Dubrulle, *Ambivalent Nation*, 60–63. Here "informal diplomacy" is distinct from "popular diplomacy" as defined by Dubrulle, as it concerns private actors working in the government interest, rather than popular opinion and the press.

12. Hubbard, *Burden of Confederate Diplomacy*. Hubbard analyzes Confederate diplomacy chiefly as a national project and emphasizes the failures of formal diplomacy.

13. See, for example, Bradlee, *Blockade Running during the Civil War*; Cochran, *Blockade Runners of the Confederacy*.

14. Saunders, "Blockade Running Era in the Bahamas"; Peters, "Blockade-Running in the Bahamas during the Civil War."

15. Bonner and McCord, "Reassessment of the Union Blockade's Effectiveness in the Civil War"; Still, "Naval Sieve"; Surdam, "Union Navy's Blockade Reconsidered"; Surdam, *Northern Naval Superiority and the Economics of the American Civil War*; Wise, *Lifeline of the Confederacy*; Ross, *Breaking the Blockade*. Wise provides a wealth of detail on the war-related traffic to and from Nassau but devotes little attention to how Confederates built their network there. Ross rectifies some of this with a very detailed popular history of blockade running in Nassau.

16. Craton and Saunders, *Islanders in the Stream*, 31–44; Bahamas Blue Book, 1860, f109–11, CO 27/59, CO 27: Colonial Office and predecessors: Bahamas, Miscellaneous, TNA; Bahamas Blue Book, 1864, f83 and f91, CO 27/62, TNA.

17. Gorman, "Adderley Family in the New World"; Nepveux, *George Alfred Trenholm and the Company That Went to War*, 6–8, 73–77.

18. Craton and Saunders, *Islanders in the Stream*, 33–40; Phillips, "Changing Role of the Merchant Class in the British West Indies," 163–84.

19. Startup, "'Guardians of Our Own Honor,'" 15–21.

20. Themistocleous, "Merchant Princes of Nassau," 145–63.

21. Peters, "American Loyalists in the Bahama Islands," 226.

22. Troxler, "Use of the Bahamas by Southern Loyalist Exiles," 185.

23. Craton, *History of the Bahamas*, 151.

24. Peters, "American Loyalists in the Bahama Islands," 228–29.

25. Will of Nehemiah Adderley, 5 Feb. 1845, Supreme Court Wills, BNA.

26. Gorman, "Adderley Family in the New World," 36.

27. Craton and Saunders, *Islanders in the Stream*, 17.

28. Gorman, "Adderley Family in the New World," 38.

29. A list of officeholders can be found in the Bahamas Blue Book, 1861, CO 27/59, TNA. Slaveowner information is available from the *Legacies of British Slavery database*, University College London, https://www.ucl.ac.uk/lbs. Nesbitt's position as colonial secretary meant he served as the chief assistant to the appointed governor and administered the government in his absence. It should not be confused with the imperial cabinet position of colonial secretary.

30. Themistocleous, "Merchant Princes of Nassau," 46–67.

31. Samuel Whiting to Robert Shufeldt, 28 July 1861, United States Consular Records for Nassau, Bahamas, 1821–1935 vol. 13, RG 84: Records of Foreign Service Posts of the Department of State, NARA II.

32. Wise, *Lifeline of the Confederacy*, appendices 5–8.

33. Lewis Heyliger to Judah P. Benjamin, 10 Dec. 1861, in *OR*, ser. 4, 1:781.

34. Winsboro and Knetsch, "Florida Slaves, the 'Saltwater Railroad,' to the Bahamas, and Anglo-American Diplomacy," 77.

35. Kerr-Ritchie, *Rebellious Passage*; Rugemer, *Problem of Emancipation*, 180–85; Guterl, *American Mediterranean*, 50–59; Jones and Rakestraw, *Prologue to Manifest Destiny*, 81–89.

36. F. I. Wilson, *Sketches of Nassau*, 5–24.

37. Craton, *History of the Bahamas*, 223.

38. Charles R. Nesbitt to the Duke of Newcastle, 21 June 1861, f343, CO 23/165, BNA.

39. Law Officers of the Crown to Lord John Russell, 7 Dec. 1860, f2–3, FO 414/17, Correspondence Relative to the Civil War in the United States, November 1860 to January 1862, FO 414: Foreign Office, Confidential Print, North America, TNA.

40. Charles R. Nesbitt to the Duke of Newcastle, 21 June 1861.

41. Charles R. Nesbitt to the Duke of Newcastle, 5 July 1861, CO 23/165, BNA.

42. Charles R. Nesbitt to the Duke of Newcastle, 11 July 1861, f480–82, CO 23/165, TNA; "Pennsylvania, U.S., Federal Naturalization Records, 1795–1931 for Archibald Forsyth," image 302 of 8483, Declarations 1001–1500 (Original)(Film), Ancestry.com, accessed March 15, 2021.

43. Colonial Office circular, 22 Oct. 1861, f415–19, CO 854/6, Circular Despatches, 1858–1861, CO 854: Colonial Office and predecessors: Colonies (General), TNA; Harry St. George Ord to the Duke of Newcastle, 15 Aug. 1861, including Colonial Office minutes, f347–50, CO 37/178, CO 37: Bermuda, Original Correspondence, TNA; Board of Trade to Undersecretary of State, Colonial Office, 3 Oct. 1861, f200–201, CO 37/180; Arthur Gordon to Lord Lyons, 14 June 1862, box 122, Letters Received, Lyons Papers, ACA.

44. Blume, "Flight from the Flag."

45. See, for example, the compiled list of blockade runners in Correspondence Respecting the Blockade of the Ports of the Confederate States, pt. 1, FO 414/20, TNA.

46. John P. Baldwin to Henry Adderley, 30 July 1861, in United States, *Message of the President of the United States to the Two Houses of Congress*, 1:154–55; Obituary of John P. Baldwin, *Bahama Herald*, 10 Dec. 1864, 2.

47. Craton and Saunders, *Islanders in the Stream*, 143–44.

48. Henry Adderley to Charles R. Nesbitt, 19 Nov. 1861, f3, Correspondence Relative to the Civil War in North America, pt. 2, FO 414/18: Confidential Print, North America, TNA.

49. Lewis Heyliger to George W. Randolph, 5 Apr. 1862, in *OR*, ser. 4, 1:1057.

50. Affidavit of John S. Howell, 16 Feb. 1869, in Alabama Claims, 6:317–18.

51. Lewis Heyliger to Judah P. Benjamin, 10 Dec. 1861, in *OR*, ser. 4, 1:781; Heyliger to Benjamin, 15 Dec. 1861, in *OR*, ser. 4, 1:798.

52. D.T. Bisbie to Judah P. Benjamin, 16 Dec. 1861, in *OR*, ser. 4, 1:800–801.

53. Lewis Heyliger to Judah P. Benjamin, 16 Dec. 1861, in *OR*, ser. 4, 1:799; Craton, *History of the Bahamas*, 215.

54. Charles J. Helm to Judah P. Benjamin, 21 Dec. 1861, in *OR*, ser. 4, 1:806–7.

55. Charles J. Bayley to the Duke of Newcastle, 11 Nov. 1861, f482, CO 23/167, TNA. In addition to having great wealth, Henry Adderley and his son, Augustus, were members of the House of Assembly. In addition, Governor Bayley nominated George D. Harris, Adderley's son-in-law and a partner in the firm, to the Executive Council in 1861.

56. Because the U.S. Army and U.S. Navy occupied or otherwise denied access to the Confederacy's other deepwater ports on the Atlantic coast, almost all blockade-running steamers traveling from Nassau and Bermuda—the two most important

colonial ports by volume of trade—went in to either Charleston or Wilmington. They had adequate coastal defenses, harbor facilities, and rail transportation inland. Only eight successful inbound steamer trips entered Atlantic Florida or Georgia ports, and none after January 1863. Schooners and other small vessels continued to use smaller ports and inlets along the coast, but the lack of transportation infrastructure inland from these locations made them of only marginal use for large-scale supply imports and cotton exports. Confederate armies, especially in Virginia, relied on rail networks to supply their needs. See Wise, *Lifeline of the Confederacy*, 233–68; Hess, *Civil War Supply and Strategy*, 328–52.

57. Lewis Heyliger to Judah P. Benjamin, 22 Feb. 1862, H-94-1862, reel 50, RG 109: Letters Received by the Confederate Secretary of War, NARA.

58. William S. Lindsay to the Duke of Newcastle, 31 Dec. 1862, with endorsements, f535–36, CO 23/170, TNA.

59. Charles O. Witte Letterbook, 1861–1867, South Caroliniana Library, University of South Carolina.

60. Witte Letterbook, f361, f399.

61. Judah P. Benjamin to Lord Lyons, 12 July 1861, box 121, Letters Received, Lyons Papers, ACA.

62. Tidwell, Hall, and Gaddy, *Come Retribution*, 91. Southerners, especially in Richmond, also received European news via the systematic smuggling of Northern newspapers.

63. W. B. Johnson, *Race Relations in the Bahamas*, xix, 3–7; Themistocleous, "Merchant Princes of Nassau," 141–45; Craton and Saunders, *Islanders in the Stream*, 26–29.

64. Charles J. Bayley to the Duke of Newcastle, 10 Sept. 1863, f140–45, CO 23/172, TNA.

65. Votes of the House of Assembly, 1862, p. 22, BNA.

66. Edward B. A. Taylor to Charles J. Bayley, 24 Mar. 1863, in Votes of the House of Assembly, 1863, pp. 90–91, 130–31, BNA.

67. *Nassau Guardian*, 7 Feb. 1863.

68. Charles J. Bayley to the Duke of Newcastle, 8 Mar. 1864, with enclosures, f353, CO 23/174, TNA. Edwin Adderley was little more than a boy at the time and was plainly used as the fraudulent "owner" of the *Ella Warley*.

69. For example, Governor Bayley deferred attempting to reform jury service rules because of anticipated opposition from the House of Assembly. Charles J. Bayley to the Duke of Newcastle, 29 Apr. 1862, CO 23/168, TNA.

70. Benton and Ford, *Rage for Order*, 26, 148–52.

71. Wise, *Lifeline of the Confederacy*, 290.

72. Henry Adderley and Co. to Charles J. Bayley, 7 May 1862, CO 23/168, TNA. Letters sent under the name of the firm usually do not indicate which partner or clerk authored them, but one may assume that one of the Adderleys or George D. Harris wrote or approved of any communications with the government.

73. Charles J. Bayley to Lord Lyons, 12 May 1862, box 122, Letters Received, Lyons Papers, ACA.

74. Lord Lyons to Alexander Milne, 26 May 1862, box 107, Private Correspondence, Lyons Papers, ACA.

75. Bernath, *Squall across the Atlantic*, 165–67; Weitz, *Confederacy on Trial*.

76. Bernath, *Squall across the Atlantic*, 65–66. Chapters 5 and 6 offer a good summary of "continuous voyage" cases.

77. Henry Adderley and Co. to Charles J. Bayley, 12 May 1862, CO 23/168, TNA; Lord Lyons to Lord Russell, 5 June 1862, f4, FO 414/26, Correspondence Respecting Interference with Trade Between New York and the Bahamas, TNA.

78. Courtemanche, *No Need of Glory*, 101–4.

79. Alabama Claims, 6:310–12.

80. Ross, *Breaking the Blockade*, 92, 96–98.

81. Affidavit of James Jenkins, 17 Feb. 1869, Alabama Claims, 6:316–17; Startup, "'This Small Act of Courtesy,'" 59. Watson and HMS *Peterel* had replaced Hickley and HMS *Greyhound* on the Bahamas station in between the seizure and the trial.

82. The Duke of Newcastle to Charles J. Bayley, 23 Dec. 1863, f366, CO 23/172, TNA; Frederic Rogers to Edmund Hammond, 29 Dec. 1863, f370, CO 23/172.

83. Speech of Charles J. Bayley to the Bahamas House of Assembly, 2 Mar. 1863, reprinted in *Liverpool Mercury*, 6 Apr. 1863.

84. *New York Herald*, 24 Mar. 1863.

85. Sir Frederic Rogers, comments on dispatch no. 18, 8 Mar. 1863, f116–17, CO 23/171, TNA.

86. The Duke of Newcastle to Charles J. Bayley, reprinted in the *New York Times*, 23 Aug. 1864.

87. The Duke of Newcastle to Charles J. Bayley, 11 Apr. 1863, Votes of the House of Assembly, 1863, 30–31, microfilm, BNA; Bayley to Newcastle, 5 May 1863, f271–78, CO 23/171, TNA.

88. Edward B. A. Taylor to Charles J. Bayley, March 1863; Receiver General to Bayley, 24 Mar. 1863 (two letters), Votes of the House of Assembly, 1863.

89. Charles J. Bayley to the Duke of Newcastle, 19 May 1864, f556, CO 23/174, TNA.

90. George D. Harris to Charles R. Nesbitt, 4 Aug. 1864, f399, CO 23/175, TNA.

91. Francis, *Governors and Settlers*, 258.

92. Charles J. Bayley to Lord Lyons, with enclosures, 9 May 1863, f31, FO 414/26, TNA. The U.S. consul in Nassau refused to cancel many of the bonds on the grounds that they were either fraudulent or had been violated.

93. James Mason to Judah P. Benjamin, 6 Aug. 1863, with enclosures, in *ORN*, ser. 2, 3:857–58; John B. Lafitte to Edmund Hammond, 21 July 1865, FO 5/1234, Case of the *Margaret* and *Jessie*, maritime jurisdiction beyond the three-mile limit, FO 5: Political and Other Departments: General Correspondence before 1906, United States of America, Series II, TNA.

94. Lewis Heyliger to Judah P. Benjamin, 6 Feb. 1863, reel 8, CSAR.

95. Charles J. Bayley to the Duke of Newcastle, 3 Feb. 1863, f73, CO 23/171, TNA.

96. Judah P. Benjamin to Lewis Heyliger, 21 Feb. 1863, in *ORN*, ser. 2, 3:697–98.

97. Wise, *Lifeline of the Confederacy*, 145–47.

98. H. Jones, *Blue and Gray Diplomacy*, 158–60.

99. Charles R. Nesbitt to Lewis Heyliger, 2 Oct. 1862, reel 8, CSAR.

100. Cleland, "Between King Cotton and Queen Victoria."

101. Sumner, *Works of Charles Sumner*, 13:85–86.

102. Wise, *Lifeline of the Confederacy*, 226.

103. Canada, for example, did so in 1864 under Union diplomatic and economic pressure. See Winks, *Civil War Years*, 138–39.

104. Kerr-Ritchie, *Rebellious Passage*, 125–44.

Chapter Three. "I Risk with All Concerned"

The epigraph is from F. M. B., "Blockade Running in Statu Quo" [*sic*], *Bahama Herald*, 23 Mar. 1864, 2.

1. John Tory Bourne to John Fraser & Co., 27 Mar. 1862, in Vandiver, *Confederate Blockade Running through Bermuda*, 10–12.

2. Vandiver, *Confederate Blockade Running through Bermuda*, xx–xxi.

3. Bensel, *Yankee Leviathan*, 95, 179–81.

4. Owsley, *State Rights in the Confederacy*, 1.

5. E. Thomas, *Confederacy as a Revolutionary Experience*, 58–59, 64.

6. E. Thomas, *Confederate Nation*, 145–55.

7. Thomas, 204–14.

8. Davis, *Look Away!*, 287–304; McCurry, *Confederate Reckoning*, 153–63; Koistinen, *Beating Plowshares into Swords*, 197–214. Davis contends that forays into "salt socialism" and other economic interventionism marked a previously "unthinkable" departure from the Confederacy's libertarian founding ideals. McCurry finds that the war forced the Confederate government into "a striking realignment of state-

citizen relations" but from the bottom up, as economic conditions, slave (and slaveowner) resistance, and the activism of women brought these previously marginal groups fully to the state's attention.

9. Bonner, *Confederate Political Economy*, 9–17.

10. Koistinen, *Beating Plowshares into Swords*, 2–7. Koistinen, in a five-volume series, periodizes American (including Confederate) mobilization for warfare into preindustrial, transitional, and industrial stages.

11. Koistinen, 271–72.

12. Wilson, *Business of Civil War*, 72–107.

13. Wilson, *Confederate Industry*, 155–79. The challenges of the Confederate Quartermaster Department's Bureau of Foreign Supplies perfectly illustrate the maze of competing contracts, purchasers, and shippers in Europe and colonies.

14. M. T. Bernath, "Confederacy as a Moment of Possibility."

15. Karp, *This Vast Southern Empire*, 1–9.

16. Balogh, *Government out of Sight*, esp. chap. 5; Novak, "Myth of the 'Weak' American State"; Edling, *Hercules in the Cradle*, 14–17, 87, 227–30.

17. Davis, *Look Away!*, 85–86, 93.

18. Thomas, *Confederate Nation*, 265. Thomas, in making this claim, cites Hill, *State Socialism in the Confederate States of America*.

19. Rao, *National Duties*, 4–12, 169–76.

20. Rao, 161–62.

21. Jarvis, *In the Eye of All Trade*, 12–18.

22. Trade data compiled from Bermuda Blue Book, 1861, CO 41/56, CO 41: Colonial Office and predecessors: Bermuda, Miscellanea, TNA. The United States was Bermuda's chief trade partner, accounting for over 60 percent of the colony's imports and 50 percent of its exports.

23. Walker, *Journal of Georgiana Walker*, 41.

24. Jarvis, *In the Eye of All Trade*, 69–70.

25. Harry St. George Ord to the Duke of Newcastle, 19 Sept. 1863, with enclosures, f209–75, CO 37/187, CO 37: Colonial Office and predecessors: Bermuda, Original Correspondence, TNA; Ord to Newcastle, 6 Nov. 1863, f276–77, CO 37/187, TNA.

26. Ord to Newcastle, 2 Nov. 1861, f214–21, CO 37/179, TNA.

27. J. T. Bourne to Daniel Draper & Son, 12 Sept. 1861, in Vandiver, *Confederate Blockade Running through Bermuda*, 5.

28. Harry St. George Ord to the Duke of Newcastle, 15 Aug. 1861, f347–50, CO 37/178, TNA; Board of Trade to Undersecretary of State, Colonial Office, 3 Oct. 1861, f200–201, CO 37/180, TNA.

29. *Bermuda Royal Gazette*, 31 Dec. 1861.

30. Charles Maxwell Allen to William H. Seward, 26 June 1862, in Allen, *Dispatches from Bermuda*, 51.

31. *Bermuda Royal Gazette*, 22 July 1862; Ord to Newcastle, 7 Aug. 1862, f111–15, CO 37/183, TNA.

32. C. M. Allen to W. Seward, 10 Jan. 1862, in Allen, *Dispatches from Bermuda*, 27.

33. C. M. Allen to Susan Allen, 24 Apr. 1862 and 15 July 1862, in Allen, *Dispatches from Bermuda*, 43, 56–57.

34. Quote is found in J. T. Bourne to A. J. M. Gilbert, 4 Jan. 1862, f259–60, CO 23/182, TNA; Ord's report on the matter is found in his dispatch of 24 Feb. 1862, f256–66, CO 37/182, TNA.

35. Ord to Newcastle, 6 Oct. 1862, f377–88, CO 37/183, TNA. Bermuda was an important naval base, but Milne's fleet was stretched thin, monitoring the blockade and events in the Caribbean and Mexico, so there was not always a warship present and ready for duty.

36. *Bermuda Royal Gazette*, 7 July 1863; Walker, *Journal of Georgiana Walker*, 44.

37. Robert Minor to Adm. Franklin Buchanan, 2 Feb. 1864, in *ORN*, ser. 1, 2:822–27.

38. Marie DeRosset to Mother [Eliza DeRosset], 27 Sept. 1864, DeRosset Family Papers #214, SHC; Armand DeRosset to Louis DeRosset, 26 Oct. 1864, DeRosset Family Papers, SHC.

39. Walker, *Journal of Georgiana Walker*, 42.

40. Walker, 78.

41. Walker, 46.

42. "The 4th of July at St. George's," *Bermuda Royal Gazette*, 7 July 1863.

43. Walker, *Journal of Georgiana Walker*, 49–50.

44. William C. J. Hyland to State Department, 21 July 1863, in Allen, *Dispatches from Bermuda*, 97.

45. Ord to Newcastle, 27 Aug. 1863, f166–75, CO 37/187, TNA.

46. Walker, *Journal of Georgiana Walker*, 86.

47. Milne to Admiral Sir Frederick Grey (First Naval Lord), 12 Dec. 1863, MLN/116/2, Sir Alexander Milne Papers, MM; Secretary of the Admiralty to Edmund Hammond, with enclosures, 4 Jan. 1864, FO 5/979, in *Milne Papers*, vol. 3. Milne described Glasse as "fragile" and "unstable."

48. Alexander Milne to the Secretary of the Admiralty, 2 Dec. 1863, f396–97, North American and West Indian Station: Admiralty out letterbook, volume "G," 18 May 1863–7 Jan. 1864, MLN/104/7, Sir Alexander Milne Papers, MM.

49. Walker, *Journal of Georgiana Walker*, 91.

50. Walker, 92.

51. *Bermuda Royal Gazette*, 17 May 1864.

52. Raphael Semmes to James Heyward North, 2 Feb. 1862, in *ORN*, ser. 2, 2:140; Luraghi, *History of the Confederate Navy*, 83–87.

53. Raphael Semmes to James Heyward North, 23 Jan. 1862 and 13 Feb. 1862, in *ORN*, ser. 2, 2:136, 145–46. Quote is from p. 145; James Mason to Judah Benjamin, 30 Oct. 1862, in *OR*, ser. 2, 4:930–31. Hester's full name was frequently misidentified in correspondence. Depositions taken from the *Sumter*'s crew identify him as Joseph Goodwyn (or Goodwin) Hester.

54. James D. Bulloch to Stephen Mallory, 25 Oct. 1862, in *ORN*, ser. 2, 2:282.

55. See depositions enclosed in Newcastle to Ord, 30 May 1863, Secretary of State's Despatches, CS 5/1/37, Bermuda Archives.

56. James Mason to Lord Russell, 21 July 1863, in *FRUS* 1864, 801.

57. Ord to Newcastle, 6 June 1863, f30–33, CO 37/187; Alexander Milne to Lord Lyons, 26 June 1863, f184, MLN 105/3, Papers of Sir Alexander Milne, MM.

58. Ord to Newcastle, 4 Aug. 1863, Governor's Despatches, 1862–1868, CS 6/1/8, Bermuda Archives.

59. John Wilkinson to Ord, 24 Aug. 1863, CO 37/187, TNA.

60. On Hester's postwar activities, see Matthew Pearl, "K Troop: The Story of the Eradication of the Original Ku Klux Klan," accessed 26 May 2017, http://www.slate.com/articles/news_and_politics/history/2016/03/how_a_detachment_of_u_s_army_soldiers_smoked_out_the_original_ku_klux_klan.html; personal correspondence with the author.

61. Outgoing cargo manifests indicate that no blockade runners left Bermuda in 1861, and only a handful in 1862, mostly late in the year. Vandiver, *Confederate Blockade Running through Bermuda*, 109–10.

62. James T. Welsman to Charles K. Prioleau, 14 July 1864, B/FT 1/159, in the Business Records of Fraser, Trenholm & Company of Liverpool and Charleston, South Carolina, 1860–1877 (microfilm), Merseyside Maritime Museum, Liverpool, UK.

63. Josiah Gorgas to James Seddon, 5 Dec. 1862, in *OR*, ser. 4, 2:227.

64. Wise, *Lifeline of the Confederacy*, 124.

65. J. T. Bourne to John Fraser & Co., 18 Sept. 1863, in Vandiver, *Confederate Blockade Running through Bermuda*, 46–47.

66. Welsman to Prioleau, 14 July 1864. Bourne had ten children, a sickly wife, and limited financial means. Welsman found him to be scrupulously honest, though perhaps not possessed with the sharpest business acumen.

67. See Bourne letters in Vandiver, *Confederate Blockade Running through Bermuda*, 31–43.

68. Petition of John T. Bourne, 30 Sept. 1861, Ship's Documents, 1860/5, Sessional and Allied Papers, 1860–1868, Bermuda Archives.

69. The *Advance* was originally dubbed the *Ad-Vance* or *A.D. Vance* but appears in contemporary correspondence under a wide variety of spellings. I have used *Advance* for the sake of clarity. Zebulon Vance to John White, 12 Mar. 1863, and White to Vance, 20 May 1863, in Vance, *Papers of Zebulon Baird Vance*, 2:84–86, 2:161; J. T. Bourne to John White, 26 Oct. 1863, and Bourne to Collie, Westhead & Co., 19 Nov. 1863, in Vandiver, *Confederate Blockade Running through Bermuda*, 49–51. Virginia owned and operated the steamer *City of Petersburg*, and South Carolina owned the *Alice*. James A. Seddon to Vance, 12 Feb. 1864, in Vance, *Papers of Zebulon Baird Vance*, 3:105.

70. Sexton, *Debtor Diplomacy*, 162–65.

71. Sexton, 172–79.

72. Abraham C. Myers to Richard P. Waller, 22 July 1863, in *OR*, ser. 4, 2:658–59.

73. James Seddon to Colin J. McRae, 26 Sept. 1863, in *OR*, ser. 4, 2:824–27.

74. Wise, *Lifeline of the Confederacy*, 136–39; Sexton, *Debtor Diplomacy*, 175–76, 182–83.

75. Colin J. McRae to Josiah Gorgas, 4 Sept. 1863, in *OR*, ser. 4, 2:889–90.

76. Davis to Herschel V. Johnson, 22 July 1864, in *OR*, ser. 4, 3:552–53. Davis explicitly blamed the congressional influence of blockade-running interests in preventing earlier attempts at trade controls.

77. Seddon to Vance, 14 Jan. 1864, *Papers of Zebulon Vance* 3:51–52.

78. For a detailed account of Confederate War Department foreign supply operations, see H. S. Wilson, *Confederate Industry*, chap. 5.

79. Vance to Seddon, 7 Jan. 1864, *Papers of Zebulon Vance* 3:23–24.

80. For a sampling of Bourne's widespread correspondence, see the John Tory Bourne Letterbooks, 1863–1869, Bermuda Archives, and Vandiver, *Confederate Blockade Running through Bermuda*.

81. *Proceedings of the First Confederate Congress, Fourth Session, 7 December 1863–18 February 1864*, 41.

82. *Proceedings of the First Confederate Congress, Fourth Session, 7 December 1863–18 February 1864*, 82, 126.

83. *Proceedings of the First Confederate Congress, Fourth Session, 7 December 1863–18 February 1864*, 226.

84. "An Act to prohibit the importation of luxuries, or of articles not necessaries or of common use," in Matthews, *Statues at Large of the Confederate States of America*, 179–81.

85. "A bill to impose regulations upon the foreign commerce of the Confederate States to provide for the public defense," in Matthews, 181–83.

86. Richard Bensel characterizes these laws as "an unprecedented imposition of central state controls on the flow of foreign trade," although a closer examination

suggests that in practice, this control was tenuous and always shared with other stakeholders. Bensel, *Yankee Leviathan*, 180.

87. Confederate States of America, *Act to Impose Regulations upon the Foreign Commerce of the Confederate States*, 4–10. The regulations, first released in March 1864, were printed alongside the act in this pamphlet.

88. Bourne to Turner Bros, Hyde & Co., 16 Apr. 1864, in Vandiver, *Confederate Blockade Running through Bermuda*, 61.

89. Quoted in Wise, *Lifeline of the Confederacy*, 146.

90. Welsman to Prioleau, 14 July 1864.

91. "Commercial," *Bahama Herald*, 16 Mar. 1864, 3.

92. "Blockade Running as It Will Be," *Bahama Herald*, 19 Mar. 1864, 2.

93. F. M. B., "Blockade Running in Statu Quo" [*sic*], *Bahama Herald*, 23 Mar. 1864, 2.

94. See *Bahama Herald* of Mar. 23, 26, and 30, 1864.

95. *Bahama Herald*, 30 Mar. 1864, 2.

96. X [Lewis Heyliger], "The Blockade," *Nassau Guardian*, 30 Mar. 1864, 2.

97. A. G. Magrath, Confederate States vs. Smuggled Liquors, 17 Dec. 1864, 17-M-9-10, Margaret and Jessie, M909—Papers Pertaining to Vessels of or Involved With the Confederate States of America: 'Vessel Papers,' NARA.

98. See cargo manifests reprinted in Vandiver, *Confederate Blockade Running through Bermuda*, 138–45.

99. Vance, *Papers of Zebulon Baird Vance*, 1:lii–lv.

100. Zebulon Vance to Jefferson Davis, 17 Mar. 1864, Vance, *Papers of Zebulon Baird Vance*, 3:151–53.

101. Jefferson Davis to Herschel V. Johnson, 22 July 1864, in *OR*, ser. 4, 3:552.

102. Vance to James A. Seddon, 8 Mar. 1864, Vance, *Papers of Zebulon Baird Vance*, 3:139–40.

103. Davis to Vance, 26 Mar. 1864, Vance, *Papers of Zebulon Baird Vance*, 3:158–60.

104. See Vance to Alexander Collie, 28 Dec. 1863, and H. Fitzhugh to Vance, 2 Dec. 1863, Vance, *Papers of Zebulon Baird Vance*, 2:335, 353–54.

105. Seddon to Vance, 12 Feb. 1864, Vance, *Papers of Zebulon Baird Vance*, 3:105.

106. William Porcher Miles to Milledge L. Bonham, 19 Feb. 1864, no. 508, William Porcher Miles Papers, SHC.

107. Joseph Brown to Vance, 13 Apr. 1864, Vance, *Papers of Zebulon Baird Vance*, 3:172–73.

108. *Proceedings of the Second Confederate Congress, First Session, 2 May–14 June 1864*, 181–82.

109. Jefferson Davis to the House of Representatives, 10 June 1864, in Richardson, *Messages and Papers of Jefferson Davis and the Confederacy*, 1:252–56.
110. Davis, *Look Away!*, 308. Davis did not address the role or influence of foreign shippers and merchants on blockade running.
111. Wise, *Lifeline of the Confederacy*, 151–52.
112. William Hamley to Edward Cardwell, 1 Sept. 1864, f368–371, CO 37/189, TNA.
113. Wise, *Lifeline of the Confederacy*, 240–41.
114. William Hamley to Edward Cardwell, 9 Sept. 1864, f380–381, CO 37/189, TNA.
115. Walker, *Journal of Georgiana Walker*, 102–3.
116. Population statistics from Bermuda Blue Book, 1864, CO 41/59, TNA; William Hamley to Edward Cardwell, 14 Dec. 1864, Governor's Despatches, 1862–1868, Bermuda Archives.
117. Wise, *Lifeline of the Confederacy*, 150–52, 156.

Chapter Four. "The Heartless Slave-Dealers in America"

The epigraph is from a speech given by Robert S. Evans, president of the Bahamas Friendly Society, on the anniversary of British emancipation, printed in the *Bahama Herald*, 6 Aug. 1859, 2.

1. British colonial censuses, official documents, and popular usage sometimes differentiated between Black people with darker skin and those of lighter complexion or mixed-race heritage by using the term "coloured" for the latter.
2. F. I. Wilson, *Sketches of Nassau*, 6.
3. Thompson, *Working on the Dock of the Bay*, 2.
4. Craton and Saunders, *Islanders in the Stream*, 11–15, 115–17; H. Johnson, "Friendly Societies in the Bahamas"; W. B. Johnson, *Race Relations in the Bahamas*, 50–69; K. E. Robinson, *Heritage, Including an Account of Bermudian Builders, Pilots, and Petitioners of the Early Post-Abolition Period*.
5. Adderley, "New Negroes from Africa," 92–125; Bradshaw, "History of the Friendly Societies"; Downing, "Friendly Planet."
6. Horne, *Negro Comrades of the Crown*, 90–114; Rugemer, *Problem of Emancipation*, 180–221; Sexton, "Anglophobia in Nineteenth-Century Elections, Politics, and Diplomacy."
7. Winsboro and Knetsch, "Florida Slaves, the 'Saltwater Railroad' to the Bahamas, and Anglo-American Diplomacy"; Kerr-Ritchie, *Rebellious Passage*.

8. Scott, *Common Wind*, 38–75; Linebaugh and Rediker, *Many-Headed Hydra*, 1–7; Payne, "'General Insurrection in the Countries with Slaves'"; Kerr-Ritchie, *Rites of August First*.

9. H. Johnson, "Friendly Societies in the Bahamas," 183.

10. Johnson, 186–87, n47. While I have used the contemporary name Out Islands to refer to the archipelago beyond New Providence, this has been renamed Family Islands in modern usage.

11. On Tucker's role, see "Report of the Young Men's Friendly Institution," *Bermuda Royal Gazette*, 16 May 1848, 4.

12. "Seizure of Slaves," *Niles' Weekly Register* 48 (1835): 41–56. The quote is from a reprint of an account in the *Bermuda Royal Gazette*, 24 Feb. 1835.

13. Kerr-Ritchie, *Rebellious Passage*, 73–76, 254.

14. Edmund Hammond to Herman Merivale, 3 Feb. 1855, with enclosures, f431, CO 37/154, TNA.

15. Freeman Murray to G. C. Lewis, 3 Oct. 1860, with enclosures, f294, CO 37/175, TNA. Williams's fate is unclear, as further efforts were interrupted by the Civil War. The British government declined to buy his freedom because it did not wish to establish such a precedent.

16. Freeman Murray to the Duke of Newcastle, 12 July 1860, with enclosures, f80, CO 37/175, TNA; "A Supposed Slaver," *Bermuda Royal Gazette*, 10 July 1860, 2.

17. *Nassau Guardian*, 1 Aug. 1849, 2; Hamer, "Great Britain, the United States, and the Negro Seamen Acts," 4. Quote is from the printed address in the newspaper.

18. *Bahama Herald*, 3 Aug. 1850, 2.

19. Robert S. Evans, speech on the anniversary of British Emancipation, *Bahama Herald*, 6 Aug. 1859, 2.

20. Kerr-Ritchie, *Rebellious Passage*, 138–48.

21. Winsboro and Knetsch, "Florida Slaves, the 'Saltwater Railroad' to the Bahamas, and Anglo-American Diplomacy," 68–69.

22. See, for example, the government inquiry into riots in Grant's Town involving West India Regiment soldiers, printed in *Nassau Guardian*, 5 Sept. 1863, 2.

23. *Bahama Herald*, 2 Aug. 1864. The newspaper reported the name as the "Baptist and Foreign Anti-Slavery Society," although it appears this was an error.

24. See, for example, Stephen Trenchard to Gideon Welles, 12 May 1863, in *ORN*, ser. 1, 2:182–83. The *Rhode Island*'s Bahamian pilot aided them in driving a blockade runner back into Nassau.

25. A. G. Clary to Charles Wilkes, 20 May 1863, in *ORN*, ser. 1, 2:199–200.

26. Affidavit of R. E. M. Solomon, Alabama Claims, 6:310–12.

27. Seth Hawley to William Seward, 24 Mar. 1863, and Hawley to Seward, 28 Mar. 1863, Microcopy T-475, roll 11, Despatches from United States Consuls in Nassau, New Providence Island, 1829–1906, RG 59: General Records of the Department of State, NARA II (hereafter cited as Consular Despatches—Nassau); report of A. G. Clary, March 23, 1863, in *ORN*, ser. 1, 2:133–34; U.S. Congress, House, 1869, *Mathew Lowe. Letter from the Secretary of State, enclosing a communication from the United States consul at Nassau, New Providence, in reference to the claim of Captain Mathew Lowe i.e., Matthew Low. January 7, 1869—Referred to the Committee on Foreign Affairs and ordered to be printed*, 40th Cong., 3rd Sess., H. Misc. Doc. No. 20, serial 1385, 1–4.

28. Hawley to Seward, 24 Mar. 1863.

29. Hawley to Seward, 24 Mar. 1863.

30. Lewis Heyliger to Judah P. Benjamin, 6 June 1863, in *ORN*, ser. 1, 2:236–37; letter from "X" [Lewis Heyliger], *Nassau Guardian*, 2 June 1862, 2.

31. Mathew Lowe to Thomas Kirkpatrick, 29 Oct. 1868, H. Misc. Doc. No. 20, serial 1385, 2–3.

32. Samuel Whiting to William H. Seward, 27 Feb. 1863, roll 11, Consular Despatches—Nassau.

33. Seth Hawley to Charles Wilkes, 27 May 1863, in *ORN*, ser. 1, 2:221–22.

34. "Our Nassau Correspondence," *New York Times*, 13 Feb. 1863, 8.

35. Samuel Whiting to Gideon Welles, 14 Feb. 1863, United States Consular Records for Hamilton, Bermuda, British West Indies ca. 1853–1940, vol. 14, RG 84: Records of Foreign Service Posts of the Department of State, NARA II. This volume was mislabeled at the archive facility when it was referenced; it actually contains dispatches from the consul at Nassau, Bahamas, from 1861 to 1864; A. G. Clary to Charles Wilkes, 2 Dec. 1862, in *ORN*, ser. 1, 1:568. Quote is from Whiting's dispatch.

36. *Bahama Herald*, 23 Jan. 1864, 2; *Bahama Herald*, 30 Jan. 1864, 2.

37. *Nassau Guardian*, 21 Jan. 1863, 2. This assertion was true for the Bahamas, but at least one case preceded it in Canada against an officer who recruited men for the U.S. Army in October 1861. See Wentzell, "Mercenaries and Adventurers," 63–64.

38. *Bahama Herald*, 20 Jan. 1863, 2.

39. Charles Bayley to the Duke of Newcastle, 29 Apr. 1862, f508–9, CO 23/168, TNA.

40. *Nassau Guardian*, 7 Feb. 1863, 2.

41. Trial information from *Nassau Guardian*, 4 May 1864, 2.

42. Samuel Whiting to William H. Seward, 27 Feb. 1863, roll 11, Consular Despatches—Nassau.

43. "Bahamas: Their Formation—Population—Geographical Position—Productions—Eligibility as a Resort for Invalids—Wrecking—Sponge Business—

Experiment of Emancipation, etc. etc.," *Merchants' Magazine and Commercial Review*, January 1861, 45–58; J. M. Wright, "Wrecking System of the Bahama Islands."

44. Seth Hawley to Charles Wilkes, 14 May 1863, in *ORN*, ser. 1, 2:192–93.

45. Seth Hawley to William H. Seward, 24 Mar. 1863, roll 11, Consular Despatches—Nassau.

46. Seth Hawley to Charles Wilkes, 14 May 1863, in *ORN*, ser. 1, 2:193.

47. For example, Charles Wilkes reported employing a Black fisherman as a spy and courier in Nassau. Charles Wilkes to Gideon Welles, 4 Dec. 1862, in *ORN*, ser. 1, 1:571.

48. Samuel Whiting to Robert Shufeldt, 8 May 1862, RG 84, Records of Foreign Service Posts, Hamilton, Bermuda, British West Indies, vol. 14, NARA II.

49. Samuel Whiting to Capt. James P. McKinstry, 15 Sept. 1862, RG 84, Records of Foreign Service Posts, Hamilton, Bermuda, vol. 14, NARA II.

50. *Decree of His Honor Judge John Campbell Lees, Esquire, Judge of the Vice-Admiralty Court of the Bahamas, in the Case of the British Steamship "Oreto," Seized for an Alleged Violation of the Foreign Enlistment Act* (Nassau: Office of the Nassau Guardian, 1862), enclosed in Samuel Whiting to William H. Seward, 18 Aug. 1862, roll 11, Consular Despatches—Nassau. Ward's race is not explicitly mentioned, but he joined the *Oreto* in Liverpool, and nonwhite cooks and stewards were commonplace on Atlantic ships in the nineteenth century.

51. Rawson W. Rawson to Edward Cardwell, with enclosures, 13 Dec. 1864, f431, CO 23/176, TNA.

52. Thomas Kirkpatrick to William H. Seward, 19 Dec. 1864, roll 12, Consular Despatches—Nassau.

53. J. Nibbs Brown to Charles R. Nesbitt, 20 Apr. 1864, f497, CO 23/174, TNA.

54. Brown to Nesbitt, 20 Apr. 1864, f499.

55. "Recollections of a Mustang," unpublished manuscript, Charles O'Neil Papers, LC, 291.

56. "Recollections of a Mustang," 312 and reverse of page.

57. George D. Harris to Jacob H. Webb, 15 Dec. 1862, enclosure in Charles Bayley to the Duke of Newcastle, 19 Dec. 1862, f467–68, CO 23/169, TNA.

58. Allen, *Dispatches from Bermuda*, 46.

59. Allen, 153.

60. Arthur G. Clary to Charles Wilkes, 28 Nov. 1862, in *ORN*, ser. 1, 1:561.

61. Charles J. Bayley to the Duke of Newcastle, 30 Aug. 1862, f202, CO 23/169, TNA.

62. Newcastle, note in margin of Bayley to Newcastle, 30 Aug. 1862, f202, and memo on the reverse of same, f203, CO 23/169, TNA.

63. Charles J. Bayley to Lord Lyons, 25 July 1863, box 123, Lyons Papers, ACA.

64. Charles J. Bayley to the Duke of Newcastle, with enclosures, 13 Jan. 1864, f34–38, CO 23/174, TNA.

65. Samuel Whiting to William H. Seward, 15 Mar. 1863, Microcopy T-475, roll 11, Consular Despatches—Nassau.

66. Extract from private journal found on board the *Florida*, Alabama Claims, 6:110. Emphasis in original.

67. Taylor, *Running the Blockade*, 143–44.

68. J. Wilkinson, *Narrative of a Blockade-Runner*, 141.

69. Affidavit of John H. McGregor, Alabama Claims, 6:313–14; affidavit of James Jenkins, Alabama Claims, 6:316–17. On the bounties offered, see affidavit of R. E. M. Solomon, Alabama Claims, 6:310–12 (quote on p. 317).

70. Bermuda Blue Book, 1864, f170, CO 41/59, TNA.

71. G. G. Walker, *Journal of Georgiana Walker*, 50.

72. Thompson, *Working on the Dock of the Bay*, 95–124.

73. K. E. Robinson, *Heritage, Including an Account of Bermudian Builders, Pilots, and Petitioners of the Early Post-Abolition Period*, 251.

74. *Bermuda Royal Gazette*, 17 May 1864; G. G. Walker, *Journal of Georgiana Walker*, 95–96. Bell was the leader of the Somers Pride of India Lodge of the Odd Fellows in St. George's.

75. G. G. Walker, *Journal of Georgiana Walker*, 50–51.

76. "The Disturbed State of St. George's," *Bermuda Royal Gazette*, 11 Aug. 1863; H. C. Wilkinson, *Bermuda from Sail to Steam*, 2:719–20.

77. *Bermuda Royal Gazette*, 18 Aug. 1863.

78. *Bermuda Royal Gazette*, 11 Aug. 1863.

79. "St. George's Fire Brigade," *Bermuda Royal Gazette*, 15 Mar. 1864, 2.

80. "A Deposed Monarch," *Bahama Herald*, 20 Feb. 1864, 2.

81. *Bahama Herald*, 17 Feb. 1864, 2; "Civic," *Bahama Herald*, 13 Jan. 1864, 2.

82. "Local," *Bahama Herald*, 15 June 1864, 2.

83. "The Late Strike," *Bahama Herald*, 29 June 1864, 2.

84. "Nassau's Future," *Bahama Herald*, 4 Feb. 1865, 2.

85. Notice of Adderley's appointment, *Nassau Guardian*, 2 July 1864.

86. Speech of Governor Rawson, *Bahama Herald*, 5 Feb. 1865, 2; Anderson, *Statute Law of the Bahamas*, 274–76.

87. "The Situation," *Bahama Herald*, 23 Mar. 1864, 2.

88. See, for example, the cascade of complaints in the *Bahama Herald*, 26 Mar. 1864, and the abuse heaped upon a correspondent who defended the new rules.

Chapter Five. "The Like Was Not Practised in the Previous Conflicts of Civilized Nations"

The epigraphs are from William H. Seward to J. Hume Burnley, 14 Mar. 1865, in U.S. Department of State, *Executive Documents Printed by Order of the House of Representatives*, 96; and James P. Holcombe to Judah P. Benjamin, 1 Apr. 1864, reel 6, CSAR.

1. British North American participation in the war on the Union side has been the subject of great contention, and although true numbers are probably impossible to determine, it is certain that large numbers, perhaps in the low thousands, served in the Union army. See Winks, *Civil War Years*, 177–85.
2. Sheehan-Dean, *Calculus of Violence*, 357.
3. Sutherland, *Savage Conflict*, 270; Sheehan-Dean, *Calculus of Violence*, 72–76.
4. *Halifax Sun*, 16 Dec. 1863, quoted in F. I. W. Jones, "Hot Southern Town," 58.
5. Sir Alexander Milne to the Secretary of the Admiralty, 2 May 1860, 26 July 1860, 13 Aug. 1860, and 7 Sept. 1860, Admiralty Letters Book, MLN 104/1, Milne Papers, MM; Lord Lyons to Lord John Russell, 31 Dec. 1861, box 107, Private Correspondence, Lyons Papers, ACA.
6. Charles J. Bayley, Speech to the House of Assembly, Mar. 1, 1864, printed in *Nassau Guardian*, March 12, 1864, 1.
7. Milne to the Secretary of the Admiralty, 2 Oct. 1860, MLN 104/1, Milne Papers, MM. Milne repeatedly sent ships to Central America in response to rumored filibustering attacks even after the Civil War began.
8. Belich, *Replenishing the Earth*, 1–14; Buckner and Francis, *Rediscovering the British World*, 1–19; Dilke, *Greater Britain*.
9. Belich, *Replenishing the Earth*, 9.
10. Ward, *Colonial Self-Government*, 111–23.
11. Many scholars of British imperialism, focused on Britain's Asian and African colonies, often assumed that political control was the chief motive for devolving political power, particularly for "collaborating elites." R. Robinson, "Non-European Foundations of European Imperialism," 120–26.
12. Francis, *Governors and Settlers*, 1, 8; Wentzell, "Mercenaries and Adventurers."
13. Wise, *Lifeline of the Confederacy*, 191–92; Marquis, *In Armageddon's Shadow*, 244–55. Manifests for outbound blockade runners frequently listed St. John or Halifax as their false destination. See, for example, the shipping notices in the *Nassau Guardian* for almost any period between 1862 and 1865.
14. Buckner, "1860s," 371.
15. Gwyn, *Excessive Expectations*, 3–9; Marquis, *In Armageddon's Shadow*, 34–35, 53–58.
16. Andrew Low and Co. to Leroy P. Walker, 24 Apr. 1861, in *OR*, ser. 4, 1:237.

17. Report of the Secretary of War, February 1861, in *OR*, ser. 4, 1:958.

18. Durham, *High Seas and Yankee Gunboats*, 31–40.

19. Larrabee, *The Dynamite Fiend*, chaps. 2 and 3; Marquis, *In Armageddon's Shadow*, 88–96. Marquis found substantial (though far from unanimous) support across the maritime colonies for the Confederacy, with frequent comparisons made between them and others attempting to throw off the "yoke" of foreign domination, such as the Italians or the Poles.

20. *Dictionary of Canadian Biography*, s.v. "Almon, William Johnston," by Allen E. Marble, accessed 15 Feb. 2025, https://www.biographi.ca/en/bio/almon_william_johnston_13E.html. Almon also had an indirect connection to slavery. His father and some other family members received compensation for slaves on a Jamaica estate after West Indian emancipation. "William Bruce Almon," *Legacies of British Slavery database*, accessed 15 Nov. 2023, https://www.ucl.ac.uk/lbs/person/view/46486.

21. F. I. W. Jones, "Hot Southern Town," 56.

22. W. C. Davis, *Look Away!*, 85–88.

23. *Dictionary of Canadian Biography*, s.v. "Wier, Benjamin," by David A. Sutherland, accessed 19 June 2019, http://www.biographi.ca/en/bio/wier_benjamin_9E.html.

24. Judah P. Benjamin to George N. Sanders, 28 Oct. 1862, reel 12, CSAR. Benjamin to Jefferson Davis, 30 Mar. 1864, reel 13, CSAR.

25. Bickham, *Weight of Vengeance*, 126–28.

26. Stephen Mallory to Jefferson Davis, 6 Jan. 1862, in *ORN*, ser. 2, 2:124.

27. Hanna, *Pirate Nests and the Rise of the British Empire*, 183–221.

28. The real John Parker, the original captain of the *Retribution*, died of yellow fever in 1861, after which Locke assumed his name in order to take over the privateer commission. Thomas B. Power to N. Irwin, 22 Feb. 1864, reel 9, CSAR.

29. Marquis, *In Armageddon's Shadow*, 135–36.

30. William H. Seward to Lord Lyons, 4 Apr. 1863, in *FRUS* 1863, 1:547. John Burnside to Charles Nesbitt, 20 Apr. 1863, in *FRUS* 1863, 1:641–43.

31. Affidavit of Isaac R. Staples, Alabama Claims, 6:736; United States, *Case of the United States, Laid before the Tribunal of Arbitration*, 261.

32. Seward to Lyons, 10 Nov. 1863, in *FRUS* 1863, supplement, cxxviii. Other sources place the bail as low as £100.

33. Bayley to Newcastle, 31 Oct. 1863, f364–65, CO 23/172, TNA.

34. Bayley to Newcastle, 22 Aug. 1863, f67–69, CO 23/172, TNA.

35. United States, *Case of the United States*, 261.

36. Marquis, *In Armageddon's Shadow*, 139–41. Some publications write Braine's name as "Brain," but as the vast majority of sources spell it in the former fashion, I have adhered to the more common spelling.

37. Stockton, *Reports of Cases Decided in the Vice-Admiralty Court of New Brunswick*, 236–38.

38. Matthews, *Statutes at Large of the Provisional Government of the Confederate States of America*, 100–104.

39. See, for example, Laurence Oliphant, *Patriots and Filibusters*, 132–242. *Blackwood's Magazine* published the book serially in its issues.

40. Testimony of Captain Issac Willett, in *ORN*, ser. 1, 2:536–38. In some correspondence, Shaffer's first name is spelled "Owen." Some pro-Confederate accounts claimed Schaffer fired shots at his attackers, wounding one, but none of the crew's statements suggest that they were armed or expecting any sort of attack. Any wounded pirates likely came by their own negligence. For a pro-Confederate account, see William Turlington to George Davis, Jan. 4 1864, in *ORN* ser. 1, 2:539-41.

41. The narrative of the capture of the *Chesapeake* is compiled from *ORN*, ser. 1, 2:512–660. For two good but slightly differing summaries, see Winks, *Civil War Years*, chap. 12; Marquis, *In Armageddon's Shadow*, chaps. 6 and 7.

42. Marquis, *In Armageddon's Shadow*, 152–54.

43. Nathaniel Gunnison to W. H. Seward, 14 Dec. 1863, in *ORN*, ser. 1, 2:523. Joseph Davis to Gunnison, 14 Dec. 1863, in House of Commons, *North America No. 9 (1864)*, 15.

44. Ward, *Colonial Self-Government*, 60–65, 172–75. Ward suggests that the *Durham Report*, published in the aftermath of the rebellions, was less important in the eventual grant of responsible government than broader changes in British society and attitudes toward settler colonies.

45. Ward, 174.

46. Buckner, *Transition to Responsible Government*, 6, 355; quote on p. 6.

47. Botting, *Extradition between Canada and the United States*, 75–91.

48. Marquis, *In Armageddon's Shadow*, 172. Charles Hastings Doyle to the Duke of Newcastle, 23 December 1863, in House of Commons, *Papers Relating to the Seizure of the United States' Steamer* Chesapeake, 10–13.

49. Arthur Gordon to the Duke of Newcastle, 1 Jan. 1864, in House of Commons, *Papers Relating to the Seizure of the United States' Steamer* Chesapeake, 34–35.

50. Marquis, *In Armageddon's Shadow*, 186–87.

51. Bale, *Chief Justice William Johnston Ritchie*, 85–89.

52. Marquis, *In Armageddon's Shadow*, 192–93.

53. Winks, *Civil War Years*, 259–62.

54. B. Wier to Maj. Norman S. Walker, 5 Jan. 1864, reel 9, CSAR.

55. J. W. Ritchie to B. Wier, 5 Jan. 1864, reel 9, CSAR.

56. Marquis, *In Armageddon's Shadow*, 145.

57. Report of Proceedings in the Vice Admiralty Court of Nova Scotia, regarding the *Chesapeake*, 15 Feb. 1864, in House of Commons, *Papers Relating to the Seizure of the United States' Steamer* Chesapeake, 83–85.

58. Doyle to Newcastle, 18 Feb. 1864, in House of Commons, *Papers Relating to the Seizure of the United States' Steamer* Chesapeake, 81.

59. Marquis, *In Armageddon's Shadow*, 198–99. See the correspondence surrounding the cargo of the *Sea Bride* in Mauritius in W. R. G. Mellen to Edward Rushworth, 4 Feb. 1864, *FRUS* 1864, 564–65.

60. Rear Admiral Sir Baldwin Walker to Lt. John Low, 27 Dec. 1863, in CSS Tuscaloosa Logs, W.S. Hoole Special Collections Library, University of Alabama.

61. Decision of Judge Alexander Stewart, enclosed in William H. Seward to Charles Francis Adams, 24 Feb. 1864, *FRUS* 1864, 198–99.

62. Charles Hastings Doyle to Lord Lyons, 17 Feb. 1864, box 123, Letters Received, Lyons Papers, ACA.

63. Marquis, *In Armageddon's Shadow*, 206–7.

64. Lewis Hutt to City Marshal of Halifax, 21 Dec. 1863, *FRUS* 1864, 484–85; Marquis, *In Armageddon's Shadow*, 209; J. W. Johnston to Doyle, 13 Jan. 1864, in House of Commons, *Papers Relating to the Seizure of the United States' Steamer* Chesapeake, 60–62.

65. Doyle to Lyons, 17 Feb. 1864, box 123, Letters Received, Lyons Papers, ACA. "*Nous verrons*" translates roughly as "we shall see."

66. W. M. Robinson, *The Confederate Privateers*.

67. Merli, *Great Britain and the Confederate Navy*, 257. Merli argues that enforcement against Confederate ships was ad hoc and driven by diplomatic and political necessity rather than a stringent interpretation of the law.

68. David Riker to Robert Toombs, 18 July 1861, in reel 12, CSAR.

69. John Yates Beall, a Southerner, was hanged for his role in ship hijackings and other clandestine attacks. A Union military tribunal did not accept a commission from Jefferson Davis as sufficient to excuse his actions. On the other hand, John C. Braine repeatedly escaped justice in colonial courts by claiming he was in the Confederate service. See Beall and Lucas, *Memoir of John Yates Beall*. W. G. Hamley to Edward Cardwell, 28 Oct. 1864, in *ORN*, ser. 1, 3:243–47.

70. Winks, *Civil War Years*, 287–91. Men who could credibly claim to be Confederates led the September 1864 attack on the *Philo Parsons*.

71. Mallory to Davis, 6 Jan. 1862, in *ORN*, ser. 2, 2:124–25; Mallory to Davis, 27 Feb. 1862, in *ORN*, ser. 2, 2:153.

72. Lester, *Digest of the Military and Naval Laws of the Confederate States*, 211–14. Congress also created a separate provisional navy, but this structure served as a way

to promote junior officers by merit rather than seniority. The quasi-privateering body was called the volunteer navy in order to differentiate the two.

73. Confederate States of America, *Journal of the Congress of the Confederate States of America*, 3:681. It is unclear how international law would have treated such a vessel, although assuming it was purchased rather than captured, the commission and letter of marque might have been legal—the CSS *Alabama* obtained a legal commission without entering a Confederate port.

74. Mallory to Col. E. C. Cabell, 10 Sept. 1863, in *OR*, ser. 1, vol. 22, pt. 2, 1001–2.

75. Merli, *Great Britain and the Confederate Navy*, 195–210.

76. Jefferson Davis, message to Congress, 2 May 1864, in Richardson, *Messages and Papers of Jefferson Davis and the Confederacy*, 1:230–31.

77. Spencer, *Confederate Navy in Europe*, 170–73; H. Jones, *Blue and Gray Diplomacy*, 307–14.

78. Alessio, "Filibustering from Africa to the Americas."

79. May, *Manifest Destiny's Underworld*, xv. May also defines filibustering as an American phenomenon, but it seems obvious that the practice is not limited to any particular nation.

80. Cusick, *Other War of 1812*, 33–37.

81. Greenberg, *Manifest Manhood*, 30.

82. Thomas E. Hogg to J. P. Benjamin, 3 May 1864, in *ORN*, ser. 2, 3:1111–12.

83. Winks, *Civil War Years*, 146–52. The first plot was far more advanced than many contemporary observers and subsequent historians realized, and its leaders canceled it only at the last moment. George W. Gift to Ellen Shackleford, 16 Nov. 1863, George W. Gift Papers #1152, Southern Historical Collection, Wilson Library, University of North Carolina at Chapel Hill.

84. James Mason to J. P. Benjamin, 12 Apr. 1864, in *ORN*, ser. 2, 3:1082–84.

85. Norman Walker to J. P. Benjamin, 15 Jan. 1864, reel 9, CSAR; Walker, *Journal of Georgiana Walker*, 61.

86. J. P. Holcombe to J. P. Benjamin, 1 Apr. 1864, in *ORN*, ser. 2, 3:1072–73.

87. See, for example, Benjamin to P. H. Aylett, 2 Mar. 1864, in *ORN*, ser. 2, 3:1044.

88. Note of Thomas F. Elliot, Under Secretary of State, 11 Jan. 1865, f47, CO 37/193, TNA.

89. Braine had obtained an acting master's commission from Mallory under false pretenses, but most of the party was recruited in Havana and was not in the Confederate service.

90. J. P. Benjamin to Charles J. Helm, 13 Sept. 1864, in *ORN*, ser. 1, 3:239–40.

91. Helm to Benjamin, 17 Aug. 1864, in *ORN*, ser. 1, 3:234–37.

92. Holbrook, "Mosby or a Quantrill?," 205–6.
93. Charles J. Helm to Don Domingo Dulce, 21 Nov. 1863, in *ORN*, ser. 1, 3:242–43.
94. S. Brownlow Gray to William G. Hamley, 24 Oct. 1864, in *ORN*, ser. 1, 3:244–47.
95. Cardwell to Hamley, 16 Jan. 1865, in *ORN*, ser. 1, 3:247–48.
96. Holbrook, "Mosby or a Quantrill?," 209–11.
97. Cano, "Salvador Affair," 77–97.
98. May, *Manifest Destiny's Underworld*, 287.

Chapter Six. "Informal Propositions Coming from Irresponsible and Unofficial Persons"

The epigraph is from James P. Holcombe to Judah P. Benjamin, 16 Nov. 1864, in *ORN*, ser. 2, 3:1238; title quote from the *Hamilton (ON) Evening Times*, 25 July 1864, 2.

1. Berwanger, *British Foreign Service and the American Civil War*, 108–24; Jenkins, *Britain and the War for the Union*, 1:300–314.
2. J. P. Benjamin to James M. Mason, 22 June 1864, in *ORN*, ser. 2, 3:1153; Jenkins, *Britain and the War for the Union*, 1:330–33; Luraghi, *History of the Confederate Navy*, 230. British officials eventually decided their seizure of the *Tuscaloosa* was not warranted on the grounds that it had previously been admitted to a British port, but the ship by then had been abandoned in the Cape Colony and never returned to Confederate hands.
3. "Manifesto by the Rebel Congress," *New York Times*, 26 June 1864. The manifesto was printed in the *Richmond Whig* on June 13, although official copies did not reach the hands of European diplomats until well into the fall of 1864.
4. Benjamin to Mason, 20 Sept. 1864, in *ORN*, ser. 2, 3:1216.
5. H. Jones, *Blue and Gray Diplomacy*, 318–19.
6. McPherson, *Battle Cry of Freedom*, 762–65; Winks, *Civil War Years*, 334–36.
7. Jenkins, *Britain and the War for the Union*, 1:362–63, 379–80.
8. Jacob Thompson to Judah P. Benjamin, 3 Dec. 1864, in *ORN*, ser. 1, 3:719; James P. Holcombe to J. P. Benjamin, 16 Nov. 1864, in *ORN*, ser. 2, 3:1239–40.
9. Sir Edmund Head to the Duke of Newcastle, with enclosures, 25 Apr. 1861, CO 42/626, reel B-447, HDL.
10. Rev. A. C. Walshe to Lord John Russell, 28 Oct. 1863, f145–48, CO 42/639, reel B-456, HDL.
11. Lord Monck to Newcastle, with enclosures, 27 Jan. 1864, f34–75, CO 42/640, reel B-457, HDL.

12. Winks, *Civil War Years*, 268–72.
13. James P. Holcombe to Lord Monck, 9 May 1864, enclosure in Monck to Edward Cardwell, 16 May 1864, f309, CO 42/641, reel B-458, HDL.
14. Herschel Johnson to Jefferson Davis, 4 Jan. 1864, in *PJD*, 10:152–53.
15. "From the Autobiography of Herschel V. Johnson," 333.
16. *PJD*, 10:153–55. "Secret service" was a catch-all term in this era for a wide variety of clandestine and diplomatic activities that the president or cabinet paid for from a budget appropriation left almost entirely to the executive's discretion.
17. *PJD*, 10:153–55.
18. Bivins, "Life and Character of Jacob Thompson," 83–88.
19. *American National Biography*, s.v. "Thompson, Jacob (1810–1885), Congressman, Secretary of the Interior, and Confederate Agent," by William L. Barney, 1 Feb. 2000, https://doi.org/10.1093/anb/9780198606697.article.0400986.
20. Rainwater, "Letters to and from Jacob Thompson," 97.
21. Nuermberger, *Clays of Alabama*, 122–39.
22. Throughout this chapter, "Northwest" or "Old Northwest" refers to the contemporary use of the term to denote the region west of the Appalachians and north of the Ohio River, especially Ohio, Indiana, and Illinois, along with the nearby states that are considered part of the modern-day Midwest.
23. Clay received a colonel's commission as a judge just before going to Canada, but he never served in the army in any meaningful sense.
24. Nuermberger, *Clays of Alabama*, 111–12, 178.
25. Clement C. Clay to Louis T. Wigfall, 29 Apr. 1864, quoted in Nuermberger, *Clays of Alabama*, 232.
26. G. G. Walker, *Journal of Georgiana Walker*, 92.
27. "Passengers Sailed," *Bermuda Royal Gazette*, 17 May 1864, 2.
28. Memorial of Thomas L. Connolly, 20 May 1864, reel 21, C. C. Clay Papers, 1811–1925, David M. Rubenstein Rare Book and Manuscript Library, Duke University.
29. Winks, *Civil War Years*, 273.
30. Denison, *Soldiering in Canada*, 58–60.
31. Thomas Connolly to James P. Holcombe, 27 May 1864, reel 21, C. C. Clay Papers.
32. Russell, *My Diary North and South*, 167; Eyal, "Romantic Realist"; Senters, "George N. Sanders."
33. Castleman, *Active Service*, 135.
34. *American National Biography*, s.v. "Sanders, George Nicholas (1812–1873), Political Booster and Confederate Agent," by Junius P. Rodriguez, Feb. 2000, https://doi.org/10.1093/anb/9780198606697.article.0400878.

35. Eyal, "Romantic Realist," 111–12.
36. Tidwell, *April '65*, 124.
37. Clement C. Clay to Judah P. Benjamin, 17 June 1864, reel 6, CSAR.
38. Spence and Winks, "William 'Colorado' Jewett," 23.
39. *Western Mountaineer* (Golden City, CO), July 5, 1860, quoted in Spence and Winks, "William 'Colorado' Jewett," 26.
40. H. Jones, *Blue and Gray Diplomacy*, 288–89.
41. Spence and Winks, "William 'Colorado' Jewett," 32–43.
42. "The Niagara Peace Negotiation: Explanation by Mr. Greeley of His Share in the Matter," *New York Times*, 17 Aug. 1865, 2. Greeley downplayed his role in the affair after the fact, attributing his visit to Niagara Falls with Lincoln's secretary John Hay as the result of a misunderstanding.
43. Nelson, *Bullets, Ballots, and Rhetoric*, 70–71.
44. Kirkland, *The Peacemakers of 1864*, 74–85.
45. J. P. Holcombe to John Hay, printed in the *New-York Tribune*, 22 July 1864.
46. McPherson, *Battle Cry of Freedom*, 766–67; Jenkins, *Britain and the War for the Union*, 1:354–55; H. Jones, *Blue and Gray Diplomacy*, 316–17. Jones called the outcome a "propaganda victory" for the Confederates.
47. Winks, *Civil War Years*, 278.
48. Quoted in Nelson, *Bullets, Ballots, and Rhetoric*, 74–75.
49. Nelson, 36–46.
50. J. P. Benjamin to James M. Mason, 25 Aug. 1864, in *ORN*, ser. 2, 3:1190–94; Nelson, *Bullets, Ballots, and Rhetoric*, 75–77.
51. Stephen Mallory to Virginia Clay, 1 Aug. 1864, quoted in Nelson, *Bullets, Ballots, and Rhetoric*, 70.
52. Jacob Thompson to Judah P. Benjamin, 3 Dec. 1864, in *ORN*, ser. 1, 3:714–19; Hines, "The Northwestern Conspiracy," January 1887, 500–501.
53. Towne, *Surveillance and Spies in the Civil War*, 89–96.
54. Nelson, *Bullets, Ballots, and Rhetoric*, 86.
55. Hines, "The Northwestern Conspiracy," pt. 2, 506–7; Nelson, *Bullets, Ballots, and Rhetoric*, 87–88.
56. J. P. Holcombe to J. P. Benjamin, 16 Nov. 1864, in *ORN*, ser. 2, 3:1239–40; Castleman, *Active Service*, 145. Bullitt was arrested and briefly exiled for pro-Confederate activity in July 1864.
57. Both Clay and Holcombe were shipwrecked on their return journeys to the Confederacy and lost much of their baggage, including records. Other records were deliberately destroyed—for example, all entries in Clay's journal from the summer and early fall of 1864 were entirely removed, and many of his letters are mutilated to remove names. Clay journal, reel 21, C. C. Clay Papers.

58. James P. Holcombe to Judah P. Benjamin, 16 Nov. 1864, in *ORN*, ser. 2, 3:1238.

59. Hines, "The Northwestern Conspiracy," pt. 2, 501–2. The Lost Cause rhetoric in Hines's account is unmistakable.

60. Keehn, *Knights of the Golden Circle*, 171–73.

61. Holcombe to Benjamin, 16 Nov. 1864, in *ORN*, ser. 2, 3:1239; Keehn, *Knights of the Golden Circle*, 173–75. Keehn misstates the date of Thompson's meetings with Vallandigham and SOL members as occurring in April 1864. Thompson did not reach Canada until late May.

62. Jacob Thompson to Mason and Slidell, 28 Aug. 1864, in Hines, "The Northwestern Conspiracy," pt. 2, 508–10.

63. Clement C. Clay to Mason and Slidell, 24 Aug. 1864, typescript copy, reel 21, C. C. Clay Papers.

64. Nelson, *Bullets, Ballots, and Rhetoric*, 86–87; Hines, "The Northwestern Conspiracy," pt. 2, 503–4.

65. Hines, "The Northwestern Conspiracy," pt. 3, 572–75.

66. Jacob Thompson to J. P. Benjamin, 3 Dec. 1864, in *ORN*, ser. 1, 3:717–18.

Chapter Seven. "Schemes of Deviltry Concocted in Canada"

1. Title quote from "Trial of the Conspirators," *Washington Evening Star*, 12 May 1865.

2. House of Commons, *North America No. 3 (1876)*; *Oxford Dictionary of National Biography*, s.v. "Burleigh, Bennet Gordon (c. 1840–1914), Journalist and Soldier," by Roger T. Stearn, 23 Sept. 2004, https://doi.org/10.1093/ref:odnb/38628. Burley changed the spelling of his last name after the Civil War and his subsequent extradition from Canada to the United States.

3. Beall and Lucas, *Memoir of John Yates Beall*, 296.

4. Beall and Lucas, 264–65.

5. Harris, *Confederate Privateer*, 24–25.

6. Shepard, "Johnson's Island Plot," 21–24.

7. The Johnson's Island raid has been recounted in detail in many publications, with varying degrees of accuracy. For good examples, see Shepard, "Johnson's Island Plot"; Winks, *Civil War Years*, 287–91; Harris, *Confederate Privateer*, 44–57.

8. Clement Clay and Jacob Thompson to Col. C. W. Hill, 22 Sept. 1864, in *OR*, ser. 2, 7:864–65.

9. Beall and Lucas, *Memoir of John Yates Beall*, 296–97.

10. Monck to Cardwell, 19 Mar. 1864, with enclosures and endorsements, f281–99, reel B-457, CO 42/640, HDL.

11. Monck to Cardwell, 26 Sept. 1864, f290–93, reel B-458, CO 42/642, HDL. Much of the correspondence around this matter was printed and can be found as CO 440, Correspondence with Canada upon the use of Armed Vessels on the American Lakes, but the printed versions omit the comments from department officials that are particularly illuminating.

12. Winks, *Civil War Years*, 298–301. Most accounts of the raid agree on the main details, although the precise number of raiders remains undetermined—it was somewhere between twenty and twenty-three.

13. Winks, 312–13.

14. Jones, *Rebel War Clerk's Diary*, 2:355.

15. Winks, *Civil War Years*, 277–78.

16. Crown Law Officers to Lord Russell, 31 Jan. 1865, enclosure in T. Frederick Elliot to Edmund Hammond, 12 Jan. 1865, f102–8, reel B-474, CO 42/652, HDL. The mismatched dating is due to the report being returned to the Foreign Office alongside the earlier-dated correspondence. The Law Officers provided legal advice to the British government and at this time usually consisted of the attorney general, the solicitor general, and the queen's advocate.

17. City Council of Montreal, *St. Albans Raid Investigation*, 5.

18. City Council of Montreal, 13.

19. Jacob Thompson to Judah Benjamin, 3 Dec. 1864, in *ORN*, ser. 1, 3:717–19.

20. Sher, *North Star*, 188–89.

21. Sher, 307–10.

22. City Council of Montreal, *St. Albans Raid Investigation*, 75.

23. Guillaume Lamothe to Henri Lamothe, 1 Mar. 1895, in Wilson, *Justice Under Pressure*, 151–78.

24. Foreman, *World on Fire*, 729.

25. Levine, *Confederate Emancipation*, 111.

26. Jenkins, *Britain and the War for the Union*, 1:339.

27. E. Hammond to F. Rogers, 1 Apr. 1865, with enclosures, f239, reel B-474, CO 42/652, HDL.

28. Winks, *Civil War Years*, 328–29.

29. Winks, 307.

30. Foreman, *World on Fire*, 717.

31. Mayers, *Dixie and the Dominion*, 135–36.

32. Winks, *Civil War Years*, 308–10.

33. Winks, 322–23; J. P. Holcombe to Benjamin, 16 Nov. 1864, in *ORN*, ser. 2, 3:1239. McMicken was the agent in Windsor for forwarding escaped prisoners of war who wished to return to the Confederacy.

34. Thompson to Benjamin, 3 Dec. 1864, in *ORN*, ser. 1, 3:718–19.

35. Bourne, *Britain and the Balance of Power in North America*, 257–70.

36. Winks, *Civil War Years*, 311. Bennett Young wrote to a Montreal newspaper after his capture to justify the St. Albans raid as retribution for Sheridan's depredations in the Shenandoah Valley.

37. Salehyan, *Rebels Without Borders*, 1–9.

38. Salehyan, 4–9.

39. Reeder, "'Sovereign Lords' and 'Dependent Administrators.'"

40. Bell, *Mosquito Soldiers*, 104. Luke P. Blackburn compiled service record, reel 24, M331, Compiled Service Records of Confederate Generals and Staff Officers, and Nonregimental Enlisted Men, RG 109: War Department Collection of Confederate Records, 1825–1927, NARA.

41. W. G. Romaine to F. Rogers, 24 Feb. 1864, f5–6, CO 37/193, CO 37, Bermuda, Original Correspondence, TNA.

42. T. Frederick Elliot to W. G. Romaine, 16 June 1865, f7–8, CO 37/193, TNA.

43. C. M. Allen to W. H. Seward, 14 Apr. 1865, in Allen, *Dispatches from Bermuda*, 180–82. The identity of the informant is not disclosed in Allen's dispatches, but it may have been George Black or one of the clerks in the Confederacy's Bermuda office.

44. "The Yellow Fever Plot," *New York Times*, 16 May 1865, 1. Several depositions related to the case are reprinted there.

45. Benjamin, *Great Epidemic in New Berne and Vicinity*, 3–4; Bell, *Mosquito Soldiers*, 5–6, 103–4.

46. *Toronto Globe*, 24 Apr. 1865; *New York Times*, 26 May 1865. Both papers printed transcripts of testimony from the trial of Blackburn in Toronto.

47. Steers, *Blood on the Moon*, 47–50. Steers finds Hyams to be a credible and convincing witness and says that charges of perjury against him were mostly a result of how his testimony in the assassination trials lined up next to other, less trustworthy figures.

48. Deposition of William W. Cleary, in Monck to Cardwell, 2 June 1865, f271, reel B-463, CO 42/649, HDL.

49. Reid, *African Canadians in Union Blue*, 2–5, 37–55.

50. *Nassau Guardian*, 7 Feb. 1863.

51. *Bermuda Advocate*, 26 Apr. 1865, reprinted in the *New York Times*, 16 May 1865, 1.

52. *PJD*, 11:119–20.

53. Rev. Kensey Johns Stewart to Jefferson Davis, 12 Dec. 1864, Prison Pens, Canada Raids, Secret Operations; Record Books of Executive, Legislative, and Judicial Offices of the Confederate Government, RG 109, NARA.

54. Kee, "Stuart Robinson."

55. Deposition of Stuart Robinson, in Monck to Cardwell, 2 June 1865, f267, reel B-463, CO 42/649, HDL.

56. Deposition of William Cleary, f272, reel B-463, CO 42/649, HDL.

57. Steers, *Blood on the Moon*, 51. Canadian courts could not try someone for a crime committed in Nova Scotia, which was still a distinct colony.

58. Romaine to Rogers, 16 Nov. 1865, f20–22, CO 37/193, TNA.

59. Headley, *Confederate Operations in Canada and New York*, 264–65.

60. *Richmond Whig*, 15 Oct. 1864, quoted in Foreman, *World on Fire*, 697.

61. Headley, *Confederate Operations in Canada and New York*, 271.

62. *New York Times*, 26 Mar. 1865; Cunningham, "'In Violation of the Laws of War.'"

63. Headley, *Confederate Operations in Canada and New York*, 274–80; For a fuller account, see Brandt, *Man Who Tried to Burn New York*.

64. Cunningham, "'In Violation of the Laws of War,'" 196–98.

65. Beall and Lucas, *Memoir of John Yates Beall*, 209–18; Headley, *Confederate Operations in Canada and New York*, 325–31.

66. Thompson to Benjamin, 3 Dec. 1864, in *ORN*, ser. 1, 3:719.

67. Holcombe to Benjamin, 16 Nov. 1864, in *ORN*, ser. 2, 3:1234.

68. Alford, *Fortune's Fool*, 195–98.

69. Steers, *Blood on the Moon*, 1–7. Steers offers a useful summary of the professional historiography of the assassination, and owing to scanty evidence, even the boldest claims do not directly implicate Davis or his cabinet.

70. Steers, 86–89.

71. Tidwell, *April '65*, 77–106. The logic of compensating civilian "destructionists" for damaging Union property and ships dates from early in the war and was linked to privateering and later efforts to create a privately funded volunteer navy. Stephen Mallory found the practice particularly attractive, and James Seddon sought to expand it to land warfare as well, beginning in 1863.

72. For a comprehensive history of the assassination, see Steers, *Blood on the Moon*, 71–118.

73. Tidwell, *April '65*, 160–96. Tidwell argues that Jefferson Davis and Judah Benjamin likely knew of and approved of plan to assassinate Lincoln and that they arranged for direct support for the operation. The evidence for this is circumstantial at best.

74. Steers, *Blood on the Moon*, 71–74, 88–89.

75. Tidwell, Hall, and Gaddy, *Come Retribution*, 328–42.

76. Lt. Robert Minor to Adm. Franklin Buchanan, 2 Feb. 1864, in *ORN*, ser. 1, 2:822–24.

77. Tidwell, Hall, and Gaddy, 333–34.

78. Wright, "Mysterious Fate of Blockade Runners"; Larrabee, *The Dynamite Fiend*.

79. Jampoler, *The Last Lincoln Conspirator*, 46–47.

80. See, for example, S. Robinson, *Infamous Perjuries of the "Bureau of Military Justice" Exposed*.

81. "The Booth Conspiracy: Letter from Beverley Tucker to the People of Canada," Toronto *Globe*, 8 May 1865, 1.

82. N. B. Tucker, *Address to the People of the United States*, 17–21.

83. Cleary, *Protest of W.W. Cleary*.

84. Winks, *Civil War Years*, 332. Monck to Cardwell, 31 Dec. 1864, with enclosures, f580, reel B-460, CO 42/644; Monck to Cardwell, 7 Jan. 1865, with enclosures, f71, reel B-461, CO 42/647, HDL.

85. Winks, *Civil War Years*, 306.

86. "From Canada; Another Attempt to Kidnap Geo. N. Sanders," *New York Times*, 9 Aug. 1865, 1.

87. Neidhardt, *Fenianism in North America*, 13–15, 30–31, 38–39, 44–49. The U.S. government proved reluctant to disturb Fenians even when they gathered near the border under arms.

88. Lord John Russell to Sir Frederic Rogers, 9 Feb. 1864, with enclosures, f69–87, reel B-460, CO 42/645, HDL; Winks, *Civil War Years*, 174.

Conclusion

The epigraph is from "That Abduction Case," *Hamilton (ON) Daily Spectator*, 11 June 1872, 2.

1. Mayers, *Dixie and the Dominion*, 212–19.

2. Mayers, 212–16.

3. Shingleton, *John Taylor Wood*, 199–206; Winks, *Civil War Years*, 372–73.

4. Holbrook, "Mosby or a Quantrill?" William Seward to Charles F. Adams, 20 July 1865, and Adams to Lord Russell, 10 Aug. 1865, in Alabama Claims, 4:350–51. Quote is from Adams's letter to Lord Russell. H. A. Parr, one of the *Chesapeake* hijackers, was reportedly along with Braine for portions of this escapade.

5. "The Ku-Klux," *Milwaukee Sentinel*, 18 Aug. 1871, 2.

6. "The Kidnapping Case," *Toronto Globe*, 18 June 1872, 4. Bratton served as an inspiration for Thomas Dixon's novel *The Clansman* and the corresponding film, *Birth of a Nation*.

7. "The Canadian Kidnapping Case," *Toronto Globe*, 21 June 1872, 1.

8. Unterman, *Uncle Sam's Policemen*.

9. Gorman, "Adderley Family in the New World," 38–39.

10. "Adderley, Henry," *England & Wales, National Probate Calendar (Index of Wills and Administrations), 1858–1995*, accessed 29 Nov. 2023, https://www.ancestry.co.uk/discoveryui-content/view/5017627:1904.

11. See correspondence in Bourne Letterbook (press), July 1865–Oct. 1869, John Tory Bourne Letterbooks, 1863–1869, Bermuda Archives. Bourne advertised widely to sell gunpowder and other stores and wrote directly to army and navy officials in charge of supplies in Bermuda.

12. Vandiver, *Confederate Blockade Running through Bermuda*, ix–x; Wise, *Lifeline of the Confederacy*, 221–26.

13. *Dictionary of Canadian Biography*, s.v. "Ritchie, John William," by Neil J. MacKinnon, accessed 15 Feb. 2025, https://www.biographi.ca/en/bio/5799; *Dictionary of Canadian Biography*, s.v. "Wier, Benjamin," by David A. Sutherland, accessed 15 Feb. 2025, https://www.biographi.ca/en/bio/wier_benjamin_9E.html.

14. Bale, *Chief Justice William Johnston Ritchie*, 85–91.

15. Connolly, "Archbishop of Halifax on the Irish and Republican America," appendix B.

16. Denison, *Soldiering in Canada*, 58–81; Berger, *Sense of Power*; Denison, *Struggle for Imperial Unity*.

17. Janney, *Remembering the Civil War*, 141.

18. Janney, 140, 234–45; Mayers, *Dixie and the Dominion*, 213–14; Davis, *Jefferson Davis, Ex-President of the Confederate States of America*, 2:796–800.

19. Foreman, *World on Fire*, 796.

20. Reid, *Louis Riel and the Creation of Modern Canada*; Read and Webb, "'Catholic Mahdi of the North West'"; Senior, *Last Invasion of Canada*, 173–87.

21. Holbrook, "Mosby or a Quantrill?," 210.

22. The Union seizure of Mason and Slidell from the *Trent* was not itself the cause of the uproar but rather taking them without proper resort to a prize court. Likewise, enemy dispatches (which would include Confederate international mail) were generally agreed to be contraband of war and liable to seizure even from a neutral vessel.

23. Charles J. Bayley to Lord Lyons, 12 May 1862, box 122, Letters Received, Lyons Papers, ACA.

24. For the Trenholm letter, see William Wilson to Lord Russell, 4 Aug. 1863, with enclosures, FO 5/1234, Case of the *Margaret* and *Jessie*, maritime jurisdiction beyond the three-mile limit, FO 5: Foreign Office: Political and Other Departments: General Correspondence before 1906, United States of America, Series II, TNA; Bernath, *Squall across the Atlantic*, 7–17; Wise, *Lifeline of the Confederacy*, 184–85; Negus, "Notorious Nest of Offence."

25. Sage, *Organization of Private Warfare*, reproduced in Tidwell, *April '65*, appendix B. The original pamphlet is held in RG 45, NARA.

26. For one example beyond the Alabama Claims and reciprocity, the lingering dispute over British and colonial culpability for Confederate attacks hindered responses to a postwar financial crisis. Sexton, "Funded Loan and the Alabama Claims."

BIBLIOGRAPHY

Primary Sources

Archival and Manuscript Materials

Arundel Castle Archives, Arundel, United Kingdom
   Lyons Papers
Bahamas National Archives, Nassau
   Colonial Office: CO 23, Bahamas, Original Correspondence (microfilm)
   Governor's Despatches, 1861–1866
   Supreme Court Wills
   Votes of the House of Assembly of the Bahamas Islands
Bermuda Archives, Hamilton, Bermuda
   Governor's Despatches, 1862–1868
   John Tory Bourne Letterbooks, 1863–1869
   Secretary of State's Despatches
   Sessional and Allied Papers, 1860–1868
David M. Rubenstein Rare Book and Manuscript Library, Duke University, Durham, NC
   C. C. Clay Papers, 1811–1925
High Density Library, University of Calgary, Calgary, AB, Canada
   CO 42: Canada: Original Correspondence, Secretary of State
Library of Congress, Manuscript Division, Washington, DC
   Charles O'Neil Papers
   Confederate States of America Records, 1854–1889
   George Nicholas Sanders Papers
Merseyside Maritime Museum, Liverpool, United Kingdom
   The Business Records of Fraser, Trenholm & Company of Liverpool and Charleston, South Carolina, 1860–1877 (microfilm)
National Archives, Kew, United Kingdom
   CO: Colonial Office and predecessors
      CO 23: Bahamas, Original Correspondence
      CO 27: Bahamas, Miscellaneous
      CO 37: Bermuda, Original Correspondence

CO 41: Bermuda, Miscellanea
CO 42: Canada, formerly British North America, Original Correspondence
CO 440: Correspondence with Canada upon the use of Armed Vessels on the American Lakes
CO 854: Colonies (General)
FO: Foreign Office
FO 5: Political and Other Departments: General Correspondence before 1906, United States of America, Series II
FO 414: Confidential Print, North America
FO 881: Confidential Print (Numerical Series)
National Archives and Records Administration, College Park, MD
RG 59: General Records of the Department of State, 1763–2002
Subject Index to Consular Despatches, Letters, and Diplomatic Correspondence, 1790–1940
Despatches from United States Consuls in Nassau, New Providence Island, 1829–1906
RG 84: Records of the Foreign Service Posts of the Department of State
United States Consular Records for Hamilton, Bermuda, British West Indies, ca. 1853–1940
United States Consular Records for Halifax, Canada, 1833–1946
United States Consular Records for Nassau, Bahamas, 1821–1935
National Archives and Records Administration, Washington, DC
RG 109: War Department Collection of Confederate Records, 1825–1927
Compiled Service Records of Confederate Generals and Staff Officers, and Nonregimental Enlisted Men
Confederate Vessel Papers, 1874–1899
Letters Received by the Confederate Secretary of War
Prison Pens, Canada Raids, Secret Operations
National Maritime Museum, Greenwich, United Kingdom
Sir Alexander Milne Papers
South Carolina Historical Society, Charleston
C.L. Burckmyer Correspondence, 1863–1865
South Caroliniana Library, University of South Carolina, Columbia
Charles O. Witte Letterbook, 1861–1867
Southern Historical Collection, Wilson Library, University of North Carolina at Chapel Hill
DeRosset Family Papers
George W. Gift Papers
Stephen Russell Mallory Diary and Recollections
William Porcher Miles Papers

State Library and Archives of Florida
  Milton Letterbooks (1861–1863)
W.S. Hoole Special Collections Library, University of Alabama
  CSS Tuscaloosa Logs

Databases and Digital Collections

Ancestry.com
Centre for the Studies of the Legacies of British Slavery Database, https://www.ucl.ac.uk/lbs
Digital Library of the Caribbean—dloc.com

Newspapers and Magazines

[Atlanta] *Southern Cultivator*
Bahama Herald
[Baltimore] *Niles' Weekly Register*
Bermuda Advocate
Bermuda Royal Gazette
Charleston Mercury
[Georgetown, Ohio] *Democratic Standard*
[Golden City, Colo.] *Western Mountaineer*
[Halifax] *Acadian Recorder*
Halifax Sun
Hamilton (ON) Daily Spectator
Hamilton (ON) Evening Times
Liverpool Mercury
[London] *Economist*
Merchants' Magazine and Commercial Review
Mobile Advertiser and Register
Mobile Evening News
Montreal Gazette
Nassau Guardian
[New Orleans] *Daily Delta*
[New Orleans] *True American*
New York Herald
[New York] *Morning Herald*
New York Times
New-York Tribune
[Raleigh] *North Carolina Standard*
[Richmond] *Daily Dispatch*
Richmond Whig
[Swanton, Vt.] *North American*
Toronto Globe
Washington Evening Star
Wilmington [N.C.] *Journal*

Pamphlets and Contemporary Printed Works

Benjamin, W. S. *The Great Epidemic in New Berne and Vicinity, September and October, 1864, by One Who Passed through It*. New Berne, N.C.: Geo. Mills Joy, 1864.

Bryan, Edward B. *Letters to the Southern People concerning the Acts of Congress and Treaties with Great Britain, in Relation to the African Slave Trade*. Charleston, S.C.: Press of Walker, Evans, 1858.

———. *The Rightful Remedy. Addressed to the Slaveholders of the South.* Charleston, S.C.: Walker and James, 1850.

Christy, David. "Cotton Is King: Or, Slavery in the Light of Political Economy." In *Cotton Is King, and Pro-Slavery Arguments: Comprising the Writings of Hammond, Harper, Christy, Stringfellow, Hodge, Bledsoe, and Cartwright, on This Important Subject*, edited by E. N. Elliott. Augusta, Ga.: Pritchard, Abbott & Loomis, 1860.

Cleary, William W. *The Protest of W.W. Cleary against the Proclamation of President Johnson, of May 2nd [. . .].* Toronto: Lovell and Gibson, 1865.

Connolly, Thomas L. "The Archbishop of Halifax on the Irish and Republican America." In *The Irish Position in British and in Republican North America: A Letter to the Editors of the Irish Press Irrespective of Party*, 2nd ed., by Thomas D'Arcy McGee, appendix B. Montreal: M. Longmoore, 1866.

Denison, George T. *A Review of the Judgments of the Bench, in the Anderson Extradition Case; or, Seven Ways of Proving That Anderson Should Not Be Remanded: With the Judgments of the Court Appended.* Toronto, 1861.

Elliott, E. N., ed. *Cotton Is King, and Pro-Slavery Arguments: Comprising the Writings of Hammond, Harper, Christy, Stringfellow, Hodge, Bledsoe, and Cartwright, on This Important Subject.* Augusta, Ga.: Pritchard, Abbott & Loomis, 1860.

Marx, Karl, and Friedrich Engels. *The Civil War in the United States.* Edited by Andrew Zimmerman. 2nd ed. New York: International, 2016.

Oliphant, Laurence. *Patriots and Filibusters, or Incidents of Political and Exploratory Travel.* Edinburgh: W. Blackwood, 1860.

Robinson, Stuart. *The Infamous Perjuries of the "Bureau of Military Justice" Exposed: Letter of Rev. Stuart Robinson to Hon. Mr. Emmons, with Postscript and Appendix.* Toronto, 1865.

Russell, William Howard. *My Diary North and South.* Boston: T.O.H.P. Burnham, 1863.

Sage, Bernard Janin. *Organization of Private Warfare: Bureau of Destructive Means and Measures.* Richmond: self-published, 1863.

Tucker, Nathaniel Beverley. *Address to the People of the United States.* Edited by James Harvey Young. Atlanta, Ga.: Emory University, 1948.

Walker, William. *The War in Nicaragua.* Mobile: S.H. Goetzl, 1860.

Wilson, Frank I. *Sketches of Nassau. To Which Is Added the Devil's Ball Alley; An Indian Tradition.* Raleigh, N.C.: The "Standard" Office, 1864.

Published Collections, Diaries, and Memoirs

Allen, Charles Maxwell. *Dispatches from Bermuda: The Civil War Letters of Charles Maxwell Allen, United States Consul at Bermuda, 1861–1888*. Edited by Glen N. Wiche. Kent, Ohio: Kent State University Press, 2008.

Beall, John Y., and Daniel B. Lucas. *Memoir of John Yates Beall: His Life; Trial; Correspondence; Diary; and Private Manuscript Found among His Papers, Including His Own Account of the Raid on Lake Erie*. Montreal: John Lovell, 1865.

Brown, William Wells. *Narrative of William W. Brown, an American Slave: Written by Himself.* DocSouth Books Edition. Chapel Hill: University of North Carolina Press, 2011. https://docsouth.unc.edu/neh/brown47/menu.html.

Calhoun, John C. *The Works of John C. Calhoun*. 6 vols. New York: D. Appleton, 1854.

Castleman, John B. *Active Service*. Louisville, Ky.: Courier-Journal Job Printing, 1917.

Davis, Jefferson. *The Papers of Jefferson Davis*. Edited by Linda Lasswell Crist, Haskell M. Monroe Jr., James T. McIntosh, Kenneth H. Williams, and Mary Seaton Dix. 14 vols. Baton Rouge: Louisiana State University Press, 1971–2015.

Davis, Varina. *Jefferson Davis, Ex-President of the Confederate States of America: A Memoir*. 2 vols. New York: Belford, 1890.

Denison, George T. *Soldiering in Canada: Recollections and Experiences*. 2nd ed. Toronto: George N. Morang, 1901.

———. *The Struggle for Imperial Unity: Recollections and Experiences*. Toronto: Macmillan, 1909.

Fremantle, Arthur J. L. *Three Months in the Southern States: April—June 1863*. Edinburgh: William Blackwood and Sons, 1863.

Headley, John W. *Confederate Operations in Canada and New York*. New York: Neale, 1906.

Hines, Thomas Henry. "The Northwestern Conspiracy." Pts. 2 and 3. *Southern Bivouac* 2, no. 8 (Jan. 1887): 500–510; 2, no. 9 (Feb. 1887): 568–75.

Hobart-Hampden, Augustus Charles. *Sketches from My Life*. New York: D. Appleton, 1887.

Jones, John B. *A Rebel War Clerk's Diary at the Confederate Capital*. 2 vols. Philadelphia: J.B. Lippincott, 1866.

Milne, Alexander. *The Milne Papers*. Edited by John Beeler. 3 vols. Burlington, Vt.: Ashgate, 2004–2023.

Sumner, Charles. *The Works of Charles Sumner*. 15 vols. Boston: Lee and Shepard, 1870–1883.

Taylor, Thomas E. *Running the Blockade: A Personal Narrative of Adventures, Risks, and Escapes during the American Civil War*. London: John Murray, 1896.

Vance, Zebulon. *The Papers of Zebulon Baird Vance*. Edited by Frontis W. Johnston and Joe Mobley. 3 vols. Raleigh, N.C.: State Department of Archives and History, 1963–2013.

Walker, Georgiana Gholson. *The Private Journal of Georgiana Gholson Walker, 1862–1865, with Selections from the Post-War Years, 1865–1876*. Edited by Dwight Franklin Henderson. Tuscaloosa, Ala.: Confederate, 1963.

Wilkinson, John. *The Narrative of a Blockade-Runner*. New York: Sheldon and Company, 1877.

Published Government Documents

Anderson, George C. *Statute Law of the Bahamas, Comprising all Acts of the General Assembly of the Bahama Islands*. Vol. 2. London: Henry Sweet, 1868.

City Council of Montreal. *The St. Albans Raid; Investigation by the Police Committee of the City Council of Montreal into the Charges Preferred by Councillor B. Devlin against Guillaume Lamothe, Esq., Chief of Police, and the Proceedings of the Council in Reference Thereto*. Montreal: Owler and Stevenson, 1864.

Confederate States of America. *An Act to Impose Regulations upon the Foreign Commerce of the Confederate States, to Provide for the Public Defence*. Richmond, Va., 1864.

———. *Journal of the Congress of the Confederate States of America, 1861–1865*. 7 vols. Washington, D.C.: Government Printing Office, 1904.

Correspondence concerning Claims against Great Britain Transmitted to the Senate of the United States in Answer to the Resolutions of December 4 and 10, 1867, and of May 27, 1863. 7 vols. Washington, D.C.: Government Printing Office, 1869–1871.

House of Commons. *North America No. 9 (1864): Papers Relating to the Seizure of the United States' Steamer Chesapeake*. London: Harrison and Sons, 1864.

———. *North America No. 3 (1876): Correspondence Respecting the Extradition of Bennet G. Burley*. London: Harrison and Sons, 1876.

Lester, W. W. *A Digest of the Military and Naval Laws of the Confederate States [. . .] Analytically Arranged*. Richmond: Evans and Cogswell, 1864.

Matthews, James M., ed. *The Statues at Large of the Confederate States of America, Passed at the Fourth Session of the First Congress; 1863–4, Carefully Collated with the Originals at Richmond*. Richmond, Va.: R.M. Smith, 1864.

———, ed. *The Statutes at Large of the Provisional Government of the Confederate States of America, from the Institution of the Government, February 8, 1861, to Its*

Termination, February 18, 1862, Inclusive. Arranged in Chronological Order. Together with the Constitution for the Provisional Government, and the Permanent Constitution of the Confederate States, and the Treaties Concluded by the Confederate States with Indian Tribes. Richmond, Va.: R.M. Smith, 1864.

Official Records of the Union and Confederate Navies in the War of the Rebellion. 30 vols. Washington, D.C.: Government Printing Office, 1894–1922.

Proceedings of the First Confederate Congress, Fourth Session, 7 December 1863–18 February 1864. Edited by Frank E. Vandiver. *Southern Historical Society Papers.* New series, no. 12, whole no. 50. Richmond: Virginia Historical Society, 1953.

Proceedings of the Second Confederate Congress, First Session, 2 May–14 June 1864. Edited by Frank E. Vandiver. *Southern Historical Society Papers.* New series, no. 13, whole no. 51. Richmond: Virginia Historical Society, 1959.

Richardson, James D., ed. *The Messages and Papers of Jefferson Davis and the Confederacy, 1861–1865.* 2 vols. New York: Chelsea House, 1983.

Stockton, Alfred A. *Reports of Cases Decided in the Vice-Admiralty Court of New Brunswick from 1879–1891.* St. John: J. & A. McMillan, 1894.

United States. *The Case of the United States, Laid before the Tribunal of Arbitration, Convened at Geneva under the Provisions of the Treaty between the United States of America and Her Majesty the Queen of Great Britain, Concluded at Washington, May 8, 1871.* Leipzig: F.A. Brockhaus, 1872.

———. *Message of the President of the United States to the Two Houses of Congress, at the Commencement of the Second Session of the Thirty-Seventh Congress.* Washington, D.C., 1861. Cited as *FRUS 1861*.

———. *Papers Relating to Foreign Affairs, Accompanying the Annual Message of the President to the Third Session of the Thirty-seventh Congress.* Washington, D.C.: Government Printing Office, 1862. Cited as *FRUS 1862*.

———. *Papers Relating to Foreign Affairs, Accompanying the Annual Message of the President to the First Session of the Thirty-eighth Congress.* Parts I and II. Washington, D.C.: Government Printing Office, 1863. Cited as *FRUS 1863*.

———. *Papers Relating to Foreign Affairs, Accompanying the Annual Message of the President to the Second Session of the Thirty-eighth Congress.* Washington, D.C.: Government Printing Office, 1864. Cited as *FRUS 1864*.

———. *Papers Relating to Foreign Affairs, Accompanying the Annual Message of the President to the First Session of the Thirty-ninth Congress.* Parts I and II. Washington, D.C.: Government Printing Office, 1865. Cited as *FRUS 1865*.

U.S. Department of State. *Executive Documents Printed by Order of the House of Representatives, during the First Session of the Thirty-Ninth Congress, 1865–'66.* Pt. 2. Washington, D.C.: Government Printing Office, 1865–66.

War of the Rebellion: The Official Records of the Union and Confederate Armies. 128 vols. Washington, D.C.: Government Printing Office, 1880–1901.

Secondary Sources

Books and Articles

Adderley, Rosanne Marion. *"New Negroes from Africa": Slave Trade Abolition and Free African Settlement in the Nineteenth-Century Caribbean*. Bloomington: Indiana University Press, 2006.

Alessio, Dominic. "Filibustering from Africa to the Americas: Non-State Actors and Empire." *Small Wars and Insurgencies* 27, no. 6 (Oct. 2016): 1044–66.

Alford, Terry. *Fortune's Fool: The Life of John Wilkes Booth*. New York: Oxford University Press, 2015.

Arielli, Nir, Gabriela A. Frei, and Inge Van Hulle. "The Foreign Enlistment Act, International Law, and British Politics, 1819–2014." *International History Review* 38, no. 4 (Aug. 2016): 636–56.

Asaka, Ikuko. "'Our Brethren in the West Indies': Self-Emancipated People in Canada and the Antebellum Politics of Diaspora and Empire." *Journal of African American History* 97, no. 3 (2012): 219–39.

Baird, Nancy Disher. *Luke Pryor Blackburn: Physician, Governor, Reformer*. Lexington: University of Kentucky Press, 2009.

Bale, Gordon. *Chief Justice William Johnston Ritchie: Responsible Government and Judicial Review*. Ottawa: Carleton University Press, 1991.

Balogh, Brian. *A Government out of Sight: The Mystery of National Authority in Nineteenth-Century America*. New York: Cambridge University Press, 2009.

Beckert, Sven. *Empire of Cotton: A Global History*. New York: Vintage, 2015.

Belich, James. *Replenishing the Earth: The Settler Revolution and the Rise of the Anglo-World, 1783–1939*. New York: Oxford University Press, 2009.

Bell, Andrew McIlwane. *Mosquito Soldiers: Malaria, Yellow Fever, and the Course of the American Civil War*. Baton Rouge: Louisiana State University Press, 2010.

Bensel, Richard Franklin. *Yankee Leviathan: The Origins of Central State Authority in America, 1859–1877*. New York: Cambridge University Press, 1990.

Benton, Lauren. *A Search for Sovereignty*. Cambridge: Cambridge University Press, 2010.

Benton, Lauren, and Lisa Ford. *Rage for Order: The British Empire and the Origins of International Law, 1800–1850*. Cambridge, Mass.: Harvard University Press, 2016.

Berger, Carl. *The Sense of Power: Studies in the Ideas of Canadian Imperialism, 1867–1914*. Toronto: University of Toronto Press, 1970.

Bernath, Michael T. "The Confederacy as a Moment of Possibility." *Journal of Southern History* 79, no. 2 (May 2013): 299–338.

Bernath, Stuart L. *Squall across the Atlantic: American Civil War Prize Cases and Diplomacy.* Berkeley: University of California Press, 1970.

Berwanger, Eugene H. *The British Foreign Service and the American Civil War.* Lexington: University Press of Kentucky, 1994.

———. "The Case of Stirrup and Edwards, 1861–1870: The Kidnapping and Georgia Enslavement of West Indian Blacks." *Georgia Historical Quarterly* 76, no. 1 (Spring 1992): 1–18.

Bickham, Troy. *The Weight of Vengeance: The United States, the British Empire, and the War of 1812.* New York: Oxford University Press, 2012.

Bivins, John F. "Life and Character of Jacob Thompson." *Publications of the Historical Society of Trinity College* 2 (1898): 83–91.

Blackett, R. J. M. *Divided Hearts: Britain and the American Civil War.* Baton Rouge: Louisiana State University Press, 2001.

Bloemendal, Albertine. "Conclusion: A Call for a New Diplomatic History." In *Reframing the Diplomat: Ernst van der Beugel and the Cold War Atlantic Community*, 319–27. Leiden, Netherlands: Brill, 2018.

Blume, Kenneth J. "Flight from the Flag: The American Government, the British Caribbean, and the American Merchant Marine, 1861–1865." *Civil War History* 32 (Jan. 2012): 44–55.

Bonner, Michael Brem. *Confederate Political Economy: Creating and Managing a Southern Corporatist Nation.* Baton Rouge: Louisiana State University Press, 2016.

Bonner, Michael Brem, and Peter McCord. "Reassessment of the Union Blockade's Effectiveness in the Civil War." *North Carolina Historical Review* 88, no. 4 (Oct. 2011): 375–95.

Botting, Gary. *Extradition between Canada and the United States.* Ardsley, N.Y.: Transnational, 2005.

Bourne, Kenneth. *Britain and the Balance of Power in North America, 1815–1908.* Berkeley: University of California Press, 1967.

Bradlee, Francis. *Blockade Running during the Civil War and the Effect of Land and Water Transportation on the Confederacy.* Salem, Mass.: Essex Institute, 1925.

Bradshaw, Michael. "True but Brief History of the Friendly Societies and Development of Black Bermudian Communities After Emancipation: Black People Seek Pride and Power in a Post-Slavery and Post-Emancipation World, the Bermuda Experience." *Africology: The Journal of Pan African Studies* 12, no. 1 (Sept. 2018): 560–78.

Brandt, Nat. *The Man Who Tried to Burn New York.* Lincoln, Neb.: iUniverse, 1986.

Brettle, Adrian. *Colossal Ambitions: Confederate Planning for a Post-Civil War World.* Charlottesville: University of Virginia Press, 2020.

Brode, Patrick. *The Odyssey of John Anderson*. Toronto: University of Toronto Press, 1989.
Brown, Charles H. *Agents of Manifest Destiny: The Lives and Times of the Filibusters*. Chapel Hill: University of North Carolina Press, 1980.
Buckner, Phillip A. "The 1860s: An End and a Beginning." In *The Atlantic Region to Confederation: A History*, edited by Phillip A. Buckner and John G. Reid. Toronto: University of Toronto Press, 1994.
———. *The Transition to Responsible Government: British Policy in British North America, 1815–1850*. Westport, Conn.: Greenwood Press, 1985.
Buckner, Phillip A., and R. Douglas Francis. *Rediscovering the British World*. Calgary: University of Calgary Press, 2005.
Cain, P. J., and A. G. Hopkins. *British Imperialism: Innovation and Expansion 1688–1914*. London: Longman, 1993.
Campbell, Duncan Andrew. *English Public Opinion and the American Civil War*. Rochester, N.Y.: Boydell Press, for the Royal Historical Society, 2003.
Chet, Guy. *The Ocean Is a Wilderness: Atlantic Piracy and the Limits of State Authority, 1688–1856*. Boston: University of Massachusetts Press, 2014.
Cochran, Hamilton. *Blockade Runners of the Confederacy*. Westport, Conn.: Greenwood Press, 1958.
Conlin, Dan. "A Historiography of Private Sea War in Nova Scotia." *Journal of the Royal Nova Scotia Historical Society* 1 (1998): 79–92.
Costello, Ray. *Black Salt: Seafarers of African Descent on British Ships*. Liverpool: Liverpool University Press, 2012.
Courtemanche, Regis A. *No Need of Glory: The British Navy in American Waters, 1860–1864*. Annapolis: Naval Institute Press, 1977.
———. "The Royal Navy and the End of William Walker." *Historian* 30, no. 3 (1968): 350–65.
Craton, Michael. *A History of the Bahamas*. 3rd ed. Waterloo, ON: San Salvador Press, 1986.
———. "The Role of the Caribbean Vice Admiralty Courts in British Imperialism." *Caribbean Studies* 11, no. 2 (1971): 5–20.
Craton, Michael, and Gail Saunders. *Islanders in the Stream: A History of the Bahamian People*. Vol. 2, *From the Ending of Slavery to the Twenty-First Century*. Athens: University of Georgia Press, 1998.
Craven, Matthew, Malgosia Fitzmaurice, and Maria Vogiatzi, eds. *Time, History and International Law*. Leiden: Brill, 2007.
Crook, D. P. *The North, the South, and the Powers, 1861–1865*. New York: John Wiley & Sons, 1974.
Cunningham, O. Edward. "'In Violation of the Laws of War': The Execution of Robert Cobb Kennedy." *Louisiana History* 18, no. 2 (1977): 189–201.

Cusick, James G. *The Other War of 1812: The Patriot War and the American Invasion of Spanish East Florida*. Athens: University of Georgia Press, 2007.
Darwin, John. *The Empire Project: The Rise and Fall of the British World-System, 1830–1970*. New York: Cambridge University Press, 2009.
Davis, William C. *Look Away! A History of the Confederate States of America*. New York: Free Press, 2002.
Deichmann, Catherine. *Rogues and Runners: Bermuda and the American Civil War*. Hamilton, Bermuda: Bermuda National Trust, 2003.
Dilke, Charles Wentworth. *Greater Britain: A Record of Travel in English-Speaking Countries*. London: Macmillan, 1888.
Dobson, Narda. *A History of Belize*. London: Longman Caribbean, 1973.
Downing, Arthur. "The Friendly Planet: 'Oddfellows,' Networks, and the 'British World,' c. 1840–1914." *Journal of Global History* 7, no. 3 (2012): 389–414.
Downs, Gregory P. *The Second American Revolution: The Civil War–Era Struggle over Cuba and the Rebirth of the American Republic*. Chapel Hill: University of North Carolina Press, 2019.
Doyle, Don H., ed. *American Civil Wars: The United States, Latin America, Europe and the Crisis of the 1860s*. Chapel Hill: University of North Carolina Press, 2017.
———. *The Cause of All Nations: An International History of the American Civil War*. New York: Basic Books, 2015.
Dubrulle, Hugh. *Ambivalent Nation: How Britain Imagined the American Civil War*. Baton Rouge: Louisiana State University Press, 2018.
Ducharme, Michael. "Closing the Last Chapter of the Atlantic Revolution: The 1837–1838 Rebellions in Upper and Lower Canada." *Proceedings of the American Antiquarian Society* 116, no. 2 (Oct. 2007): 413–30.
Durham, Roger S. *High Seas and Yankee Gunboats: A Blockade-Running Adventure from the Diary of James Dickson*. Columbia: University of South Carolina Press, 2005.
Edling, Max M. *A Hercules in the Cradle: War, Money, and the American State, 1783–1867*. Chicago: University of Chicago Press, 2014.
———. *A Revolution in Favor of Government: Origins of the U.S. Constitution and the Making of the American State*. New York: Oxford University Press, 2003.
Eichhorn, Niels. *Liberty and Slavery: European Separatists, Southern Secession, and the American Civil War*. Baton Rouge: Louisiana State University Press, 2019.
Eyal, Yonatan. "A Romantic Realist: George Nicholas Sanders and the Dilemmas of Southern International Engagement." *Journal of Southern History* 78, no. 1 (Feb. 2012): 107–30.

Finkelman, Paul. "International Extradition and Fugitive Slaves: The John Anderson Case." *Brooklyn Journal of International Law* 18, no. 3 (1992): 765–810.

Fitzmaurice, Andrew. "Liberalism and Empire in Nineteenth-Century International Law." *American Historical Review* 117, no. 1 (Feb. 2012): 122–40.

Fleche, Andre. *The Revolution of 1861: The American Civil War in the Age of Nationalist Conflict.* Chapel Hill: University of North Carolina Press, 2012.

Foreman, Amanda. *A World on Fire: Britain's Crucial Role in the American Civil War.* New York: Random House, 2010.

Francis, Mark. *Governors and Settlers: Images of Authority in the British Colonies, 1820–60.* London: Macmillan, 1992.

"From the Autobiography of Herschel V. Johnson, 1856–1867." *American Historical Review* 30, no. 2 (1925): 311–36.

Gerriets, Marilyn, and Julian Gwyn. "Tariffs, Trade, and Reciprocity: Nova Scotia, 1830–1866." *Acadiensis* 25, no. 2 (Spring 1996): 62–82.

Gobat, Michel. *Empire By Invitation: William Walker and Manifest Destiny in Central America.* Cambridge, Mass.: Harvard University Press, 2018.

Gorman, John. "The Adderley Family in the New World." *Journal of the Bahamas Historical Society* 22 (Oct. 2000): 31–41.

Greenberg, Amy S. *Manifest Manhood and the Antebellum American Empire.* New York: Cambridge University Press, 2010.

Greer, Allan. *The Patriots and the People: The Rebellion of 1837 in Rural Lower Canada.* Toronto: University of Toronto Press, 1993.

Greer, Allan, and Ian Radforth, eds. *Colonial Leviathan: State Formation in Mid-Nineteenth Century Canada.* Toronto: University of Toronto Press, 1992.

Guterl, Matthew Pratt. *American Mediterranean: Southern Slaveholders in the Age of Emancipation.* Cambridge, Mass.: Harvard University Press, 2008.

Gwyn, Julian. *Excessive Expectations: Maritime Commerce and the Economic Development of Nova Scotia, 1740–1870.* Toronto: McGill-Queen's University Press, 1998.

Hall, Catherine. *Civilising Subjects: Colony and Metropole in the English Imagination, 1830–1867.* Chicago: University of Chicago Press, 2002.

Hall, William Edward. *The Rights and Duties of Neutrals.* London: Longmans, Green, 1874.

Hamer, Philip M. "Great Britain, the United States, and the Negro Seamen Acts, 1822–1848." *Journal of Southern History* 1, no. 1 (1935): 3–28.

Hanna, Mark G. *Pirate Nests and the Rise of the British Empire, 1570–1740.* Chapel Hill: University of North Carolina Press, 2015.

Harris, Steven M. "The Global Construction of International Law in the Nineteenth Century: The Case of Arbitration." *Journal of World History* 27, no. 2 (2016): 303–25.

Harris, William C. *Confederate Privateer: The Life of John Yates Beall*. Baton Rouge: Louisiana State University Press, 2023.

Harrold, Stanley. *Border War: Fighting over Slavery Before the Civil War*. Chapel Hill: University of North Carolina Press, 2010.

———. "Romanticizing Slave Revolt: Madison Washington, the Creole Mutiny, and Abolitionist Celebration of Violent Means." In *Antislavery Violence: Sectional, Racial, and Cultural Conflict in Antebellum America*, edited by Stanley Harrold and John R. McKivigan, 89–107. Knoxville: University of Tennessee Press, 1999.

Head, David. *Privateers of the Americas: Spanish American Privateering from the United States in the Early Republic*. Athens: University of Georgia Press, 2015.

Herring, George C. *From Colony to Superpower: U.S. Foreign Relations since 1776*. New York: Oxford University Press, 2008.

Hess, Earl J. *Civil War Supply and Strategy: Feeding Men and Moving Armies*. Baton Rouge: Louisiana State University Press, 2020.

Hill, Louis B. *State Socialism in the Confederate States of America*. Charlottesville: University of Virginia Press, 1936.

Hoffman, Elizabeth Cobbs. "Diplomatic History and the Meaning of Life: Toward a Global American History." *Diplomatic History* 21, no. 4 (Fall 1997): 499–518.

Holbrook, Francis X. "A Mosby or a Quantrill? The Civil War Career of John Clibbon Braine." *American Neptune* 33, no. 3 (July 1973): 199–211.

Hopkins, A. G. *American Empire: A Global History*. Princeton, N.J.: Princeton University Press, 2018.

Horne, Gerald. *Negro Comrades of the Crown: African Americans and the British Empire Fight the U.S. before Emancipation*. New York: New York University Press, 2012.

Hubbard, Charles M. *The Burden of Confederate Diplomacy*. Knoxville: University of Tennessee Press, 1998.

———. "James Mason, the 'Confederate Lobby' and the Blockade Debate of March 1862." *Civil War History* 45, no. 3 (Sept. 1999): 223–37.

Hunt, Michael H. "Internationalizing U.S. Diplomatic History: A Practical Agenda." *Diplomatic History* 15, no. 1 (1991): 1–11.

Hurt, R. Douglas. *Agriculture and the Confederacy: Policy, Productivity, and Power in the Civil War South*. Chapel Hill: University of North Carolina Press, 2015.

Hutton, T. R. C. "Sleuthing for Mr. Crow: Detective William Baldwin and the Business of White Supremacy." *Journal of Southern History* 85, no. 2 (2019): 285–320.

Huzzey, Richard. *Freedom Burning: Anti-Slavery and Empire in Victorian Britain.* Ithaca, N.Y.: Cornell University Press, 2012.

Jampoler, Andrew C. A. *The Last Lincoln Conspirator.* Annapolis: Naval Institute Press, 2008.

Janney, Caroline E. *Remembering the Civil War: Reunion and the Limits of Reconciliation.* Chapel Hill: University of North Carolina Press, 2013.

Jarvis, Michael. *In the Eye of All Trade: Bermuda, Bermudians, and the Maritime Atlantic World, 1680–1783.* Chapel Hill: University of North Carolina Press, 2010.

Jenkins, Brian. *Britain and the War for the Union.* 2 vols. Montreal: McGill-Queen's University Press, 1974–80.

Johnson, Howard. "Friendly Societies in the Bahamas, 1834–1910." *Slavery and Abolition* 12, no. 3 (1991): 183–99.

Johnson, Ludwell H. "Abraham Lincoln and the Development of Presidential War Making Powers: Prize Cases (1863) Revisited." *Civil War History* 35, no. 3 (1989): 208–24.

Johnson, Wittington B. *Race Relations in the Bahamas, 1784–1834.* Fayetteville: University of Arkansas Press, 2000.

Jones, Francis I. W. "A Hot Southern Town: Confederate Sympathizers in Halifax during the American Civil War." *Journal of the Royal Nova Scotia Historical Society* 2 (1999): 52–69.

Jones, Howard. "Anglophobia and the Aroostook War." *New England Quarterly* 48, no. 4 (1975): 519–39.

———. *Blue and Gray Diplomacy: A History of Union and Confederate Foreign Relations.* Chapel Hill: University of North Carolina Press, 2010.

———. "The Peculiar Institution and National Honor: The Case of the Creole Slave Revolt." *Civil War History* 21, no. 1 (Mar. 1975): 28–50.

Jones, Howard, and Donald A. Rakestraw. *Prologue to Manifest Destiny: Anglo-American Relations in the 1840s.* Wilmington, Del.: Scholarly Resources, 1997.

Jones, Wilbur Devereux. "The Influence of Slavery on the Webster-Ashburton Negotiations." *Journal of Southern History* 22, no. 1 (Feb. 1956): 48–58.

Karp, Matthew. *This Vast Southern Empire: Slaveholders at the Helm of American Foreign Policy.* Cambridge, Mass.: Harvard University Press, 2015.

Kaye, Anthony. "The Second Slavery: Modernity in the Nineteenth-Century South and the Atlantic World." *Journal of Southern History* 75, no. 3 (Aug. 2009): 627–50.

Kee, Kevin. "Stuart Robinson: A Pro-Slavery Presbyterian in Canada West." In *Historical Papers*, edited by Bruce L. Guenther, 5–23. Canada: Canadian Society of Church History, 1996.

Keehn, David C. *Knights of the Golden Circle: Secret Empire, Southern Secession, Civil War*. Baton Rouge: Louisiana State University Press, 2013.

Kelly, Patrick. "The Lost Continent of Abraham Lincoln." *Journal of the Civil War Era* 9, no. 2 (June 2019): 223–48.

Kerr-Ritchie, Jeffrey R. *Rebellious Passage: The "Creole" Revolt and America's Coastal Slave Trade*. New York: Cambridge University Press, 2019.

———. *Rites of August First: Emancipation Day in the Black Atlantic World*. Baton Rouge: Louisiana State University Press, 2007.

Kert, Faye. *Trimming Yankee Sails: Pirates and Privateers of New Brunswick*. Fredericton, NB: Goose Lane Editions, 2005.

Kilbride, Daniel. "The Old South Confronts the Dilemma of David Livingstone." *Journal of Southern History* 82, no. 4 (Nov. 2016): 789–822.

Kirkland, Edward. *The Peacemakers of 1864*. New York: Macmillan, 1927.

Kiser, William S. *Illusions of Empire: The Civil War and Reconstruction in the U.S.-Mexico Borderlands*. Philadelphia: University of Pennsylvania Press, 2022.

———. "'We Must Have Chihuahua and Sonora': Civil War Diplomacy in the U.S.-Mexico Borderlands." *Journal of the Civil War Era* 9, no. 2 (June 2019): 196–222.

Koistinen, Paul A. C. *Beating Plowshares into Swords: The Political Economy of American Warfare, 1606–1865*. Lawrence: University Press of Kansas, 1996.

Koskenniemi, Marttii. *The Gentle Civilizer of Nations: The Rise and Fall of International Law 1870–1960*. Cambridge: Cambridge University Press, 2001.

Krein, David F. *The Last Palmerston Government: Foreign Policy, Domestic Politics, and the Genesis of "Splendid Isolation."* Ames: Iowa State University Press, 1978.

Laidlaw, Zoe. "Breaking Britannia's Bounds? Law, Settlers, and Space in Britain's Imperial Historiography." *Historical Journal* 55, no. 3 (Sept. 2012): 807–30.

———. *Colonial Connections, 1815–1845: Patronage, the Information Revolution, and Colonial Government*. Manchester: Manchester University Press, 2005.

Larrabee, Ann. *The Dynamite Fiend*. Halifax, NS: Nimbus, 2005.

Lemnitzer, Jan. *Power, Law, and the End of Privateering*. London: Palgrave MacMillan, 2014.

Levine, Bruce. *Confederate Emancipation: Southern Plans to Free and Arm Slaves during the Civil War*. New York: Oxford University Press, 2006.

Linebaugh, Peter, and Marcus Rediker. *The Many-Headed Hydra: The Hidden History of the Revolutionary Atlantic*. Boston: Beacon, 2000.

Luraghi, Raimondo. *A History of the Confederate Navy*. Translated by Paolo Coletta. Annapolis: Naval Institute Press, 1996.

Lyall, Gordon Robert. "From Imbroglio to Pig War: The San Juan Island Dispute, 1853–1871, in History and Memory." *BC Studies*, no. 185 (Summer 2015): 73–95.

MacDonald, Helen G. *Canadian Public Opinion on the American Civil War*. New York: Columbia University Press, 1926.

Mahin, Dean. *One War at a Time: The International Dimensions of the Civil War*. Washington, D.C.: Brassey's, 1999.

Maier, Charles S. *Leviathan 2.0: Inventing Modern Statehood*. Cambridge, Mass.: Harvard University Press, 2014.

Majewski, John. *Modernizing a Slave Economy: The Economic Vision of the Confederate Nation*. Chapel Hill: University of North Carolina Press, 2009.

Manning, F. E. "Nicknames and Number Plates in the British West Indies." *Journal of American Folklore* 87, no. 344 (June 1974).

Marler, Scott P. "'An Abiding Faith in Cotton': The Merchant Capitalist Community in New Orleans, 1860–1862." *Civil War History* 54, no. 3 (2008): 263–67.

———. *The Merchants' Capital: New Orleans and the Political Economy of the Nineteenth-Century South*. Cambridge: Cambridge University Press, 2013.

Marquis, Greg. *In Armageddon's Shadow: The Civil War and Canada's Maritime Provinces*. Montreal: McGill-Queen's University Press, 1998.

May, Robert E. "The Irony of Southern Diplomacy: Visions of Empire, the Monroe Doctrine, and the Quest for Nationhood." *Journal of Southern History* 83, no. 1 (Jan. 2017): 69–106.

———. *Manifest Destiny's Underworld: Filibustering in Antebellum America*. Chapel Hill: University of North Carolina Press, 2002.

Mayers, Adam. *Dixie and the Dominion: Canada, the Confederacy, and the War for the Union*. Toronto: Dundurn Press, 2003.

McCurry, Stephanie. *Confederate Reckoning: Power and Politics in the Civil War South*. Cambridge, Mass.: Harvard University Press, 2010.

McLaren, John. *Dewigged, Bothered, and Bewildered: British Colonial Judges on Trial, 1800–1900*. Toronto: University of Toronto Press, for the Osgoode Society, 2011.

McPherson, James. *Battle Cry of Freedom: The Civil War Era*. New York: Oxford University Press, 1988.

Merli, Frank J. *Great Britain and the Confederate Navy, 1861–1865*. Bloomington: Indiana University Press, 1970.
Montgomery, Skye. "Reannealing of the Heart Ties: The Rhetoric of Anglo-American Kinship and the Politics of Reconciliation in the Prince of Wales's 1860 Tour." *Journal of the Civil War Era* 6, no. 2 (June 2016): 193–219.
Moore, J. H. "New South Wales and the American Civil War." *Australian Journal of Politics and History* 16, no. 1 (Apr. 1970): 24–38.
Morgan, Cecilia. *Building Better Britains? Settler Societies in the British World, 1783–1920*. Toronto: University of Toronto Press, 2017.
Moss, Kenneth B. *Marque and Reprisal: The Spheres of Public and Private Warfare*. Lawrence: University Press of Kansas, 2019.
Munsell, F. Darrell. *The Unfortunate Duke: Henry Pelham, Fifth Duke of Newcastle, 1811–1864*. Columbia: University of Missouri Press, 1985.
Murray, Alexander L. "The Extradition of Fugitive Slaves from Canada: A Re-Evaluation." *Canadian Historical Review* 43, no. 4 (Dec. 1962): 298–314.
Myers, Phillip E. *Caution and Cooperation: The American Civil War in British-American Relations*. Kent, Ohio: Kent State University Press, 2008.
Neely, Mark E., Jr. "The Perils of Running the Blockade: The Influence of International Law in an Era of Total War." *Civil War History* 32, no. 2 (June 1986): 101–18.
Neff, Stephen C. *War and the Law of Nations*. New York: Cambridge University Press, 2005.
Negus, Samuel. "A Notorious Nest of Offence: Neutrals, Belligerents, and Union Jails in Civil War Blockade Running." *Civil War History* 56, no. 4 (Dec. 2010): 350–85.
Neidhardt, W. S. *Fenianism in North America*. University Park: Pennsylvania State University Press, 1975.
Nelson, Larry E. *Bullets, Ballots, and Rhetoric: Confederate Policy for the United States Presidential Contest of 1864*. Tuscaloosa: University of Alabama Press, 1980.
Nepveux, Ethel Trenholm Seabrook. *George Alfred Trenholm and the Company That Went to War, 1861–1865*. Charleston, SC: self-published, 1973.
Novak, William J. "The Myth of the 'Weak' American State." *American Historical Review* 113, no. 3 (June 2008): 752–72.
Nuermberger, Ruth Ketring. *The Clays of Alabama: A Planter-Lawyer-Politician Family*. Lexington: University of Kentucky Press, 1958.
Obert, Jonathan. *The Six-Shooter State: Public and Private Violence in American Politics*. New York: Cambridge University Press, 2018.
O'Brien, Michael. *Conjectures of Order: Intellectual Life in the Old South, 1810–1860*. Chapel Hill: University of North Carolina Press, 2004.

O'Connor, Peter. *American Sectionalism in the British Mind, 1832–1863.* Baton Rouge: Louisiana State University Press, 2017.

Owsley, Frank Lawrence, Jr., and Gene A. Smith. *Filibusters and Expansionists: Jeffersonian Manifest Destiny, 1800–1821.* Tuscaloosa: University of Alabama Press, 2004.

Owsley, Frank Lawrence, Sr. *King Cotton Diplomacy: Foreign Relations of the Confederate States of America.* 3rd ed. Revised by Harriet Chappell Owsley. Tuscaloosa: University of Alabama Press, 2008.

———. *State Rights in the Confederacy.* Chicago: University of Chicago Press, 1925.

Packwood, Cyril Outerbridge. *Detour—Bermuda, Destination—U.S. House of Representatives; the Life of Joseph Hayne Rainey.* Hamilton, Bermuda: Baxter's Limited, 1977.

Paterson, Thomas G. "A New Diplomatic History: The Domestic Side." *Social Studies* 62, no. 4 (Apr. 1971): 156–59.

Payne, Samantha. "'A General Insurrection in the Countries with Slaves': The US Civil War and the Origins of an Atlantic Revolution, 1861–1866." *Past and Present* 257 (Nov. 2022): 248–79.

Peters, Thelma. "Blockade-Running in the Bahamas during the Civil War." *Tequesta: The Journal of the Historical Association of Southern Florida* 1, no. 5 (1945): 16–29.

———. "The American Loyalists in the Bahama Islands: Who They Were." *Florida Historical Quarterly* 40, no. 3 (Jan. 1961): 226–40.

Pierce, Michael. "'Adventures. Escape of a Slave': An Account of the Flight of Nelson Hackett, May 27, 1842." *Arkansas Historical Quarterly* 79, no. 2 (2020): 133–41.

Platt, Stephen. *Autumn in the Heavenly Kingdom: China, the West, and the Epic Story of the Taiping Civil War.* New York: Alfred A. Knopf, 2012.

Rainwater, P. L. "Letters to and from Jacob Thompson." *Journal of Southern History* 6, no. 1 (Feb. 1940): 95–111.

Rao, Gautham. *National Duties: Customs Houses and the Making of the American State.* Chicago: University of Chicago Press, 2016.

Read, Geoff, and Todd Webb. "'The Catholic Mahdi of the North West': Louis Riel and the Metis Resistance in Transatlantic and Imperial Context." *Canadian Historical Review* 93, no. 2 (2012): 171–95.

Reeder, Tyson. "'Sovereign Lords' and 'Dependent Administrators': Artigan Privateers, Atlantic Borderwaters, and State Building in the Early Nineteenth Century." *Journal of American History* 103, no. 2 (Sept. 2016): 323–46.

Reid, Jennifer. *Louis Riel and the Creation of Modern Canada.* Albuquerque: University of New Mexico Press, 2008.

Reid, Richard M. *African Canadians in Union Blue: Volunteering for the Cause in the Civil War.* Kent, Ohio: Kent State University Press, 2015.

Robinson, Kenneth E. *Heritage, Including an Account of Bermudian Builders, Pilots, and Petitioners of the Early Post-Abolition Period, 1834–1859.* London: Macmillan Education Limited, for the Berkeley Educational Society, 1979.

Robinson, Ronald. "Non-European Foundations of European Imperialism: Sketch for a Theory of Collaboration." In *Studies in the Theory of Imperialism*, edited by Roger Owen and Bob Sutcliffe, 117–42. London: Longman, 1972.

Robinson, William Morrison. *The Confederate Privateers.* Columbia: University of South Carolina Press, 1928.

Ross, Charles D. *Breaking the Blockade: The Bahamas during the Civil War.* Jackson: University Press of Mississippi, 2021.

Rugemer, Edward Bartlett. *The Problem of Emancipation: The Caribbean Roots of the American Civil War.* Baton Rouge: Louisiana State University Press, 2008.

Salehyan, Idean. *Rebels without Borders: Transnational Insurgencies in World Politics.* Ithaca, N.Y.: Cornell University Press, 2009.

Saunders, Gail. "The Blockade Running Era in the Bahamas: Blessing or Curse?" *Journal of the Bahamas Historical Society* 10, no. 1 (Oct. 1988): 14–18.

Schoen, Brian. *The Fragile Fabric of Union: Cotton, Federal Politics and the Global Origins of the Civil War.* Baltimore: Johns Hopkins University Press, 2009.

Scott, Julius S. *The Common Wind: Afro-American Currents in the Age of the Haitian Revolution.* London: Verso, 2020

Senior, Hereward. *The Last Invasion of Canada: The Fenian Raids, 1866–1870.* Toronto: Dundurn Press, 1991.

Sexton, Jay. "Anglophobia in Nineteenth-Century Elections, Politics, and Diplomacy." In *America at the Ballot Box: Elections and Political History*, edited by Gareth Davies and Julian E. Zelizer, 98–117. Philadelphia: University of Pennsylvania Press, 2015.

———. *Debtor Diplomacy: Finance and American Foreign Relations in the Civil War Era, 1837–1873.* New York: Oxford University Press, 2005.

———. "The Funded Loan and the Alabama Claims." *Diplomatic History* 27, no. 4 (Sept. 2003): 449–78.

———. "Steam Transport, Sovereignty, and Empire in North America, circa 1850–1885." In "Crises of Sovereignty in the 1860s." Special issue, *Journal of the Civil War Era* 7, no. 4 (2017): 620–47.

Sheehan-Dean, Aaron. *The Calculus of Violence: How Americans Fought the Civil War.* Cambridge, Mass.: Harvard University Press, 2018.

Shepard, Frederick J. "The Johnson's Island Plot: An Historical Narrative of the Conspiracy of the Confederates, in 1864, to Capture the U.S. Steamship Michigan on Lake Erie, and Release the Prisoners of War in Sandusky Bay." *Proceedings of the Buffalo Historical Society* 9 (1906): 1–51.

Sher, Julian. *The North Star: Canada and the Civil War Plots Against Lincoln.* Toronto: Alfred A. Knopf Canada, 2023.

Shingleton, Royce Gordon. *John Taylor Wood: Sea Ghost of the Confederacy.* Athens: University of Georgia Press, 1979.

Smith, Andrew. *British Businessmen and Canadian Confederation: Constitution Making in an Era of Anglo-Globalization.* Montreal: McGill-Queen's University Press, 2008.

Spence, Clark C., and Robin W. Winks. "William 'Colorado' Jewett of the Niagara Falls Conference." *Historian* 23, no. 1 (Nov. 1960): 23–53.

Spencer, Warren F. *The Confederate Navy in Europe.* Tuscaloosa: University of Alabama Press, 1983.

Startup, Kenneth M. "'The Guardians of Our Own Honor': Confederate Sympathies and the Pew Controversy in Christ Church." *Journal of the Bahamas Historical Society* 30 (Oct. 2008).

———. "'This Small Act of Courtesy': Admiral Sir George Willes Watson, Trouble, Trials, and Turmoil in Bahama Waters." *Journal of the Bahamas Historical Society* 31 (Oct. 2009): 57–62.

Steers, Edward. *Blood on the Moon: The Assassination of Abraham Lincoln.* Lexington: University of Kentucky Press, 2001.

Still, William N., Jr. "A Naval Sieve: The Union Blockade in the Civil War." *Naval War College Review* 36, no. 3 (June 1983): 38–45.

Stout, Joseph Allen. *Schemers and Dreamers: Filibustering in Mexico, 1848–1921.* Fort Worth: Texas Christian University Press, 2002.

Stuart, Reginald C. *United States Expansionism in British North America, 1775–1871.* Chapel Hill: University of North Carolina Press, 1988.

Surdam, David G. *Northern Naval Superiority and the Economics of the American Civil War.* Columbia: University of South Carolina Press, 2001.

———. "The Union Navy's Blockade Reconsidered." *Naval War College Review* 51, no. 4 (September 1998): 85.

Sutherland, Daniel E. *A Savage Conflict: The Decisive Role of Guerillas in the American Civil War.* Chapel Hill: University of North Carolina Press, 2009.

Thomas, Emory. *The Confederacy as a Revolutionary Experience.* Englewood Cliffs, N.J.: Prentice-Hall, 1971.

———. *The Confederate Nation: 1861–1865*. New York: Harper & Row, 1979.
Thomas, William G. *The Iron Way: Railroads, the Civil War, and the Making of Modern America*. New Haven, Conn.: Yale University Press, 2011.
Thompson, Michael D. *Working on the Dock of the Bay: Labor and Enterprise in an Antebellum Southern Port*. Columbia: University of South Carolina Press, 2015.
Thomson, Janice E. *Mercenaries, Pirates, and Sovereigns: State-Building and Extraterritorial Violence in Early Modern Europe*. Princeton, N.J.: Princeton University Press, 1994.
Thorp, Daniel B. "New Zealand and the American Civil War." *Pacific Historical Review* 80, no. 1 (Feb. 2011): 97–130.
Tidwell, William A. *April '65: Confederate Covert Action in the American Civil War*. Kent, Ohio: Kent State University Press, 1995.
Tidwell, William A., James O. Hall, and David Winfred Gaddy. *Come Retribution: The Confederate Secret Service and the Assassination of Lincoln*. Jackson: University Press of Mississippi, 1988.
Towne, Stephen E. *Surveillance and Spies in the Civil War: Exposing Confederate Conspiracies in America's Heartland*. Athens: Ohio University Press, 2015.
Troxler, Caroline Watterson. "Uses of the Bahamas by Southern Loyalist Exiles." In *The Loyal Atlantic: Remaking the British Atlantic in the Revolutionary Era*, edited by Jerry Bannister and Liam Riordan, 185–208. Toronto: University of Toronto Press, 2012.
Tucker, Ann L. *Newest Born of Nations: European Nationalist Movements and the Making of the Confederacy*. Charlottesville: University of Virginia Press, 2020.
Tuffnell, Stephen. "Expatriate Foreign Relations: Britain's American Community and Transnational Approaches to the U.S. Civil War." *Diplomatic History* 40, no. 4 (Sept. 2016): 635–63.
Turner, Michael J. *Stonewall Jackson, Beresford Hope, and the Meaning of the American Civil War in Britain*.
Unterman, Katherine. *Uncle Sam's Policemen: The Pursuit of Fugitives Across Borders*. Cambridge, Mass.: Harvard University Press, 2015.
Van Alstyne, Richard W. "American Filibustering and the British Navy." *American Journal of International Law* 32, no. 1 (Jan. 1938): 138–42.
Vandiver, Frank E., ed. *Confederate Blockade Running through Bermuda, 1861–1865: Letters and Cargo Manifests*. Austin: University of Texas Press, 1947.
Ward, John Manning. *Colonial Self-Government: The British Experience, 1759–1856*. London: Macmillan, 1976.

Weitz, Mark A. *The Confederacy on Trial: The Piracy and Sequestration Cases of 1861.* Lawrence: University Press of Kansas, 2005.

Wentzell, Tyler. "Mercenaries and Adventurers: Canada and the Foreign Enlistment Act in the Nineteenth Century." *Canadian Military History* 23, no. 2 (2014): 1–21.

Wilkins, Joe. "Window on Freedom: South Carolina's Response to British West Indian Slave Emancipation, 1833–1834." *South Carolina Historical Magazine* 85, no. 2 (1984): 135–44.

Wilkinson, Henry Campbell. *Bermuda from Sail to Steam: The History of the Island from 1784–1901.* 2 vols. London: Oxford University Press, 1973.

Wilson, Dennis K. *Justice under Pressure: The St. Albans Raid and Its Aftermath.* New York: University Press of America, 1992.

Wilson, Harold S. *Confederate Industry: Manufacturers and Quartermasters in the Civil War.* Jackson: University Press of Mississippi, 2002.

Wilson, Mark R. *The Business of Civil War: Military Mobilization and the State, 1861–1865.* Baltimore: Johns Hopkins University Press, 2006.

Winks, Robin W. *The Civil War Years: Canada and the United States.* 4th ed. Montreal: McGill-Queen's University Press, 1998.

Winsboro, Irvin D. S., and Joe Knetsch. "Florida Slaves, the 'Saltwater Railroad' to the Bahamas, and Anglo-American Diplomacy." *Journal of Southern History* 79, no. 1 (Feb. 2013): 51–78.

Wise, Stephen R. *Lifeline of the Confederacy: Blockade Running during the Civil War.* Columbia: University of South Carolina Press, 1988.

Wright, James M. "The Wrecking System of the Bahama Islands." *Political Science Quarterly* 30, no. 4 (1915): 618–44.

Wright, J. W. A. "Mysterious Fate of Blockade Runners." *Overland Monthly* 7, no. 39 (Mar. 1886): 298–302.

Unpublished Theses and Dissertations

Cano, Alexander S. "The Salvador Affair: Anatomy of a Confederate Naval Expedition to Central America." Master's thesis, Angelo State University, 2006.

Childs, Travis. "In Liberating Strife: American Filibusters in the Texas Revolution 1835–1836 and the Canadian Rebellion 1837–1839." Master's thesis, University of Texas at Arlington, 2005.

Cleland, Beau. "Between King Cotton and Queen Victoria: Confederate Informal Diplomacy and Privatized Violence in British America during the American Civil War." PhD diss., University of Calgary, 2019.

Phillips, Glen O. I. "The Changing Role of the Merchant Class in the British West Indies, 1834–1867." PhD diss., Howard University, 1976.
Senters, Melinda J. "George N. Sanders: A Political Confidence Man." PhD diss., University of Kentucky, 2006.
Themistocleous, Rosalyn. "The Merchant Princes of Nassau: The Maintenance of Political Hegemony in the Bahamas, 1834–1948." PhD diss., University of Kent at Canterbury, 2000.

INDEX

Page numbers in italics denote figures.

abolition: anxieties around, 16–20, 206n16; contingency of, 8; legal disputes over slavery, 22–26, *23*; Niagara peace negotiations and, 158–60; post-emancipation mutinies, 20–22. *See also* slavery
Adams, E. D., 5
Adderley, Augustus, 60, 117
Adderley, Edwin, 60
Adderley, Henry "King Conch," *46*; opposition to emancipation, 50–51; pro-Confederate influence, 5, 45–46, 48, 54–57, 61, 63, 65; retirement, 195; William Seward's critique of, 44–45
Alien Act (1864), 176, 178, 184, 191
Allen, Charles Maxwell, 76, 77, 80, 110
Almon, William J., 125, 134, 135, 136, 137–38
Anderson, George, 20–21, 50, 62, 106–7, 207n31
Anderson, John, 22–26, *23*, 32, 41
Andreae, Theodore, 93
Andrews, William, 84
antebellum era: filibustering, 27–30; informal diplomacy, 13–16, 42; kidnapping, 32–34; King Cotton diplomacy, 35–38; legal disputes over slavery, 22–26; public opinion, 16–20; responses to privatized violence, 38–41; slave mutinies, 20–22; state centralization, 72
Aroostook War (1838–39), 29, 31
Ashbrook, John, 187

Bahamas: attitudes toward Southerners, 17–18; author's terminology and, xv, 12, 205n24; Confederate connections in, 182–83, 198; *Creole* mutiny, 20–22; friendly societies and activism, 100–101, 102; kidnappings, 32–33; labor disturbances, 113–18, *117*; Union support in, 103–8. *See also* Black colonials; blockade running, Bahamas
Bahamas Friendly Society, 99
Baldwin, John P., 54
Balogh, Brian, 72
Bayley, Charles John, 59, 60, 61–64, 82, 106, 111, 129–30
Beall, John Yates, 168–70, 186, 230n69
Beauregard, Pierre G. T., 88
Bell, Inkel, 114
Benjamin, Judah P.: belief in international recognition, 64–65, 160; blockade running and, 57, 58; detention of Joseph Hester and, 84;

267

Benjamin, Judah P. (*continued*)
  promotion of cotton embargo,
  37–38; response to *Tuscaloosa*
  seizure, 150; support for privatized
  violence, 9, 29, 30, 119
Benton, Lauren, 4
Bermuda: attitudes toward Southerners, 17–18; author's terminology and,
  xv, 12, 205n24; Confederate
  connections in, 182–83, 198; friendly
  societies and activism, 100, 114; labor
  disturbances, 113–18, *117*; Union
  support in, 110. *See also* Black
  colonials; blockade running,
  Bermuda
Bernath, Michael, 72
biological warfare, 179, 180–84
Black, Jeremiah S., 163
Blackburn, Luke Pryor, 126, 135,
  180–84
Black colonials: Confederate attitudes
  toward, 70, 97–98; conflicting
  motivations of, 6, 41–42, 182–83;
  kidnapping of, 32–33; labor disturbances, 113–18, *117*; solidarity and
  self-protection, 98–103; support for
  Confederate cause, 110–12; support
  for the Union, 103–10, 118
Blackett, R. J. M., 17
blockade running: aftermath of, 195;
  importance of colonial partners, 3,
  5–7, 15; labor disturbances affecting,
  98, 113–18, *117*; role of Black colonials
  in, 102–3. *See also* blockade running,
  Bahamas; blockade running,
  Bermuda
blockade running, Bahamas: centrality
  of informal relations, 43–49, 66–67,
  211n10, 211n15; communication
  tactics, 58; development of, 52–54;
  impact on Civil War, 44, 65–66;
  motivations for Bahamian cooperation, 49–52; public-private partnerships, 56–57, 213n56; tensions and
  divisions, 59–65
blockade running, Bermuda: attitudes
  toward Union government, 76–77;
  covert interactions, 83–85; decline
  of, 95; development of, 73–78; social
  networking and hospitality, 79–83,
  80; state involvement, 70–73, 86–94;
  strategic advantages, 68–70
Bonham, Milledge L., 94
Bonner, Michael Brem, 71
Booth, John Wilkes, 1, 187–90, 192
Bourne, John Tory: 1863 dockworkers
  strike and, 115; blockade running
  and, 74, 85–86, 90; dedication to
  Southern cause, 68, 77, 95; extensive social networks, 89, 96; later
  years, 195
Braine, John C., 106, 126, 130–31, 134,
  143–46, 194, 196
Bratton, Rufus, 194
Britain: advocating for international
  law reform, 4; antebellum attitudes
  toward, 16, 19; attitude toward
  United States, 16–17; *Creole* mutiny
  and, 20–22; neutral stance on
  foreign policy, 7–8; response to
  privatized violence, 39, 40–41.
  See also Black colonials; blockade
  running, Bahamas; blockade
  running, Bermuda; informal
  diplomacy; maritime violence;
  privatized violence
British America: interpretation of
  international law, 4; motivations for

Confederate support, 6; term usage herein, xv, 12, 205n23. *See also* Bahamas; Bermuda; Canada
British and Foreign Anti-Slavery Society, 103
British North America: antebellum-era public opinion, 17; Bermuda as access point for, 82–83; divided sovereignty in, 7; interpretation of international law, 4; participation in Union army, 227n1; as postwar fugitive refuge, 193–96; push for Confederation, 177–78; "Settler Revolution" in, 124; support for Confederate cause, 120–21, 228n19; term usage herein, xv, 12, 205n24. *See also* Canada; maritime violence
Brown, Albert Gallatin, 29
Brown, George, 17
Brown, James Nibbs, 109
Brown, John, 9, 19, 21
Brown, Joseph, 71, 94, 159
Brown, William Wells, 32
Browne, William Montague, 13–14
Bryan, Edward B., 18–19
Buckalew, Charles, 163
Bullitt, Joshua, 163
Burley, Bennet G., 168, 170, 176
Butterfield, Nathaniel, 86

Calhoun, John C., 19, 21
Canada: abolitionist stance, 17; John Anderson extradition case, 22–26, *23*; attack on New York and, 185–87; author's terminology, xv, 12; Confederate operations in, 152–56; cross-border raids and plots, 167–74, *173*, *178*; decrease in pro-Confederate sentiment, 175–77; erosion of warfare norms, 178–80; increased precarity and violence, 149–52; Johnson's Island plot and, 167–70, 171; kidnapping attempts in, 32; Lincoln assassination and, 187–90; Niagara peace negotiations, 156–60; as postwar fugitive refuge, 193–96; postwar violence, 196–97; self-governing status, 124; St. Albans attack and, 171–74, *173*; Thompson's "Northwest Conspiracy," 160–66; yellow fever plot and, 180–84. *See also* British North America; *and individual cities and provinces*
Canadian rebellions (1837–38), 17, 27, 124
Cardwell, Edward, 170
Caroline affair (1837), 31
Cartier, George-Etienne, 175
Cass, Lewis, 24
Catholic Church, 83, 126, 155–56, 174, 195–96
Chase, Salmon P., 63
Chesapeake, hijacking of, 120–21, 123, 128–39, *132*, 168, 194
Civil War (1861–1865): Bermuda as base of operations, 69; centrality of grassroots actors, 2, 43–44, 65–66, 197–99; privatized violence and, 10, 14
Clarendon, George William Frederick Villiers, 27
Clark, Frederick, 33
Clary, Arthur, 103, 132, 134
Clay, Clement C.: Confederate operations in Canada, 149, 154–59, 163–66, 171, 175–76; Lincoln assassination and, 188, 190, 200; social connections, 83

Clayton-Bulwer Treaty (1850), 14
Cleary, William W., 155, 184, 188, 190
Cockburn, George, Sir, 20
Cole, Charles H., 168–70
colonials: as active Civil War participants, 14; antebellum-era public opinion, 16–20; divided sovereignty, 7; interpretation of international law, 4; motivations for Confederate support, 6; term usage herein, 12. *See also* Black colonials; blockade running, Bahamas; blockade running, Bermuda; informal diplomacy; maritime violence; privatized violence
Coney, Richard, 75
Confederate States of America (CSA): antebellum-era public opinion, 16–20; Bahamian cultural connections, 49–50; Black colonial support for, 110–12; development of maritime networks, 122–28, *127*; embracing of private violence, 139–47, 150–51; extent of government centralization, 70–73, 216n8; Lost Cause myth, 196; recognition of colonial support, 2–3. *See also* Black colonials; blockade running, Bahamas; blockade running, Bermuda; informal diplomacy; maritime violence; privatized violence
Connolly, Thomas, 83, 126, 156, 195–96
Copperheads (Peace Democrats), 150, 159, 162–63, 165, 177, 185, 186–87
cotton: blockade-related traffic in, 45, *48*, 58, 66, 88, 94–95; cotton embargo, 3, 6, 15, 35–38, 42
Coursol, Charles J., 172, 175

Creole mutiny (1841), 20–22, 52, 193, 207n31
CSS *Alabama*, 84, 137
CSS *Florida*, 62, 81, 103, 199
CSS *Tuscaloosa*, seizure of, 150, 232n2
Curry, Thomas, 106, 107
"cut-outs" (neutral proxy figures), 6–7, 58

Dahlgren raid (1864), 188, 190
Dames, Thomas, 105, 106
Davis, Jefferson: 1864 appeal for recognition, 175; ambivalence toward filibustering, 15, 29, 30; blockade running interventions, 70, 73, 90, 92–94; Confederate operations in Canada, 153–54; cotton embargo and, 35; Dahlgren raid, 188, 190; expanding government intervention, 71; Johnson's Island raid and, 170; Lincoln assassination and, 1; on Niagara peace negotiations, 159–60; postwar refuge in Canada, 193, *197*; recognition of British American support, 2; response to *Chesapeake* affair, 139, 143–44; support for privateering operations, 9, 39, 141–42, 150; yellow fever plot and, 183–84
Davis, Varina, 79
Davis, W. C., 216n8
Declaration of Paris (1856), 4, 15, 27, 40
Democratic National Convention (1864), 150, 160–66
Denison, George Taylor, 25, 176
DeRosset, Louis H., 79
DeRosset, Marie, 79
Dickson, John, 125
Dillet, T. W., 106–7

Dix, John A., 186
Doyle, Charles Hastings, 133, 134, 137, 138

Early, Jubal, 196
Edling, Max, 72
Edwards, Samuel, 33
Emancipation Proclamation (1863), 98
Evans, Robert S., 97, 101

Fenian Brotherhood, 177, 191–92, 196
filibustering: ambivalence to, 13, 14–15; British concerns over, 123; government approval of, 142; proslavery expansionism and, 8–9; ubiquity of, antebellum era, 27–30. *See also* maritime violence; privatized violence
Flanner, James H., 87
"flight from the flag," 54
Ford, Lisa, 4
Foreign Enlistment Act (1819), 41, 105, 106, 134, 135
Forsyth, Archibald, 53–54
Fraser, John, 48, 57
Freemasons, 99, 114
Fugitive Slave Law (1850), 17

Georgian (steamer), 176
Giddings, Joshua, 152
Gladiator (blockade runner), 56–57
Gordon, Arthur, 135–36
Gorgas, Josiah, 86, 87–88
Graff, E. B., 101
Grant's Town Friendly Society, 99–100
Gray, John Hamilton, 135
Greeley, Horace, 157–58
Gunning, James, 24

Hackett, Nelson, 22
Halifax, Nova Scotia: *Chesapeake* hijacking, *132*, 132–38; Confederate support in, 2, 5, 44, 65, 83, 86, 120, 122, 124–28, 156; mail communication through, 78; Walker family in, *80*
Hall, Catherine, 206n16
Hammond, James Henry, 35
Harkaway (schooner), 64
Harris, George, 63, 195
Hawley, Seth, 104, 105
Headley, John W., 185
Hebe (schooner), 33–34
Helm, Charles J., 56, 145
Henry, William Alexander, 125
Hermosa (slave ship), 20
Hernandez, Tom, 125
Hester, Joseph Goodwyn, 83–85, 194–95
Heyliger, Lewis: blockade running, 56–57, 65, 92; on *Harkaway* seizure, 64; response to Union supporters, 105, 107; on *Trent* affair, 51
Hickley, Henry, 61–62
hijacking. *See* maritime violence
Hill, Philip Carteret, 138
Hines, Thomas Henry, 162–65
Hogg, Thomas, 143, 145, 146–47
Holcombe, James P., 2, 120, 143–44, 149, 153–59, 163–64, 184, 186–87
Hubbard, Charles, 47
Hunt, Washington, 163
Huzzey, Richard, 206n16
Hyams, Godfrey, 181–84
Hyland, William C. J., 81

informal diplomacy: antebellum-era public opinion, 16–20; British neutrality and, 7–8; British response

informal diplomacy (*continued*)
to privatized violence, 40–41;
Canada as postwar refuge, 193–96;
centrality of grassroots actors,
43–44, 197–99; characterized, 3–4,
47; Confederate operations in
Canada, 152–53; crucial role of, 1–7,
13–16, 34–35, 42, 200–201; increasing chaos and violence, 149–52; King
Cotton diplomacy, 35–38, 198; legal
disputes over slavery, 22–26; Niagara
peace negotiations, 156–60;
post-emancipation slave mutinies,
20–22; postwar violence, 196–97;
private and public violence, 8–10;
relations with Black colonials and,
113–14, 118–19; responses to privateering, 38–39; Thompson's
"Northwest Conspiracy," 160–66.
See also Black colonials; blockade
running, Bahamas; blockade
running, Bermuda; maritime
violence; privatized violence
Ireland, 177, 191–92, 196

Jenkins, Brian, 151, 211n10
Jewett, William "Colorado," 157–59
John Fraser and Co., 48, 57, 68, 85
John Hancock (schooner), 53
Johnson, Andrew, 188, 190
Johnson, Herschel V., 153–54
Johnson's Island, Ohio, 78, 141, 143, 167–68, 171, 176, 185, 189
Johnston, James William, 136
Jones, Howard, 5, 211n10
Joseph R. Gerrity hijacking, 143, 147, 168

Karp, Matthew, 72
Keith, Alexander, 86

Keith, Alexander, Jr., 125, 134, 137–38, 189
Kennedy, Robert Cobb, 185–86
Kenner, Duncan, 37–38, 150, 175
kidnappings, 32–34
King Conch. *See* Adderley, Henry "King Conch"
King Cotton diplomacy, 35–38, 198. *See also* cotton; informal diplomacy
Kirkpatrick, Thomas, 108–9
Knights of the Golden Circle (KGC), 163–65
Koistinen, Paul A. C., 71
Kossuth, Lajos, 29
Ku Klux Klan, 194

labor: disturbances, Bermuda and Bahamas, 113–18, *117*; mistreatment and malignment of Black workers, 6, 97. *See also* Black colonials
Lafitte, John Baptiste, 5, 56, 57, 86, 108
Lamothe, Guillaume, 174–75
law: blockade running and, 59–60; colonial-metropolitan conflict, 22–26; filibustering and, 29–30; positivism, 4; unequal treatment of Union supporters, 106–7, 130; white elite exploitation of, 50–51
Lee, Edwin Gray, 189–90
Lees, John Campbell, 62
Lees, Stephen, 106, 107
Lemmon & Co., 87
Lemnitzer, Jan, 4
Lincoln, Abraham: assassination of, 1, *178*, 180–81, 187–90, 192, 201; attack on New York and, 186; attempted kidnapping of, 179, 188, 200; declaration of Union blockade, 2, 53; Niagara Falls Conference and, 158–60; response to privateering, 39

Locke, Vernon Guyon, 106, 126, 128–31, 134, 142, 146, 194, 228n28
Lost Cause myth, 196
Low, Andrew, 125
Lowe, Matthew, 104, 105
Loyalists (American Revolution), 49–50
Lyons, Richard Bickerton Pemell: anxiety over Bahamas, 43; blockade running and, 61, 63, 199; Confederate communication tactics and, 58; response to Bahama kidnappings, 33

Macdonald, John A., 24, 176–77
Mackenzie, William Lyon, 31
Maffitt, John Newland, 81
mail, communication by, 58, 68, 102
Main, cross-border violence, 29, 31
Mallory, Stephen R.: blockade running and, 54; critiquing colonial Britain, 19; on neutrality, 13; on Niagara peace negotiations, 160; response to *Chesapeake* affair, 119, 139; support for filibustering, 13, 29, 30; support for naval warfare, 9, 128, 141, 142, 145, 146, 147, 199
Margaret and Jessie affair, 64
maritime violence: adventurism and private capital, 147; *Chesapeake* hijacking, 120–21, 123, 128–39, *132*; Confederate embracing of, 139–47; development of maritime networks, 122–28, *127*
Marler, Scott, 36
Marquis, Greg, 228n19
Martin, Patrick C., 189
Martin, Robert, 185–86
Marx, Karl, 8–9
Mason, James, 51, 61, 64, 76–77, 143, 147, 175

Maury, Matthew Fontaine, 78
McClellan, George B., 164, 165
McCurry, Stephanie, 216n8
McLean, Washington, 163
McMicken, Gilbert, 177
McPherson, James, 151
McRae, Colin, 88
Mercer, John, 135–36
Merchant Shipping Act (1854), 53
Miles, William Porcher, 94
Milne, Alexander, 28, 41, 61, 69, 77, 82, 85, 123
Milton, John, 38
Monck, Charles Stanley Monck, Viscount, 153, 170–71, 174, 175–76
Monroe Doctrine, 164
Montreal, Quebec: Anglo-French tensions in, 174–75; Confederate support network in, 65, 164; Jefferson Davis in, *197*; Lincoln assassination and, 1, 189, 190; St. Albans attack and, 171–74, *173*
Moore, Thomas, 38

Nassau Friendly Society, 102, 103
Negro Seaman Acts, 101
Nesbitt, Charles R., 50, 53–54, 76, 117, 212n29
New Brunswick: Aroostook War, 29, 31; *Chesapeake* hijacking, 120–21, 123, 128–39, *132*; political independence, 124; prominent pro-Confederate figures, 195
New York City, attack on, 179, 185–87
Niagara Falls Conference (1864), 150, 156–60
Nicaragua, 27–30
Novak, Robert, 72

Nova Scotia: *Chesapeake* hijacking, 120–21, 123, 128–39, *132*; political independence, 124, 133; prominent pro-Confederate figures, 195–96; support for Confederate cause, 2, 122, 124–28, *127*, 156; yellow fever plot and, 184. *See also* Halifax, Nova Scotia

O'Connor, Peter, 17
Odd Fellows (fraternity), 99, 114
Ord, Harry St. George, 74–76, 77, 78, 81–82, 85, 113
Order of American Knights (OAK), 161, 163–64
Oreto (CSS *Florida*), 62, 103, 108, 112
Orr, James L., 154
Owsley, Frank L., 36, 70–71

Palmerston, Lord, 7, 16
Parker, John, 129, 228n28
Parr, Henry A., 130, 134, 136
Partisan Ranger Act (1862), 122
Peace Democrats, 150, 159, 162–63, 165, 177, 185
Pegram, Robert, 75
Pelham-Clinton, Henry, 62
Pemberton, John C., 155
Pendleton, George, 163
Perpall, John, 50
Perpall, Mary Ann, 50
Philo Parsons, hijacking of, 169, 176, *178*
Pickett, John T., 13
Pinkertons (Pinkerton National Detective Agency), 10, 194
Pope, John H., 32
Porterfield, John, 174, 190
positivism, in international law, 4
Price, Alexander, 105, 106–7

privateering: antebellum embracing of, 15; Britain's response to, 40–41; maritime warfare and, 139–40; piracy vs., 38–39; privatized warfare and, 9. *See also* maritime violence
privatized violence: assassination of Abraham Lincoln, 187–90; attack on New York, 185–87; border violence, 30–32; British response to, 40–41; Civil War as inflection point in, 10; Confederate embracing of, 139–48; crucial role of, 13–16, 34–35, 42, 191–92; decline in pro-Confederate sentiment, 175–78; erosion of warfare norms, 178–80; filibustering, 27–30; kidnapping, 32–34; piracy vs. privateering, 38–39; proslavery expansionism and, 8–9; raid on Johnson's Island, 167–70; St. Albans attack, 171–74, *173*; violence at sea, 120–21; yellow fever plot, 180–84. *See also* filibustering; informal diplomacy; maritime violence; privateering

Rainey, Joseph Hayne, 182–83
Rao, Gautham, 73
Rawson, Rawson W., 146
Reciprocity Treaty (1854), 151, 177, 201
Richmond, Leigh, 163
Riel, Louis, 192, 196
Rightful Remedy, The (Bryan), 18–19
Riker, David, 140
Ritchie, John W., 135–36, 195
Ritchie, William Johnston, 135–36, 195
Roanoke hijacking, 30, 121, 139, 140, 144–46, 194
Roberts, Stephen, 106, 107
Robinson, Stuart, 184
Ross, Charles D., 211n15

Rugemer, Edward, 19
rules-based international order, 4
Rush-Bagot Agreement (1817), 170
Russell, John, 7, 61, 63, 172, 175
Russell, William Howard, 13–14

Sage, Bernard Janin, 199
Saint-Jean-Baptiste Society, 174
Salvador, hijacking of, 146–47
Sanders, George N., *161*; Lincoln assassination and, 188, 188–91; networking in Canada, 126, 153, 163, 164; Niagara peace negotiations, 156–60; St. Albans raid, 171, *173*
Saunders and Son, 58
Schaffer, Orin, 120, 131, 229n40
Schoen, Brian, 36
secret societies, 161, 163–65, 186–87
Seddon, James A., 87–89, 94, 171
Semmes, Raphael, 84, 126
"Settler Revolution," 124
Seward, William H., 3, 7, 44–45, 81, 120, 129, 188
Sheehan-Dean, Aaron, 121
Sheridan, Philip H., 185
Sir Robert Peel (steamer), 31
slavery: *Creole* mutiny, 20–22; filibustering and proslavery expansionism, 8–9; friendly societies and fraternal groups, 99–100, 114; kidnapping of enslaved people, 32; legal disputes over, 22–26, *23*; motivations for Confederate support and, 6; opposition to emancipation, 50–52; slaveholder control over foreign policy, 72. *See also* abolition; Black colonials
Slidell, John, 30, 51, 76–77
Smith, Peleg, 134, 137–38
social networking and hospitality, 79–83, *80*

Sons of Liberty (SOL), 161, 164
Southern Rights Association, 19
sovereignty, maritime violence and, 133–35
St. Albans attack, 171–77 *173*
Stephens, Alexander, 30, 154, 159
Stewart, Alexander, 137
Stewart, Kensey Johns, 183–84
Stirrup, John, 33
St. Mary (schooner), 146, 194
Sumner, Charles, 3, 66, 155
Surratt, John Harrison, 174, 189–90
Sweeting, James, 106, 107

Taylor, Thomas, 112
Thomas, Emory M., 71, 72
Thompson, Jacob S.: as Confederate operative in Canada, 149, 154–57; Johnson's Island raid, 168–69; Lincoln assassination and, 188, 191; New York arson scheme, 184–87, 200; "Northwest Conspiracy," 160–66; social connections, 83; St. Albans attack and, 175–77; yellow fever plot and, 181
Toombs, Robert, 29, 140
Toronto, Ontario: attitudes toward Godfrey Hyams, 181–82; Confederate support network in, 44, 156, 164, 184, 185
trade: blockade aftermath, 195; cotton embargo, 3, 6, 15, 35–38, 42; importance of colonial partners, 3, 5–7, 15; labor disturbances affecting, 98, 113–18, *117*; Union blockade function, 2. *See also* blockade running, Bahamas; blockade running, Bermuda
Trenholm, George A., 64, 199
Trent affair (1861), 17, 28, 51, 76, 77, 199

Tucker, Nathaniel Beverley, 153, 163, 164, 188, 190
Tucker, Richard, 100
Tucker, William Tudor, 114
Tupper, Charles, 125, 133
Tyler, John, 21

Union government: Bermudian attitudes toward, 76–77; Black colonial support for, 103–10, 118; Niagara Falls Conference, 156–60; response to Confederate activity in Bahamas, 44–45; Union blockade function, 2. *See also* Black colonials; blockade running, Bahamas; blockade running, Bermuda; informal diplomacy; maritime violence; privatized violence
United Fruit Company, 10
U.S. Marine Corps, 10
USS *Chesapeake*, 128
USS *Dacotah*, 132
USS *Ella and Annie*, 131–32
USS *Flambeau*, 56
USS *Michigan*, attack on, 168–69, 176
USS *Tioga*, 103–4, 105, 106, 109–10

Vallandigham, Clement, 78, 158, 162–63, 164
Vance, Zebulon Baird, 71, 86–87, 89, 92–94
Varina, Davis, 196, *197*
Vattel, Emer de, 39
Virginia Company, 73

Wade, George, 131, 134, 137–38
Walker, Georgiana Gholson, 79–83, *80*, 95, 113, 114, 143, 156
Walker, John C., 163

Walker, Norman S., 5, 78, 86, 113, 114–15, 136, 143
Walker, William, 15, 27–30, 41, 123, 147
Waller, Richard P., 87
Walshe, A. Crawford, 152
Ward, Charles, 108, 225n50
Washington, Madison, 20, 21
Webster-Ashburton Treaty (1842), 21–25, 133, 176
Weller, John, 163
Wells, Frederick B., 75
Welsman, James T., 85
West Indies, 16, 205n24
Wheaton, Henry, 39
Whiting, Samuel, 51, 62, 107, 111–12
Whiting, W. H. C., 88
Wier, Benjamin, *127*; *Chesapeake* hijacking and, 131, 136; as Nova Scotia senator, 195; as pro-Confederate network anchor, 5, 125, 126–28, 156
Wilkes, Charles, 77–78
Wilkinson, John, 85, 112
Williams, Patrick, 100
Wilson, Frank, 97
Winks, Robin, 151, 159
Wise, Stephen R., 211n15
Witte, Charles O., 58
women, facilitating social networking, 79–81, *80*
Wood, Benjamin, 163
Wood, John Taylor, 194

Yancey, William Lowndes, 154
yellow fever, 69, 89, 95, 179, 180–84, 187, 191
Young, Bennett H., 171, 172
Young Men's Friendly Institution, 100

Zuill, William, 195

UNCIVIL WARS

Weirding the War: Stories from the Civil War's Ragged Edges
edited by Stephen Berry

Ruin Nation: Destruction and the American Civil War
by Megan Kate Nelson

America's Corporal: James Tanner in War and Peace
by James Marten

The Blue, the Gray, and the Green: Toward an Environmental History of the Civil War
edited by Brian Allen Drake

Empty Sleeves: Amputation in the Civil War South
by Brian Craig Miller

Lens of War: Exploring Iconic Photographs of the Civil War
edited by J. Matthew Gallman and Gary W. Gallagher

The Slave-Trader's Letter-Book: Charles Lamar, the Wanderer, and Other Tales of the African Slave Trade
by Jim Jordan

Driven from Home: North Carolina's Civil War Refugee Crisis
by David Silkenat

The Ghosts of Guerrilla Memory: How Civil War Bushwhackers Became Gunslingers in the American West
by Matthew Christopher Hulbert

Beyond Freedom: Disrupting the History of Emancipation
edited by David W. Blight and Jim Downs

The Lost President: A. D. Smith and the Hidden History of Radical Democracy in Civil War America
by Ruth Dunley

Bodies in Blue: Disability in the Civil War North
by Sarah Handley-Cousins

Visions of Glory: The Civil War in Word and Image
edited by Kathleen Diffley and Benjamin Fagan

Household War: How Americans Lived and Fought the Civil War
edited by Lisa Tendrich Frank and LeeAnn Whites

Buying and Selling Civil War Memory in Gilded Age America
edited by James Marten and Caroline E. Janney

The War after the War: A New History of Reconstruction
by John Patrick Daly

The Families' Civil War: Black Soldiers and the Fight for Racial Justice
by Holly A. Pinheiro Jr.

Sand, Science, and the Civil War: Sedimentary Geology and Combat
by Scott Hippensteel

A Man by Any Other Name: William Clarke Quantrill and the Search for American Manhood
by Joseph M. Beilein Jr.

A Continuous State of War: Empire Building and Race Making in the Civil War–Era Gulf South
by Maria Angela Diaz

Between King Cotton and Queen Victoria: How Pirates, Smugglers, and Scoundrels Almost Saved the Confederacy
by Beau Cleland